HAROLD MACMILLAN

A Biography by NIGEL FISHER

HAROLD MACMILLAN

A Biography by NIGEL FISHER

Weidenfeld and Nicolson   London

To my son Mark

First published in Great Britain by
George Weidenfeld & Nicolson Ltd
91 Clapham High Street, London sw4 7ta
1982

ISBN 0 297 77914 1
Printed and bound in Great Britain by
Butler & Tanner Ltd, Frome and London

CONTENTS

CONTENTS

ILLUSTRATIONS

Daniel Macmillan, Harold Macmillan's grandfather (*Hulton Picture Library*)
Harold Macmillan at the age of eight (*Camera Press*)
Lady Dorothy and Harold Macmillan after their wedding (*Hulton Picture Library*)
Lady Dorothy and Harold Macmillan in the 1920s (*Popperfoto*)
Anthony Eden, Winston Churchill and Harold Macmillan in North Africa, 1943 (*Camera Press*)
Macmillan at Birch Grove House (*Keystone*)
Selwyn Lloyd, President Eisenhower, Harold Macmillan and Foster Dulles (*Keystone*)
Macmillan and Khrushchev in Moscow, 1959 (*Popperfoto*)
The Prime Minister in 10 Downing Street (*Camera Press*)
Harold Macmillan's Cabinet in October 1959 (*COI/Crown copyright*)
During the 1959 General Election (*Popperfoto*)
Macmillan and Duncan Sandys in 1963 (*Mirrorpic*)
Harold and Maurice Macmillan at Birch Grove (*Camera Press/Alan Clifton*)
At a pheasant shoot in 1969–70 (*Camera Press/R. Slade*)
As Chancellor of Oxford University receiving Her Majesty The Queen (*Popperfoto*)
Harold Macmillan and Margaret Thatcher in 1979 (*Keystone*)

ACKNOWLEDGEMENTS

I am much indebted to Christopher Barnett, Ann Somerset and Mark Eldridge for the invaluable help they gave me by their efficient research work for this book and to Mrs R. Kloegman for typing the manuscript with speed and complete accuracy. My thanks are also due to my wife for her suggestions and corrections, and to my secretaries, Patricia Sydney-Smith and Shirley Ann, Lady De Freyne, for the extra work the book entailed.

I am very grateful indeed to the following who worked with or for Harold Macmillan at different periods of his career, or who knew him well, and have kindly talked to me about him: His personal secretary, Miss Aimetti; his daughter and son-in-law, Catherine and Julian Amery; Jeffrey Archer; Lord Barber; Humphry Berkeley; Sir Frederick Bishop; Lord Boothby; Viscount Boyd of Merton; Samuel Brittan; Lady Mairi Bury; Lord Caccia; Sir Alec Cairncross; Neil Cairncross; Lord Carrington; Norman Collins; Quentin and Susan Crewe; Sir Philip and Lady de Zulueta; Piers Dixon; Sir Douglas Dodds-Parker; Lady Egremont; Lord Erroll of Hale; Sir Harold Evans; Julian Faber; Lord Fraser of Kilmorack; Sir Hugh Fraser, MP; Lord Gore-Booth; Raymond Grumbar; Lord Harlech; Mrs Hermione Hichens; Lord Hill of Luton; Lord Home of the Hirsel; Douglas Jay, MP; Lord Kaldor; J. L. Lambart; Kenneth Lewis, MP; Kenneth Lindsay; Alan Maclean; Sir Fitzroy Maclean; Alexander Macmillan; Dame Katherine Macmillan; Lord Margadale; Lord Molson; Lord Rawlinson; Lord Robbins; Lord Roberthall; Lord Sherfield; W. Shimwell; Sir Peter Smithers; Lord Soames; Lord Thorneycroft; Lord Trend; Frank Whitehead; Sir Harold Wilson, MP; Sir Hugh Wontner; Philip Woodfield.

The following, who have since died, were also most helpful in talking to me about Harold Macmillan: Viscount Amory; Lord Armstrong; Lord Boyle of Handsworth; Sir Robert Cary; Sir Harwood Harrison; George Hutchinson; Malcolm MacDonald; Reginald Maudling; Lady Anne Montagu; Lord Selwyn-Lloyd; Lord Snow.

PREFACE

I have always been an admirer of Harold Macmillan as a successful and sophisticated leader of the post-war Conservative Party and as a distinguished world statesman. It was his book *The Middle Way* which led me to become a Conservative, and I have been much influenced by the progressive 'One Nation' approach to politics, of which he and Rab Butler – and later Iain Macleod – were the chief exponents.

It has not been my purpose to write a political history of the period or even a detailed account of Harold Macmillan's prominent part in it. He has provided that himself in his own six-volume memoirs. This book is a much shorter study of an outstanding statesman, which attempts to assess his contribution to the country and to the Tory Party, as seen through the eyes of a younger colleague in Parliament – assisted by the comments of those who worked with and for him and who have been good enough to talk to me about him.

I have been greatly helped by Harold Macmillan himself. He has kindly read every chapter and made factual amendments where these have been necessary; but he has never attempted to influence any personal opinion or assessment I have formed.

I have experienced only one disappointment. I had hoped to write a definitive biography of this complex and remarkable man. He preferred it to be a political biography, so some of the more personal aspects of his life have been omitted at his request. I am content to respect his privacy.

NIGEL FISHER

1
THE EARLY YEARS

Harold Macmillan was born at his parents' home in Cadogan Place on 10 February 1894. He can remember seeing the great procession of troops in 1897 which marked the sixtieth anniversary of the reign of Queen Victoria, on whose Empire the sun never set. By the time he entered Parliament thirty years later the security and apparent permanence of that era had been threatened and then eroded by the First World War and, when he retired from public life at the age of seventy, had virtually vanished in the aftermath of the Second World War. The Empire itself had disappeared, its dissolution deliberately hastened by Macmillan's own policies.

In his life-time the world – and Britain's place in it – had radically changed, partly because of the rapid advance of science and technology, partly because of the social conscience of some of its leaders and the nationalist ambitions of others.

Such a prospect could not have entered the minds of Harold Macmillan's parents as they welcomed the arrival of the new addition to their family. The red on the map of every school atlas, the power of the British Navy and the continuing commercial and industrial prosperity of the nation, still led largely by its land-owners and aristocracy, seemed to ensure a settled future for their three small sons, of whom Harold was the youngest.

The stability of the Victorian age was enlivened by the opportunities it offered to the enterprising and the ambitious, and no family provided more evidence of this than Macmillan's own. Although aristocratic in manner, Harold Macmillan was paradoxically proud of his humble highland ancestry and later in life loved to boast that his forebears had been crofters on the Isle of Arran. He always kept a small sketch of the cottage in which his grandfather was born in his room at No. 10 Downing Street and had a strong feeling for his family background, perhaps because, like his experiences in the First World War, it was a link with ordinary people.

His grandfather, Daniel, born at Arran in 1813, was the tenth of twelve children and, despite chronic ill-health, he was determined to succeed in the world through his own endeavours. At the age of ten he became apprenticed to a bookseller for a wage of 1s 6d a week, which rose by 1s a week for each of the next six years. By the time he was eighteen he had found work in a bookshop in Glasgow; but England (and preferably London) was his objective and he eventually obtained employment in Cambridge with another bookseller called Johnson, who paid him £30 a year for a day which started at half-past seven in the morning and did not finish till seven at night.

Daniel Macmillan died at the age of forty-four, but by that time – with the help of his younger brother, Alexander – he had founded the family firm which was to grow and prosper for the next century and become, as it is today, one of the leading publishers in Britain. Daniel was a man of ability and character whose life and work is recorded in a biography by Thomas Hughes, and in *The House of Macmillan* by Charles Morgan.

Harold's father, Maurice, was only four years old when Daniel died, but Alexander brought up his brother's family of three sons and a daughter with his own children and developed the business so successfully that within a few years there was enough money to send Maurice to Uppingham and then to Christ's College, Cambridge, where he obtained a 1st Class Honours Degree in Classics in 1875. After six years as a classical master at St Paul's, Maurice joined the family firm and was responsible for extending its scope by establishing branches overseas and by beginning the educational publications which have been a valuable side of the business ever since.

Maurice was an able man, kind, generous and devoted to his children, who loved and respected him; but Harold Macmillan's mother was an even greater influence in his life. She was the daughter of Dr Tarleton Belles of Spencer, Indiana, and was born there in 1856. At the age of nineteen she married a musician, who died six months later, and soon afterwards she left the United States for Paris, where she studied sculpture, exhibited some of her own work, developed a talent for singing, and met and married Maurice Macmillan. Although a good hostess who enjoyed mixing authors, artists and politicians at her parties, she was also a loving mother, ambitious for her children and concerned – perhaps over-concerned – with every aspect of their lives. She was a strong character, and a tower of strength and encouragement to Harold Macmillan in any dangers or disappointments which befell him.

The way of life of children in an upper-middle-class household was secure and ordered for at least the first quarter of this century and was scarcely altered even by the First World War. Harold Macmillan recalls the straw put down in the roadway to deaden the noise of traffic when some distinguished resident in Sloane Street or Cadogan Place was dying or giving birth to a baby. He remembers Mr Vigo's fish shop and Mr Macpherson's gymnasium, both still Sloane Street features twenty years later; the walks with Nanny in Hyde Park; the Sunday ritual of morning service at Holy Trinity Church, often followed by a visit to the zoo in the afternoon (weekends out of London only came into fashion as cars became more reliable); the visiting-cards on a silver salver in the hall (turned up at the corner if they had been left in person); the staff of eight indoor servants to look after a family of four or five. Almost the only difference after the First World War was the gradual replacement of the horse-drawn drays, hansom-cabs and carriages by the motor-car.

The atmosphere at the Macmillans' Cadogan Place home was agreeable but somewhat austere and a high standard of application and academic achievement was expected of the children. Harold Macmillan was sent to Gladstone's, the day-school near Sloane Square, and by the time he went on to Summerfields in 1903, at the age of nine, he had already gained a good grounding in the classics. Later in life he became a governor of the school and when *A Century of Summerfields* by Richard Usborne was published in 1964, the headmaster asked Macmillan to write a foreword. 'I could not refuse,' he records, 'for I still stand in great awe of a headmaster.' In the foreword he wrote: 'I think all Summerfields boys ... will agree on this: whether we were happy or not, successful or not, scholars or not, athletes or not, we did somehow get into our heads that, if a thing was worth doing at all, it was worth doing as well as possible. ... Even in the heyday of the Eton scholarship list, the all-round boy was regarded as the ideal. Our school motto (*Mens sana in corpore sano*) may seem to some people rather trite. But the idea is really very sensible.'

Many of his contemporaries at Summerfields were killed in the First World War, but among those who survived it were Harry Crookshank, later to be a Minister in several Conservative Governments and a life-long friend of Macmillan's at Eton, in the Grenadier Guards and in the House of Commons; Evelyn Baring, who became Managing Director of Baring Bros.; Eric Ward, subsequently a Member of Parliament till he succeeded his father as 3rd Earl of Dudley; and Sir Olaf Caroe, later a Governor of the North-West Frontier Province of India.

Caroe recalls that, although Harold Macmillan was a year younger, they were in the Fifth Form together: 'He was a youth of a rather withdrawn taste; he had striking good looks and elegance and a conscious distinction of mind and person. He had the makings of a passable bowler, but I cannot see him in the hurly-burly of the football field. I remember thinking that, even then, he had a way of ordering affairs as he thought they should be ordered. And he was a firm friend.'[1]

Another contemporary, A.D. Finney, wrote that during their last year they were all in the Fifth Form working for scholarships: 'We certainly had to work hard, for if we did not, corporal punishment might follow. ... In the Fifth Macmillan was certainly the best Classic. The Doctor wished us to be original and brilliant and he couldn't have had a more apt pupil. In the end they gave the 1st Eton scholarship to a mathematician, also from Summerfields. Macmillan was 3rd and Crookshank 6th.'[2] Lieutenant-General Lord Norrie later described Macmillan as 'a very attractive, slim, modest boy, perhaps a trifle reserved'.[3]

A book of *Fairy Story Plays* was discovered recently on a Summerfields shelf. It shows the casting for a school play with the boys' names written against the parts they were to take. It was an augury for the future that Harold Macmillan played the part of the Prime Minister.

Macmillan went to Eton in 1906. The 'election' to College that year was of a high standard, but he always managed to maintain a good place in his classical division, although overshadowed by his eldest brother, Daniel, who was a brilliant classicist, won the Newcastle Prize and gained the senior scholarship to Balliol. In later life Harold always acknowledged his brother's intellectual superiority.

Eton in those days was a snobbish place and the Oppidans, instead of recognizing the greater ability of those in College, tended to look down on them because the fees their parents paid were lower. In Macmillan's case his father could no doubt have afforded the Oppidan scale, but he was proud that his sons were clever enough and had worked hard enough to gain scholarships.

During his three years at Eton, Harold Macmillan lived in the Tudor building on the north side of School Yard opposite College Chapel. Looking back on his time there, he recalls that 'it was plain living and high thinking, but I was brought up to both'.[4] He got his College Wall colours, but this was his only distinction at games, perhaps because he left Eton early owing to ill-health. His close friends there included Harry Crookshank; Henry Willink, later Minister of Health and then Master of Magdalene College, Cambridge, and Vice-Chancellor; and Julian Lambart, who became successively a housemaster, Lower Master and finally Vice-Provost of Eton.

Lambart and Macmillan have remained friends ever since and still stay with each other periodically at Birch Grove in Sussex and at Lambart's house at St David's in South Wales. They both had the same tutor, the legendary A.B. Ramsay, known as 'the Ram', who later took them on an Hellenic Society cruise and gave them their first sight of the Parthenon. Lambart remembers Harold Macmillan's 'great charm and intelligence' as a boy, but recalls that his subsequent interest in and feeling for history were not evident at school. Surprisingly, Macmillan devoted only one paragraph of his six-volume autobiography to his time at Eton.

When an overstrained heart forced him to leave school in 1909, his education was continued at home under the tutorial guidance of A.B. Ramsay, who journeyed to London once or twice a week to correct his Latin and Greek compositions. Another tutor, who had a great influence on Macmillan and became a close friend, was Ronald Knox. Harold's mother, brought up as a Methodist, disapproved of Knox's High Church (and later Roman Catholic) beliefs and forced him to leave when he would not undertake to refrain from discussing religion with her son. Knox thought Macmillan would follow him into the Roman Catholic Church,[5] but Harold wrote to him in 1915:

I'm going to be rather odd. I'm not going to 'Pope' until after the war (if I'm alive).
1 My people. Not at all a good reason, which weighs.
2 My whole brain is in a whirl. I don't think God will mind.[6]

Their friendship lasted unimpaired and Knox went to stay at Downing Street just before he died of cancer in 1957. Harold Macmillan remained a High Church Anglican of deep religious convictions.

In 1912, after gaining a classical Exhibition at Balliol, Macmillan went up to Oxford. For him, as it has been for almost every young man before and since, the University was a liberating and exhilarating experience after the restrictions of any school, even Eton. Among the friends he made there, many of whom were killed in the First World War, Alan Herbert, Bobbety Cranborne (later 5th Marquess of Salisbury) and Vincent Massey were to survive and make their mark in later life.

Oxford was a mixture of comfort and hardship. A hot breakfast and lunch, served in one's room by an attentive 'scout', were luxurious; but a walk of 200 or 300 yards to the nearest bath was less agreeable, especially in winter. Until elected to one or more of the social clubs, it was usual to dine in Hall, where the food, accompanied by a glass or two of claret, was 'tolerably good'. Whisky in those days cost 2s 6d or 3s a bottle.

Harold Macmillan loved Balliol, which he regarded as the mecca of intellectual life and as a microcosm of the world in its variety and catholicity. Its undergraduates, drawn from every class, were rich and poor, scholars and athletes, but in those days it was 'an entirely masculine, almost monastic, society ... there were women's colleges with women students. But we were not conscious of either ... they played no role at all in our lives.'[7]

Macmillan joined innumerable Oxford societies, including the Union. He was already interested in politics, and had somewhat confused sympathies which ranged, as he himself described them, between Tory-Democrat, Liberal-Radical and Fabian Socialist. In the Union he usually supported the Liberal Government of the day, especially in its more radical measures, but like many young men he was attracted to Socialism and in October 1912 he and Harry Strauss (who became a Conservative MP and Minister, and later Lord Conesford) supported a motion that 'This House approves the main principles of socialism.' Four months later he spoke critically of the public school system – a line he was to follow in his book *The Middle Way*, in which he argued that shared schooling would lead to greater understanding between people of different backgrounds.

In December 1913 Macmillan supported a motion of confidence in Asquith's Government and during his time at Balliol the Prime Minister came to dine in Hall and made the speech in which he referred to 'the tranquil consciousness of effortless superiority which is the mark of the Balliol man'. An even more memorable occasion was a speech at the Union by David Lloyd George, whose personality and performance made such a deep impression on Macmillan that he recalled sixty years later 'the rapid changes from grave to gay, from slow to quick, now menacing, now seductive. I can still see the tremendous head, with the long raven-black hair.'[8]

Lloyd George's visit was an opportunity for Tory Oxford to stage a demonstration, but the attempt was admirably controlled by Gilbert Talbot, then President of the Union, and the evening was a success. In a letter to Hermione Lyttelton, written sixty years later, Harold Macmillan recalled Talbot's 'great coup in bringing Lloyd George to Oxford, which was then as if he had brought Cromwell to Oxford during the royalist occupation'.

During his time at Balliol, Macmillan acquired the intellectual mastery which contributed so much to his success in later life. He does not seem to have excelled in debate, but his speeches were frequent, carefully thought out and well prepared. The *Isis* commented on one of them that it was 'in many ways a model paper speech' but recommended 'more originality' for the future. He was elected Secretary of the Union in November 1913, Treasurer in March 1914 and, but for the outbreak of war, he would have been a strong candidate for the presidency in his last year at Oxford.

In 1965, Sir Colin Coote, who was a Balliol contemporary, wrote: 'He has hardy changed at all in the last fifty years. Probably wrongly, I always imagined that he modelled himself on A.J. Balfour – tall, willowy, languid, never at a loss, seldom at a height, ready at any time to make a "defence of philosophic doubt".'[9]

Despite Macmillan's Liberal/Labour tendencies, Disraeli was always his political hero. Macmillan was steeped in biographies of the former Conservative leader and especially in the great work of Moneypenny and Buckle. Books were the inevitable background to his life; he read voraciously himself and was intensely proud of the family firm.

In spite of the social distractions of Oxford, he worked hard, especially in the vacations, and achieved a First in Honour Moderations in the Easter term of 1914. During the glorious summer of that year, with week after week of cloudless blue skies, Macmillan played tennis and cricket, punted on the river and bathed, read Dostoyevsky, went to luncheon and dinner parties and occasionally to the opera or ballet in London; but this idyllic existence was soon to be cut short by the onset of war. Unlike Anthony Eden, he did not return to Oxford when it was over. Of his friends and contemporaries few had survived, and to Macmillan Oxford had become a city of ghosts. He could not bring himself to visit the University for many years.

2
THE FIRST WORLD WAR

Harold Macmillan emerged from a London ballroom in June 1914 to hear a newspaper boy calling out the morning news headline: 'Serbia's reply to the ultimatum. Archduke murdered.' Franz Ferdinand had been assassinated at Sarajevo. This meant little or nothing to the *jeunesse dorée*, so soon to sacrifice their lives on the Western Front, but within a few weeks the Great War had begun.

Macmillan joined the Artists' Rifles and was posted to Southend as a 2nd Lieutenant in the King's Royal Rifle Corps. No weapons were yet available for issue to his unit and he feared the war might be over before he could take part in it. He need not have worried. Through his mother's influence he obtained a transfer to the Grenadier Guards in March 1915 and by August he was in France with the newly-formed 4th Battalion.

Six weeks later the Guards Division fought its first action at the battle of Loos, which Lord Kitchener described as a substantial success. In fact there were 45,000 casualties for a gain of rather less than one mile. The battalion lost 11 officers and 350 other ranks and Macmillan had a head wound and a bullet through his right hand. He was evacuated to England, to a hospital in Lennox Gardens, and thereafter joined the Reserve Battalion at Chelsea Barracks, from which he mounted King's Guard at St James's Palace and spent an enjoyable convalescence. By April 1916 he was back in France with a new draft for the 2nd Battalion, then in the line in the Ypres salient, where he was joined by his old friend Harry Crookshank.

Those who fought in the Second World War (and still less the younger generation who have no experience of war at all) cannot easily imagine 'the desolation and emptiness' of the battlefield – described by Macmillan in a letter to his mother in May 1916 – where nothing was visible except 'a few shattered trees and three or four thin lines of earth and sandbags'. Yet thousands of men, concealed 'like moles or rats' in their dug-outs, were busy planning death and launching missiles of destruction against each other.

Night patrols were often used at this period to take prisoners or identify German regiments and, in leading one of these, Macmillan suffered severe concussion and a slight wound when a bomb exploded on the side of his tin helmet. At the end of July, the Guards Division left Ypres to take part in the Battle of the Somme. After a successful company assault against a German machine-gun post on the Ginchy–Flers road, Macmillan was hit by shrapnel in the right knee during the march south, but the wound was not serious and he was able to continue. Worse was to follow.

After heavy fighting and the capture of a line of trenches, Macmillan took out a small party to deal with some troublesome machine-gun fire from the left flank. He was shot at short range and seriously wounded by bullets which entered his thigh below the hip and lodged in his pelvis. He lay dazed but still conscious in a shell-hole and, as he was not in pain, was able to pass the time by reading *Prometheus* in the Greek, a copy of which he carried, somewhat improbably, in his pocket. A counter-attack was mounted and could have proved fatal, but he pretended to be dead and the German soldiers took no notice of him. He remained there all day without food or water and was eventually rescued by a search party under cover of darkness. By this time his right knee was stiff and painful and his left leg unusable owing to the wound in his thigh. A stretcher party was detailed to carry him to a dressing station, but the shelling was so heavy in Ginchy that Macmillan thought it wrong to risk the lives of the stretcher-bearers and sent them back to the battalion. He was now alone, without the need to set an example of courage he did not feel. Fear is a powerful incentive and, although in theory unable to move, he somehow crawled out of Ginchy and rolled himself into a ditch by the road-side, where he was later picked up by some transport of the Sherwood Foresters. He was taken to a dressing station and thence to a hospital at Abbeville. Unfortunately his wound was allowed to heal without first being drained, so that abscesses formed inside and his whole body became poisoned.

Some weeks later he was sent back to England, arriving at Victoria Station dangerously ill and with a high temperature. He should have been taken to Essex, but he persuaded the ambulance driver to go to Cadogan Place instead. His mother immediately took charge, drove with him to a hospital in Belgrave Square and telephoned a surgeon she knew called Sir William Bennett, who performed an immediate operation, which saved his life.

For Macmillan the war was over. Apart from a period of sick leave and a short spell of light duty at Chelsea Barracks, he was in hospital for over two years, undergoing a series of operations to remove pieces of metal and bone from his thigh. The wound was not completely healed until early in 1920.

In August 1918 he wrote light-heartedly from hospital to Hermione Lyttelton about a League of Individuals 'which Bobbety Cranbourne and I are going to start. We are going to go about refusing to do things. Also we are to have no telephones; in fact we are going to start a telephonoclastic heresy. I think it will be rather soothing.'

He went on to describe his companions in hospital: 'The man in the bed next to me is stone deaf as a result of shell shock. He is a very voluble talker, but, as he can hear absolutely nothing that one says, it's one of the easiest conversations to maintain. He is talking all the time to me now. I just say "Rhubarb, Mr Benson" from time to time and he is quite delighted. ... The man on the other side is much more trying. He speaks with a strange kind of Midland accent which is quite unintelligible ... so far all I have gathered is that he has a profound admiration for ... Joseph Chamberlain, which I pretend (rather hypocritically, but for the sake of peace) to share.'

Macmillan had had what is known as 'a good war' and was unlucky not to have been awarded a Military Cross for his part in it. Decorations in wartime are often almost a matter of chance and depend on how well the citation is written. They were usually more difficult to obtain in the Brigade of Guards than in most other units. Colin Coote wrote: 'What only a few may remember is his immense physical courage. I have been told that there was a saying in the Guards Brigade "as brave as Macmillan".'[1]

In 1916 Asquith had been replaced as Prime Minister by Lloyd George, and in France the useless slaughter of Passchendaele, with its 400,000 casualties, had been followed by the German Spring offensive of 1918 and then by the turn of the tide and final victory for the Allies.

Harold Macmillan learnt much from the First World War – the discipline of the Brigade of Guards and the superb fighting qualities it produced; the involuntary feeling of contempt for those 'gentlemen in England now abed' who did not take their part in the battle; the companionship of shared danger and discomfort with those who did; and the better understanding of the soldiers he led, their humour and their steadfast endurance.

Young men whose only experience hitherto had been the pursuit of learning or of pleasure now knew keener perceptions, more mature motivations, and they felt the need to close the gap between the 'two nations'[2] and make a better world for the less privileged. Harold Macmillan was one of them.

3

CANADA AND MARRIAGE

During the long months of illness, Macmillan read widely and thought deeply of the contribution he could make both to his family firm and to the country. But business and politics were in the future. He wanted, first, to see more of the world. An opportunity seemed to arise when George Lloyd (later Lord Lloyd of Dolobran) was appointed Governor of Bombay and invited Macmillan to join his staff as an ADC. Unfortunately Macmillan was not yet fully recovered from his wound and the doctors declined to pass him as fit for service in India. He was disappointed but an alternative soon arose. His mother, so often a decisive help in his early life, had heard that the Duke of Devonshire, then Governor-General of Canada, needed some young ADCs to replace the older men who had filled this role during the war. She was a friend of the Duke's mother and the appointment was speedily arranged. It was to be an important one for Macmillan.

For a young man of twenty-five, after four years of war, life at Rideau Hall in Ottawa was an agreeable experience. The work was light, the other members of the staff friendly, and the family and their guests created the atmosphere of a large and enjoyable country-house party. The visit of the Prince of Wales to Canada in the autumn of 1919 added a little to the work and a great deal to the interest. Macmillan had the opportunity to travel from coast to coast on both the Canadian Pacific and Canadian National railway systems and to see the vast plains of Manitoba, the breath-taking beauty and grandeur of the Canadian Rockies, the developing city of Vancouver and the surprisingly 'English' island of Victoria.

The Duke of Devonshire had sat in the House of Commons for nearly twenty years and had been a junior Minister in the Governments of Balfour and Asquith before going to Canada in 1916, so his advice was often sought and always welcome. He was a popular and successful Governor-General, who enjoyed the affection and respect of the Canadian people. When he became aware of Macmillan's interest in politics, he made a practice of discussing the problems of the day with his young ADC, who learnt much from him and from the political leaders with whom he came in contact.

Mr Shimwell, who had started life as a garden boy at Chatsworth and ended as Clerk of the Works there, recalls hearing the Duke telling his military secretary, Colonel Henderson, at Government House, that Harold Macmillan was thinking of going into politics and that, if he did, he would probably become Prime Minister of England. The Duke was devoted to Harold and would have been proud and pleased if he had lived long enough to see his prophesy come true.

The Governor-General was more than a figure-head in those days. He was the main channel of communication with the British Government and was consulted by the Canadian ministers on any matter of importance to the two countries. It was an interesting period in Canada both domestically and internationally. The Liberal leader, Sir Wilfred Laurier, had just died and was succeeded by Mackenzie King. The Prime Minister, Sir Robert Borden, was away for much of the time at the Paris Peace Conference, but Arthur Meighen acted effectively for him in his absence. On Borden's return an unsuccessful attempt was made to continue the wartime coalition, a situation comparable to that which Lloyd George was soon to face in Britain. The representation of Canada and the other Dominions at the Peace Conference was the fore-runner of their separate membership of the League of Nations and of their own independent embassies to foreign countries. The process was completed by the Statute of Westminster in 1931.

During his year in Canada, Harold Macmillan fell in love with Dorothy Cavendish, then aged nineteen. Her youngest sister, Anne, who was only nine, remembered acting as a go-between and taking notes and messages from Harold to Dorothy. In return she was rewarded with books like *Call of the Wild* and *Jock of the Bushveld*, and sometimes even with small pieces of bone from the wound in Harold's leg.

Dorothy, slim and faun-like, was the third and the prettiest of the Duke of Devonshire's five daughters. She was not well educated because it was unusual in those days for girls to go to boarding-school, or even day-school, and she and her sisters had been taught, rather inadequately, by a succession of English, French and, until the war, German governesses. She was not at all sophisticated and had met few young men, so propinquity made it probable that she would marry one of her father's ADCs – as her eldest sister, Maud, had already done. She was in love with Harold and this made his time in Canada a period of 'unalloyed enjoyment – in many ways the happiest of my life'.

They returned to England to be married at St Margaret's, Westminster, on

21 April 1920. It was a grand society wedding, typical of the time but seldom seen nowadays. Among the guests were Queen Alexandra, the Duke of Connaught, the future King George VI and several Macmillan authors, including Rudyard Kipling, Thomas Hardy, Lord Bryce and Lord Morley. Harold observed later to Anne Montagu: 'You had all the royalty and Dukes and Duchesses on your side of the Church, but I had three OMs on mine.' The reception, one of the last to be held there, was at Lansdowne House, owned by Dorothy's grandfather.

It has been suggested that one of Harold Macmillan's motives in marrying Dorothy was the fact that she was the daughter of a Duke. There is no truth in this story. He did not marry her for her social position, but because he was deeply in love.

The newly-married couple bought the lease of a house in Chester Square and lived there for the next sixteen years. They had no country house at this period, because Harold had not yet inherited his parents' home, Birch Grove House, in Sussex, but they often went there for weekends and Dorothy was very fond of it. She loved gardening and became an enthusiastic golfer. After the deaths of his father and mother, Harold Macmillan succeeded to the property, which was a secure family base for their children as they grew up. There and at Chester Square they had a happy childhood. Dorothy was an adoring mother and gave them more time and care than parents usually did in those days. She was admirably assisted by Nanny West, who joined the family when their only son, Maurice, was born in 1921, and she remained with the Macmillans for more than forty years till she died at Birch Grove at the age of eighty. There were three daughters – Carol, who married Julian Faber; Catherine, who married Julian Amery; and Sarah, who died unmarried in her thirties. Nanny West looked after them all with loyalty and devotion and was much loved by the whole family. The Macmillans had a good staff, an admirable cook and an adequate income, so they were able to entertain their friends in comfort both in London and at Birch Grove.

The great country-house parties were still a feature of upper-class life in England in the years between the wars and, after their marriage, the Macmillans were frequent visitors at Bowood, Hatfield, Wynyard and Cliveden, and even more often at the Devonshire homes, Chatsworth and Bolton Abbey. Harold Macmillan much enjoyed the shooting, although at that time he had had relatively little practice and was not yet a good shot. John Morrison (later Lord Margadale) tells the story of a visit to Chatsworth in the 1920s when, although still a schoolboy at Eton, he was given a better place in the line of guns than Harold Macmillan, by then a Member of Parliament. He modestly attributes this to the fact that the head keeper at Chatsworth had started life as a kennel-boy at the Morrisons' home at Islay in Argyll. In later years Macmillan became a good grouse shot and a very good pheasant shot. He brought down his last high pheasant in January 1978 at the age of eighty-four. In recalling the incident, he remarked: 'And you know, it was a very high bird!'

The country-house parties were an agreeable and convenient opportunity for conversation and argument and the great political families like the Cecils, Churchills, Stewarts and Stanleys met frequently and entertained their friends and colleagues in their own homes, both in London and in the country. The extent and intimacy of these close personal contacts, based on the same social background, developed their ties of kinship, friendship and mutual interests as well as the political views they shared.

Macmillan's marriage gave him an earlier entrée into this world than he might otherwise have achieved. Anthony Sampson considered that 'in his early married years, relationships with the Devonshires were never very easy: the family patronized him and were bored by his intellectual talk.'[1] I have been unable to discover any evidence to support this observation, rather the reverse, and I do not believe it to be true. Sampson wrote that the Duke, whose second daughter had already married Colonel John Cobbold, a member of the brewing family, 'muttered gloomily on hearing the news of Lady Dorothy's engagement: "Well, books is better than beer." ' Despite this remark, the Duke was in fact fond of Harold and, although the Duchess might have preferred a grander marriage, the Cavendish family were devoted to him and regarded him, in Anne Montagu's words, as 'a very loveable character'. He became a close friend of the Duke's heir, Lord Hartington, and was popular at Chatsworth with the staff as well as with the family.

Large gatherings for Christmas, lasting two or three weeks, were a feature of life at Chatsworth. They were always attended by the seven Cavendish sons and daughters, accompanied by their wives and husbands and all their children. The inclusion of a few cousins and occasionally an old friend of the family meant that the house party usually consisted of at least thirty people. The guests brought their children's nannies and their own menservants and ladies-maids and, including the resident staff, not less than a hundred people were fed at Chatsworth for every meal. It was customary to bake twelve Christmas cakes and a thousand mince-pies before the guests arrived. In addition to the indoor servants, there were up to fifty gardeners, estate workers and foresters and a dozen keepers. A huge Christmas tree was surrounded with presents for every member of the staff.

Chatsworth was always the centre of the family's life. Hardwicke was seldom used and Bolton Abbey only during the month of August for the grouse-shooting. After leaving the Colonial Office in 1923, the Duke seldom visited London and, in his estimation, England scarcely existed south of the Trent.

Harold Macmillan's relationship with his children was neither more intimate nor more remote than was usual in those days. Although, when they were young, Lady Dorothy was closer to them than most mothers of her generation, their early years were spent largely in the care of Nanny West. Their father sometimes swam with them in the pool at Birch Grove House and on one occasion plunged into it fully clad to save a pig - which had inexplicably fallen in - from drowning. In London Macmillan was always busy at the publishing house and in Parliament, but he took Catherine and Carol to school on his way to the office, went for walks with the four of them at weekends and read to them in the evenings whenever he was at home. Catherine did not feel that she got to know him really well until she accompanied him to Strasbourg in 1949, a year before her marriage to Julian Amery.

4

THE HOUSE OF MACMILLAN

Harold Macmillan has described the period between 1920 and 1923 as his 'years of apprenticeship' as a publisher and as a politician. As soon as he returned from Canada, he entered the family firm and began to learn the business of publishing.

There were three senior partners: his uncle, Sir Frederick, his father, Maurice, and a cousin called George. The junior members were George's son, Will, and Harold's brother, Daniel. The older Macmillans were typical Victorians of their class and much resembled John Galsworthy's Forsytes in their outlook and in many of their individual characteristics. The partners solemnly shook hands with each other every morning and lunched together every day. Although they occasionally invited a guest, much of their general business was transacted over the meal.

Macmillan worked for the firm for twenty years until he joined the Government in 1940 and again, when in Opposition, between 1945 and 1951. In the course of time he handled the books of many of its leading authors, including Thomas Hardy, Rudyard Kipling and Hugh Walpole.

Daniel and Alexander Macmillan, Harold Macmillan's grandfather and great-uncle, had founded the firm by opening a bookshop at Cambridge, with the help of a loan from a friend, Archdeacon Hare, who also provided them with valuable introductions to some of the leading University personalities. Religious books were selling well and profitably at the time and they developed their church links and extended the business by taking over another Cambridge bookseller.

The two brothers published their first book in 1843. This was Daniel's real goal. He wrote to a friend in 1852: 'The retail business will keep as good as ever, but my great hopes are in the publishing. I am convinced that we shall gradually, in a few years, have a first rate and capital paying publisher's trade.' His optimism was justified and, in 1855, the Macmillans produced their first big seller, Charles Kingsley's *Westward Ho!*, which was followed

16

by Thomas Hughes's *Tom Brown's Schooldays* in 1857. In the previous year Hughes had written to Alexander Macmillan: 'My chief reason for writing is that, as I always told you, I'm going to make your fortune and you'll be happy to hear that the feat is almost, or at least more than half done. I've been and gone and written, or got in my head, a one volume novel for boys, to wit Rugby in Arnold's time.'

Daniel died in 1857, but Alexander at once took over the leadership and opened a branch of the firm in London. Although Cambridge remained the centre of activity, Alexander came to the capital for the 'Tobacco Parliaments', when he was 'at home to all and sundry' in Henrietta Street, Covent Garden. Tennyson and many of the other leading figures in the literary world were frequent visitors.

Soon *Macmillan's Magazine* was started as a monthly publication. Its contributors were to include George Eliot, Thomas Carlyle, George Meredith, Mrs Gaskell, Herbert Spencer, Professor T.S. Huxley, Robert Louis Stevenson, Matthew Arnold and Thomas Hardy. Henry James's *Portrait of a Lady* and Kingsley's *Water Babies* first appeared in the magazine.

Palgrave's *Golden Treasury* was published in 1861, and the *Cambridge Shakespeare* and the *Globe Shakespeare* in the 1860s. In 1865 Macmillans produced the first edition of *Alice in Wonderland*, but Charles Dodgson (Lewis Carroll) was dissatisfied with the printing and recalled the edition, so that only a few presentation copies survived and have become rare collectors' pieces. The author bore no resentment and later paid this tribute to Macmillans:

The publisher contributes about as much as the bookseller in time and bodily labour, but in mental toil and trouble a great deal more. I speak with some personal knowledge of the matter, having myself, for some twenty years, inflicted on that most patient and painstaking firm, Messrs Macmillan & Co, about as much wear and worry as ever publishers have lived through. The day when they undertake a book for me is a *dies nefastus* for them.... To say that every question gets a courteous and thoughtful reply – that they are still outside a lunatic asylum – is to speak volumes in praise of their good temper and of their health, bodily and mental.[1]

An important scientific journal, named *Nature*, was first published in 1869 and by the 1880s and 1890s the partnership was producing a wide range of books by economists, philosophers, psychologists and scientists.

The business was expanding rapidly and, after a preliminary visit to the United States, Alexander wrote that 'a great international publishing house is possible and would be a grand idea to be realized'. An American branch was opened in 1869, and Frederick, Daniel's elder son, was sent out to help establish it. A corresponding enterprise was launched in Canada in 1905.

Following Alexander's death in 1896, the American company became a separate entity, though retaining close links with the parent organization until 1951. After six years as a classical master at St Paul's School, Daniel's younger son, Maurice (Harold Macmillan's father), joined the firm in 1883, as did Alexander's son, George. Another important recruit was John Morley, who came in to read and edit new manuscripts.

Macmillans did not think highly of Bernard Shaw's early novels, which they declined, and an office report in 1884 noted that 'he has some promise of writing in him if he did not disgust us by his subject'. Morley thought they would not have much financial success with his work, 'but the writer, if he is young, is a man to keep one's eye upon'. Despite their unfavourable reaction, Shaw wrote sixty years later: 'Macmillans were very much ahead of the older publishers (I tried them all) in recognizing my talent.'[2]

H.G. Wells was less complimentary. The partners had turned down *The New Machiavelli*, and Wells found them insufficiently adventurous: 'I like your firm in many ways,' he said in a letter. 'I don't think you advertise well and I think you're out of touch with the contemporary movement in literature. I don't think you have any idea of what could be done for me ... But on the other hand you are solid and sound and sane.'[3] His criticism seemed justified when, after selling only 180 copies of *Mr Kipps* in a whole year, he persuaded them to let Nelsons bring out a cheaper edition, which sold 43,000 copies in a few months.

Macmillans also rejected some of Thomas Hardy's early books and sent him letters suggesting improvements in his writing and the choice of better subjects. Hardy was not discouraged and later became one of their most renowned authors, although it was only towards the end of his life that he grew fashionable and gained a wide readership. Harold Macmillan, who did some business with him in this period and used to visit him occasionally in Dorset, recalls that 'he was rosy-cheeked like an apple; and one felt he had the slight acidity of a good Cox's Pippin'. Sir Frederick Macmillan liked telling the story of a lunch party, at which a gushing lady exclaimed: 'Oh, Mr Hardy, dear Mr Hardy, tell us about Tess. Tell us what Tess meant to you.' Hardy, looked across the table to Sir Frederick: 'Lady Blank wants to know about Tess. What shall I say? Anyway, Tess has been a good milch cow to you and me, Fred!' The firm had another major success with Morley's *Life of Gladstone* in 1903.

After Alexander's death at the end of the century, control of the business passed to Daniel's sons, Frederick and Maurice, and to Alexander's son, George. In his book *The House of Words*, Lovat Dickson refers to them as 'bluff Christian gentlemen, dispensing good and making a satisfactory profit out of it'.

Frederick was largely responsible for the Net Book Agreement, a milestone in the history of publishing, which prevented under-selling and the stocking of only a small selection of books. Its purpose was to ensure that books were sold at the listed price instead of at a discount. Macmillans would only sell to bookshops which undertook not to cut the price and this policy was gradually adopted by other publishers, whose trade association circulated a draft of the Net Book Agreement in 1899. Soon afterwards a battle took place with the Times Book Club, in the course of which Frederick led the way in stopping the sale of nearly new books at high discounts a few months after publication. Success in this book war led to the tightening of the Net Book Agreement.

Harold Macmillan recalls that 'George was serious and his spiritual home was the Athenaeum.... He took a great part in developing the theological, classical and higher technical side of our publications.' George was a good editor of classical text-books and was responsible, through a friend, for bringing out *Grove's Dictionary of Music*.

Harold's father, Maurice, allowed himself few holidays – not more than a fortnight or three weeks in a year – and devoted all his energies to the business. He was especially concerned with the educational side of the work and with expansion overseas. An Indian branch was opened in Bombay in 1901 and an Australian branch in Melbourne three years later. In 1898, Richard Bentley's entire publishing business was bought by Macmillans.

It has been said that Harold Macmillan's mother made a formidable impact on the firm's fortunes and helped to start its specialization in text-books, but Harold Macmillan doubts that this was so. Apart from entertaining the authors, she took little part in the publishing business, although her charity school for orphaned boys was useful in providing staff, including several subsequent managers, for the firm. Her only direct involvement arose from having read the American proofs of *Gone with the Wind*, which so much impressed her that she insisted on the purchase of the British rights. The book became the best-selling novel in the history of the partnership.

Harold Macmillan was the last of his generation to join the family firm. His uncle, Frederick, handed over to him the duty of looking after the affairs of many of their leading authors, including Thomas Hardy, Rudyard Kipling, Hugh Walpole, W.B. Yeats and Maynard Keynes. Harold Macmillan met Kipling from time to time at the office or at a club, and occasionally visited him at Bateman's, his house in Sussex. Business matters were dealt with by his wife or by his literary agent, but he sometimes consulted Macmillan for advice on the format of a book or its illustrations. Kipling was very reserved and, partly, no doubt, owing to the death of his only son in the war, he always seemed to Harold 'a somewhat sad figure'.

Macmillan's relationship with Hugh Walpole was much closer. He looked after the publication of Walpole's successful novels, saw him frequently and formed an intimate friendship with him. Walpole lacked confidence and was sensitive to any criticism, especially from fellow authors, but Macmillan remembers that 'he was very kind and thoughtful to others, a delightful companion and a loyal friend'.[4] Charles Morgan, another of the firm's authors, was a close friend of Daniel, but Harold saw him often, too, and found his 'grave dignity and delicacy attractive'.

James Stephens, who wrote *The Crock of Gold*, seemed himself 'like a leprechaun', but his success as a journalist and broadcaster discouraged serious writing in his later years. Sean O'Casey, another great friend in the Irish group, used to stay at Birch Grove and, although claiming to be a communist and an atheist, had, in Macmillan's words, 'a truly Christian nature; one of the kindest and most genuine men that I have known. He and Ronald Knox – in their very different ways – were saintly men.' Yeats was another Irish author with whom Macmillan had dealings: 'He used to come in unannounced to my room in St Martin's Street: I can recall his splendid figure, his tie flowing through a fine ring, his somewhat dramatized appearance of the poet and dreamer. But he was also a practical man and by no means despised the mundane problems of publishing.'

As time went on, Harold Macmillan's growing interest in politics and economics led him to encourage the firm to publish more books on these subjects than was usual in those days, including the works of Maynard Keynes. Later, he was instrumental in adding Sir John Wheeler-Bennett to the firm's list of authors.

Sir Frederick, Maurice and George Macmillan all died in 1936. As Harold Macmillan has written: 'The death of the three senior partners and chief proprietors within a period of four months naturally threw a very heavy burden upon my brother and me. As regards day-to-day management, there was little difficulty, for we were already in active and effective control.'[5] The real problem was the death duties and the retention of the family ownership. As the business had built up, the profits had been reinvested and there were few liquid resources to draw upon. In those days, however, estate duty was not as punitive as it is now and the two brothers resolved to raise the money and keep the business. In the years since then, 'closed companies' have been subjected to continually rising taxation and to save and reinvest, once regarded as a virtue, has become almost a vice to be penalized.

On 17 September 1939, the following announcement appeared in the press:

Macmillan & Company Ltd., in response to numerous enquiries from authors, booksellers and members of the public, wish to state emphatically that they propose to carry on their business at St. Martin's Street, London, WC2, until they are either taxed, insured, ARP'd or bombed out of existence.

It was a statement typical of the spirit of the partners and their staff and of the British people as a whole in this crisis of their affairs.

When Harold Macmillan was in office between 1940 and 1945 and from 1951 until his retirement in 1963, the chief burden fell inevitably upon 'my devoted brother, Daniel, who was to me throughout his life a protecting and loving friend'. Their affection was mutual and Daniel always spoke with pride and admiration of Harold's achievements.

Daniel Macmillan had been a scholastic star at Eton and Oxford and would certainly have had a distinguished career as an academic. As a publisher he was not outstanding. C.P. Snow, a well-known Macmillan author, considered that 'his judgement of men and of books was indifferent and he made no mark as a publisher'.[6] But this is a post-war view and perhaps over-critical. He was a shy, kind, very private man, who could be difficult to work for; however, those who liked him and whom he liked enjoyed working with him. He was often autocratic, discussed very little with his colleagues and made all the decisions himself.

Macmillan's autumn list in 1939 was a fine one, but by the 1950s, their best authors were aging and Daniel's recruitment of Alan Maclean was important for the future, since he later became managing director of the British branch of the business.

The family flair for publishing, so evident in the two earlier generations, had faded a little in the third; but Harold Macmillan inherited his share of it and would have made a considerable contribution had he been able to give more time to the business. He has real literary insight of a rather old-fashioned kind and is a good judge of a book, although not an innovator. Throughout his life he has been an insatiable reader and even when he was Prime Minister he would often telephone the firm to give his opinion of a new book or a new author. His comments were always shrewd and usually of more value than those of any of Macmillan's regular readers. His staff enjoyed his unfailing sense of humour and found him kind and considerate to work for.

5
APPRENTICESHIP TO POLITICS

If the years 1920 to 1923 were those of Macmillan's apprenticeship in publishing, they were also a period of growing interest, leading to active involvement, in politics. His brother-in-law, Lord Hartington, had been an unsuccessful candidate in the 1922 election and had been invited to stand again;
other friends from Eton, Oxford or the Army were contemplating political
careers. He was tempted and fell.

The post-war period was a fluid and interesting time in public affairs.
Following the Coalition Government's massive victory in the 'Coupon Election' of December 1918, the Liberal Party, deeply divided between the followers of Asquith and Lloyd George, was already in the process of a disintegration from which it has never recovered. A move to form a centre party drawn
from the Conservative and Liberal supporters of the Coalition did not materialize and the Government gradually lost popularity. The Conservative
leader, Bonar Law, retired in 1921, due to ill-health; unemployment rose to
two million; the peace treaties were widely criticized and the problem of war
reparations appeared insoluble. After difficult and prolonged negotiations,
the Irish Treaty, giving independence to Eire while retaining the six northern
counties within the United Kingdom, was eventually signed in December
1921. But the failure of the important international conference at Genoa in
1922 was a blow to the Prime Minister's prestige; and the prospect of British
involvement in war between Greece and Turkey, though averted by the
Chanak settlement, shook people's confidence in Lloyd George's judgement.
In the end it was his style of government, as much as any specific issue, which
undermined his position. This was exemplified in the sale of honours, which
escalated into a national scandal and gave rise to Baldwin's condemnation of
the 'morally disintegrating' effect of Lloyd George's leadership.

Lord Curzon, ambitious for the premiership, was ambivalent and although
the other senior Conservative Ministers – Austen Chamberlain, Balfour and
Birkenhead – loyally supported the Prime Minister, many members of the
Parliamentary Party, including several junior Ministers, were determined to

bring about the break-up of the Coalition. They were led by Stanley Baldwin, the relatively unknown President of the Board of Trade, and they might not have achieved their purpose but for the re-emergence of Bonar Law, whose health had improved and who was persuaded by Lord Beaverbrook to return to active politics.

A Party meeting at the Carlton Club was convened for 19 October 1922 to resolve the matter. Bonar Law was present and spoke against continued Conservative participation in the Government. His intervention was decisive and the vote was 187 to 87 against remaining in the Coalition. Lloyd George resigned at once, never again to hold office, and the King invited Bonar Law to form a Government. As soon as he had done so, Bonar Law dissolved Parliament and won the ensuing election for the Conservatives by a majority of 203 over the Labour Party.

Macmillan's father-in-law, the Duke of Devonshire, became Secretary of State for the Colonies and established the principle of paramountcy for British East Africa by which, in any conflict between the interests of the settlers and those of the Africans, the latter would prevail. This progressive policy set a pattern for the future which was to culminate in the important decolonization decisions Macmillan himself took as Prime Minister forty years later.

The new Government was soon beset with problems. Against the advice of Bonar Law and Curzon, France – under her new Premier, Poincaré – occupied the Ruhr; and Baldwin, as Chancellor of the Exchequer, negotiated an un-favourable debt settlement with the United States, which Bonar Law was, with difficulty, dissuaded from repudiating. At home, deflationary policies prevailed and unemployment persisted at over one million. In May 1923 Bonar Law, who was suffering from cancer, was again obliged to retire; he died five months later.

The succession lay between Baldwin and Curzon. Many commentators regarded Curzon as the obvious choice and a generation earlier he would almost certainly have gained the prize; but it became apparent that Stanley Baldwin was more acceptable to most of the Conservative Members of Parliament. King George v exercised the royal prerogative and sent for Baldwin, who accepted the King's commission to form a Government without waiting to be formally elected as Leader of the Party.

Faced with the high and continuing level of unemployment, Baldwin de-cided that the introduction of industrial protection offered the best hope of reversing this trend, but he had no mandate for such a major change of policy and felt obliged to go to the country for its endorsement. The General Election was to be held on 6 December 1923.

Harold Macmillan was invited to stand as Conservative candidate for

Stockton-on-Tees. This constituency, with its strong Liberal tradition, seemed a hopeless prospect, but that did not trouble Macmillan: he was more concerned about taking time away from his publishing commitments and only wished for experience of the hustings. He did not expect or want to win. He had no practical knowledge of political campaigning and had done no work, not even a day's canvassing, for the Party. From listening to his father's friends, John Morley, James Bryce and Lord Robert Cecil, he knew a little about political philosophy and, through his father-in-law, something about the post-war problems of the Coalition; but he had no experience of public speaking, of the way an Association works or of how an election campaign is conducted. With so slight a record he would not nowadays have been a likely choice even for an unwinnable seat; but at that time social background counted for more in the Conservative Party than work for the cause or knowledge of the issues. The General Election was imminent, Stockton had no candidate and the chairman of the local Association was delighted to have found someone who was as clever and well connected as Macmillan.

Macmillan himself had misgivings: 'It seemed almost impudence for me, without experience of industrial life, without close contact with the sufferings of unemployment or poverty, without technical knowledge of the problems besetting industry, to come before these people and solicit their suffrage.'[1] But the die was cast.

Lady Dorothy, with her family's political background, had helped at earlier elections, but only in rural areas, where the conditions were very different from those in the industrial North-East. She canvassed assiduously and Macmillan made innumerable speeches. In those pre-television days, meetings were much more important than they are now. In an election in which his Party fared badly, Macmillan did remarkably well and was surprised when his Liberal opponent defeated him by only 73 votes, with the Socialist candidate in third place 1,000 votes behind.

Macmillan had enjoyed his first experience of electioneering, but he had learned much more than how to run an election campaign – he had learned, or begun to learn, about the privations of poverty and the soul-destroying effect of prolonged unemployment. The hardships of an industrial area, after four years of war and another four without work, were a shock and a revelation to someone who had never encountered them before. Stockton was an extreme example. In the years between 1924 and 1929 the level of unemployment in Durham and Northumberland varied between 20 per cent and 25 per cent, and at the worst point in the Depression half the male population of Stockton was without work.

Industry, especially ship-building, was contracting and, although the introduction of unemployment relief by Lloyd George's post-war Government did much to alleviate the distress – and perhaps saved the nation from a near-revolution – it was in itself inadequate to cope with the high unemployment in the distressed areas. It was soon to be supplemented by the 'dole' and even, in extreme cases, by the humiliation of the old Poor Law. It was during this period that the effects of mass unemployment began to haunt Harold Macmillan and the memory of them remained in his mind and influenced his policies for the rest of his life.

In the House of Commons, the 258 Conservatives led Labour by 67 seats, but the Liberals, temporarily united though mutually mistrustful, held the balance of power. Baldwin met Parliament and was at once defeated by the combined Opposition. The Labour Party formed a Government for the first time in British history; it was not to last for long.

The Prime Minister, Ramsay MacDonald, was his own Foreign Secretary and it was in the field of foreign affairs that the Government soon lost credit and credibility. The negotiations for a treaty with Russia were mishandled and the Attorney-General's prosecution in the Campbell case added to the impression of muddle and indecision. Asquith's call for a Select Committee into the latter was rejected by MacDonald and the Liberals joined the Conservatives to defeat the Government in the House of Commons. Another General Election, the third in three years, became inevitable, but the ground on this occasion was much more favourable to the Conservatives than it had been a year before.

The Liberals were discredited, as they have been in similar circumstances since, for having sustained in office an unpopular and unsuccessful Government. The Labour Party looked incompetent and unfit to govern and would probably have lost seats in any event, but the *coup de grâce* came with the publication of the Zinoviev Letter to the British Communist Party. This letter encouraged subversion of the Armed Forces. It may or may not have been a forgery; but it fell into the hands of the Foreign Office and, as the *Daily Mail* had obtained a copy, MacDonald would have been wise to publish it and send a strong note of protest to the Soviet Government in order to allay suspicion of guilt by association. He did not do so, and the incident was an added bonus for the Conservative Party.

In the event, Labour did not lose as heavily as might have been expected and it was the Liberals who suffered most severely; 419 Conservative Members and 151 Labour Members were elected, while the Liberal parliamentary representation was reduced to 40. At Stockton Macmillan achieved a majority of 3,215 over his Labour opponent with the Liberal in third place. Harold Macmillan had embarked on a career in Parliament which, with the exception of two years between 1929 and 1931, was to continue until his retirement nearly forty years later.

6

THE FIRST TWO PARLIAMENTS

For any new Member of Parliament there is a sense of excitement and exhilaration about entering the Palace of Westminster for the first time as of right. He may imagine, with the general election safely over, that his troubles are over too; in fact, they have barely begun.

Harold Macmillan appeared to have acquired a fascinating job – lounging comfortably on the leather benches, listening to great orators in a glamorous atmosphere, talking in the Smoking-Room to the leaders of the nation on terms of equality about affairs of state and enjoying the amenities of what, in his time, was still 'the best club in the world'.

The reality, however, is rather different. The assiduous young Member soon finds that he has to listen to many dull speeches and relatively few that are eloquent or even informative. There is much hard, unpublicized committee work upstairs. The mail is heavy and grows larger every year as Government legislation impinges more directly on the daily lives of the people. Constituents arrive at the House of Commons for interviews or in deputations, usually without appointments and at inconvenient times. A Member is expected to visit his constituency every weekend to attend meetings, 'socials' or civic and charity functions, and to hold 'surgeries' (a post-Second World War development), in order to listen to the problems of the unfortunate and the dissatisfied. The sittings can be late and the hours long, especially in the summer, and the work is often a classic example of scientific drudgery on a grand scale.

In addition, the new Member's words will often be misrepresented; he may be torn to shreds by his political opponents and vilified in the local press. The fierce glare of publicity beats upon his life, both public and private, and blackens every blot. However conscientious he may be, his career is the most precarious in the world; it may be cut short at any election by the unpopularity of his Party or the volatility of his constituents.

That is the black side of the picture, but the atmosphere and much of a

Member's work in Parliament has an extraordinary fascination. It is like a drug which, once experienced, is difficult to give up; and, on great occasions, the drama far transcends that in any theatre in the land.

Disraeli used to describe the House of Commons as the most chilling and nerve-destroying audience in the world. The Member's maiden speech is a considerable ordeal. Sheridan's was so bad that he was advised to give up politics and stick to writing plays – yet he became one of the great orators of his time. The younger Pitt's, on the other hand, was a personal triumph, which justified Burke's tribute: 'This is not a chip off the "old block"; it is the old block himself.'[1] Edward Gibbon, who wrote *The Decline and Fall of the Roman Empire*, never made a single speech, although he was a member for twelve years.

One of the initial problems for a new Member is that of learning the complicated rules of procedure. Towards the end of the last century a new arrival asked in despair, 'How can I ever learn the rules of this place?' – to which one of the Irish members replied, 'By breaking them.'

The essence of Parliamentary procedure lies in the allocation of time and is governed by the maxim that the minority must have its say but the majority must have its way. It is the duty of the Speaker, who interprets the rules, to keep the balance between the rights of the Executive and those of the private Member.

It was this new world that Harold Macmillan entered on 2 December 1924. He had often listened to debates from the Strangers' Gallery, but now he took his own place on the floor. He felt like a new boy at school – there seemed to be so much to learn and to absorb. He watched and listened to the leading personalities: David Lloyd George, who could always fill the House when he rose to speak; Stanley Baldwin, who loathed Lloyd George and warned the younger Members not to fall under his spell; Winston Churchill; Austen and Neville Chamberlain; the Liberal leaders, Herbert Samuel and John Simon; and, on the Labour benches, Ramsay MacDonald, still in his prime, Philip Snowden, Arthur Henderson, and the famous Clydeside rebels led by James Maxton. James Wheatley, David Kirkwood, Campbell Stephen and Geordie Buchanan were the other notable Clydesiders. There were more 'characters' in the House in those days and far fewer technocrats than there are today.

Most new Members like to get rapidly off the mark with their maiden speeches. Harold Macmillan was an exception: he waited for five months before entering the fray. The occasion he chose was the debate on the Budget resolutions on 30 April 1925.

Philip Snowden, the former Labour Chancellor, had criticized Winston Churchill's first budget intemperately and somewhat inaccurately as 'a rich man's budget' and Macmillan described this as a 'monstrous statement'. In fact, the new Chancellor had announced the introduction of contributory pensions for widows, orphans and old people, of which the Opposition approved, and his reduction in the income tax included special remissions for those in the lower income range. 'That is where the shoe pinches,' Macmillan declared. 'If these proposals had been made ... when they were still in office, all would have been well. ... [The] Honourable Gentlemen opposite are in a dilemma. They are not quite certain whether to take the line that we have been stealing their clothing while they ... went to bathe in the muddy waters of Russian intrigue, or whether they are to say the clothes are no good anyway.'

As a maiden speech it was rather more controversial than usual, but it was well received in the House and by the national press, and it led to invitations to contribute articles, many of which were syndicated in provincial newspapers. These dealt mainly with rating reform and housing, including unconventional building methods. One of his maxims in 1925 – 'Housing is not a question of Conservatism or Socialism. It is a question of humanity' – became a Macmillan slogan when he was appointed Minister of Housing twenty-six years later. Baldwin, whom Macmillan much admired, always advised young Members to specialize in a particular group of problems and, with the Stockton background, it was natural for Macmillan to concentrate on social, economic and industrial issues. Unlike Anthony Eden and Duff Cooper, he did not at that time concern himself with foreign affairs.

In the early months of the new Parliament he joined a group of progressive younger Members, who became known as the Young Men's Christian Association, the YMCA. In approximate terms they were the forerunners of, and comparable to, later left-wing Conservative discussion groups like Tory Reform after the Second World War and One Nation in the 1950 and succeeding parliaments. The nucleus of those who worked closely together in this way consisted of their leader, Noel Skelton, Oliver Stanley, John Loder, Rob Hudson and Bob Boothby. Their antithesis were the Industrials, known to the YMCA as 'the Forty Thieves', and the pre-war die-hards led by Colonel Gretton. To the younger Members both these groups represented the forces of reaction in the Party.

In 1925, not for the first time or the last, a serious crisis developed in the coal industry. Almost every coalfield in the country was operating at a loss and, due to the deepening industrial depression, the falling demand for coal at home and abroad made it impossible for the mine-owners to maintain the post-war rates of pay. However, the miners stuck solidly to their slogan: 'Not a penny off the pay, not a minute on the day.' The Government appointed a Royal Commission under the chairmanship of Sir Herbert Samuel and paid a subsidy of £23 million to the industry while the Commission carried out its enquiry. Its report, published in March 1926, was a constructive one, broadly favourable to the miners' case; but the problem of pay was unresolved.

The attitude of both sides in the dispute was inflexible and all negotiations proved abortive. Reluctantly and under strong pressure from the Miners' Federation, the TUC issued instructions for a General Strike in support of the miners, which began on Monday 3 May. Three days later Sir John Simon made a notable speech in which he declared that the strike was illegal and that every trade union leader would be 'liable in damages to the uttermost farthing of his possessions'. Winston Churchill took over the offices of the Morning Post for the production of the British Gazette, and volunteers in every walk of life came forward in large numbers to man the essential services. On 12 May the General Strike was called off.

Baldwin's words and actions had been moderate and fair-minded throughout the crisis and, once it was over, he intervened firmly to prevent attempts by some of the owners to victimize their workers. The TUC leaders recognized and trusted his honesty of purpose and the public had responded to his leadership. In the aftermath of the dispute his position was therefore a strong one; yet he failed to use it to bring about a lasting settlement. The men drifted sullenly back to work but, as Macmillan commented, 'a great opportunity was missed'.[2] Conscious of this, the YMCA turned their minds to relations between industry and the Government in the post-war world. They were impatient of the old laissez-faire attitudes, recognized the growing importance of the trade unions and pleaded for a sense of partnership in industry and for statutory schemes for arbitration and conciliation between management and men.

In September 1926, Harold Macmillan made a speech on this theme which attracted attention and some criticism in the right-wing press. As a result, the YMCA went to work on these questions during the winter and, in the spring of 1927, Macmillan, with Oliver Stanley, Bob Boothby and John Loder as co-authors, published a slim and unpretentious book entitled Industry and the State, which rejected both Socialism and unrestrained individualism as being inimical to Conservative principles. Its concept was an industrial society, the strategic control of which would rest with the State, while the tactical management remained in private hands; public and private industry would work together in a mixed economy. Laissez-faire, concluded Macmillan, 'leads inevitably to socialism. The only anti-socialist programme that has any chance of success is the organization of a social and industrial structure which shall be neither capitalist nor socialist, but democratic; where the wage-earner shall be neither slave nor tyrant, but truly and in the widest sense partner.'[2]

These ideas, now generally accepted, were considered visionary, almost revolutionary, fifty years ago. The book was an attempt to find a *via media* between collectivism and unrestricted private enterprise, and it was the prelude to the more important and influential *The Middle Way*, which Macmillan published in 1938. *Industry and the State* was regarded as representative of the views of the progressive wing of the Party and, though deplored by the die-hards, it evoked a long letter of congratulation and comment from Neville Chamberlain, who considered it an interesting and stimulating contribution to Conservative thought.

The Times described it as 'admirably written and dominated by a sincere and thoughtful endeavour to lay aside outworn prejudices and catchwords'[4]: but the predominantly right-wing press was almost universally hostile: 'What it preaches is nothing more or less than thinly-veiled socialism,' commented the *Sunday Pictorial*,[5] and the *Daily Mail* wondered why 'these gentlemen still figure in the Conservative Party'.[6] The fact that they, Anthony Eden, R.A. Butler and, in the next generation, Iain Macleod, held these views and implemented them when their turn came, ensured the evolution and modernization of the Conservative Party after the Second World War.

In the wake of the General Strike, the Trades Disputes Bill, or something like it, became inevitable. It was preceded by discussion of the Washington Eight-Hour Day Convention, on which the Government was dragging its feet. The Minister responsible, Sir Arthur Steel Maitland, had nothing to say and did not say it very well. Harold Macmillan was caustic: 'I could only draw the conclusion that his speech was not intended to have any particular meaning.' He classified Steel-Maitland as 'a Minister who meant well, but listened too much to the advice of his Department. Whether in Cabinet or in the House, he followed the brief. This is not what Ministers are for.'[7]

The Trade Disputes Bill was introduced in May 1927. It declared illegal any strike or lock-out designed to coerce the Government or by men who were not themselves employed in the industry concerned. Intimidation was made illegal and the Bill substituted 'contracting in' for 'contracting out' of the political levy.

Macmillan conceded the need for legislation along these lines. He did not question the Bill's intentions, but he thought its psychological effects were 'likely to be dangerous to the well-being of the community'. He believed that its secondary results would depend 'not so much on the Bill itself but on the temper in which it is passed. . . . If this Bill is to be the prelude to a general swing to the right, if it means the beginning of reactionary policy, then it means the beginning of the end of this Party . . . and it means also the end of all the members of the moderate Party opposite. It means that the Parties . . . are captured by the extremists.' He thought that much would depend on whether the Bill was regarded by the electorate as 'a revengeful Bill passed in a spirit of reaction' or as 'a wise Bill passed with the genuine desire to put right a real wrong'.[8]

An amendment put down by Sir Leslie Scott and supported by Lloyd George and Sir Alfred Mond sought a system of delay and conciliation before strikes in public utility services could take place. Macmillan strongly supported this and called for a more positive approach to economic and industrial conditions. The debate had no practical result, but it helped to improve the atmosphere. Unknown to Back-Benchers at the time, Chamberlain's 1927 diary[9] revealed that he had advocated the same proposal in Cabinet without success. The Act was repealed by the Labour Government in 1945.

During 1927 Macmillan became interested and active in the reform of the rating system as a way of assisting industry without either the political embarrassment of resurrecting protection or the risk of inflation, about which the Treasury was always apprehensive. Churchill's fertile mind was moving in the same direction. Trade had not recovered, exports were static and the unemployment figures remained high. Some new stimulus must be found and the relief of the rate burden by means of direct Exchequer subsidies was a clear candidate for consideration. It was partially incorporated in Churchill's 1928 budget.

The natural life of the 1924 Parliament was drawing to its close by the Spring of 1929. It was dissolved on 10 May. In a leading article after the General Election, *The Times* took the view that 'In the Parliaments of the last fifty years only two or three will be found to rival in quality and quantity the output of the past four and a half years.' There was much truth in this assessment but, from an electoral point of view, it was only one side of the picture. Baldwin's slogan – 'Safety First' – was ill-chosen and uninspiring; and Lloyd George's 'Yellow Book', entitled *We can conquer unemployment*, captured the imagination of a significant proportion of the uncommitted centre vote which might otherwise have remained loyal to the Conservative Party.

Although, owing to the unfair weighting of Britain's first-past-the-post electoral system, only fifty-nine Liberal MPs were returned to the House of Commons, this was enough to deprive the Conservatives of victory. For a popular vote of $8\frac{1}{4}$ million they obtained 260 seats, while the Labour Party, with fewer than $8\frac{1}{2}$ million, secured 288. The Liberals, temporarily united under Lloyd George's leadership, again held the balance of power.

Macmillan's own 1924 majority of 3,215 disappeared and his Labour opponent won Stockton by 2,389 votes. Most of the YMCA Group suffered the same fate: Duff Cooper, Rob Hudson, John Loder and Terence O'Connor were all defeated and only Boothby and Oliver Stanley remained in the

House of Commons. Many newspapers, like *The Times*, the *Daily Telegraph* and the *Observer*, regretted the elimination of these younger Members, but the *Daily Mail* was delighted and hoped that no vacant seats would be found for 'semi-Socialists such as Captain Harold Macmillan'. The *Saturday Review* described Duff Cooper and Macmillan as 'only Socialists in disguise'.

Some commentators were kinder and James Johnstone, the Parliamentary correspondent of the *Yorkshire Post*, referred to the YMCA as 'the young enthusiasts in the Conservative Party who have devoted themselves to the advocacy of social reform'. Of Harold Macmillan personally, he wrote:

In the Group ... Captain Harold Macmillan is a prominent figure; he is indeed its most frequent and most efficient spokesman. He is a model YMCA man. His correctness of manner and bearing, his moderation of speech, the suggestion of the 'good boy' ... are all typical of the general idea of what a YMCA Member should be.... His tall, debonair figure and his fresh, youthful face predispose the House in his favour. He has charm, marred perhaps by a touch of smugness.... He is sincere.... He is an enthusiast who does not enthuse. There is no declamation in his speeches, no skilful manipulation of voice, no display of studied gesture.... He holds his ideas and is not held by them. ... He has them always under control.... He has a grace of style ... he is never formless or slovenly or unpolished. He dresses his ideas with the same taste and care with which he dresses his body. He is one of the best tailored men in the House and he is also one of the most polished speakers in it.... Some enthusiasts for reform deal in vague general phrases ... Captain Macmillan is full of plans for the necessary repair and reconstruction of society ... he is not merely an idealist, he is also a practical student of social affairs ... and he is also in personal contact with the realities of life ... his interest is essentially human. His governing impulse is the desire to give to the mass of the people the fullest possible individual life. He is one of the few promising men whom this Parliament has produced. He has the affinity with the spirit of the age and the understanding of Parliamentary ways which guarantee success in the political life of the future. Some day he will be one of the guiding forces of the Conservative Party, a capable and persuasive Minister.[10]

This was not only prescient; it was a fair, if favourably disposed description of Macmillan at the end of his first Parliament. He had already made a mark in politics which augured well for the future; but his hope of office was delayed longer than could have been expected. Lloyd George had said to Macmillan in 1928, 'You are a born rebel' and, as Macmillan himself admitted, 'lack of promotion was my own fault and the result of my deliberate determination to pursue my own plans and purposes'.[11]

For the time being he was in political limbo, but this did not prevent him voicing his views outside Parliament. Writing in the *Saturday Review* in November 1929, he was strongly critical of the lack of direction in Conservative policy:

The fundamental weakness of the Unionist Party to-day lies in its present confusion of thought ... it has no clear goal towards which it feels itself to be striving. It has too many 'open questions' and too many closed minds. It is at once Protectionist and Cobdenite: imperialist and internationalist; reforming and static. At some moments it favours State interference with the conditions of industry, at others it embraces *laissez-faire* ... Sometimes dominated by the memories of Shaftesbury and Disraeli, it seems about to revive Young England; at other times it appears far more nearly a twentieth-century edition of nineteenth-century Liberalism. Now almost cheese-paring, now almost prodigal, its financial policy presents a series of baffling contradictions.

It was a damning condemnation of his own Party at this period and there was much truth in it.

In a second article he summarized his own objectives:

There are three great aims upon which Unionism must concentrate – the modernization of our economic methods, the humanization of our industrial relations, and the expansion of our foreign and primarily of our imperial markets.[12]

Newspaper articles and speeches outside Parliament kept Macmillan's name before the public, but he was naturally anxious to return to the House of Commons as soon as possible, in order to gain the experience of Opposition, which always provides the opportunity for an ambitious young man to make his reputation. The American economic depression had not yet spread to Britain, and at first the Labour Government appeared to be doing well. There seemed to be no reason why the Parliament should not run its full course and Macmillan was therefore anxious to contest a by-election if the occasion arose. The Hitchin division of North Hertfordshire appeared a likely prospect. Between the wars it was a safe Conservative seat and only fell to Labour in the 1945 landslide. The sitting Member, Major Guy Kindersley, wanted to retire for business reasons and, in December 1929, Macmillan was invited to become prospective Conservative candidate, with the probability of a by-election in the Spring of 1930. When the time came, however, Kindersley changed his mind. There were good reasons for his decision, notably the danger of holding a by-election when the Beaverbrook campaign against Baldwin was at its height; but it left Macmillan in an awkward position. He had only withdrawn from Stockton in order to secure an early return to Parliament. Now that prospect had receded.

It so happened that the new candidate at Stockton, who had been adopted in Macmillan's place, was himself obliged to retire owing to ill-health, and in March 1931 the Executive Committee asked Macmillan to return. His heart was in the North-East and he was delighted to accept the invitation. He was received with great enthusiasm at his adoption meeting in May 1931. As matters turned out, he had only a few months to wait before being re-elected to Parliament.

While Macmillan's political fortunes were undergoing these vicissitudes, his leader's were equally at issue. In Juiy 1929 Lord Beaverbrook, in uneasy alliance with Lord Rothermere, began his campaign for Empire Free Trade. Baldwin yielded partially to this pressure by accepting a policy of imperial preference for manufactured goods, but his rejection of food taxes was unacceptable to Beaverbrook, who continued his attacks on the Party leadership. The economy was deteriorating and the unemployment figures, just over one million in the summer of 1929, had risen to 2,700,000 two years later. The Treasury was obliged to increase its contribution to the unemployment fund, but the socialism of the Chancellor, Philip Snowden, had by this time virtually vanished and he was more interested in retrenchment than in reform. He had agreed that four of his Ministerial colleagues should examine the unemployment problem, but he did not intend to spend public money on its solution, and when their proposals, known as the Mosley Memorandum, were submitted to the Cabinet, they were rejected. Their principal author, Sir Oswald Mosley, then resigned from the Government, insisted on a vote he could not win and published a Manifesto supported by seventeen other Labour Members, including Aneurin Bevan. This demonstration should have been enough, but early in the following year Mosley announced the formation of his New Party. It was a major error of judgement, which brought his Parliamentary career to an abrupt end.

Many of Mosley's original proposals had been constructive and reasonable, and a few of them original, and Harold Macmillan, who was strongly attracted by Mosley, had written to *The Times* on 27 May 1930 in his defence. This letter, described in one newspaper as 'brilliantly indiscreet', did not endear him to the Conservative leadership and was, no doubt, a further check to his political ambitions. Rab Butler and two or three co-signatories answered it the following day and advised Macmillan to find 'a pastime more suited to his talents'. It was the first clash between the two men.

In his autobiography, Mosley observed: 'It was always to me a mystery why Eden was so assiduously groomed for the leadership by the Conservative Party, as his abilities were much inferior to the abilities of Stanley and Macmillan.'[13] This was probably true, but Eden had a nine-year start in office. He had specialized in the relatively calm and then uncontroversial waters of foreign affairs and had been scrupulously loyal to Baldwin, whereas Macmillan had often been at odds with the Party leadership over the major domestic issues of the day.

For a time, Macmillan even contemplated working with the New Party, before it took its later turn towards Fascism, but the flirtation was short-lived. He was shrewd enough to realize that the traditional parties would survive and that it was wiser to work within one of them than to join a man who had no real political base.

When Thomas Jones, a Deputy Secretary to the Cabinet under four Prime Ministers, was asked to recommend a speaker to represent the point of view of the younger Conservatives for an important speech in Washington in 1931, he said he would choose from Walter Elliot, Robert Boothby, Oliver Stanley, Duff Cooper and Terence O'Connor. He described Macmillan as 'quite able, but I think rather pedestrian' and concluded in favour of Walter Elliot.[14]

In February 1931 a committee was appointed under the chairmanship of Sir George May to advise on the cuts it considered necessary in the worsening economic situation. The Committee's Report was published on 31 July, the day after Parliament had adjourned for the summer recess. It recommended a reduction in national expenditure of £120 million. This shook the nation's confidence and itself caused a run on the pound. Snowden agreed with the Committee's findings but, although the majority of the Cabinet willed the end, they shrank from implementing the means. Ramsay MacDonald made no serious attempt to convince them, and only Snowden, Sankey, the Lord Chancellor, and J.H. Thomas remained with him when the Government resigned.

Following talks with King George v and with the leaders of the other political parties, MacDonald then formed a National Government to put the May Committee recommendations into effect. It was 'a Ministry of nearly all the talents', as Churchill is said to have described it. He himself was excluded, no doubt because of his views on India, and Lloyd George was seriously ill at the critical time and unable to serve. The National Government was formed as an emergency administration to carry through the essential economies and was only intended to remain in office for a short time. In fact it continued under MacDonald's premiership for four years and under that of Baldwin, and later Chamberlain, for a further five.

The immediate crisis had been overcome and a General Election now became necessary – but on what programme? The Conservatives were insistent on a general tariff; the Liberals were still adamant for free trade: MacDonald was undecided. Eventually Neville Chamberlain devised the formula of the 'Doctor's Mandate', by which Ministers would go to the country as a 'united' Government, free to decide upon policy after being returned to power. National unity was the theme, but within it Baldwin could argue for protection, Samuel for free trade. This somewhat bizarre arrangement worked surprisingly well, because most people were by this time a little bored by the old tariff controversy and merely wanted the best men available in public life to work together in the national interest and restore the country's prosperity. Polling Day was fixed for 27 October.

Macmillan was suffering from neurasthenia in a clinic in Germany. He was weak and walking with the aid of two sticks, but he returned to Stockton at once and offered to stand down if the Labour Member would support Ramsay MacDonald. Fortunately for Macmillan the Labour Member declined to do so. The Liberal candidate then withdrew to avoid splitting the anti-Socialist vote. Although the means test and the cuts in unemployment benefit were naturally unpopular in an area so dependent on the dole, the people of Stockton put the national interest before their own and, after an exceptionally rowdy election, Harold Macmillan was returned with a majority of over 11,000. In fact, the Labour vote had remained remarkably steady, but the Liberals had voted for Macmillan almost to a man.

The same pattern prevailed all over the country, with the result that no less than 473 Conservatives were elected, with 68 Liberals (some of whom supported Sir John Simon and some Sir Herbert Samuel) and 13 National Labour followers of the Prime Minister. The official Labour Party was reduced to 52 Members in the House of Commons. It was the greatest landslide in political history and is never likely to be seen again.

7

THE NATIONAL GOVERNMENT

From 1931 to 1935 the House of Commons presented a strange appearance. The Labour Party occupied the Opposition benches above the gangway, but did not of course fill them. The Liberal followers of Sir Herbert Samuel sat (after the Ottawa Conference) on two of the Opposition benches below the gangway, with the Conservative Party overflowing from the Government side of the House on to the remaining Opposition benches. Harold Macmillan took his place with the overflow on the fourth bench below the gangway, facing the Government Front Bench. This was a suitable position for someone who was more often critical of than complimentary to the Ministers in his own Party.

George Lansbury, who had held the relatively minor office of Minister of Works in the Labour Government, was now leader of the Opposition, with Clement Attlee, the former Postmaster-General, as his deputy. They were the only Ministerial survivors of the landslide. The occupants of the Government Front Bench were more distinguished and far more experienced.

The Prime Minister's position was a painful one. He was regarded as a Judas by his old friends and former colleagues in the Party he had done so much to create; but he had acted courageously and in the national interest and his character and career have been much underrated. He had a high reputation abroad and spoke well and persuasively on foreign affairs. Harold Macmillan wrote that at the beginning of the Parliament he 'commanded not only our affection but our respect'. As the years passed his eyesight deteriorated and his mental and physical powers began to fail. Towards the end, his speeches became tortuous, incoherent and almost meaningless: 'Always high-minded, he became woolly-minded.' But he had a noble appearance, great charm and dignity and 'was a much more considerable man than it is now the fashion to admit'.[1]

The real power lay with Baldwin even before he succeeded MacDonald in 1935. He was the leader of by far the largest Party in Parliament and has been described as the first 'modern' Conservative Prime Minister. He did much, both to educate the Tory Party for its role in the second half of the twentieth century and to ensure that the Labour Party would be a safe and responsible alternative Government. He was trusted and respected by the Labour Members in the House of Commons and by the trade union leaders outside it, and he did more than anyone else to lower the tensions between the social classes in the inter-war years. He was a good House of Commons man and sat in the Chamber more than any other Prime Minister before or since. This was the secret of his mastery of the House and of his ability to reduce the temperature if it became over-excited or unruly. Macmillan described him as 'a great Peace Minister, in many ways comparable to Walpole'[2] and Jan Smuts thought him 'a good Englishman, a bad European' – by which he meant that Baldwin was skilful in his handling of domestic issues, but not so successful over foreign affairs, in which he was less interested. Baldwin's appeal was to the heart rather than to the head and he attracted the young by his idealism and his sincerity. Above all, he was a patriot, devoted to his country and with an instinctive appreciation of the character and aspirations of its people.

The most effective and efficient Minister was Neville Chamberlain. Able and immensely hard-working, he had proved an outstanding administrator as Minister of Health, with a genuine desire to improve and reform. Harold Macmillan has described him as corvine in his facial appearance, and 're-spected and feared, rather than loved'.[3] He had a harsh, rasping voice and, although always clear and logical, he was not an inspiring speaker. A man of limited imagination and little personal charm, he was cordially disliked by his opponents, mainly because of an ungracious and somewhat supercilious manner. He was a kind man, but outside his immediate family circle lacked warmth and friendliness. He was intellectually arrogant and always sure that he was right; but as Chancellor of the Exchequer during much of the 1931 and 1935 Parliaments, he became the key figure in the National Government.

Of the Liberal Ministers, Sir John Simon had a clear lawyer's mind. Macmillan thought him 'agreeable and friendly', but he longed to be loved and was not, partly because of an unattractively unctuous manner. Sir Herbert Samuel was the leader of the other Liberal faction, which withdrew its support from the Government on the issue of imperial preference. Macmillan records that 'his speeches were always admirably and even persuasively argued, but they had no fire'.[4]

The two outstanding figures of the time were not included in the adminis-tration: Lloyd George's great days as leader of the nation were over; Chur-chill's were yet to come. Lord Boothby has described their relationship at this period as one of 'mutual admiration, mutual fear, but not of mutual affection'. Harold Macmillan was dazzled by Lloyd George, as were many of the younger men between the wars. Even in his decline, he was a towering figure, whose personal charm and magnetism were equalled only by the poetry and force of his Celtic oratory. Churchill's position was formidable but frustrating. Through his strong and persistent opposition to the Government's India policy he became isolated from the main stream of Conservative opinion and he alienated the progressive element in the Party, to whom his attitude seemed reactionary and unrealistic. He was out of office for a whole decade at the height of his powers, a politician with a past but apparently no future – a man of courage, eloquence and bad judgement.

On the back benches, the YMCA membership had changed considerably since the 1924 Parliament. Anthony Eden, Duff Cooper, Oliver Stanley, Rob Hudson and Terence O'Connor had all become Ministers, but a successor group, which concentrated on policy, included Rob Bernays, Anthony Crossley, Paul Emrys-Evans, Edward Grigg (later Lord Altrincham), Hamilton Kerr, Richard Law (later Lord Coleraine), Kenneth Lindsay, Hugh (later Lord) Molson and Charles Peat, with Tom Martin as its secretary. Lord Eustace Percy was a most helpful later addition. Macmillan was a prominent member and was also active in a new Northern Group of Conservative Members who represented seats in the North of England and whose purpose was to bring pressure upon the Government in the interests of their region.

The Cabinet was soon faced with a divisive issue. In 1931, the Statute of Westminster had formally recognized the independence of the old Dominions, now linked only by their common allegiance to the Crown; but under Conservative pressure new economic ties were negotiated at Ottawa in 1932. The Conference was only partially successful because Britain was unwilling to face taxes on food; but the acceptance of imperial preference was more than the free traders could stomach, and Snowden, Samuel and Sinclair resigned from the Government in September 1932, a year after its formation. The Liberal followers of Sir John Simon, less intransigent on tariffs, remained in support of the Ministry. Although known as Liberal Nationals, they were gradually absorbed in, and became indistinguishable from, the Conservative Party.

At home, unemployment was still the overriding problem. By June 1931, 21 per cent of the working population were unemployed and the figures were destined to rise even higher, to nearly three million, before the tide turned. As Macmillan wrote later:

Whole families had been without work and wages for long periods. . . . Their clothes were worn out, their furniture in disrepair, their savings gone, their homes dilapidated. Weekly sums of money . . . which might have been adequate for a man out of work for a few weeks, were cruelly insufficient for men involved in what had become almost permanent unemployment. . . . I shall never forget those despairing faces . . .[5]

After the hardship and horror of the wartime battlefields of Loos and Ginchy and the Somme, Macmillan was faced by the industrial battlefield at Stockton. His compassion was aroused and his conscience moved.

This was the period of the 'hunger marches' – especially the poignant Jarrow march. Those who lived in comfort in the South of England had no idea of the suffering and hopelessness of so many of their less fortunate fellow citizens. But Macmillan was well aware of it and deeply distressed by it. 'These grim conditions filled the background of my life and thoughts,' he recorded.[6] He never forgot the experience, which greatly influenced his economic policies in the years ahead.

In 1931, 'transitional benefit' (in effect a subsidy by the tax-payers to the unemployed) amounted to about £40 million and was, as it had to be, means-tested, though this was resented in the country and constantly debated in Parliament. The use of the old Poor Law to supplement unemployment benefit was also criticized as an unfair local burden to meet a national need; but this was largely resolved by the Unemployment Act of 1934, which transferred 95 per cent of the responsibility to the central Government. The process was completed by the establishment of the Unemployment Assistance Board, which developed later into the National Assistance Board.

There still remained the problem of the so-called 'special areas', which included the North-East; this was due primarily to the collapse of the heavy industries. During the winter of 1932–3, unemployment reached 27% in Macmillan's part of the country and was even worse elsewhere. In Merthyr Tydfil it rose to 62% and in Jarrow to 67%. Speaking in the House of Commons in March 1934, Macmillan forecast: 'We shall have to take great powers in the hands of the State to direct in what localities and areas fresh industrial development will be allowed.' Nowadays regarded as normal, this suggestion was considered almost revolutionary forty years ago.

Under pressure, the Government appointed four Commissioners to investigate conditions in certain parts of the country – including Tyneside. Captain Euen Wallace, the Civil Lord of the Admiralty, produced an imaginative and constructive report which was discussed in the debate on the Address in November 1934. Macmillan pointed out that there could be no justification for excluding Tees-side from the enquiry while including Tyneside, but he also ridiculed the idea of regional research. Quoting and adapting Disraeli's phrase 'the key of India is not Herat or Kandahar; the key of India is London',[7] he said, 'So it is with the problem of unemployment. The key lies, not in South Wales or in Durham, but in Downing Street and Threadneedle Street.' He pointed out that industry was making money but not investing it: 'We are neither investing the surplus abroad nor at home. Money is, therefore, "all dressed up and nowhere to go".'[8]

The Special Areas Bill, which followed, was welcomed by Macmillan as far as it went, although he thought its scope too limited: 'At no stage have I attempted to minimize the importance, which I believe to be great, of this Bill,' he said, 'but in comparison with the problems before us this is a mouse – a nice mouse, a good little mouse, a profitable and helpful little mouse, but a ridiculous, microscopic, Lilliputian mouse.' He accused the Government of having no comprehensive policy; of saying, in effect, 'that the system demands $2\frac{1}{2}$ million unemployed'.

In June 1935, Ramsay MacDonald yielded the premiership to Baldwin and himself became Lord President of the Council, the post Baldwin had held hitherto. In the reshuffle, Sir John Simon left the Foreign Office for the Home Office, to which he was better suited and in which he was more successful, and Sir Samuel Hoare succeeded him as Foreign Secretary. It was not a position he was to occupy for very long.

The change of Prime Ministers made no difference to the policy for the special areas and in another debate on this subject in July, Stanley Baldwin merely advocated the transfer of population as a solution. In other words, Macmillan commented curtly, we are to say to these people: 'You are now depressed – you must become derelict.'[9] He pressed for the extension of public works to cover not only the necessities but also the amenities of life, including the provision of parks, recreational facilities and public buildings: 'When was this ... dismal view invented', he asked, 'that a legitimate public work must always earn its exact amount of revenue? On that basis Pericles would not have built the Parthenon unless he could have shown ... that the revenue from tourists ... would pay interest on it for all time.'[10]

Although Macmillan's speeches were often critical of the Government, he was careful to confine his complaints to the subjects in which he had specialized and of which his personal experience was probably greater than that of the Minister concerned. He held sincere views and expressed them fearlessly, but he did not attack the Government over a wide range of other issues and was therefore not regarded as disloyal or as a professional rebel. Nevertheless, promotion continued to elude him. This was not surprising because, apart from his speeches inside and outside Parliament, he was busy throughout the 1930s with the production of books and pamphlets which must, in those days, have seemed very left-wing in character.

After the acceptance by the British people of the 1931 crisis measures, which temporarily reduced their standard of living, much had been achieved in the four years of the 1931–5 Parliament. In 1931 there was an adverse trade balance of £104 million. By 1935 this had become a credit balance of £32 million. Production had risen and unemployment, though still high, had fallen from three million to two million and by July 1936 was down to

1,600,000. The cuts in unemployment benefit and public salaries were restored and income tax was reduced by 6d in the pound. With the passage of the 1932 Wheat Act and the introduction of other cereal subsidies, agriculture became more prosperous.

These were helpful measures, but Macmillan thought that more should be done. In March 1932 he wrote a pamphlet, *The State and Industry*, in which he argued that increased Government intervention in industry had so far been by *ad hoc* methods and, with the new machinery tariffs made necessary, should now be put on a more organized basis. He advocated the establishment of Councils of Industry operating in partnership with the Government and co-ordinated by an Industrial Development Board.

A few months later he produced a more ambitious document on the same lines entitled *The Next Step*, which stressed the need for a comprehensive national policy covering the whole field of politics, industry and finance. In June 1932, Maynard Keynes wrote to him saying he liked the pamphlet very much, but added: 'My criticisms are really due, I expect, to the sort of middle position you occupy.... My main feeling is that you are not nearly bold enough with your proposals for developing the investment functions of the State....'[11]

Keynes put the main emphasis on reflation; Macmillan considered this only part of the policy and that the rationalization of industry was just as important. But in March 1933 he advanced a strong Keynesian argument in the House of Commons: 'In a period of boom individuals are investing freely. ... During that time the Government should ... save, it should pull in its horns. On the other hand, a period of depression, when individuals are unwilling to invest, is the time for capital investment on the part of the Government.' He quoted houses as an example, pointing out that when money and building costs were high 'we built hundreds of thousands of them. Now, in a period of depression, when we can borrow money cheaply and build houses cheaply, we are a little reluctant to invest capital sums from Government sources.'[12]

In the same month he pleaded for greater capital expenditure, lower taxes to increase consumption and stimulate investment, and an unbalanced budget. After a discussion at Macmillan's house, Tom Jones recorded that: 'He talks very much like a Professor of Economics.'[13] He was thinking along the same lines as Keynes at a time when these views were unfashionable. A decade or so later they had found general acceptance.

In December 1933, he published a book called *Reconstruction*, which developed the theme he had put forward in the earlier pamphlets. 'The only thing ... more dangerous than a mistaken policy is to have no policy at all,' he wrote, and 'the machines which enabled man to conquer scarcity now threaten to plunge him deeper and deeper into poverty'. But he added that he thought 'the idea of planning is slowly but definitely gaining ground'. The book was well received by the press and by many of his political colleagues, including several Ministers, and had useful sales to the public.

In the summer of 1934 Macmillan launched the Industrial Reorganization League with the help of Lord Melchett, Sir Robert Horne, Sir Felix Pole, Sir William Firth and Sir Valentine Crittall. Others associated with the League included Israel Sieff, Sir Francis Goodenough, Oliver Lyttleton and Seebohm Rowntree. Melchett introduced a Private Member's Bill in the House of Lords and Macmillan and others addressed meetings all over the country.

In March 1935, with the support of fourteen Parliamentary colleagues, Macmillan produced another book entitled *Planning for Employment*. In the meantime a group in which Macmillan took a leading part had been formed under the leadership of Lord Allen of Hurtwood. It brought together a large number of distinguished men and women of all political affiliations and none, who published a book called *The Next Five Years* in July 1935, which was signed by 153 well-known political and literary personalities. Its economic policy, as Macmillan acknowledged, was a compromise between Socialists and anti-Socialists, but 'a compromise very much to my taste'. Its subtitle was 'An essay in political agreement' and it included proposals for the public control of transport, gas and electricity and for the nationalization of the Bank of England. Hours of work were to be reduced, the means test abolished, the school leaving-age raised and death duties increased. All these measures took effect over the following forty years, mostly under Labour Governments, but Macmillan's description of the book as 'a little to the left of centre' was a euphemism which to most Conservatives in the 1930s must have seemed a remarkable understatement.

In the autumn of 1932 Macmillan paid a visit to Russia, an event that was less usual in those days than it has since become. He was there during the period of the first Five-Year Plan, when Stalin was consolidating his personal power. During his stay in Leningrad he was struck by the overcrowded trams and the almost complete absence of motor-cars or even carts. In Moscow there were more cars, more new buildings and better dressed people. The police were helpful and everyone seemed interested in and well disposed towards foreigners. He had a talk with Maxim Litvinoff, then Commissar for Foreign Affairs; and later, at Nizhni-Novgorod, attended a meeting of the local Communist Party.

On a river steamer *en route* to Stalingrad he talked to fellow passengers who were enthusiastic about conditions in the country, which they assured him were much better than under the Czars. He visited a tractor factory in Stalingrad, where keen and adaptable Russian peasants were being taught new skills by American instructors. At Rostov he saw a large mechanized farm of 250,000 acres, divided into units of 20,000 acres each, where about 3,000 peasants were employed as hired labour. The countryside was reminiscent of the prairie provinces of Canada and the people friendly and hospitable. The south of Russia seemed more prosperous than the north. At a Rostov factory making agricultural machinery and employing 18.000 people, he noticed that the rates of pay varied widely between 75 roubles a month for the least skilled and 278 roubles for the highest category of workers. Piece work was almost universal.

Everywhere in Russia 'anti-religion' was taught as an important subject in the schools. Wherever he went in the cities, Macmillan saw long queues for everything. It was a period of rapid industrialization, when (as since) the people were forced to accept low living-standards in order to allow the development of capital goods and productive capacity; they were trying to achieve in five years what in other countries had taken several generations.

Lord Strang, who had spent three years at the British Embassy in Moscow, commented that 'in the 1930s the truth about the Soviet Union was a subjective phenomenon',[14] depending on how the visitor's mind was conditioned before he got there; and after a talk with Macmillan at that time, Tom Jones noted: 'He has just returned from Russia, much impressed by what he saw.'[15] Nevertheless, Macmillan wrote that when he crossed the frontier on his way home, he felt as though he was 'stepping back from a kind of nightmare world into the world of reality'.[16]

If he is to be an effective influence it is impossible for a Back-Bench Member of Parliament to cover the whole spectrum of politics. On international issues Macmillan had been content to follow the guidance of contemporaries like Anthony Eden, who had specialized in foreign affairs; but as these assumed a graver significance, his interest was inevitably aroused.

Between the wars, the world's hopes for peace rested on the efficacy of the newly-established League of Nations. The world was destined to be disappointed. As early as 1931, Japan's invasion of China – known as the Manchurian crisis – was a serious blow to the League, which was seen to be ineffective in preventing aggression by a major power. There were excuses: America lacked the will to act against Japan, Britain alone was not strong enough and was in any case 10,000 miles away. It was a set-back, but it did not destroy belief in the League as the basis of British foreign policy, and Germany's admission to it in 1926 was welcomed as an important accretion.

Nevertheless, the security of Europe depended on Anglo-French strength and resolution, and Britain was disarming unilaterally while France's armaments were becoming obsolescent. The Disarmament Conference, which sat assiduously between 1932 and 1934, eventually collapsed without result.

From the moment that Hitler became Chancellor of the German Reich, in January 1933, the prospects of permanent peace began to recede. Hitler took Germany out of both the Disarmament Conference and the League of Nations by the end of that year.

In October the Fulham by-election, fought largely against any strengthening of our defences, resulted in a Labour victory, which made a deep impression on Stanley Baldwin. A year later the assassinations of King Alexander of Yugoslavia and of the resolute and realistic French Foreign Minister, Barthou, were a blow to the democracies and, as matters turned out, a bonus for the dictators. Barthou was succeeded by Pierre Laval.

In March 1935 the British Government published a White Paper outlining its plans for modernizing the equipment of the Army and Navy and increasing the size of the Air Force. Hitler retaliated by announcing the creation of the Luftwaffe and the introduction of conscription to produce an Army of 500,000 men. The Anglo-German Naval Agreement, thought at the time to be a success for the Admiralty, proved gravely mistaken in allowing Germany to build up her submarine fleet until it was on a level with the British. Again and again Churchill warned that the Luftwaffe was approaching the strength of the RAF. Baldwin had, correctly, denied this but he felt obliged to acknowledge later that the Government had been misled as to the respective *future* strengths of the two air forces: 'There, I was completely wrong,' he said. This frank admission disarmed the House of Commons, which always likes and accepts a candid confession of error.

In June 1935, the Peace Ballot organized by the League of Nations Union produced over $11\frac{1}{2}$ million answers, 10 million of which favoured economic sanctions by the League in the event of aggression by one nation against another. This ballot was held against the background of mounting military preparations by Italy against Abyssinia and public opinion was strongly anti-Italian.

The British Government was faced with a clear choice: it could support Mussolini's ambitions and thus perhaps keep Italy neutral in the event of war against Germany. This would have been cynical but realistic; the League would have failed but Hitler might have been contained. The alternative policy was to take the lead in supporting effective action against Italian aggression. The British and French fleets could have deprived the Italians of the use of the Suez Canal and oil sanctions against Italy would have prevented her waging a successful war against Abyssinia. This was a more respectable moral position and, just before the House rose for the summer recess, the Foreign Secretary, Sir Samuel Hoare, stated firmly that the Government would stand by the Covenant of the League. At Geneva, Anthony Eden rallied support for the sanctions policy and Hoare made a stirring speech to the Assembly pledging Britain's opposition to any act of unprovoked aggression. Next day words were followed by action, when the battle-cruisers *Hood* and *Renown* arrived at Gibraltar.

The Labour Party was torn between the pacifism of its leader, George Lansbury, and Ernest Bevin's robust support for sanctions and the League. When a large majority at the Party Conference voted for sanctions, Lansbury resigned and Clement Attlee was elected Leader of the Party. By the time the House of Commons reassembled on 23 October 1935, Italy had launched her attack upon Abyssinia, and Eden was organizing positive measures against the aggressor with the general approval of the British people. Two days later Parliament was dissolved for the General Election, which was to be held on 14 November.

In the summer of 1935 Macmillan had received an informal offer from a Parliamentary colleague, who was not standing again, of his safe seat in the south of England. In declining this proposal, he wrote that he would rather not leave Stockton 'because one does not like giving up anything until one is beaten and because I now feel that I have a good chance of holding the seat against the Socialist. ... I prefer to take the risk of being beaten in the North.'[17]

On the home front Macmillan fought the election on 'The Next Five Years' manifesto and was associated with the 'New Deal' policy put forward by Lloyd George's Council of Action. Both movements had the same objective of a more positive attack on unemployment. At Stockton he was faced not only by a formidable Socialist opponent, Miss Susan Lawrence, who had been a successful Minister in the previous Labour Government, but also by a Liberal candidate. Lloyd George referred publicly and most generously to Macmillan's work in Parliament and his views on unemployment and he was supported by some of the leading Liberals in the constituency, as well as by Professor Gilbert Murray, a prominent Liberal, who wrote: '... if I were an elector in Stockton, I should without hesitation give you my vote'.[18] All this was helpful, but the presence of an official Liberal candidate in the field made the outcome uncertain.

On the foreign affairs issue of sanctions against Italy, Macmillan seemed on safer and more orthodox Conservative ground. He was a convinced supporter of the League and had written a letter to *The Times* welcoming the Foreign Secretary's strong statement at Geneva and expressing the hope that a similar policy would be pursued by Great Britain 'in the case of a future threat to peace arising elsewhere'.[19] During the course of the campaign Lloyd George attacked the Government for using the international crisis to win an election and warned the nation that Ministers would not hold to the course on which they were apparently set: 'They are too late to save Abyssinia,'

Lloyd George declared, 'but are just in the nick of time to save the Government.'[20] This prescient observation did not, however, cause Macmillan undue anxiety. The Conservative Manifesto was unequivocal and he believed in the Government's sincerity of purpose.

Lord Allen went to Stockton to speak for him and paid an influential public tribute: 'He could have earned the ordinary plaudits of his Party. He could have gained a career, honour and comfort; instead, he has insisted in making an independent contribution to the whole of our national political life.'[21] The result of the election in Stockton was better than Macmillan expected. He had a majority of 4,000 over Susan Lawrence and the Liberal lost his deposit. The local Press stressed the independence of his campaign and he thanked the electors 'for the freedom they have given me'.

In the country as a whole, although Labour recovered some of the ground lost in 1931, the National Government, with 432 seats in the House of Commons, still had a massive majority of 249. When Baldwin formed his new administration, Churchill and Lloyd George, the two outstanding figures in Parliament, were still excluded from it.

Baldwin's timing of the election had been skilful. In Leo Amery's somewhat cynical words, the Government had sailed 'back into office on a wave of virtuous indignation as the true champions of collective security'.[22] Few doubted that the intention was to stop Mussolini and that, in this objective, the Government was sincere.

By this time Baldwin was conscious of the need to strengthen the national defences. As Macmillan wrote: 'By combining a realistic approach to our defence requirements with the idealistic wave of enthusiasm which had been built up in support of the collective power of the League, he hoped to achieve rearmament by consent.'[23] It was a respectable posture and the Prime Minister's prestige had never stood higher than when Parliament met on 3 December. Yet such are the swift vicissitudes of politics that within a week the Government was in disarray, its credit destroyed and its authority most grievously damaged.

On 7 December 1935, Sir Samuel Hoare, who was in bad health and in need of a rest, set out for a skating holiday in Switzerland. He broke his journey in Paris for discussions with the French Foreign Minister, Pierre Laval. Together they concocted a plan – for which Hoare had no Cabinet authority – the effect of which was to hand two-thirds of Abyssinia's territory to Italy. Hoare initialled a document incorporating this agreement and at once left by train for Switzerland. The story was leaked to the French Press on 9 December and taken up by the British newspapers the following day.

The Cabinet was in serious difficulty. The Foreign Secretary was not there to explain and defend his decision and, mistakenly, Baldwin did not summon him back to England. In fact, a summons would have made no difference because Hoare had a fall on the ice that same morning and broke his nose, so he could not in any case have travelled back that day.

Attlee put down a Private Notice question to the Prime Minister, to which Baldwin had no adequate reply, and a short but tense debate followed. Eden did the best he could in such an unpromising situation, but the press, led by *The Times*, launched a ferocious attack on the Government. Its supporters in Parliament as well as in the country, at first puzzled, became genuinely angry as the days passed without any convincing explanation of the Hoare–Laval Agreement. The Opposition put a motion on the Order Paper to repudiate its terms and when Austen Chamberlain strongly criticized the Government in the Conservative Party's Foreign Affairs Committee, the Chief Whip, David Margesson, advised the Prime Minister that he could no longer hold the Parliamentary Party together in support of Hoare's policy. It was clear that, in order to save the Government, the Foreign Secretary must be sacrificed. He had by this time returned to England, and he at once resigned his office. In the debate which followed he advanced a dignified justification of his actions, for which he declined to apologize. As Macmillan has pointed out: 'In a sense he proved too much. . . . While sanctions were relatively ineffective, they were safe; as soon as they began to bite, they became too dangerous.'[24]

Hoare was an efficient Minister, but he had no doubt been over-influenced by the devious Laval. He was trying to follow two policies at the same time – support for the League and appeasement of Mussolini – and, as they were incompatible, he was bound to fail. Having to choose between two quite different, indeed opposite courses – either of which could have been justified and either of which, if pursued with clarity and conviction, might have been successful – the Government fell clumsily between two stools. Macmillan accurately summarized the dilemma when he wrote: 'They would not go ahead and risk trouble with Mussolini and they were ashamed to go backwards and make a deal with him.'[25]

Eden, who succeeded Hoare as Foreign Secretary, would have taken the risk and supported the League. He would have imposed oil sanctions, which might have compelled Mussolini to abandon the enterprise, but the opportunity was missed. By the beginning of May 1936 the war in Abyssinia was over and the Emperor, Haile Selassie, had fled into exile in England.

After an unwise and ill-timed speech by Neville Chamberlain in June, there was a fierce debate in the House of Commons, made memorable by a bitingly scornful speech by Lloyd George, which was described by Churchill as one of the greatest Parliamentary performances of all time. The Labour Front Bench moved a vote of censure and Macmillan, who had trusted the Government's pledge and fought the Stockton election in support of it, took the serious step of voting in the Opposition lobby. Although the Chief Whip took no action, Macmillan thought it honourable to resign the whip and wrote accordingly to the Prime Minister on 29 June. Baldwin replied curtly in a letter of two short sentences, regretting 'this decision which you have thought it necessary to take'. Macmillan continued to sit as an independent Conservative for the next eleven months until Baldwin relinquished office. He thought that Chamberlain, who succeeded to the premiership, would pursue a stronger foreign policy; he was soon to be disillusioned.

Meanwhile, on 7 March, Hitler re-occupied the Rhineland in contravention not only of the Treaty of Versailles, which had been imposed upon Germany, but also of Locarno, to which she had voluntarily acceded. This flagrant violation of a clear international commitment evoked no retaliatory action by France or Britain. There had been no contingency planning, a French general election was to take place a few weeks later and the public mood in both countries was one of peace at almost any price. Although Churchill regarded the re-militarization of the Rhineland as the fatal step which made war inevitable, he was almost alone in this assessment. Even Eden excused the Anglo-French inaction; all he could obtain from the situation were staff talks between the two allies and even these proved perfunctory.

Harold Macmillan was uneasy. He expressed his fears in a newspaper article on 20 March, in which he bluntly ascribed to MacDonald and Baldwin the responsibility for a foreign policy of drift: 'They have elevated inactivity into a principle and feebleness into a virtue,' he wrote. '... There will be no war now. But.... there will be war in 1940 or 1941 ..., Let us settle with Germany now or coerce her now. But don't let us purchase an uncertain peace at a terrible price to be paid later.'[26]

Hitler proceeded at once to rearm Germany and to fortify the Rhineland. Baldwin's only response was to invite the easy-going and undynamic Solicitor-General, Sir Thomas Inskip, to co-ordinate the defence of Britain. It was a most curious and unlikely appointment, received, in Churchill's words, 'with astonishment by Press and public'.[27] It had few, if any, positive results.

While these events, menacing the peace of Europe, were taking place, an ideological civil war had broken out in Spain. The dictators – Hitler and Mussolini in support of General Franco, and Stalin on the side of the Spanish Government – were very ready to fish in troubled waters and supplied arms and volunteers to the combatants. Britain and France wisely maintained a policy of non-intervention; but opinion in both countries was bitterly divided.[28]

At home, division of a different kind developed during the summer and autumn of 1936 due to the domestic difficulties of King Edward VIII, who had succeeded to the throne on the death of George V. The King had fallen in love with Mrs Simpson, an American divorcée, whom he wished to marry. This project was unacceptable to the Prime Minister and the Government, to the Established Church, to the majority of the British people and to the Governments and people of the Dominions. When the extent of the opposition to his hopes became obvious, the King determined to abdicate. It was a painful situation, handled with skill and care by Stanley Baldwin, who emerged with credit from what might have become a grave constitutional crisis.[29]

8

THE MIDDLE WAY

The year 1936 was marred by bereavements in Harold Macmillan's family. His cousin George died in February, his father in March and his uncle Frederick in June. The firm thus lost its three senior partners within four months and the business burden fell upon his elder brother, Daniel, and upon Harold himself. The death of his mother eighteen months later was an even greater personal blow.

In spite of the darkening scene in Europe and the time and energy required by the family firm, Macmillan continued, until 1938, to devote his main political efforts to the country's economic and industrial problems. The Next Five Years Group was re-formed as a pressure, propaganda and research organization; but, within it, different views were held as to its future role. Macmillan wanted it to make a practical, political contribution, in association with Lloyd George's Council of Action. Lord Allen preferred it to remain academic and educational. He resented what he saw as an attempt to take over the group, but Macmillan secured a majority for his views and Allen's influence was greatly curtailed. It was decided to publish a monthly journal called *The New Outlook*, which ran for a year from June 1936 under Macmillan's chairmanship, and to separate this from the Next Five Years Group. The journal, though not financially profitable, put forward a specific programme, including collective security, the abolition of the means test, action in the special areas and an extension of public ownership and control. After publishing another booklet entitled *A Programme of Priorities*, the Next Five Years Group was dissolved in November 1937 and Lord Allen himself died in 1939.

In a speech on the Finance Bill in May 1936, Macmillan argued that the economic purpose of savings was to replace obsolescent capital goods; but if this was overdone, as had happened in Russia, insufficient consumer goods would be produced, so a balance must be struck between the two. The real problem was to ensure that savings were channelled, not into gilt-edged stocks, but into industrial investment; the improvement in the social services was helpful, he suggested, not only on humanitarian and political grounds but also because it reduced the motivation to save for security and encouraged the circulation and investment of the savings of the people as society became more prosperous. He stressed the need to have plans prepared in advance in order to be able to turn on the reflationary tap in good time.

The exclusion of Tees-side from the special area category persisted and it still rankled in Macmillan's mind. Even in the conditions of relatively full employment in later years, he was always on the side of the borderline cases. In his own area he made a substantial personal contribution towards the purchase of a derelict shipyard for use as a recreational centre.

During 1936 and 1937 Macmillan was writing a serious and important 400-page book, *The Middle Way*, which was published in May 1938. Its theme was the same as he had been developing for many years in his speeches, articles, pamphlets and other publications. It brought all his ideas together in a single volume and supported them with tables and statistics drawn from the work of Seebohm Rowntree and Sir John Boyd Orr. The evidence he collected that the incomes of many in the lower wage brackets were insufficient to provide a minimum standard of food, warmth and shelter were not seriously challenged; and he underlined the truth (at that time) that '... our system of public health, environmental and social services falls very far short of providing an adequate basis of physical well-being and security'. He set out as his aim the achievement of higher standards in these areas: 'The object of all our endeavours must be to lift the burdens of poverty and distress that weigh so heavily upon great masses of the people, in order to build up a secure and adequate standard of life for all.'[1]

All this was unexceptionable. It was not until he turned to the remedies that his proposals became controversial: '... society should be organized in such a way as to bring the economic system under conscious direction and control,' he wrote, and he believed that 'the whole trend of development is in the direction of greater integration and the supersession of unrestrained competition by methods of co-operation'. This led him to consider the large-scale distribution of many foods, such as milk, butter, margarine, cheese, eggs, bread and flour, potatoes and sugar. He thought the retail price of milk in England, in relation to people's wages, was disproportionately high, as compared to its cost in the United States or Sweden; and he outlined a scheme for its distribution:

... by the elimination of competitive redundancy and by the creation of a single national organization concerned only with delivery by the shortest and most economical route. ... There is a strong case for placing in the hands of the community an instrument of distribution that would provide a direct contact with the nutritional requirements of every household. The organization for supplying these elementary human needs should be non profit-making . . .[2]

He maintained that the eradication of malnutrition was so important that every theoretical prejudice must be made to give way to practical necessity.

Any Conservative could have been forgiven for criticizing some of Macmillan's proposals for going a long way down the road, if not towards Socialism, at least towards the Labour Party's objective of an egalitarian society. His ideas on education, for instance, were far removed from orthodox thought at that time and even today would be considered controversial by many Conservatives:

In so far as snobbery and class alienation exists in this country, it is largely a product of class differences in education. . . . It would do nothing but good to the children of every class if the early years of life were spent in the same school. . . . The class differences which now tend to go according to incomes might in future be replaced by . . . intellectual differences, but these would be superimposed upon a common training upon which mutual understanding could be preserved.[3]

Macmillan stressed the importance of planning: 'I believe it to be politically wise and economically urgent for us now to devise a comprehensive system of national planning. . . .' He thought the weakness of partial planning arose 'from the incomplete and limited application of the principles . . .' and that the lesson of these errors of limitation 'is not that we should retreat. On the contrary, we must advance more rapidly and still further upon the road of conscious regulation.'[4]

Although he was well aware of the weaknesses of the capitalist system, Macmillan believed they could be corrected by a measure of Government intervention and that this was far preferable to the imposition of full-blooded Socialism, which he rejected because it would destroy human diversity, variety and liberty. 'Our task', he wrote, 'is to prove that it is both unwise and unnecessary to sacrifice democracy, political liberty and individual freedom in order to deal with our economic problems.' But he warned that 'it is not enough to deplore and condemn the political excesses and the economic inadequacies of the totalitarian States. We must prove that democracy can do better.'

Macmillan concluded that 'it is both possible and desirable to find a solution of our economic difficulties in a mixed system which combines State ownership and regulation or control of certain aspects of economic activity with the drive and initiative of private enterprise. . . .'[5] Since the Second World War, this mixed economy has developed very much along the lines he had in mind and now finds general acceptance, but forty years ago his ideas were *avant-garde* and were the subject of suspicion and often disapproval in more conventional Conservative circles. For this reason he was especially pleased, after the publication of the book, to receive an agreeable letter from Leo Amery, whose position in the Party was somewhat different from his own: 'It is full of good stuff and points substantially in the right direction,' Amery wrote. 'I am not sure that I agree with every one of your detailed proposals, but there clearly is a middle way between theoretical socialism and diehard individualism.'[6]

Although, not surprisingly, there was criticism from both the Left and the Right, the book had a remarkably good press and aroused much interest, not only among politicians and political commentators, but also among economists and students. It had a great appeal for the young and uncommitted and was influential in converting many, including myself, to Conservatism. Edward Heath, then an Oxford undergraduate, was another young man who was much influenced by the book. In Macmillan's own generation Derick Heathcoat Amory (later Viscount Amory), who had hitherto been a Liberal, became a Conservative mainly as a result of reading *The Middle Way*. Many colleagues wrote warm letters of congratulation. Harold Nicolson said he thought it 'a book of real importance'. J.L. Garvin was characteristically enthusiastic and Macmillan was gratified by a generous letter from Lord Allen, who praised the 'high quality' of the book and its detail and precision. He thought it 'one of the finest productions of its kind I have seen'.

Many years later, in 1958, Harold Macmillan – by then Prime Minister – addressed the Conservative Political Centre:

Everyone in this hall tonight who is more than twenty-five years of age has actually lived in a period when there were $2\frac{3}{4}$ million unemployed in this country, when 60% of the workers in the ship-building and allied industries were out of work and nearly 50% of all workers in the iron and steel trades. ... I was a Member of Parliament in those days on Tees-side. As long as I live I can never forget the impoverishment and demoralization which all this brought with it. I am determined, as far as it lies within human power, never to allow this shadow to fall again upon our country. ... Between the Scylla of inflation and the Charybdis of deflation we must therefore steer a middle way.[7]

Macmillan was always haunted by the spectre of unemployment and has been blamed by some critics for a tendency to encourage expansion when a more cautious approach might have been wiser. But in this, as in two other basic policies – his advocacy of a middle position in politics and, especially in times of crisis, of the need for national unity – he has always been consistent.

He followed, instinctively, the example of Stanley Baldwin.

'I believe today, as surely as I believed twenty years ago, that the only position in politics that we Conservatives can occupy with honour is the middle ground. . . . We Conservatives must believe above all in national unity.'[8]

9

PRELUDE TO DISASTER

For the first two years of the 1935 Parliament, Macmillan was still absorbed by the economic and social problems in which he had specialized for so long; but by 1937, his mind was beginning to turn to the German danger and to the urgent need for British rearmament. Neville Chamberlain, now Prime Minister, took a different view. He believed that peace could be preserved by conciliation and his first objective was to detach Italy, the weakest of the dictatorships, from the German orbit.

If Baldwin had taken too little interest in foreign affairs, his successor soon showed a disposition to take too much – in the sense that he began to communicate directly or indirectly with foreign governments without even informing the Foreign Secretary. This was not only discourteous but dangerous. In July 1937, unknown to Anthony Eden, Chamberlain wrote a personal letter to Mussolini. 'I did not show my letter to the Foreign Secretary,' he noted in his diary, 'for I had the feeling that he would object to it.'[1] It was an extraordinary way in which to conduct Government business. During the autumn the Prime Minister carried on a correspondence with his sister-in-law, Austen Chamberlain's widow, who was living in Rome and had developed an intense admiration for Mussolini. She was indiscreet in her conversations with Ciano, the Italian Foreign Minister, and her private reports to Downing Street were unreliable. To make matters more difficult, Chamberlain was turning for advice on these issues to the Government's Chief Industrial Adviser, Sir Horace Wilson, who had no experience of foreign affairs. This did not help to improve the atmosphere between Downing Street and the Foreign Office.

As the dictatorships increased their military strength and the relative unpreparedness of France and Britain became more apparent, Eden realized the importance of working as closely as possible with the United States in order to wean her from too firm an adherence to the Monroe doctrine. He was having some success in establishing a close relationship with President

Roosevelt when a most untoward incident occurred. The President had proposed an international conference which would have had the effect of aligning American opinion more closely with the democracies. This idea was strongly supported by Sir Ronald Lindsay, the British Ambassador in Washington, and was submitted in advance to Neville Chamberlain, who should certainly have responded to it, if only for psychological reasons. Unfortunately Eden was away in France and, contrary to the advice of the Permanent Secretary, Sir Alexander Cadogan, Chamberlain sent a discouraging reply, described by Sumner Wells as a 'douche of cold water', to the President's initiative. Eden was neither consulted, nor even informed, until he returned to London three days later. Chamberlain's action in again going behind the back of his own Foreign Secretary was reprehensible and the reason for it, though no doubt well-intentioned, was ill-advised. He thought he could trust the dictators and do business with them. His own upright character was such that he did not realize they would cheat. He was still determined to open direct negotiations with Mussolini, although the Duce himself had made no gesture to indicate that the outcome might be successful.

The clash of personalities and of policies between Eden and Chamberlain now came to a head and after an unfortunate and, for Eden, humiliating interview with the Italian Ambassador, Count Grandi, the Foreign Secretary felt that his position had become impossible. He resigned on 20 February 1938 and his Under-Secretary, Lord Cranborne, followed him to the Back Benches. After a debate on an Opposition motion of censure, about twenty Conservatives, including Harold Macmillan, abstained in the division. It was a portent of things to come.

Eden was replaced at the Foreign Office by the more pliable Lord Halifax, a much-respected former Viceroy of India. R.A. Butler succeeded Cranborne as Under-Secretary of State, a position of some importance on the political ladder because his chief was in the House of Lords; but increasingly, Chamberlain replied for the Government in foreign affairs debates and, as Macmillan commented: 'Since his style of argument, although powerful, was never conciliatory, the result was an increasing bitterness at the very time when the largest degree of unity and understanding was desirable.'[2] The Opposition's dislike of Chamberlain ensured that when, in 1940, a coalition government became inevitable, the Labour leaders would decline to serve under him.

Three weeks after Eden's resignation, Hitler annexed Austria. The Russians proposed a four-power conference to discuss the deteriorating situation, but Chamberlain rejected this initiative. Czechoslovakia was clearly the next country on Hitler's list. Her three million Sudeten Germans gave him an excuse to stir up trouble. He exaggerated their grievances and demanded their 'return' to Germany, to which they had never in fact belonged. His real objective was the destruction of the Czech State.

Under pressure, President Beneš conceded the Sudeten demand for local autonomy. In reply, Hitler made an hysterical and abusive speech at Nuremberg, despite or because of which Chamberlain decided to visit the German dictator at Berchtesgaden. At this meeting Hitler insisted on self-determination for the Sudeten area. The French and British Governments then induced, virtually compelled, Beneš to capitulate and the cession of the Sudetenland to Germany was agreed. Chamberlain returned to Godesberg to report this to Hitler, only to be met by a further demand that, instead of a peaceful transfer of the territory, the German troops should march in as conquerors. This was too much even for the British Government and belated preparations began in London in case of the early outbreak of war.

In a final effort to preserve the peace, Chamberlain proposed a four-power conference. The House of Commons met on 28 September 1938 in a tense and anxious atmosphere, but during the Prime Minister's speech a dramatic message was passed to him that Hitler and Mussolini had accepted his proposal and invited him and the French Premier, Daladier, to meet them at Munich. The House rose to cheer Chamberlain and wish him God-speed on his journey.

On the afternoon of 30 September an agreement was signed in Munich and Chamberlain returned, having avoided an immediate war and carrying with him a declaration which he and Hitler had signed, pledging their countries to a policy of consultation to save the peace of Europe. Carried away by the relief and excitement of the crowds in Downing Street, the Prime Minister waved this piece of paper and declared that he had brought home 'Peace with honour. I believe it is peace for our time.' In fact there was not much honour and the peace lasted for a little less than one year.

To the large majority in the House of Commons and in the country as a whole, Chamberlain was the hero of the hour. The people believed what they wanted to believe. Only one Minister, Duff Cooper, the First Lord of the Admiralty, resigned in protest against the Munich Agreement. Harold Macmillan was firmly against appeasement and therefore against Chamberlain as the architect and chief exponent of this policy. It was a family custom to make a big bonfire at Birch Grove on 5 November and that year the centrepiece was an effigy of the Prime Minister, for which 'a black Homburg hat in quite good repair, as well as a rolled umbrella'[3] were sacrificed. The presence of forty or fifty Czech refugees, to whom the Macmillans had given shelter in cottages on the estate, added poignancy to the scene.

After Eden's resignation Macmillan had joined a group of dissident Conservatives which became known as the Eden Group and was sometimes derisively described by the Government whips as 'the glamour boys'. Eden took the chair at their meetings and, although small at first, the Group gradually grew, especially after the fall of Prague in the spring of 1939. It eventually comprised between twenty and thirty Conservative Members of Parliament, including Leo Amery, Duff Cooper, Lord Cranborne, Lord Wolmer, Richard Law (later Lord Coleraine), Jim Thomas (later Lord Cilcennin), Edward (Louis) Spears, Sydney Herbert, Mark Patrick, Ronnie Tree, Hubert Duggan, Derrick Gunston, Robert Bower, Paul Emrys-Evans, and Anthony Crossley and Ronnie Cartland, both of whom were soon to be killed in action. A National Labour Member, Harold Nicolson, also joined the Group, and Mark Patrick became its secretary. Its members met once a week, when Parliament was sitting, at the houses in Westminster of Ronnie Tree, Jim Thomas or Mark Patrick. The purpose of these gatherings was to discuss the menacing international scene and to consider what could be done to avert its dangers.

The much smaller Churchill Group, which shared the same objectives, consisted of Churchill, Brendan Bracken, Bob Boothby and Duncan Sandys. Churchill and Eden were on good terms and they and their followers often combined forces for debates of mutual concern. In retrospect it is strange that the two Groups remained distinct and had little contact with each other.

After Churchill and Eden joined the Government on the outbreak of war, the Group continued to meet, usually under the chairmanship of Leo Amery; and an all-Party group was also formed by Clement Davies, who later became leader of the Liberal Party. This group, for which Bob Boothby acted as secretary, was important as a bridge to the Labour leadership. With Churchill's knowledge and approval, Macmillan had himself been in touch with Hugh Dalton in the aftermath of Munich to ascertain the reaction of the Labour Party in the rumoured event of a snap General Election.

There is no doubt that Chamberlain still believed, in the face of all the evidence to the contrary, that a settlement with Germany could be reached and the peace of Europe saved. The British people wanted to believe it too and there was an almost universal feeling of gratitude to the Prime Minister for sustaining their hopes and relieving their fears. Nevertheless, there was a general realization that rearmament was now vital and should be achieved as rapidly as possible.

It is still a matter of argument forty years later whether it would have been wiser to resist in 1938 than to wait for another year. The advice of the Chiefs of Staff that Britain's armed forces, especially the Air Force, were unready and inadequate was unequivocal. The French, though bound to Czechoslovakia by treaty, which Britain was not, were reluctant to honour their commitment. The Dominions were hesitant. On the other hand, the Czech Army and her formidable defences were lost without a shot being fired. Had the British Government shown more resolution, the Russians might have supported the United Kingdom and the German generals might themselves have overthrown their own Führer if his bluff had not been so triumphantly successful.

Macmillan's own view, at the time and since, was that Britain ought to have fought in 1938 rather than yield at Munich. He began at once to campaign vigorously for the introduction of National Service, at first in his own constituency and then at a by-election at Oxford, which was fought mainly on the Munich policy. The official Conservative candidate, Quintin Hogg (now Lord Hailsham), was opposed by an independent, Dr A.D. Lindsay, the Master of Balliol, who had the support of the Liberals, Lord Cecil of Chelwood, Harold Macmillan and most of his friends from the Next Five Years Group, as well as an enthusiastic young undergraduate called Edward Heath. Speaking at a public meeting, Macmillan declared that the foreign policy of the Government had been one of retreat and that it was not always possible to appease lions by throwing them Christians. He wrote to Lindsay to say that 'the times are too grave and the issue is too vital for progressive Conservative opinion to allow itself to be influenced by Party loyalties....'⁴ Although Quintin Hogg won the election, the Government majority was almost halved and there were suggestions, which did not materialize, that Macmillan should be deprived of the Conservative whip and asked to resign from the Carlton Club – of which he was to become Chairman nearly forty years later.

A movement was already developing that winter to change the Government and bring in Churchill as Prime Minister. Macmillan wrote a pamphlet, *The Price of Peace*, criticizing the Munich policy and calling for rearmament and an alliance of Britain, France and Russia. This was reproduced in February 1939 as part of a booklet on the economic aspects of defence, which had good reviews and sales. In it Macmillan warned that it was no longer a question of efficiency, but of survival.

By this time the refugee problem was becoming acute. The Government did little, but Macmillan was able to give private help in Sussex to a group of Czechs, mostly Jews, who had escaped to England. A little later, the Macmillans moved out of Birch Grove into a cottage on the estate and made the house available for children evacuated from London. Between sixty and seventy of them remained there throughout the war.

Gradually the public mood, influenced by the brutalities of Hitler's persecution of the Jews, was beginning to change; and when, on 15 March 1939, the German troops marched into Prague, the scales finally fell from the eyes of the British people. Even Chamberlain was disillusioned and, although he rejected a Russian proposal for an international conference to co-ordinate means of resisting aggression, he issued a guarantee that, in the event of action threatening the independence of Poland, the British Government would give the Poles all the support in its power. In fact, Britain had no power to help Poland, so the only meaning of this guarantee was that any further German aggression would mean war in Europe. It was followed by similar guarantees to Rumania and Greece. Even these did not deter Mussolini from invading Albania on 7 April – about which Lord Halifax is said to have exclaimed characteristically 'And on Good Friday too!'

Macmillan wrote a letter to *The Times* calling for the immediate formation of a National Government 'on the broadest possible basis',[5] and on 29 March, a House of Commons motion along the same lines was supported by nearly thirty signatures. Harold Nicolson recorded that Macmillan 'is enraged that Chamberlain should remain on. He thinks that all we Edenites are too soft and gentlemanlike. That we should have clamoured for Chamberlain's removal. That no man in history had made such persistent and bone-headed mistakes, and that we shall go on pretending that all is well.'[6] At the end of April the principle of National Service, though still bitterly opposed by the Labour Party, was accepted by the House, and in the summer a Ministry of Supply was at last created.

On 16 April, Russia offered Britain and France a Tripartite Alliance. Its acceptance might have changed the course of history; it was certainly the last chance of preventing war. But the proposal was rejected and its originator, Litvinoff, was promptly dismissed and replaced by Molotov as Russian Foreign Minister. Stalin had decided that co-operation with Britain and France was no longer worth pursuing in the face of consistent discouragement and vacillation by the two democracies. On 22 August the German–Russian pact, ensuring Russia's neutrality in the event of war, was signed.

At dawn on 1 September, German mechanized troops invaded Poland. In a debate in the House of Commons the following day, the Prime Minister's statement sounded equivocal and was a disappointment to those who expected an immediate ultimatum to Germany. There were fears of another Munich and, when Arthur Greenwood rose for the Opposition, Leo Amery called from the Conservative benches, 'Speak for England, Arthur.' In fact, Neville Chamberlain had already made the fateful decision and the delay was due to an attempt to synchronize his announcement with that of the French. Britain's ultimatum to the German Government was despatched next morning. There was no reply and at 11 a.m. on Sunday, 3 September, the Prime Minister broadcast the news to the nation that Britain was at war with Germany. After an air-raid warning which proved to be a mistake, Chamberlain made a statement to the House of Commons which Amery described as 'good, but not the speech of a war-leader', and he added, 'I think I see Winston emerging as PM out of it all by the end of the year.'[7]

Appeasement has become a term of reproach, but Chamberlain's policy in the years before the Second World War, and especially at the time of Munich, undoubtedly reflected the hopes and wishes of the British Parliament and people, by whom it was fully supported and endorsed. He was a man of peace, sincere and dedicated in his efforts to preserve it; but he did not possess the qualities required to lead a nation at war, and just as Asquith, for the same reason, had to give place to Lloyd George, so it was inevitable that Churchill should succeed Chamberlain. Sorrowfully, he summed up his personal tragedy to the House of Commons on the day the war began: 'Everything that I have worked for, everything that I have hoped for, everything that I have believed in during my public life has crashed in ruins.' It was a sad valediction to the years of toil.

10

THE TWILIGHT WAR

As long ago as 1931, Harold Nicolson wrote of Churchill: 'He is a man who leads forlorn hopes and when the hopes of England become forlorn, he will once again be summoned to leadership.'[1] It was a prescient observation nine years before the event and at a time when Hitler was not known to the world.

Churchill's passionate pleas for British rearmament had been ridiculed and largely ignored until they were shown to have been justified when war broke out. His strong advocacy of unpopular policies had kept him out of office for ten years, and many people thought that, at the age of sixty-five, his ministerial career was over. From the Prime Minister's point of view it was questionable whether it would be more troublesome to have Churchill in the Government or outside it, but on 2 September 1939 he was invited to join the War Cabinet as First Lord of the Admiralty. He had held the same post twenty-five years earlier at the outbreak of the First World War. Anthony Eden, who also rejoined the Government as Secretary of State for the Dominions, had been reluctant to do so, but was persuaded by Churchill that together they could effect more from within the administration than from outside it.

Macmillan's claims to office were still disregarded. 'What could I do?' he wrote despondently:

I was too old to fight. I had already tried to get back into the Reserve Battalion of my regiment, but they did not want officers of my age and physique ... and unless there was fighting on a prodigious scale, I saw no hope of employment.... I held no post, even in the lowest ranks of the administration. In these opening weeks, Parliament did not seem likely to play a great role in the drama that was unfolding. The prospect, therefore, seemed flat and uninspiring.[2]

Family history was repeating itself throughout the land, and Harold Macmillan's only son, Maurice, abandoned Oxford, as his father had done in the previous generation, and joined the Army within a few days of the declaration of war. In London there was work to be done organizing the firm to meet its new wartime problems and at home Harold supported his wife in her efforts to look after the child evacuees who were already being harboured at Birch Grove.

In October, Macmillan took part in a debate in the House of Commons on economic warfare. He reminded Members that war 'means that the total energy of the nation has to be organized and directed ... and that every error of policy or administration ... will be paid for by a prolongation of the struggle and the consequent sacrifice of additional lives'.[3] Government controls and the planning of industry, which he had urged for so long, were now essential and would have to be greatly extended. Conscription between the ages of eighteen and forty-one was at length introduced, but industrial mobilization was slow, and by January 1940 there were still nearly 1,300,000 unemployed.

The war at sea began badly with the losses of the liner *Athenia*, the *Rawalpindi* and the aircraft-carrier *Courageous*. The *Royal Oak* was torpedoed by a German submarine in Scapa Flow and attacks on merchant shipping were ruthless and continuous. But in December British morale received a welcome boost with the dramatic action off the River Plate, when the heavily-armed German pocket battleship, *Graf Spee*, was humiliated by the light cruisers, *Ajax*, *Achilles* and *Exeter*, and scuttled by her own crew.

On land no military action was undertaken by France or Britain, despite Hitler's initial preoccupation in Poland and the fact that seventy-six Anglo-French divisions confronted only thirty-two German divisions on the Western Front. It is fair to add that only four of the allied divisions were British, but their inactivity was of no help to Poland, on whose behalf the war had ostensibly begun. As Hugh Dalton observed, 'We were letting them down and letting them die, while we did nothing to help them.'[4] Geographically, there was in fact no effective aid Britain could ever have given to Poland. But the half-hearted and unenterprising conduct of the war was giving rise to criticism of Chamberlain at home, as much from within the Conservative Parliamentary Party as from the Opposition side of the House of Commons.

In a speech to his constituents, Macmillan foresaw and warned them of the inevitability of a German attack on Holland and Belgium; and in the House of Commons he said it was unwise to gloat over the news that Germany had introduced rationing: 'We ought to have had rationing of almost every article from the very beginning of the war. That is no reason for us to laugh at the Germans; we should have done it ourselves.'[5]

In January 1940, Macmillan had his first chance of a more active involvement in the war. Despite the recently concluded pact with Germany, the Soviet Government, like its Tzarist predecessors, was anxious to protect its western borders – in this case from the possibility of a German attack. Russia therefore occupied the Baltic States of Estonia, Latvia and Lithuania without resistance at the beginning of the war. Finland was a tougher proposition, but the Russian invasion of her territory was duly launched on 30 November. It was a brutal, unprovoked assault on a small neutral country which shocked Western opinion, and the Soviet Union was expelled from the dying and by now discredited League of Nations.

The Finns resisted with great gallantry and a movement was formed, with the approval of the British Government, to send them aid, including the recruitment of a small international volunteer force. A Committee was set up under the chairmanship of the Finnish Minister in London, with Leo Amery, Lord Balfour of Burleigh, Lord Phillimore, Lord Davies, General Macdonogh and Harold Macmillan as the other members. Five hundred volunteers were recruited in Britain and the total force eventually amounted to two battalions. It was decided to send a small delegation, consisting of Lord Davies and Macmillan, to Finland and they set out on 10 February 1940. It was an intensely cold winter, and on the way through Sweden Macmillan bought a white fur hat, which he wore again twenty years later when he visited Russia as Prime Minister.

Soviet superiority in the air was complete, and the Finns desperately needed aircraft and artillery. Harold Macmillan sent a telegram to the Prime Minister and the Foreign Secretary urging the Government to send immediate aid. Almost miraculously the Finns had by this time shot down 387 Russian airplanes and destroyed 400 Russian tanks, but at the end of February the Russians broke through the Mannerheim Line and Finland was obliged to accept the peace terms she was offered. The fighting ended on 13 March.

Back in England, Macmillan took part in a two-day debate on Finland in the House of Commons on 19–20 March. The Prime Minister had claimed in his opening speech that 'no appeal that was made to us by the Finnish Government remained unanswered'. Macmillan was able to disprove this with a list of the meagre supplies of airplanes, anti-tank guns and small-arms ammunition that had been sent, and he drew attention to the long delays between authorization and despatch even of those supplies which did actually leave England. The British Government had been asked for 100 anti-tank guns, but had been unable to send any: 'We could only send 25 howitzers out of 150 asked for; only 30 field-guns out of 166 asked for, and these were despatched one month after the request.' Macmillan used his eye-witness knowledge to describe the heroism of the Finnish struggle and to make the point that if more men and materials had been supplied sooner, the Finns could have held out for much longer. He did not criticize the intentions of the British Government so much as its competence: 'This episode', he said, throws 'a piercing light on the present machinery and the method of government.

The delay, the vacillation, changes of front ... before a decision is given – these are patently clear to anyone. The moral of the history of these three months to be drawn for the future is, to use the phrase of Burke, "a proof of the irresistible operation of feeble counsel".'[6] These strictures and the evidence in support of them impressed the House and were a prelude to the criticisms of the Government which were to be made in the more important debate on Norway six weeks later.

Early in April, another group of dissident Conservatives came into existence. It was known as the Watching Committee and was concerned with inadequacies in the war effort. Lord Salisbury, a senior ex-Minister, acted as chairman and the meetings took place at his London house in Arlington Street. The peers included Lord Astor (the owner of the *Observer*), Lord Cecil of Chelwood, Lord Hailsham (a former Lord Chancellor), Lord Lloyd, Lord Londonderry, Lord Swinton and Lord Trenchard. The House of Commons membership overlapped with that of the other disaffected groups. Leo Amery, Robert Cranborne, Duff Cooper, Richard Law, Harold Macmillan, Harold Nicolson, Louis Spears, Patrick Spens and Lord Wolmer were all active contributors to the discussions, and Emrys Evans acted as secretary. The Committee made private representations direct to the Prime Minister, but one of its strongest recommendations, for a smaller War Cabinet, whose members should not be burdened with departmental duties, was brusquely dismissed by Chamberlain. These various groups, working on much the same lines, were unsuccessful in changing or even influencing Government policy. Their importance lay in the organized criticism they were able to generate within the Party, which laid the foundation for the Conservative defections in the decisive Norway debate the following May.

Germany's supplies of iron ore came from the Swedish mines and were shipped from the Norwegian port of Narvik through the Leads, a deep-water channel within the safety of Norway's territorial waters. Churchill wished to mine this channel, and, after considerable discussion and indecision, the project was at length approved.

It was at this moment that Chamberlain, in a speech to the Central Council of the Conservative Party on 4 April, made the ill-advised assertion that Hitler had 'missed the bus' by not using the initial advantage of his greater military preparedness to attack the Allies before they were ready. Five days later the Germans invaded Norway and Denmark. Hitler had pre-empted Britain's intervention in Scandinavia.

The enemy's invasion plans had been prepared with meticulous care; Britain's were improvised and continually altered. The Norwegians appealed for help at Trondheim, but the naval assault upon this port was postponed and finally abandoned altogether at the beginning of May. The British troops lacked naval and air support, and the Navy had been unable to prevent the landing of German tanks. The War Cabinet agreed to the evacuation of central Norway on 26 April and Narvik was eventually evacuated on 8 June. The British Government had been forestalled and outwitted and the failure in Norway was a shock to public opinion which provoked a political crisis at home.

From a military standpoint the Scandinavian set-back was not a major disaster and did not damage Britain's prospects of ultimate victory. Its significance lay in the apparent lack of efficiency and foresight with which the war was being waged. Although Churchill was more directly involved than Chamberlain, it was the Prime Minister's reputation which suffered most and Churchill emerged almost unscathed in the public estimation. The scuttling of the *Graf Spee* and the boarding of the *Altmark* were remembered to his credit and he seemed to personify the drive and energy which the people were looking to their leaders to supply.

The Opposition asked for a debate, ostensibly on the Norwegian reverse, in reality on the general conduct of the war. This was arranged for 7 and 8 May, on a motion for the Whitsun adjournment. Newspaper comment did not predict important political changes as a result of the debate and Ministers were equally optimistic. Chamberlain recorded, 'I don't think my enemies will get me down this time,'[7] and Halifax, while admitting 'considerable political clamour',[8] doubted if it would amount to much in the end. The Chief Whip was confident that he could keep the Party in line and Macmillan was one of the few Members who believed (and hoped) that the Government would fall. The House was crowded and its mood critical when the Prime Minister came in at question time and he was greeted from the Labour benches with cries of 'Resign' and 'The man who missed the bus'. He opened the debate with an appeal for unity and for the support and co-operation of all Parties, but he rejected suggestions for a reorganization of the War Cabinet and, although partly successful in lowering the temperature in the House, he failed to allay the anxieties and growing hostility of his critics.

Clement Attlee followed him from the Opposition Front Bench. 'I am not in the least satisfied', he declared, 'that the present War Cabinet is an efficient instrument for conducting the war. . . . We cannot afford to have our destinies in the hands of failures or men who need a rest.'

Sir Roger Keys appeared in the House bemedalled and resplendent in the uniform of an Admiral of the Fleet. He was usually a poor speaker and on this occasion asked Harold Macmillan's advice about the form his speech should take. Macmillan suggested that he should make it short, write it out beforehand and deliver it exactly from the text. He did so with simplicity, sincerity and great effect. Although critical of the Government, he expressed confidence in Churchill and his contribution made a considerable impact on the House.

The strongest and most damaging condemnation of Chamberlain was yet to come. Leo Amery, small in stature, combative and tenacious, did more than anyone to destroy the Government in the best speech of his career. Macmillan thought it 'the most formidable philippic'[9] he had ever heard. The Prime Minister had said nothing, Amery declared, 'which suggested that the Government either foresaw what Germany meant to do or came to a clear decision when it knew what Germany had done or acted swiftly or consistently throughout this whole lamentable affair'. In his peroration, he quoted Cromwell, using – with devastating effect – the Protector's savage attack on the Long Parliament: 'You have sat here too long for any good you have been doing. Depart, I say, and let us have done with you. In the name of God, go.'[10] As Churchill was to comment: 'These were terrible words coming from a friend and colleague of many years, a fellow Birmingham Member and a Privy Councillor of distinction and experience.'[11]

That evening Chamberlain saw the King and said he still hoped to be able to reconstruct his Government by bringing the Labour leaders into a national coalition. He did not realize the degree of personal hostility they felt towards him.

Leo Amery recorded an important conversation between Attlee and Brendan Bracken the same evening,[12] when Attlee intimated that, in any change of Government, his Party would favour Halifax as Prime Minister, with Churchill as Minister of Defence. On his own responsibility, Bracken argued that Churchill could not accept a situation in which he would have no real control but would be blamed if things went wrong. He persuaded Attlee not to refuse to serve under Churchill if a coalition government was formed. This would certainly have been reported to Churchill and no doubt strengthened his hand when the issue of who should become Prime Minister developed two days later. Perhaps more influential with Attlee was a message on the same lines from Clement Davies, who telephoned him from Bob Boothby's flat in London.

It is surprising that some Labour opinion at that time was more favourably disposed towards a national leader from the House of Lords than from the House of Commons. The succession, if there was to be a change, lay between Churchill and Halifax.

Herbert Morrison opened for the Opposition on the second day of the debate and announced that his Party would force a vote at the end of it. This was an important decision. It is unusual to divide on an adjournment and some Conservatives had felt less inhibited in their criticisms of the Government than would have been the case had it been clear from the outset that the debate would culminate in a division. The Conservative rebels would not on their own have divided the House.

Chamberlain made an unprepared and injudicious intervention in reply to Morrison's attack: 'I do not seek to evade criticism, but I say to my friends in the House – and I have friends in the House – no Government can prosecute a war efficiently unless it has public and Parliamentary support. I accept the challenge ... and I call on my friends to support us in the lobby to-night.'[13] The reference to his friends was ill-advised. It seemed to personalize a great issue in which the national interest was at stake and many Members felt that the appeal for loyalty to the Party and to himself fell below the level of the occasion.

Morrison, who was anxious to show that the challenge to Chamberlain extended beyond the ranks of the Labour Party, had been working behind the scenes to persuade Lloyd George, 'the energetic leader of the First World War, to make a vigorous speech against the feeble leader of the Second'.[14] Lloyd George agreed to speak from the Opposition Front Bench. Such was his dislike of Chamberlain that he could scarcely have resisted the temptation to contribute to his downfall. It was the last great speech he was to make in the House of Commons:

It is not a question of who are the Prime Minister's friends; it is a far bigger issue. ... He has appealed for sacrifice. The nation is prepared for every sacrifice, so long as it has leadership. ... I say solemnly that the Prime Minister should give an example of sacrifice, because there is nothing which can contribute more to victory in this war than that he should sacrifice the seals of office.

Lloyd George's target was Chamberlain and he warned Churchill, who was to wind up the debate, not to allow himself 'to be converted into an air-raid shelter to keep the splinters from hitting his colleagues'. Duff Cooper took the same line and forecast that 'those who so often trembled before his sword will be only too glad to shrink behind his buckler'.

As the debate progressed, the whips became anxious about the number of dissident Conservatives who might abstain or even vote against the Government and were busy in the Smoking-Room and corridors trying to persuade the doubtfuls not to join the incipient revolt; but Emrys Evans rejected these pleas on behalf of the Amery Group and at an emergency meeting held later that evening, Evans's action was endorsed by his associates, who agreed unanimously to vote against the motion. This decision proved fatal for Chamberlain's chances of weathering the storm.

Winston Churchill wound up the two-day debate for the Government.

He accepted his full share of responsibility for the failure to sustain Norway and loyally defended the Prime Minister and the conduct of the war. The moral and intellectual position of the Socialists, who had voted consistently against conscription and the pre-war Service Estimates, was not a strong one, but their anger now was uninhibited and it was directed less against Churchill than against Chamberlain.

At eleven o'clock the House divided. Conservative Members in uniform mixed with Labour pacifists in the 'No' lobby for what Macmillan described as the most tense division he had ever known. When the figures were announced the normal Government majority of over 200 had fallen to 81; the Prime Minister had lost the confidence of a substantial section of his own Party in the House of Commons. Macmillan recalls that a Labour Member '"Josh" Wedgwood ... started singing *Rule Britannia*. I tried to join in. But as neither of us could sing, it was not a very successful effort.'[15]

With his usual frosty smile to some of his supporters, Chamberlain rose and walked slowly to his room, where he asked Churchill to join him. Churchill advised him to strengthen the Government and continue at its head, but Chamberlain remained uncomforted and unconvinced. Such a large fall in his majority was almost the equivalent of a defeat, especially in wartime, when a dissolution of Parliament was unthinkable. He knew he must resign.

As often happens at Westminster after a controversial debate and a dramatic division, groups of Members met the following day to discuss the situation and decide what line to follow. Lord Salisbury's Watching Committee was agreed that Chamberlain must go, but there was doubt as to whether Churchill or Halifax should succeed him. Macmillan spoke out strongly in favour of Churchill both at this meeting and at a gathering of the Amery committee later in the day. The Davies and Amery Groups, meeting separately, resolved that there must be an all-Party National Government. These decisions were conveyed to Chamberlain, and Amery issued a public statement to the same effect. Clement Davies acted as a liaison between the Conservative critics and the Labour leadership.

It was clear that the Chamberlain administration could not continue in its existing form and that he was himself the main obstacle to any reconstruction on an all-Party basis. The real question now crystallizing was whether Churchill or Halifax should follow him as Prime Minister. Lord Halifax, who had been a liberal-minded Viceroy of India, was a man of the highest character but he would not have made an inspiring leader in time of war. On the morning of 9 May, he received a report from R.A. Butler, his Under-Secretary at the Foreign Office – who had talked to both Dalton and Herbert Morrison the previous evening – that the Labour leaders would join the Government under himself, but not under Chamberlain. Halifax, though gratified, was unenthusiastic: 'If I was Prime Minister', he told Butler, 'Winston would run it. He might consult me, but he would be in charge.' Halifax recognized that Churchill's drive and determination made him the obvious choice.

The Prime Minister saw Halifax at ten o'clock. They agreed that an all-Party Government was now needed and that the prospects of forming one under Chamberlain's leadership were negligible. The Prime Minister wanted Halifax to succeed him, but this prospect was so unattractive that Halifax 'experienced a feeling of physical sickness in the pit of his stomach'[16] even in discussing the suggestion. He argued that the position of a Prime Minister in the House of Lords, especially in wartime, would be an impossible one.

The other candidate for the leadership was much less unwilling to assume it: 'The prospect neither excited nor alarmed me,' Churchill wrote characteristically. 'I thought it would be by far the best plan. I was content to let events unfold.'[17] They were soon to do so. Kingsley Wood, one of the Prime Minister's closest political friends, warned Churchill that Chamberlain would like him to concur in the choice of Halifax. 'Don't agree,' was Kingsley Wood's advice, 'and don't say anything.' Brendan Bracken also counselled Churchill to say nothing if his views were invited.

At 4.30 that afternoon Chamberlain saw Churchill and Halifax at Downing Street. The Prime Minister reiterated his resolve to resign and added that he would be willing to serve under either Halifax or Churchill. Acting on the advice he had received, Churchill said nothing. A long and crucial silence ensued. It was eventually broken by Halifax, who argued against himself, re-stating his opinion that, quite apart from Churchill's outstanding qualities, it was out of the question for the Prime Minister not to be a Member of the House of Commons. Winston then intervened briefly to say he had reached the same conclusion. It was now clear that the responsibility would fall upon him – a situation accepted regretfully by Chamberlain and evidently with much less reluctance by his probable successor. The most important interview of Churchill's life and perhaps the most momentous for the nation in the whole course of the war was now over.

At 6.15, Attlee and Greenwood arrived at Downing Street. Chamberlain asked if they would serve in a National Government under him or under someone else. The conversation was courteous but there was little doubt of their disinclination to join a Government still led by Neville Chamberlain. They said they would consult their Party Executive and telephone their decision the following day.

The early morning of 10 May brought with it the awesome news of Hitler's invasion of the Low Countries. The German armies had violated the frontiers of Belgium, Holland and Luxembourg. Three Cabinets were held that day, at the second of which Chamberlain told his colleagues of his original intention to resign, but indicated that the German attack meant a temporary deferment of this decision. Some Ministers, including Kingsley Wood, disagreed; they thought the immediate formation of a National Government was more essential than ever to deal with the new and menacing situation. During the third meeting, the Prime Minister's private secretary telephoned Attlee, who said that his Party would not join a Government under Chamberlain but would do so under another Conservative leader; no stipulation was made as to who this should be. This message was decisive, and shortly after receiving it Neville Chamberlain drove to Buckingham Palace to tender his resignation. The King accepted it with genuine regret as he was loyal to his Prime Minister, whom he thought had been unfairly treated. They then discussed the succession; King George VI's preference was for Halifax, but Chamberlain explained the Foreign Secretary's lack of enthusiam for the task and advised the King to send for Churchill. At six p.m. Winston Spencer Churchill was summoned to the Palace and invited to form a Government.

Lord Boothby considers that three men played a major part in bringing Churchill to power: Leo Amery, who became Secretary of State for India, Kingsley Wood, who was made Chancellor of the Exchequer, and Clement Davies, who received no reward. Brenden Bracken, Churchill's closest political associate, became Parliamentary Private Secretary to the new Prime Minister and, unusually in that position, was given a Privy Councillorship.

Chamberlain accepted Churchill's invitation to remain in the War Cabinet as Lord President of the Council, an offer which was at first coupled with the post of leader of the House of Commons; but the Labour Party objected to the second of these appointments and Chamberlain willingly withdrew from it. He behaved throughout with dignity and magnanimity. Under the circumstances, Churchill retained the leadership of the House in his own hands, with Attlee as his deputy and *de facto* leader.

By ten p.m. on 10 May, Churchill had sent the list of his key Ministerial appointments to the King. Attlee became Lord Privy Seal; Greenwood, Minister without Portfolio; Eden, Secretary of State for War; A. V. Alexander, First Lord of the Admiralty; and Sir Archibald Sinclair, Secretary for Air. Lord Halifax continued as Foreign Secretary. The War Cabinet consisted initially of Churchill, Chamberlain, Attlee, Greenwood and Halifax. Churchill could boast that he had formed 'the most comprehensive Administration in history',[18] stretching from Lord Lloyd of Dolobran on the extreme right of the Conservative Party to Miss Ellen Wilkinson, who had red hair and was so far to the left in the Labour Party that she was known as 'Red Ellen'.

On the commemorative medal which Churchill presented to every Minister who had served under him in the war were engraved the words 'The Great

Coalition'. It was not misnamed. Party affiliations and loyalties no longer mattered. Churchill personified the nation at war and achieved a unity at this moment of crisis more complete, perhaps, than ever before in Britain's long island story. Now, no one was for the Party and all were for the State.

11

THE MINISTRY OF SUPPLY

Within a few days Churchill was able to announce the junior appointments in his Government. Among them was that of Harold Macmillan as Parliamentary Secretary to the Ministry of Supply. He was forty-six years old when he left 'the carefree although sometimes frustrating irresponsibility of the Back Benches'.[1] For the next twenty-three years, whether in office or in Opposition, he was never to leave the Front Bench until his resignation as Prime Minister in 1963. It was a late start, but it heralded a long stay.

In the earlier years of his parliamentary career, Macmillan had acquired a reputation that was very different from that of the urbane, witty, sometimes cynical statesman of his premiership. Always hardworking, he had given the impression of being an earnest, idealistic, perhaps over-critical intellectual. To the inter-war Establishment he seemed a well-informed irritant, but to his Back-Bench contemporaries he was distinguished in appearance, stimulating and agreeable to work with and well worth listening to in the House of Commons. Most of them thought he should have been taken more seriously, and much sooner, than he had been.

In the course of the few weeks after he became Prime Minister, Churchill was faced not only by the withdrawal of the British Army from Dunkirk but by the capitulation of France and the beginning of the Battle of Britain. For over a year England and the Empire stood alone against the dictators. Britain survived and it was no doubt her finest hour, but it was followed by a further eighteen months of hard, unremitting effort, with scarcely a single success to sustain the nation's endeavours. It was not until October 1942 that the tide began to turn and, as Macmillan recorded, 'it might almost be said that before Alamein we never had a victory; after Alamein we never had a defeat'.[2] During the whole of this period Macmillan was working hard as a junior Minister, for most of it at the Ministry of Supply.

The Department's main task was to provide the weapons and other needs of the British Army and Air Force. The Admiralty continued to control most of its own sources of supply and the Ministry of Aircraft Production, under the dynamic leadership of Lord Beaverbrook, was responsible for the manufacture of aircraft; but the enormous and rapid expansion of the Army meant a corresponding increase in its demands. The list of contractors and sub-contractors had to be extended, tools adapted and factory manpower trained. Dunkirk multiplied the problems. Almost all the weapons Britain possessed had been shipped to France and the equipment for five divisions now had to be replaced, because although the men had been saved, their arms were for the most part lost. Despite this and the imminent danger of invasion, Churchill courageously despatched convoys of tanks and munitions to save the situation in the Middle East.

The Department organized the supply and control of all the means of production, including factory space, machine-tools and raw materials, whether home-produced or imported. At the beginning of the war Britain paid in cash for all her imports, but by the autumn of 1940 her dollar reserves were much depleted and she was only saved by the introduction of Lend-Lease, which President Roosevelt carried through Congress in March 1941. Under this scheme, described by Churchill as 'the most unsordid act in the history of any nation',[3] Britain obtained future supplies from the United States without payment.

One of the Department's duties was the collection of scrap of all kinds, including metal and paper. Eventually Macmillan was able to persuade the then Minister of Works, Lord Reith, to take over this task; but the range of the Ministry's activities is illustrated by the sort of questions Macmillan had to answer in the House of Commons. These covered the collection of kitchen waste and of gates and railings from the parks and people's private houses; the provision of steel helmets for the Home Guard and of nurseries in which women workers could leave their children; the possibilities of making paper out of straw, the supply of lavatory paper and of newsprint for Polish periodicals; the salvaging of bottles and of rubber; the use of railway workshops for munitions; and the requisition of material on the Welsh Highland Railway.

Macmillan was an effective Minister. His earlier enthusiasm for economic planning helped him to organize the war production machine; and for the first time he could apply his pre-war ideas to a practical task. He did much to bring about a closer relationship between Government, industry and labour. New Area Boards were established, with representatives from different Ministries, which were responsible to the Industrial Capacity Committee of which Macmillan was chairman. Anthony Sampson described the organization as 'a planner's paradise'.[4] He wrote that Macmillan 'lovingly explained the new system in a speech on 7 August 1940 and jokingly remarked that he would try to introduce State Socialism in the country if he did not have to put up with the tremendous resistance of the Labour movement'.

The Director-General of Production in the Department was Sir Harold Brown, for whom Macmillan developed a great admiration. Another important figure was Lord Weir, who was in charge of the explosives programme for all the services. Stores were in the able hands of Sir Frederick Marquis (later Lord Woolton), who was soon to become well known as a successful Minister of Food. Sir Walter Layton was the Director of Statistics, responsible for production schedules; Percy Mills, who became one of Macmillan's closest friends, was in charge of the Machine Tool Control; and Colonel J.J. Llewellyn was chairman of the important Raw Materials Allocation Committee. The Ministry was well served by all these key men, who discharged their duties with dedication and efficiency.

During his twenty months in the Department, Macmillan worked under three successive Ministers – Herbert Morrison, Sir Andrew Duncan and Lord Beaverbrook. Their backgrounds and personalities were very different. Macmillan used to say that, working with a Cockney, a Lowland Scot and a Canadian, he 'never heard a word of English spoken correctly from the Minister's chair'.[5]

Morrison understood the political importance of public relations, of which Macmillan became such a successful exponent as Prime Minister many years later. In this respect Morrison was his mentor. He was fascinated to find that

... the most important person in his private office appeared to be the Public Relations Officer, a figure of whom up till then I had never heard.... I did my best to second his efforts to keep our Minister in the lead, for he was subject to a good deal of cross-fire between Ernest Bevin, the powerful Minister of Labour, and Beaverbrook, the somewhat anarchic head of the newly-formed Ministry of Aircraft Production.[6]

Morrison appreciated Macmillan's loyalty and recorded that 'his advice for my advancement tended to occupy his mind to such an extent that I had to remind him that we had a war job to do and that personal careers were not important'.

Macmillan described his chief as 'tough, imaginative and resilient', a good administrator, open-minded and fair, who 'set about his task with vigour and courage', but he doubted whether Morrison really understood the problems which confronted the Department, 'for he had no practical knowledge of business or production ... he was really out of his depth and was not unwilling to move'.[7] Churchill made some Cabinet changes in October 1940 and Morrison went to the Home Office – renamed the Ministry of Home Security – for which Macmillan thought him better suited. He was succeeded at Supply by Sir Andrew Duncan.

The new Minister had all the characteristics of a Lowland Scot – 'cautious, diligent, orderly, unimaginative, but efficient'.[8] He had useful experience of organization, good judgement and a grasp of detail, which Macmillan admired, but although a kind man, agreeable and easy to work for, he lacked the dynamic drive and gift for improvisation of his successor. Duncan went to the Board of Trade in June 1941 and Lord Beaverbrook took over the Department.

The new appointment caused anxiety and concern, but also some excitement among officials, who had suffered from raids on their resources by the former Minister of Aircraft Production. Macmillan described his arrival as 'a thrilling event'. There were immediate changes. Beaverbrook did not care for the rather dismal offices which the Ministry occupied and at once took over Shell-Mex House 'with a speed and a ruthlessness which commanded, if not the approval, at least the admiration' of his staff. The whole atmosphere changed too. 'There was a general sense of bustle, excitement and even confusion,'[9] but also of energy and determination.

Macmillan detected 'a streak of vindictiveness and even cruelty' in his new chief but found him also capable of great kindness. 'He sometimes seemed almost a Jekyll and Hyde.' His charm, when he wished to exert it, was proverbial and irresistible and Macmillan enjoyed being 'in close and daily contact with this extraordinary man'. His working methods usually left the heads of departments to their own devices for most of the day, until about six or seven o'clock, when they attended a conference in his room to discuss the problems and arrive at decisions. After a short break for dinner at 9.00 or 9.30, the meeting would continue till midnight or one in the morning.

After Andrew Duncan's departure, Macmillan became solely responsible for questions and debates in the House of Commons, and in July 1941 he received a letter from Beaverbrook:

May I send you warmest congratulations on your speech in the House to-day. On all hands I hear immense praise of it as a most splendid Parliamentary performance.

I count myself a most fortunate Minister in having so able and persuasive an advocate in the House of Commons.

This was typical of Beaverbrook, who well understood the importance of praise and encouragement when it was deserved.

In his role as chairman of the Industrial Capacity Committee, Macmillan worked for a time under Ernest Bevin, the redoubtable Minister of Labour. This dual loyalty to two very different men proved difficult. The atmosphere between Bevin and Beaverbrook was always strained and became increasingly so. It was a clash of personalities rather than of principles and, given goodwill, the issues in dispute could easily have been resolved; but Macmillan's attempts to improve the relationship were not successful and matters came to a head over the creation of a Ministry of Production.

For some time the need for a central control had been apparent and in February 1942 this new Department, under the leadership of Lord Beaverbrook, came into existence. By then the whole civilian population, including the maximum number of women, was fully deployed. There were logical arguments for placing the allocation of labour under the Minister of Production, but this was strongly resisted by Bevin, whose power in Cabinet and Parliament was greater than Beaverbrook's. Partly owing to this disagreement, but mainly because of a collapse in his own health, Beaverbrook resigned from the Government a fortnight later. By then Macmillan had left the Ministry of Supply to serve as Under-Secretary of State at the Colonial Office.

Throughout his time at the Ministry he had had to contend with opposition in the House of Commons, mainly over production problems. This was led by Emanuel Shinwell, Clement Davies, Lord Winterton, Richard Stokes, Garro-Jones and Leslie Hore-Belisha, with the occasional support of Sir John Wardlow-Milne. Shinwell's speeches were always critical, often acid and usually well informed. He and Eddie Winterton formed a close if somewhat incongruous working association. The sight of the tall, angular aristocrat and the small, left-wing agitator walking through the lobby together reminded Macmillan of Don Quixote and Sancho Panza. A play called *Arsenic and Old Lace* was running in London at the time and the two men were soon given these soubriquets.

One of the main targets for criticism was the supply and quality of armoured vehicles. The Army had lost all its tanks in France in the summer of 1940 and the fighting in North Africa called for large numbers of bigger, better armoured and better gunned replacements than had ever been made in Britain before.

There were continual complaints about performance, breakdowns in action and the lack of spares. Much of this criticism was justified. For some time the Department could not supply what the Army needed in the quantity or at the rate required, and Macmillan acknowledged that 'we fell perhaps in between the search for perfection and the call for profusion'.[10] Gradually the problems were overcome, and by the time he left the Department both design and production had greatly improved. After becoming Minister of State in North Africa he was able to record in his diary that the new Churchill tanks were a success and were doing well in battle.

By the middle of September 1940, the Battle of Britain had been won, as much by the decisions and dynamism of Lord Beaverbrook as by the heroism of the air crews. In spite of the heavy losses in machines, production had risen to such an extent that Fighter Command had more aircraft in service at the end of the battle than when it began.

The next ordeal for the British people was the Blitz, which lasted from September 1940 until May 1941. In almost the last of the raids on London, the House of Commons was destroyed on 10 May. Macmillan was knocked down by a taxi one night in the darkness of the black-out, but no bones were broken and he was back at work within a few days. On another occasion he was at the Carlton Club when it was destroyed and later the same evening, when he was talking to his brother-in-law in Pratt's Club, a message was brought to the Duke that his house in Carlton Gardens was on fire. As soon as the fire was under control they carried out the best pieces of furniture into the garden, from where they were retrieved next day by Lady Dorothy. Macmillan's own top floor flat in Piccadilly was bombed, but he was able to move into another belonging to Hugh Walpole on the first floor of the same building. The top floors of Macmillans Publishing Company were used as storage space for stock, and his brother, Daniel, commented with a wry smile that there were some very slow-selling books there and he doubted whether any German bomb could get through them. Macmillan was sometimes able to get down to Sussex on a Saturday or Sunday and calculated afterwards that one bomb for every ten acres had fallen on the Birch Grove estate. The only casualties were a cow and a pheasant, which were duly entered in the game-book – the cow under the heading of 'various'.

At the offices of the Ministry, little working-time was lost after the alert system was altered on the Prime Minister's instructions. It was the duty of the spotter on the roof to sound the alarm and when Macmillan asked him how he interpreted his instructions, he replied: 'When I sees 'em over the Coliseum, I rings me bell.' The Parliamentary Secretary took his turn at fire-watching in London, and in the course of his duties travelled all over the country to meet the Regional Representatives of the Department. He was at Woolwich, Cardiff and Bristol on the nights of exceptionally heavy attacks, but there was never any panic and the ARP organization worked well. Although several buildings were destroyed and casualties caused, the damage to production was relatively slight and, even after bad raids, the factories were usually working again within a few days.

The Blitz on Britain had barely ended when, on 22 June 1941, the Germans attacked Russia. Churchill's immediate decision to send weapons, ammunitions and materials in large quantities to the Soviet Union was undoubtedly the right one, but it made heavy additional demands on the Ministry of Supply.

Following the treacherous attack on Pearl Harbour, Britain declared war on Japan on 8 December 1941, and Germany reacted by a declaration of war against the United States. This was a benefaction for Britain – and for President Roosevelt. From the earliest days of the conflict he had done everything in his power to be helpful. In return for bases in the West Indies, he had given the United Kingdom fifty obsolescent destroyers, at that time almost essential to her survival; he had policed half the Atlantic against German submarines; and he had saved Britain financially by the system of Lend-Lease. But he was not all-powerful. Many members of Congress and of the American public wished to avoid actual involvement in the European war. The Monroe doctrine, long a principle of United States foreign policy, died a slow death and there was a still a strong isolationist instinct which even Roosevelt could not easily eradicate. Hitler's declaration of war removed all these inhibitions. The people of the Great Republic now rallied enthusiastically to the cause of freedom and thereafter held tenaciously to its support. From this moment final victory was no longer in doubt.

An important element in Anglo-American co-operation, both before and after the United States' entry into the war, was the close personal relationship which had grown up between Churchill and Roosevelt. There was only one fly in the ointment of accord between them. Like so many Americans at even the highest political level, the President was suspicious of and instinctively hostile to, the existence of the British Empire. It may have been a subconscious legacy from his country's colonial past, but he did not believe in Britain's commitment to confer political independence on her colonies. Nevertheless, as Macmillan put it: 'While the Russian alliance brought us a welcome diversion, the American alliance brought us an almost fraternal partnership.'[11] To the son of an American mother and a British father, this relationship between the two nations was a thrilling and emotional event.

12

THE COLONIAL OFFICE

On 5 February 1942 Macmillan was appointed Under-Secretary of State for the Colonies. At the same time he was made a member of the Privy Council. This is the highest political honour, automatic for a member of the Cabinet, but a special and unusual compliment for a junior Minister. As the Secretary of State was Lord Moyne, Macmillan was still answerable for his Department in the House of Commons. He recorded that to 'exchange the heat and bustle of life at Shell-Mex House under Lord Beaverbrook for the cool dignity of the old Colonial Office in Downing Street was a curious experience.'[1] At the modern, characterless offices of the Ministry of Supply the hours had been long, the atmosphere hectic and the sense of urgency paramount and pervasive. The large high-ceilinged rooms of Whitehall with their marble chimney-pieces and antique furniture were in striking contrast, and the pace of work seemed correspondingly slower. To Macmillan 'it felt like leaving a madhouse in order to enter a mausoleum',[2] though he acknowledged that this description was somewhat unfair to both Departments.

Soon after his arrival, Lord Moyne was succeeded as Colonial Secretary by Lord Cranborne, who was an old friend of Macmillan's. They were already connected by marriage and that summer Harold's son Maurice married Katie Ormsby-Gore, one of Cranborne's nieces. Their partnership in the office was therefore close and agreeable; but Macmillan knew nothing about the Colonies or how they were governed, so there was much to learn.

India was separately administered by the India Office, but there were fifty-five Colonies, with a total population of sixty million people of different races and religions. Many of them joined the Armed Forces in their own territories or for service overseas, but the main need was to mobilize the materials and potential resources of the Colonial Empire for the more effective prosecution of the war. Increased production, especially of tin, rubber, sisal, sugar and tea, was urgently required and there were demands from Macmillan's former Department and from the Ministry of Aircraft

Production for bauxite, wolfram, copper, zinc, manganese, chrome, iron ore and industrial diamonds. Macmillan was given responsibility for all economic and trade problems.

To sustain the Colonial production effort, imports of consumer goods for the workers, and capital equipment for roads and railways had to be obtained. Bicycles, the only method of personal transport in most of the territories, were also in great demand. Owing to the continual sinkings by German submarines, the provision of shipping for both imports to and exports from the Colonies was a major problem and local agriculture had to be developed to feed the people. Every ton of food that could be grown in a Colony saved a ship to transport it there.

Despite the demands of war, the long-term needs of the Colonies were not entirely neglected. Indeed, much of the capital development made necessary by the war effort was a gain for the future; and the passage through Parliament of the Colonial Development and Welfare Act was the foundation on which many extensive, though overdue, post-war projects were based.

In June 1942 Macmillan made a speech in the House of Commons, during the course of which he pointed out that the Colonies

... are poor because they are just beginning. They are four or five centuries behind. Our job is to move them, to hustle them, across this great interval of time as rapidly as we can.... The Empires of the past have died because they could not change with the times.... By contrast our Empire has had the great quality of adaptation.... The governing principle of the Colonial Empire should be the principle of partnership between the various elements composing it. Out of partnership come understanding and friendship. Within the fabric of the Commonwealth lies the future of the Colonial territories.[3]

He used the word partnership deliberately to express the relationship he envisaged between Britain and her Colonies when the war was over. A newspaper noted that partnership 'implies the gradual elevation of every Colony into something like Dominion status'.[4] Macmillan had already anticipated the future developments in which he was himself to play such a leading and progressive part. He foresaw, too, the difficulties which the British settlers in the East African Colonies might have to face and he put forward a scheme, far ahead of its time, by which the local Governments should buy the freehold of the larger farms – retaining their existing owners as managers or tenants – and the smaller farms for resale to Africans. All this could have been done far more cheaply and easily then, or soon after the war, than proved possible twenty years later.

Macmillan records an interesting conversation between the Colonial Secretary and Mr Foster Dulles in July 1942,[5] in which the future American Secretary of State is quoted as saying that 'embedded in the mind of most

Americans was a fundamental distrust of ... British Imperialism'. Although Dulles personally disclaimed such a view, subsequent events showed that anti-Colonialism was certainly embedded in his own attitude, and he went on to say that:

... the only way in which we could remove this deep-seated prejudice would be to invite the co-operation of the United States in the development of our Colonies after the war.... They were merely concerned with the welfare of the indigenous populations and the development of the material resources of the territories.

Dulles did not believe that co-operation between Britain and the United States could be based only on sentiment, because that would not be enduring. A task to be done together should be the basis and 'no ideal would more appeal to the American people ... than the advancement of backward peoples'. If Britain and the United States could combine in this work, especially in Africa, he believed it would be a solid foundation for future co-operation.

In the meantime the war was still going badly for Britain: Hong Kong had been lost, so had the Straits Settlements, the Malay States, North Borneo and Sarawak – and later Burma. On 15 February 1942, Singapore surrendered with the capitulation of 85,000 British troops. In the summer of 1942, 23 ships out of 36 were sunk in one convoy to Russia and 18 out of 37 in the next. Stalin's only reaction was a demand, unrealistic but often repeated, for the opening of a 'Second Front'.

In North Africa, Tobruk fell on 21 June. This was followed by a motion of censure in the House of Commons, expressing no confidence in the central direction of the war. Aneurin Bevan made a bitter interjection: 'The Prime Minister wins debate after debate and loses battle after battle'; but Churchill wound up with a powerful defence of the Government and obtained an overwhelming majority in the division which followed.[6]

Within four months the tide of fortune had begun to turn. On 23 October the church bells were rung in England for the first time during the war to celebrate the great victory of El Alamein, which was followed by the pursuit of the German and Italian forces into Libya and Tripoli. On 8 November came the Allied landings in North Africa. Thereafter the British and American forces operated under the single unified command of General Eisenhower. Although he did not know it at the time, these events were to be the background of Harold Macmillan's life for the next two and a half years.

In a Government reshuffle on 22 November 1942, Cranborne left the Colonial Office and was succeeded by Oliver Stanley. Like his predecessor, the new Secretary of State was an old friend of Macmillan's; but whereas Cranborne had devolved authority over a wide area of the Department's activities to his Under-Secretary, who also answered for the Office in the

House of Commons, Macmillan feared that this would not continue under his new chief. Stanley was himself a skilled Parliamentarian, renowned for his wit and speaking ability, and would clearly take the lion's share of the House of Commons work. Under these circumstances Macmillan drafted a letter of resignation, but was wise enough to show it to Brendan Bracken before sending it off. Bracken strongly advised him to delay doing so. This was good advice, which Macmillan took. Exactly one month later his patience was rewarded.

On 22 December the Prime Minister offered him the post of Minister of State in North Africa. He was to be of Cabinet rank, reporting direct to Churchill and working at Allied Forces Headquarters in Algiers. His task was to represent the Prime Minister's views, especially on the political issues, to the Commander-in-Chief and to convey General Eisenhower's thoughts to Churchill. As Britain's forces in North Africa were more numerous than America's, the British Government had every right to express its opinions on the use of all troops and on the strategy of the war, but success in doing so would clearly depend on the extent to which the Minister Resident could influence the Supreme Allied Commander. It was an independent diplomatic and political assignment of significance and great potential importance. Macmillan accepted it with alacrity – and carried it out superbly well. He was lucky to be given this opportunity, but he had earned it and his success was to establish him in the first rank of post-war British politics.

Churchill enquired if he would go in uniform. After a moment's thought, he declined.

'Why not?' said Churchill angrily.

'Among all those generals, admirals and air marshals, an infantry captain, even in the Grenadier Guards, would not cut a very impressive figure,' Macmillan replied.

'I see your point,' Churchill agreed. 'You mean that between the baton and the bowler there is no middle course.'[7]

13
NORTH AFRICA

With modesty and good sense, General Eisenhower realized that he and his American officers had no experience of commanding troops in war. He much admired the brilliant successes the British Army had recently achieved in the desert and himself suggested that all the British and American forces in North Africa should be combined under a single unified command, with himself as Supreme Allied Commander, but with the joint land, sea and air forces each under the direction of the respective British leaders, General Alexander, Admiral Cunningham and Air Marshal Tedder. He made this suggestion to Duncan Sandys, then a junior Minister at the War Office on a visit to Algiers, who at once conveyed it to Churchill. The Prime Minister and the War Cabinet accepted the idea with alacrity, and within a few weeks the combined Allied Command was successfully established.

Nevertheless, the political background to Macmillan's new appointment was difficult and potentially divisive. Although the staff of Eisenhower's Headquarters was completely integrated, with British and American officers serving as members of a single team, there were inevitable differences of view between the two allies, which it was Macmillan's task to minimize, whether they arose from London and Washington or from local circumstances. He was admirably assisted in this objective by his American counterpart, Robert Murphy, whose advice carried considerable weight in Washington; but a most awkward situation had arisen just before Macmillan's arrival in Algiers, mainly because there was no real agreement at the highest level as to how to handle the French problem.

In June 1940, in order to sustain the crumbling morale of the French Government, Churchill had made the imaginative offer of complete union between Britain and France. This was declined and Marshal Pétain formed a Government of collaboration with the Germans. Churchill still hoped that the French fleet would be handed over to Britain, but when Admiral Darlan, the head of the French Navy, joined Pétain's Cabinet, his undertaking to move the fleet to a place of safety was rescinded. As a result, the British had had to seize or destroy as many French ships as possible in order to prevent them falling into German hands and being used against the Allies. The United States had recognized and been represented with the Vichy Government ever since the fall of France, whereas Britain supported the Free French under the leadership of de Gaulle. This patriotic young General had established a 'French National Committee' in England and secured the adherence of some of the French colonial territories. These did not include the important Colonies in North and West Africa.

Unfortunately the Americans distrusted de Gaulle and, although by 1942 they had recognized his Committee as being in effective control of the French Pacific and French Equatorial Africa, they would not permit him to take part in or even be informed of the Anglo-American invasion of North Africa until the night before the landings.

The Americans pinned their faith in General Giraud, who was senior to de Gaulle and had recently escaped from a German prisoner-of-war camp. The Americans hoped he would rally the French in North Africa to the Allied cause, but in fact they remained loyal to Vichy, would not accept Giraud's authority and opposed the landings.

It so happened that Admiral Darlan was in Algiers at the time and in order to stop the fighting General Mark Clark, Eisenhower's Second-in-Command, made a deal with him to order a cease-fire throughout North Africa. By this means, the Allies gained control of Morocco, Algeria and most of Tunisia without serious opposition. Darlan was repudiated by Pétain, but nevertheless he was regarded with contempt as a collaborator and a man of Vichy, and the American arrangement with him was an unpopular and controversial one in Britain. Churchill loyally upheld Eisenhower's action in a debate in the House of Commons in secret session, and on military, as opposed to moral, grounds it was no doubt defensible.

After Darlan's assassination outside his office in Algiers on Christmas Eve 1942, Eisenhower fell back on Giraud as the substitute French leader. French opinion in North Africa was now divided between those who still supported Pétain, those who accepted Giraud and those who saw de Gaulle as the only Frenchman who represented the honour of France.

It was this difficult political situation that faced Macmillan on his arrival in Algiers. He left England on 31 December, accompanied by his Private Secretary, John Wyndham (later Lord Egremont), two typewriters and two young ladies who were to use them. After a night at Gibraltar they arrived in Algiers on 2 January 1943. Macmillan's first interview with the Commander-in-Chief, who had been hurt by the unfavourable reaction to the Darlan arrangement, was rather cool. Eisenhower was somewhat suspicious of his role; but this was soon to change and Macmillan quickly developed a real respect and affection for the Allied Commander and for his Chief of Staff, General Bedell Smith, which was entirely mutual.

The following day Macmillan called on Giraud, who was no doubt a good divisional commander, but out of his depth in the political complications of his new position and an unsuitable leader of the civil and military French administration in North Africa. Macmillan's next important contact was Robert Murphy, Eisenhower's political adviser and President Roosevelt's personal representative at Allied Headquarters, with whom it was vital for him to work in close accord. The two men developed a good relationship, based on complete frankness, which proved invaluable. Murphy was a professional diplomat with no political experience and although Macmillan's weight in London was far greater than Murphy's in Washington, he had the good sense not to use it. Indeed, by seeming not to exercise undue influence at Allied Forces Headquarters, he gradually acquired it. This was made easier because the Foreign Office procedures, superior to those of the State Department, kept him much better informed than Murphy of decisions taken in Washington. Murphy wrote later: 'We got along famously together ... he did not bring to Algiers any exceptional knowledge of French or African affairs. What he did bring was exceptional common sense and knowledge of British politics.... Macmillan – in dignity, voice, manners, dress and personality – was and still is almost the American popular image of an English gentleman.'[1]

On 4 January, Macmillan was joined in Algiers by Pierson Dixon (later to be British Ambassador to the United Nations and then to France), as his Foreign Office Chief of Staff. At first the small British team lived at a hotel overlooking the port and worked in the hotel bedrooms. This was not a convenient arrangement because the lights went out whenever there was an air-raid alert, so after a few days two offices were made available at Allied Headquarters in the Hotel St George. One of the offices was used by Macmillan and the other shared by Dixon, Wyndham and their two typists. As early as 10 January, Wyndham was writing home to his mother with an affectionate reference to Macmillan as 'Uncle Harold' and describing him as 'being a great success. He is much liked, his sincerity is admired, and he has made constructive suggestions which have been hungrily welcomed.'

Wisely, Macmillan was content to spend the first two weeks listening, learning, getting to know his new colleagues and gradually earning their trust and confidence. One small task was, however, delegated to him and Murphy, acting together for the first time.

The Comte de Paris was said to be in Algiers and Eisenhower decided that his presence and the possibility of a *coup* on his behalf by French monarchist elements was an unnecessary complication. The two political advisers were therefore invited to secure his departure from French North African territory. They went to see General Giraud, giving the danger of public unrest as the reason for Eisenhower's request, and Giraud agreed to make the necessary arrangements.

A few days later, a telegram arrived informing Allied Headquarters that a secret conference between the President and the Prime Minister was to be held on 15 January at Casablanca in Morocco. Before leaving for this meeting, Macmillan gave a press conference in Algiers, which was much welcomed by the British and American correspondents for whom it was held, because a period of press censorship in North Africa had given them little or nothing to write about for the previous six weeks. In answer to questions, Macmillan gave full support on military grounds to Eisenhower's deal with Darlan, without which, he pointed out, there would have been heavy opposition and loss of life during and after the Allied landings. He dwelt upon the paramount need for the closest Anglo-American accord and for co-operation between Giraud and de Gaulle. This press conference was well timed and well handled and did much to win Eisenhower's confidence. Meanwhile, in preparation for Casablanca, Macmillan and Murphy obtained the General's approval of a plan designed to unify the various French groupings by bringing about a meeting between Giraud and de Gaulle.

Macmillan and Dixon left for Casablanca at six a.m. on 15 January, without the benefit of breakfast. The Conference was held in an armed camp four miles from the town. It comprised a dozen villas, which housed President Roosevelt, the Prime Minister and their principal advisers, including Macmillan, and a hotel where the rest of their large staffs were accommodated. Among those present on the British side were General Alexander, Admiral Cunningham, Air Marshal Tedder, General Ismay and Lord Leathers. Averell Harriman and Harry Hopkins accompanied the President. The camp was surrounded by a barbed-wire fence with American sentries posted at intervals of a few yards. The two entrances were guarded by strong pickets and at night the inside of the camp was patrolled by sentries and dogs.

The talks between the principals were conducted in a holiday atmosphere, those taking part being sustained by plentiful supplies of well-cooked food and unlimited quantities of drink, free of charge. Churchill spent most of the day in bed and much of the night conferring with his advisers. He seldom went to bed before three a.m., which was a little trying for his staff, who had to work all day as well as at night. Macmillan recollects that Churchill 'ate and drank enormously all the time, played bagatelle and bezique by the hour and generally enjoyed himself'.[2]

After a talk with the Prime Minister on the afternoon of 15 January,

Macmillan was invited to the President's villa the following morning. Roosevelt was in bed and Churchill, who had had three eggs, the wing of a chicken and several glasses of white wine for breakfast, was in his famous 'rompers' and smoking a cigar. General Eisenhower and Murphy were also in attendance. The President greeted Macmillan cordially by his Christian name, which much impressed Eisenhower, who had not realized until then that they had even met before. 'How strange you English are,' he said afterwards. 'If you had been an American, you would have told me you were on Christian name terms with the President of the United States.'

Roosevelt and Churchill were anxious to announce a settlement of the French question by the time the conference broke up and had agreed to invite Giraud and de Gaulle to meet each other in Casablanca to settle their differences. Macmillan expressed the view that the French Generals might resent being summoned by foreign leaders to a meeting in an armed camp on French territory. The invitation to de Gaulle was sent through Anthony Eden in London, but Macmillan's fears proved well founded. To Churchill's indignation de Gaulle declined to come. 'He may refuse even to see Anthony,' Pierson Dixon suggested, to which Churchill replied 'There *are* men who refuse to cash a cheque.' Further persuasive telegrams eventually met with a reluctant acceptance and de Gaulle arrived on 22 January. As on so many occasions, he was most difficult to deal with.

Giraud, who was much more amenable, had already arrived from Algiers. Dixon described him as 'a reasonable and honest man with antiquated military ideas and an instinct for fair play in politics'. Diana Duff Cooper looked upon him as 'a more wooden Kitchener of Khartoum'. He had a genuine affection for the British, but was convinced that 'no Anglo-Saxon could penetrate the intricacies of the Latin temperament'.[3] In mourning for the defeat of France, he did not wear any of his four rows of decorations.

The Allied proposal was for a merger of the two French groups in a 'Directing Committee', with Giraud and de Gaulle as its joint Presidents. De Gaulle wanted a Provisional Government in exile, with Giraud in command of the French Army of Liberation, but himself as the political leader. He saw his role as the Clemenceau to Giraud's Foch. He also insisted on the dismissal of any leading Frenchman who had been connected with the Vichy regime. This was a real difficulty because, although Giraud was passionately anti-German, he was not anti-Vichy.

Macmillan and Murphy framed draft after draft of an agreement for the two French leaders to sign, but each in turn, though accepted by Giraud, was rejected by de Gaulle. It was Macmillan's first experience of high-level diplomacy and he was determined to persevere in the hope of at least partial success: 'I found myself in the embarrassing position of continually trying to persuade Churchill and Roosevelt to give de Gaulle another chance, which he seemed always unwilling to grasp.'[4] The President was prejudiced against de Gaulle and Churchill often followed his lead. Macmillan, who had a more far-sighted appreciation of the Frenchman's position during the war and of his potential importance after it, persisted patiently and it was a notable achievement that he was able to sustain de Gaulle's cause and Churchill's support for it, while avoiding a conflict with Roosevelt, who was becoming increasingly irritated by the obstructive attitude de Gaulle always adopted. Even Murphy began to feel that it was useless to continue the negotiations, but at last de Gaulle consented to a *comité de guerre*, with himself and Giraud as co-chairman, and the two Generals were left together to produce a joint statement. No real agreement was possible in the short time available, but Macmillan had at least prevented an open rupture.

The Conference was about to break up and the President and the Prime Minister had arranged to give a press conference on 24 January, before they left Casablanca. This presented Macmillan with an opportunity that he was quick to seize. As Roosevelt and Churchill took their seats, he and Murphy almost forcibly pushed the two Generals forward. Extra chairs were quickly provided and, after the President and the Prime Minister had made their statements, Giraud and de Gaulle – much photographed by the press in the process – shook hands publicly with the nearest approach to a smile they could each muster. In the end they produced a joint declaration which was interpreted as a closer concordat than had in fact been achieved.

It was, as the President described it, a shot-gun wedding and Macmillan never thought they would get de Gaulle to the church. Giraud was an honest, straightforward man, anxious to help the Allies as a soldier, but unwilling to be involved in politics. De Gaulle, on the other hand, had become a statesman, concerned almost entirely with the renaissance of France as a major power in the post-war world.

The secret of the Conference had been well kept. The Axis powers never guessed that the President had even left the United States and in Casablanca no one knew that he and Churchill were meeting a few miles away. Churchill was the dominating personality at the conference. For its duration, his assumed name was Air Commodore Frankland, derived from a friend called Frankland, who had saved his life in the South African war and was subsequently killed at Gallipoli. On the only occasion that he went into Casablanca, Churchill wore his Air Commodore's uniform. At the Conference, he dressed in his siren suit during the day and a dinner-jacket in the evening. He was usually in high spirits and only showed annoyance after a meal with the Sultan of Morocco when he had been given nothing stronger to drink than sherbet. He liked to take three baths a day and was irritated when the water was not hot enough. One evening, to the relief of his staff, he decided to dine in bed and went to sleep after dinner; but at midnight he awoke, had another bath, dressed and played picquet with Harry Hopkins till three o'clock in the morning. His French was a constant joy. The loyalty of the French Governor of Morocco was suspect, and Churchill was heard to address him with the remarkable admonition: '*Il faut garder mon secret. Ne dites rien à l'ennemi. La lune est bon pour les attaques. Mais si les bombes tombent, ils tombent sur vous aussi bien que sur moi.*'[5]

Pierson Dixon recorded in his diary that, on the last night of the Conference, the President was dictating the communiqué while Churchill was planning a picnic for the following day. Sonorous phrases were interrupted by an order for *foie gras*; but the Prime Minister was listening with one ear to the drafting, which did not please him. 'Have I your permission, Mr President, to make some amendments?' he asked. It was then two in the morning, but Churchill proceeded to re-write the whole communiqué and by four a.m. he had agreed the final version with Roosevelt before they went to bed. Dixon noted that Macmillan, whose admiration for Churchill was immense, modelled his method of working on that of the Prime Minister. He enjoyed talking late over dinner and at about midnight would settle down to two hours of serious work.

After the press conference on 24 January, Roosevelt and Churchill left for Marrakesh and the next day Macmillan returned to Algiers. At the end of the month Dixon handed over to Roger Makins (later Lord Sherfield), who had arrived from London as the new Foreign Office adviser.

The Casablanca Conference had ended with Roosevelt's sudden and controversial announcement that the Allies would enforce 'unconditional surrender' on all their enemies, which some people believe prolonged the war. To Churchill, close accord with the United States was of far greater concern than the future of France. Sir Douglas Dodds-Parker, who was in Algiers at this period, thought Macmillan learned much more quickly than the Prime Minister that de Gaulle was the key to the French situation in North Africa, and probably to *rapprochement* with France when the war was over. Roosevelt never learned this at all. Another basic difference in the strategic thinking of the Allies soon arose. The United States, like the Russians, favoured a frontal assault on northern France, which Churchill rightly believed to be premature. The British preferred to attack the weaker enemy flank through Italy.

Soon after the Casablanca Conference, Macmillan became involved in the problem of the French warships, known as Force X, lying in the port of Alexandria. Their commander, Admiral Godfroy, was anti-German but loyal to Pétain as his Head of State. Churchill and, on his instructions, R.G. Casey, the Minister Resident in Cairo, had adopted a bullying attitude towards

Godfroy which had had no effect. Macmillan was now instructed to arrange for the transfer of the French fleet to the Allied side 'by guile or force'. He decided to go to Alexandria in order to meet and talk to Godfroy personally and, leaving Roger Makins in charge in Algiers, he and John Wyndham went to the airport on 21 February. No sooner had the airplane gathered speed down the runway than a fault developed and it was throttled back by the pilot, but it was too late; the aircraft ran on off the tarmac into a field, where it burst into flames. The pilot emerged through an emergency exit and John Wyndham, who was travelling in the back of the plane, managed to crawl out, but Macmillan was trapped in the front.

Wyndham recalled the incident:

Suddenly a familiar figure was seen to be struggling to get out of the pilot's side window, his moustache burning with a bright blue flame. He was quite out of reach. We shouted 'Push, Minister, push.' He landed on the ground with a thump, very badly burnt.[6]

Macmillan described his predicament in his diary:

Middle-aged and rather portly publishers, encumbered by the weight of their own dignity and a large green Ulster overcoat, trying to spring through a smallish hole ... to be reached by scrambling over a confused mass of driving-wheels, levers and other mechanical devices of a jagged and impeding kind, if they are to achieve success in such an operation, must be inspired by a powerful and overwhelming motive. For lesser exertions, such as to enter Parliament, to struggle through years of political failure and frustration, lesser motives may serve. Ambition, patriotism, pride – all these can impel a man and finally bring him within the hallowed precincts of the Privy Council and the Cabinet. But to do what I did in the early hours of last Monday morning, only one motive in the world is sufficient – FEAR (not fame) is the spur.[7]

With a final effort he emerged, just before the plane exploded. He had some superficial leg wounds and his face was severely burned. He was taken to the Military Hospital in Algiers, where he was forced to remain for a week.

By 6 March Macmillan felt well enough to resume his journey and he met Godfroy that evening. He listened patiently to the Admiral's complaints against Churchill and Casey, explained fully and objectively the situation in North Africa since the Allied landings and made some suggestions as to the future which were not ill-received. They dined together, discussed mutual friends and partridge-shooting, and exchanged reminiscences about the First World War. Macmillan felt that a better atmosphere had been established and progress had been made. While awaiting Churchill's reaction to his report, he paid a short visit to Malta, where he found a splendidly buoyant spirit, despite the terrible damage done by the air bombardment of the island.

By the middle of May an agreement was finally concluded with Godfroy, who moved his ships to join the Allies in August. Macmillan attributed the ultimate success of this negotiation to the changed circumstances following the Allied victories in North Africa.[8] These no doubt contributed, but his own tact and diplomacy had certainly played an important part.

Meanwhile, the French administration in Algiers and in the French territories of Algeria, Morocco and Tunisia had to be handled with equal care. Giraud had beautiful manners, an upright character and a hatred of the Germans, but he was totally ignorant of politics and was incapable of taking a strong line on anything. In fact, as Macmillan wrote, 'except under extreme pressure from Murphy and me, he does nothing at all'.[9] They pressed Giraud to dismiss the remaining Vichy officials, to introduce more civilians into the administration and to release the Gaullist political prisoners. A genuine Giraud–de Gaulle fusion was becoming essential.

At the end of February, Jean Monnet arrived from Washington. This remarkable man was strongly anti-Vichy, anxious to work for French unity and was trusted by Giraud. He was, therefore, a helpful and hopeful new influence. Macmillan described him as 'vital to any solution. He was the lubricant, or even catalyst'[10] between the opposing factions. His high moral and intellectual qualities were invaluable to North Africa and later to France and to the European movement. His presence in Algiers, the rapid improvement in the military situation, due largely to Alexander's leadership, and Macmillan's own skilful handling of the problems and personalities – to which he modestly makes no reference in his memoirs – all combined to bring about a dramatic change in Giraud's attitude. By the middle of March he had agreed to almost all the Allied demands.

At the end of March, General Catroux arrived in Algiers as the leader of de Gaulle's emissaries from London. He was a reasonable, reliable and patient man, an old friend of Giraud's and himself a five-star General, who also enjoyed the confidence and admiration of de Gaulle. He therefore had an important role in the relationship between the two French leaders. Unfortunately, at this moment de Gaulle proposed a visit to Algiers for personal discussions. The Americans were opposed to this, as was Catroux, who threatened to resign if he was not allowed quietly to continue the negotiations. He agreed, however, to take Giraud's latest suggestions to London. These were rejected by de Gaulle and Catroux returned to Algiers, where the discussions continued. At length, guided by Macmillan and Monnet, Giraud sent further proposals for a French Cabinet with collective responsibility and a joint premiership with de Gaulle. Catroux was to go to London to explain this and Macmillan decided to accompany him. They found de Gaulle in an unusually calm and benevolent mood. He accepted the new basis for future French collaboration without demur and, in return, it was arranged that he should visit Algiers at the end of May.

Earlier in the month, General Alexander had been able to report to the Prime Minister that the Tunisian campaign was over and all enemy resistance had collapsed. This ended the war in Africa. A great victory parade was held in Tunis in which 30,000 troops took part.

De Gaulle brought with him from England René Massigli and André Philip, who were to be his two nominees on the Executive Committee which was to be formed. When its seven members met, the proceedings were mismanaged: De Gaulle insisted on the immediate dismissal of the formerly pro-Vichy Colonial Governors. Monnet and Catroux tried to build a bridge between the differing views of Giraud and de Gaulle, but without success, and the meeting broke up without the Committee even being formally constituted. In a talk with Macmillan and Murphy the next day, de Gaulle was more amenable and impressed Murphy as 'a more powerful character than any other Frenchman in or outside France'.[11]

A new crisis immediately arose however because of the resignation, probably due to Gaullist pressure, of Peyrouton as Governor of Algeria. His letter of resignation was sent to de Gaulle, who accepted it with alacrity and, without consulting Giraud, issued the correspondence to the Press. Giraud, who imagined that de Gaulle was planning a *coup d'état* against him, lost his head, appointed Admiral Muselier to maintain order in Algiers, called in some colonial troops and wrote an hysterical letter to de Gaulle. To smooth this over, Macmillan had a long private talk with de Gaulle, which helped to pave the way for a more successful meeting of the Committee next morning. The central authority was formally established, Catroux was appointed Governor of Algeria to replace Peyrouton, and the meeting ended with de Gaulle and Giraud embracing each other.

Churchill, who was in Algiers at the time, gave a lunch party for the French Committee, at which suitable speeches, all of them in French, were made by the Prime Minister, Giraud, de Gaulle and Eden. At the end of luncheon, Churchill was photographed with the two Generals by the Press. The French union was well received and much credit for it was rightly accorded to Macmillan; one paper referred to his 'good knowledge of French and an imperturbability which it is almost impossible to rattle'.

The French Committee at once applied for official recognition by the British and United States Governments. It did not, however, make a convincing start. Within a week there was a dispute about the command and control of the French forces, which led to an impetuous letter of resignation from de Gaulle. Giraud was delighted and wanted to accept this at once; but Macmillan wisely pointed out the possible grave repercussions and counselled delay. He was supported by Monnet and Catroux, and Giraud's letter of acceptance was not sent.

A visit to Algeria by King George VI was about to take place and this helped to defuse the situation. He arrived on 12 June, gave a successful dinner for Eisenhower, to whom he presented the insignia of the GCB, and then held a lunch party the following day for Giraud and de Gaulle. Churchill had advised the King not to hold this unless the French Generals were behaving well; Macmillan was obliged to tell him that they were not. 'What, then, shall I do?' asked the King. 'I should go on with it, Sir,' Macmillan replied. 'It may do good and can do no harm.'[12] In fact, it was a great success.

Afterwards, de Gaulle suggested that he should spend the rest of the day with Macmillan, who was going to bathe at Tipasa. They talked for three and a half hours and, while Macmillan swam naked in the sea, de Gaulle sat on a rock, fully clad in uniform. They dined together at the local inn and Macmillan persuaded him to remain on the Committee. 'It is very difficult to know how to handle him,' Macmillan recorded in his diary:

I do my best and I know that he likes me and appreciates having somebody whom he trusts and with whom he can talk freely.... But I am afraid he will always be difficult to work with. He is by nature an autocrat. Just like Louis XIV or Napoleon. He thinks in his heart that he should command and all others should obey him ... it is authoritarian.[13]

Churchill sent a reply to the Committee's request for recognition, quoting St Matthew, Chapter VII, verse 16: 'Ye shall know them by their fruits. Do men gather grapes of thorns or figs of thistle?' He declined to give recognition until he knew what he had to recognize. Macmillan replied with Revelations, Chapter II, verses 2-4, which ended with the words '... I have somewhat against thee, because thou hast left thy first love'.

There was considerable prejudice against de Gaulle at the White House and Churchill was disinclined to upset the President; but by this time Eisenhower, Bedell Smith and Murphy were all on Macmillan's side. They had become disillusioned by Giraud's vacillations; he always preferred 'the discomforts of a fence to the horrors of a decision'.[14] They advised the President to accept de Gaulle and to recognize the Committee as the Provisional Government of France. Streams of telegrams arrived from the White House and from Downing Street, many of which Eisenhower and Macmillan exchanged and compared. The Commander-in-Chief now consulted Macmillan, not only as the British political representative, but as a friend. It was a far cry from Eisenhower's suspicious attitude at their first meeting and the concern of the American State Department and War Department. In the early days the Assistant Secretary for War had complained, 'You simply cannot have a

Cabinet Minister on the ground, particularly one of Macmillan's character and ability, without his taking part in the play.'[15] It was a tribute to Macmillan's tact that these doubts had disappeared and that, in the words of the official history, 'in the creation of this Anglo-American instrument of Government, much was owed to the efforts of General Eisenhower and Mr Macmillan'.[16] Lord Sherfield thinks that Eisenhower's contribution in North Africa has been underrated. Although politically inexperienced at that time, the General had very good judgement and he and Macmillan worked increasingly well and closely together.

At a meeting with de Gaulle, Eisenhower was impressed by the Frenchman's powerful personality. He was 'strong but uncertain; Giraud was reliable but weak'.[17] Eventually, a formula was accepted, establishing a Military Committee responsible for the unification and training of the French Armed Forces, while the National Committee was entrusted with the general control of the French war effort. Giraud was to be Commander-in-Chief in North and West Africa, and de Gaulle of the other parts of the French Empire.

Meanwhile, Macmillan accompanied King George VI on a visit in the cruiser *Aurora* to Malta, where there was a tremendous reception by the garrison and the civilian population, who turned out in thousands with flowers, flags, confetti and cheers to greet the King. His safe passage to and from the island was the answer to Mussolini's empty boast that the Mediterranean was '*Mare Nostrum*'.

On his return to Algiers, Macmillan found an awkward issue had arisen over the resignation of another Colonial Governor, General Boisson of French West Africa. This man seemed to the Gaullists 'a double-dyed traitor; to the English mildly antipathetic ... by the Americans greatly admired. The President unfortunately is ... determined to see Boisson kept in his position.... I am in some difficulty since I personally think the President's demands outrageous, but I am instructed to support them. General Eisenhower shares my view and is trying to get some compromise out of the White House.'[18] The Commander-in-Chief expressed his opinion firmly and with effect, the Committee behaved sensibly and appointed an unexceptionable successor to whom the President could not reasonably object, and the problem was thus resolved.

On 2 July, Giraud departed for a visit to the United States – unwisely, because this left the local situation in de Gaulle's hands; but the question of recognition still remained undecided. De Gaulle much resented the delay, which was indeed unrealistic and due entirely to White House prejudice and a reluctance to face the facts. Churchill had at length become convinced that it would be wise to recognize the Committee and he sent a most helpful telegram to Roosevelt. Meanwhile, Macmillan mollified de Gaulle by giving him advance notice of the invasion of Sicily, which was about to be launched. He had received no instructions to convey this information and thought it best not to ask for any; he was by then sufficiently confident to take his own decisions on North African affairs.

On 23 July, Giraud returned from America. Rather surprisingly, he agreed to a new plan, under which he was to be Commander-in-Chief of the French forces but responsible only for military matters, while de Gaulle became sole President of the Committee in control of all political issues. Throughout July and August the recognition debate continued. It was discussed at the conference in Quebec, where Eden did his best to secure the agreement of Cordell Hull, the American Secretary of State. At last the matter was resolved by the expedient of two texts, the American form of words being rather less explicit and forthcoming than the British. Jean Monnet took the chair at a press conference and skirted skilfully over the discrepancies. The British candidate had in the end prevailed and de Gaulle was, in effect, Prime Minister of the Provisional Government of France.

By this time Macmillan had been given new instructions: he was to continue, as before, to work closely with Eisenhower, but in future his political advice was to be concerned more with Italian than with French affairs. This was made necessary by the successful Allied invasion of Sicily, soon to be followed by that of Italy. Meanwhile, his time was almost equally divided between Algiers, where a number of French problems still remained unresolved, and Tunis, where Eisenhower's new Headquarters had been established.

As Macmillan's responsibilities increased, so too did his personal staff, which had been augmented by the arrival of Harold (now Lord) Caccia and Sir Anthony Rumbold. John Wyndham commented: 'I doubt whether any foreign mission in peace or war contained so much ability concentrated in so few people.'[19] This small staff was soon supplemented by Eric Duncannon (now Lord Bessborough), whose perfect French was a linguistic asset to the team.

For some days in October, Harold Macmillan was seriously ill with a fever brought on by exhaustion; but, at Eisenhower's request, he made the effort to go to Tunis to meet Cordell Hull. He was, however, cheered by the news of the birth of his first grandchild, Maurice's son Alexander. In the same month Field Marshal Smuts called in at Algiers on his way to England. He was due to leave after luncheon and said suddenly to Macmillan: 'Why don't you come too, so that we can finish our talk?' This appealed to Harold, who happily travelled thousands of miles to complete their discussions.

In Algiers, the initial meeting of the partly (and indirectly) elected French Consultative Assembly was held on 3 November and three days later a debate took place deploring the number of Generals on the National Committee and urging the appointment to it of more civilians. Giraud resigned from the Committee but remained Commander-in-Chief.

The next crisis, and a major one, suddenly arose in the Lebanon. A Free French administration had been established there in 1941; but elections had recently been held which resulted in the majority of French candidates being defeated and the new Government was pledged to secure independence as soon as possible. The Lebanese Parliament proceeded to pass an Independence Bill, but the French authorities promptly arrested the Ministers and closed the Parliament. Riots followed and the situation was complicated by the presence in Beirut of the British representative, General Spears, who had quarrelled with the French.

Churchill demanded the release of the arrested Lebanese Ministers. De Gaulle took the opposite line and urged Catroux, who was in Beirut, to make no concessions. Anglo-French relations were seriously threatened, but Massigli handled the problem with great skill. Against the wishes of de Gaulle, he persuaded the National Committee to order the release of the President of the Lebanon and his Ministers. This saved face, as it appeared to be a voluntary decision by the Committee rather than one imposed by the British. The outstanding difficulty was the reinstatement of the Ministers; this was recommended by Catroux and again Massigli contrived to carry it in the Committee. No British ultimatum had to be issued on either point. Thanks mainly to Massigli, the result was achieved without humiliating the French.

On 15 November, Macmillan was ordered to HMS *Renown*, which was lying off Gibraltar with the Prime Minister on board *en route* to a conference with President Roosevelt in Cairo; this was a preliminary to the even more important meeting with Stalin in Teheran. Churchill asked Macmillan's opinion about the structure of the high command in Italy when Eisenhower left the area to organize the invasion of France and the campaign in north-west Europe. Macmillan advised that General Alexander should be given the Mediterranean appointment; but the choice fell on General Maitland Wilson, who held it until November 1944 when he went to Washington; he was then succeeded by Alexander. Churchill also decided that Casey was to leave Cairo and would not be replaced, so it was evident that the political responsibility for the whole Mediterranean theatre would fall to Macmillan. Duff Cooper, who had been appointed Ambassador to the Provisional French Government, would take charge of Anglo-French relations in Algiers as soon as he arrived there.

A final French crisis arose because of the arrests by the National Committee of the former Vichy supporters, Peyrouton, Boisson and Flandin. The United

States Government felt a responsibility for the first two and Flandin was a personal friend of Churchill's. It was an awkward situation. On 23 December a telegram arrived for Eisenhower from the President, which read: 'You shall direct the French Committee of National Liberation immediately to set free and discontinue the trial of Peyrouton, Boisson and Flandin.' Macmillan recorded in his diary:

The President hates de Gaulle and the French Committee. He would seize on any excuse to overthrow them and restore Giraud. The PM's sentiments are more complex. He feels about de Gaulle like a man who has quarrelled with his son. He will cut him off with a shilling. But (in his heart) he would kill the fatted calf if only the prodigal would confess his faults.[20]

Had the President's orders been carried out, they would have precipitated a most serious situation, because the Committee would have refused to obey them. Telegrams and telephone calls poured in. Churchill even telephoned the Chief of Staff to say: 'Keep Harold up to the mark. He is much too pro-French. He will not carry out my policy or my wishes. I rely on you.'[21] The President's message was held in abeyance and Macmillan went to Tunis to see Churchill on Christmas Day. They had a talk that night, at the end of which Churchill said: 'Well, perhaps you are right. But I do not agree with you. Perhaps I will see de Gaulle. Anyway, you have done very well.'[22]

Back in Algiers next day, the situation was transformed by another telegram from Roosevelt, who, in Macmillan's words, 'has completely backed down. There was to be no ultimatum, no intervention by Eisenhower.'[23] In his turn, de Gaulle agreed to villa custody for the Vichy men as opposed to imprisonment, and no trial until after the liberation of France. The last of the many Algerian crises in the year 1943 had been successfully surmounted.

During December, Churchill fell ill in Tunis with pneumonia and shortly afterwards suffered a slight heart attack, but within ten days had made a remarkable recovery. In the New Year, he moved to Marrakesh to convalesce and de Gaulle paid him a successful visit there. Eisenhower left for Washington *en route* for London, where he wanted Macmillan to help him organize 'Operation Overlord'. They had formed a lasting friendship and Macmillan, who sincerely regretted his departure, wrote admiringly of

... his truly noble character.... His services to the Allied cause were immeasurable. The experiment of a fully integrated staff, where British and American officers served side by side, was unique. Only Ike could have made it succeed.... When big decisions had to be taken, Eisenhower never flinched.[24]

On 4 January 1944, Duff Cooper arrived in Algiers to take over the conduct of Anglo-French relations. The most difficult part of the French assignment had been Macmillan's relations with de Gaulle:

I had no doubt at all of his greatness ... nothing could have prevented him becoming leader ... of post-liberation France.... De Gaulle had, in spite of many faults, real genius. Passionately devoted to France ... insular, half revolutionary, half reactionary ... [he was] in the front rank of French statesmen.[25]

Macmillan, who got on better with de Gaulle than anyone else, was mainly responsible for the solution of the French problem. His outstanding talent for diplomacy ensured his success both with the Americans and with the French. In the light of Roosevelt's antipathy to de Gaulle, this was a remarkable achievement. During the year Macmillan spent there, Lord Sherfield was scarcely exaggerating when he described Algiers as 'the crossroads of the world'.[26] Macmillan does not refer to his own contribution to the Allied cause, but others have done so. Lady Diana Cooper wrote: 'Harold Macmillan is our saviour. He's a splendid man.... One day he'll be Prime Minister. I've put my money (nay, my shirt) on him. He's my horse.'[27] When he did become Prime Minister thirteen years later, she often referred to him as 'my horse'. L.A. Siedentrop wrote:

He turned a secondary and precarious position ... into nothing less than the overlordship of the Mediterranean theatre of war. Macmillan's extreme importance is often unwittingly revealed in American accounts of the North African and Italian campaigns.... [His] extraordinary achievement ... has not been widely appreciated. And the fact is interesting in itself. For it suggests how much more he was interested in the substance of power than in its mere form. Without drawing attention to himself or offending the *amour propre* of Eisenhower and his colleagues, Macmillan overcame the Americans' suspicions, gained their confidence and saw to it that the British had a part in making decisions. Indeed, he soon came to dominate many of those decisions. He did this by sheer ability to anticipate circumstances, careful planning, subtlety, persistence and patience.[28]

A revealing illustration of these qualities and methods is contained in an account by Richard Crossman, when he arrived in Algiers as Director of Psychological Warfare:

Macmillan sent for me straight away.... 'Remember,' he said, 'when you go to the Hotel St George, you will regularly enter a room and see an American colonel, his cigar in his mouth, his feet on the table.... You will see in a corner an English captain, his feet down, his shoulders hunched, writing like mad, with a full in-tray and a full out-tray, and no cigar.

'Mr Crossman, you will never call attention to this discrepancy. When you install a similar arrangement in your own office, you will always permit your American colleague not only to have a superior rank to yourself and much higher pay, but also the feeling that he is running the show. This will enable you to run it yourself. We, my dear Crossman, are Greeks in this American empire. You will find the Americans much as the Greeks found the Romans – great big vulgar, bustling people, more vigorous than we are and also more idle, with more unspoiled virtues, but also more corrupt. We must run AFHQ as the Greeks ran the operations of the Emperor Claudius.'[29]

Crossman described Macmillan at this time as 'a dashing man of action' and was especially struck by

... his buoyancy. And no wonder. Not even the Prime Minister in Britain enjoyed quite such unquestioned prestige as Harold Macmillan had earned for himself both in his own British staff and in Ike's entourage.... I suspect it was in Algiers, where he could do all the thinking and take all the decisions while Ike took all the credit, that Harold Macmillan first realized his own capacity for supreme leadership and developed that streak of intellectual recklessness which was to be the cause both of his success and of his failure when he finally reached No. 10.[30]

Macmillan returned the compliment when he referred to Crossman as 'intelligent, humorous and loyal' and as 'a very able chap and working splendidly. The Americans (rather unexpectedly) like him, although he is a Socialist, which usually terrifies them.'[31]

The Americans liked Macmillan, too; and Robert Murphy, who worked so closely with him, recalled that he knew how not to appear to be influencing the Americans 'but he did indeed exercise greater influence upon Anglo-American affairs in the Mediterranean than was generally realized'.[32] In conceding the appearance, he was able to secure a large part of the reality of power. This, from the beginning, had been his objective and was exactly what Churchill had hoped he would do.

Macmillan's role was not appreciated by everyone. Sir Alan Brooke (later Lord Alanbrooke), the Chief of the Imperial General Staff, was less than enthusiastic about Macmillan's attempts to influence the Prime Minister:

All my good work with him [Churchill] is gone. He is now back again wanting Alexander as Supreme Commander for the Mediterranean and has pushed old 'Jumbo' Wilson aside.... The trouble has been caused by Macmillan, who has had a long talk with the PM suggesting Alex as the man for the job and that he, Macmillan, can take the political load off him ... he evidently does not understand what the functions of a Supreme Commander should be.'[33]

There can be little doubt that Macmillan's judgement on this subject was in fact sounder than that of Brooke.

After Alexander had succeeded Wilson, Brooke seems to have tried to make trouble between him and Macmillan. On 31 January 1945 he referred in his diary to a conversation with Alexander: 'I told him that some of us had doubts as to whether Macmillan or Alexander was Supreme Commander of Mediterranean.' This attempt to inject grit into the relationship of the two men was unsuccessful; they had become close friends and worked together in complete trust and confidence.

Macmillan's success in North Africa was the real foundation of his career. He never sought to take the credit; he knew he could do the job and he did it supremely well. His influence on Eisenhower can scarcely be exaggerated and, because of the imagination and breadth of his strategic assessments, this influence was entirely beneficial to the Allied cause. Although he had still barely been heard of by the British public, his contribution was acknowledged by his colleagues and, from 1944 onwards, his place in the highest echelons of politics was assured.

14
ITALY AND GREECE

For the last six months of 1943 Harold Macmillan had been involved as much with the new Italian problems as with the French. The attack on Sicily had been authorized at the Casablanca Conference, but President Roosevelt was determined not to divert for the Italian enterprise any forces which were already earmarked for the invasion of France. Yet even the Sicilian assault in July was a formidable undertaking. Alexander was in command of the ground troops, Tedder of the Allied Air Force, and Admiral Cunningham of the Fleet; they all served under Eisenhower as Supreme Commander.

Macmillan moved to Tunis, where the High Command for the Sicilian expedition was established. He found the atmosphere agreeable; it was rather like living in a large country-house. He records that the conversation usually consisted of 'a little history, a little politics, a little banter, a little philosophy. ... I have never enjoyed so much the English capacity for restraint and understatement.'[1] Alexander always invited Macmillan to his morning conferences in the war room, where all the maps and the latest information about the campaign were available.

On 25 July 1943 came the news of the fall of Mussolini. He was succeeded by Marshal Badoglio as head of the Italian Government. The people of Italy wanted peace, but no one knew how to obtain it. Eight divisions of German troops were being rapidly augmented and 10,000 German agents were said to have permeated the Italian machine of Government.

Allied Forces Headquarters were without any instructions and Macmillan drafted two telegrams to the American and British Governments suggesting a declaration to the Italian people and ten conditions for an armistice. The latter became known as the 'short terms'; they were purely military and were to be supplemented later by the 'long terms', which were still the subject of discussion between the State Department and the Foreign Office.

After some tentative soundings, a peace approach was made by the Italians, following which it became clear that they wished to change sides and join the Allies. Macmillan's 'short terms' were acceptable to them in principle, but the Italian emissary thought the 'long terms' brutal and humiliating for Italy and said they would require more careful consideration. As the German forces were being increased every day, it was greatly to the advantage of the Allies to obtain a quick military armistice with the Italians before the landings were launched, and Macmillan urged this view on his colleagues in London. He quietly shelved – indeed suppressed – the 'long terms', lest they should be made a pretext for delay. This was important because by this time the Germans had nineteen divisions in Italy and the Italians sixteen, whereas Alexander could only make eight available for the first two weeks following the landings. Italian co-operation was therefore essential and urgent.

At the beginning of September, armistice discussions with envoys sent from Italy were held secretly in a Sicilian olive grove. The Allied representatives were Macmillan, Murphy and Eisenhower's Chief-of-Staff, General Bedell Smith. After four days of Italian procrastination in the conference tent, General Alexander, who had been kept in reserve, took charge of the negotiations. His entrance had been planned with care and was carried out with panache. Although his own tent was only a few yards away in the same olive grove, he arrived by car, immaculately dressed and escorted by several be-medalled Staff Officers. He greeted the Italians with cold courtesy and informed them that they would not be permitted to leave the tent until they had signed the armistice terms and that, if they did not do so immediately, the Allies would bomb Rome. This dramatic intervention was decisive and they signed at once.

As soon as the armistice terms were accepted, it was decided to send an airborne division to Rome to help the Italian troops in that area. Eisenhower rather reluctantly agreed to Macmillan and Murphy flying in with this division: 'Well, all right,' he said. 'There's nothing in the regulations which says diplomats are not expendable.'[2] Unfortunately, at the last moment, the Italians withdrew their support for the airborne landing, because large German troop movements into Rome meant that Badoglio could no longer guarantee the airfield. The expedition, to Macmillan's disappointment, was therefore cancelled and it was not until nine months later that the Allied armies at last entered Rome.

When the armistice agreement was announced, the Germans disarmed the Italian troops in the Rome area and King Victor Emmanuel and Marshal Badoglio were forced to flee to Brindisi. But the armistice was of value because it secured the surrender of the Italian fleet, which withdrew to the Grand Harbour in Malta. Taranto was seized and the port of Naples was in Allied hands by the beginning of October.

Shortly afterwards, Macmillan and Murphy flew into Taranto, from which the Germans had retired a day or two before, to see King Victor Emmanuel.

His only request was for some fresh eggs for the Queen. 'So, with a dozen eggs,' Macmillan recalled, 'we sealed our concord with the thousand-year-old House of Savoy.'[3] Macmillan and Murphy talked to Badoglio and called upon Prince Umberto, the heir to the throne, who Macmillan thought might play a useful role in the future of Italy.

The next point at issue was Italian acceptance of the 'long terms', which were onerous, no longer very relevant and contained the contentious phrase 'unconditional surrender', which was politically difficult for Badoglio's Government. Finally, Badoglio was persuaded to sign and Italy declared war on Germany on 13 October.

By changing sides, the Italians had hoped to obtain peace, but the result was that their country became a battlefield for the next eighteen months. At the outset of this prolonged campaign, Italy was divided: the Germans held the territory from the north of Naples to the Alps, comprising the industrial, prosperous, most populated part of the country; while the Allies occupied the southern part from Naples to Brindisi, which was soon sub-divided into the forward areas, directly administered by the military authorities, and the back areas, which were transferred as soon as possible to the Italian Government.

Macmillan proposed that General Alexander should be appointed Military Governor, with himself and Murphy as political advisers. An Allied Control Commission was established to supervise the activities of the Italian Government in the part of the country which they were to administer. General Mason-Macfarlane, an unfortunate choice because he never got on well with Macmillan, was made head of this Commission, with Harold Caccia as Macmillan's representative on it. Superimposed on this organization, the Allied Foreign Ministers had agreed in Moscow to set up an Advisory Council for Italy, the members of which would be nominated by the United States, Britain, Russia and France.

As in Algiers, there was a basic difference of approach to the Italian problem: the Americans favoured direct military government of the whole country; the British preferred to change this to indirect control as early as possible, with detailed administration devolving to the Italians as and when more areas came under Allied occupation. The population was friendly and there was no difficulty in co-operating with the local civilian authorities, including the police.

The initial problem was the provision of food, most of which had been either destroyed by the military operations or removed by the Germans as they retreated. There was no electric power to mill the grain and no transport to move it. A black market flourished and, at first, near-starvation – and certainly malnutrition – faced the poorer people in the Naples area. Outbreaks of cholera and typhus were inevitable and for a time there was virtually no water until the British engineers distilled sea water from the bay. Genral Brian (later Lord) Robertson, described by Macmillan as 'the most efficient "Q" officer since Marlborough's Cadogan',[4] was put in charge, and gradually the physical difficulties were overcome.

The political problems were less easily resolved. Count Sforza, who had been Italian Foreign Minister before Mussolini came to power, arrived in Italy from America, where he had some influence on the Italian vote. He demanded the abdication of King Victor Emmanuel in favour of the six-year-old Prince of Naples. His plan was to make Badoglio Regent, so that he could himself become Prime Minister, and he was supported in this ambition by the philosopher Benedetto Croce. The Americans, including Murphy, wanted to dismiss the King. Macmillan had no guidance from London, but thought it unwise for the Allied Governments to be either for or against the King at this stage. He believed it would be best for the Italians if they could solve their own internal problems without Allied interference. It was difficult to estimate the effect on Italian opinion of a forced, as opposed to a voluntary, abdication and the repercussions might be adverse. He conveyed this advice to the Prime Minister.

In addition to his other appointments, Macmillan was now given the title of United Kingdom High Commissioner and he sat as such on the Advisory Council for Italy. The Russians sent Vyshinsky to represent them; he was Deputy Commissar for Foreign Affairs and a powerful personality in the Soviet Government. Macmillan though he looked like Pickwick: '... genial ... the image of every Conservative mayor or constituency chairman ... the eyes, however, are ... hard. And behind the geniality one detects a certain toughness....'[5] He was reputed to have been responsible for the deaths of hundreds of thousands of people in the Stalin purges. The Russian were more interested in politics than in food supplies and Vyshinsky thought only 1,500 British Fascists in prison (and none shot) was a poor record. He was incensed by the news that Oswald Mosley, whom he considered should have been liquidated, had been released from prison. At dinner one evening with Macmillan, he expressed the view that 'Democracy is like wine. It is all right if taken in moderation.' He thought free speech was all right too 'so long as it does not interfere with the policy of the Government'.[6]

The principle of indirect government, which Macmillan believed wise, was adopted by the Advisory Council and it was agreed that the Allies should be committed to the support of King Victor Emmanuel and Badoglio only up to the time of the capture of Rome.

In January 1944 Macmillan was invited to Marrakesh to meet Churchill. The Prime Minister was in a mellow mood and asked him whether he would like a Cabinet post at home or if he would prefer to stay in the Mediterranean.

Without hesitation, Macmillan opted to stay. 'Well, in spite of our tiffs, we have got on well together,' Churchill observed. 'You have done very well, very well indeed.'[7]

A few days later Macmillan visited Caserta for the first time. It was to be Allied Headquarters for the rest of the war and he had been allocated accommodation there. Lord Alexander wrote later:

Caserta is ... associated in my mind, and very pleasantly, with Harold Macmillan ... he acted as adviser to the Commander-in-Chief on all political issues.... Thus, in my own command in the Mediterranean, I was never brought into direct collision with an Allied Government on a political issue.... For a time in Italy Mr Macmillan shared my mess at Caserta and during this period he and I would go to the front in my open desert-car to visit the troops. Those were happy days for me. I had a delightful companion who was both wise in advice and always amusing; a man of great intellect, morally and physically brave....[8]

The Anzio landings were about to take place and when these fared ill, Alexander took personal charge and restored the position. The bridgehead was held against German counter-attacks, but the 'break-out' was delayed.

The State Department now sent a strong but foolish demand, in support of a French move on the same lines, for the immediate abdication of King Victor Emmanuel. In Murphy's absence on leave, Macmillan persuaded his deputy, Reinhardt, not to carry out the instructions he had received to inform Massigli and Sforza of this. He was also able to dissuade General Wilson from taking any action against the King with the argument that this was better left for Churchill and Roosevelt to decide. The Prime Minister supported his plea for delay and spoke in this sense in the House of Commons.

Macmillan was suffering from eczema during this period and was in poor general health; he felt the need for some leave and left in February for four weeks in England. This gave him the opportunity of useful talks with Churchill and with the Foreign Office. On his return he found that General Wilson had not had the same success in winning American support as Eisenhower had had with the British. Paradoxically, therefore, the fact that there was now a British Commander-in-Chief was not to Britain's advantage. Roger Makins had, however, handled the local situation skilfully in Macmillan's absence; and, following messages from Churchill, Roosevelt instructed the State Department to take no further action for the time being about changes in the Italian Government.

Another difficulty soon arose, this time of Russian making. The Soviet Government informed Badoglio that they would exchange Ambassadors with Italy. Macmillan insisted on a meeting of the Advisory Council to consider this unilateral action by Russia, taken without any prior consultation with her allies; but in the end the United States, Britain and France had to accept the arrangement – it was a warning of future Soviet tactics. At the same time there was growing activity on the part of the local Communist leaders and the Russians were beginning to exploit the differences in British and American policy, especially evident after Eisenhower's departure. It seemed the right moment to send Allied Ambassadors to Italy who could also represent their governments on the Advisory Council. Sir Noel Charles was chosen for Britain and Alexander Kirk for the United States.

The military deadlock at Cassino, the impending Presidential election in America, and party pressures in Italy combined to convince Macmillan that some political advance was now desirable. The base of the Government needed broadening and the six Italian parties seemed prepared to enter it. As long as Badoglio retained the premiership and kept his commitments to the Allies, the position of King Victor Emmanuel was relatively less important. It was still necessary, however, that he should agree to retire and appoint Prince Umberto as Regent. Macmillan and Murphy went to see the King at Ravello on 10 April. After some discussion he said he was willing to withdraw in favour of his son 'on the day on which the Allied troops enter Rome'. Badoglio thought the Italian politicians would agree to this and that the Allies should also accept it. Murphy would have liked an immediate abdication, but Macmillan persuaded him to concur in the compromise and the King drafted his declaration, which was submitted to and amended by Macmillan.

The six political parties then entered the Government. Badoglio remained Prime Minister and Foreign Secretary and the Service Ministers were also unchanged, but the political leaders, including Croce, Sforza and the Communist Togliatti, took office as Ministers without Portfolio; the other posts were divided equally between the six parties. The new Government undertook to adhere to the commitments made by its predecessor. After the satisfactory conclusion of this problem Macmillan went to stay with General Alexander for a few days at Caserta. He was glad when, shortly afterwards, Lady Dorothy came out from England on a four-month visit.

On 4 June, the Allied armies entered Rome. Macmillan was in Algiers at the time, where an Old Etonian dinner was held that evening. The following telegram was sent to Alexander: 'Many congratulations on the successful development of your battle and all good wishes for its exploitation. It was, moreover, thoughtful of you, as an Old Harrovian, to capture Rome on the Fourth of June.' Alexander replied: 'Thank you. What *is* the Fourth of June?'[9]

Two days later came the news of the landings in France. 'Operation Overlord' had been launched and the war in Europe was entering its final phase.

On 8 June, following the publication of the King's declaration, Prince Umberto, General Badoglio and seven members of his Cabinet were flown to Rome. It soon became clear that Badoglio had been outmanœuvred by his colleagues and he was now persuaded to retire. Bonomi became Prime Minister and Sforza Minister for Foreign Affairs.

Macmillan had warned Mason-Macfarlane and Noel Charles against allowing the Ministers to come to Rome, and he sent the same advice to the Foreign Office; but Churchill was angry with him for leaving this decision to Mason-Macfarlane and it is indeed odd that he should have done so. It was, however, Mason-Macfarlane's fault. He was used to making his own arrangements and had not appreciated that in any dealings with London it was best to work through Macmillan. On this occasion he needed Harold Macmillan's help and would have received it if he could have brought himself to ask for it. In trying to extricate himself from the difficulty, Mason-Macfarlane made matters worse by expressing the opinion that the appointment of Sforza as Foreign Minister 'would not meet with much approval on the part of the Allied Governments'.[10] In fact, the Americans did approve and the State Department sent a protest to London complaining that they had not been consulted about Mason-Macfarlane's statement. No one else had been either. Macmillan had never worked easily with Macfarlane, whose health was now failing, and Macmillan persuaded him to go home on sick leave and thereafter to resign on grounds of ill-health.

The first stage of the Italian operation was now over and Macmilan returned to London in order to see Churchill and to explain and advocate an ambitious proposal, conceived by Alexander, for the future use of his forces. The plan was to split the German Army in half, destroy it and then march on Vienna; if Hitler detached sufficient forces from the north to prevent this, nothing would be more helpful for the success of 'Operation Overlord'. The alternative Allied plan, favoured by the Americans, was 'Operation Anvil' – the invasion of the South of France. At first the Combined Chiefs-of-Staff were indecisive and left it to Eisenhower to decide which of these operations would best assist 'Operation Overlord'.

After Macmillan had talked to Churchill, it was decided to discuss the matter more fully the following day with the British Chiefs-of-Staff. Macmillan made the case for Alexander's proposal and, on Sunday 25 June, he was invited to Chequers, where the Prime Minister was preparing a paper on the subject. The following day the Chiefs-of-Staff sent their formal advice, recommending Alexander's plan; but despite Churchill's powerful advocacy, the Americans disagreed and expressed their strong preference for 'Operation Anvil'. Reluctantly, the Prime Minister concurred and seven of Alexander's divisions, as well as 70% of his Air Force, were removed from his command to make the new operation possible. He was left with twenty divisions in Italy against Germany's twenty-six.

'Operation Anvil' made little difference to the success of 'Operation Overlord', but the American decison had fatal implications for the future of eastern Europe. It suited Russia to keep her Allies in the West, and Roosevelt's policy at that time was to please Stalin at almost any price. The ultimate cost was high and Macmillan 'looked back on this decision of June 1944 as one of of the sad turning-points of history'.[11]

Ever since the invasion of Italy, the official Allied attitude towards her had been ambivalent. They were undecided whether to treat her as a defeated enemy subject to the doctrine of unconditional surrender, or whether to accept her as an ally against Germany. The military campaign was slow, due to the overriding demands of 'Operation Overlord', and this made the political position more difficult. Macmillan also had to contend with serious economic problems, the chief of which was inflation. The German system had been to live off the country and let its people starve. The Allies, who were less ruthless, in fact did more damage to the economic structure of Italy by printing paper money to pay for the supplies they needed. It became necessary to establish an Allied anti-inflation committee to formulate plans for increasing the bread ration, breaking the black market and stabilizing wages. Against strong opposition from the Combined Chiefs of Staff, the bread ration was raised from 200 to 300 grammes and within three weeks Macmillan was able to report that black-market bread had fallen in price from 160 to 60 lire and flour from 300 to 40 lire per kilo. This made it easier to resist inflationary rises in wages. Electric power was another difficult deficiency. Provision had to be made and priorities allocated between military and civil needs; Macmillan worked out a system, based on his Ministry of Supply experience earlier in the war, which gradually became operative under the guiding hand of General Brian Robertson.

In July 1944, King George VI visited Naples and stayed for a few days at the Villa Emma (named after Emma Hamilton). King Victor Emmanuel had arrived in Naples at about the same time, but Macmillan had omitted to inform the Commander-in-Chief of his presence and early one morning a picket boat arrested a suspicious-looking couple who were fishing near the Villa Emma. They protested vigorously and the noise woke King George VI, who put his head out of the window to ask the cause of the trouble.

'Says he's the King, sir,' explained the young officer in charge of the picket boat.

'What King?'

'The King of Italy, sir.'

Eventually, Queen Helena produced as proof of identity an enormous visiting-card of Alice in Wonderland proportions, which King George kept as a souvenir of this vicarious encounter.[12]

The following month Churchill arrived in Rome for a discussion about the future status of Italy, prompted by a request from the Italian Government that the armistice arrangements should be replaced by a preliminary peace treaty. The Prime Minister thought this premature, but he accepted Italy as a 'friendly co-belligerent and no longer an enemy state',[13] and agreed that her export trade should be revived and that greater responsibilities should be given to the Italian administration. He wanted Macmillan to become head of the Control Commission and run this new and more relaxed policy. This was in accord with Macmillan's own views. He had been scathing about the Commission's military emphasis after the invasion:

Planning of the Allied Control Commission by academic methods ... without comprehension of the situation likely to exist in conquered and largely devastated territory has produced an organisation ill-conceived, ill-staffed and ill-equipped for its purpose.[14]

He welcomed the new civilian concept and the constructive assistance the remodelled Commission could give to the Italian people. In these discussions 'Winston was like a dog worrying at a bone,' Macmillan reported;[15] and when it became clear that the Foreign Office wished to elevate Sir Noel Charles's position at the expense of his own, the Prime Minister gave the idea short shrift. 'But what am I to do?' asked Charles. 'What do Ambassadors ever do?' replied Churchill scornfully.[16]

In his new capacity as Acting President of the Allied Commission (from the title of which the word 'control' had now been dropped) Macmillan took many decisions on his own authority. The American elections were helpful because President Roosevelt wished to make sure of the Italian vote, and he even assumed responsibility for increasing the bread ration. Gradually, the economy improved and the Commission's role became one of friendly counsel instead of control.

By this time Macmillan's advice on Italian affairs carried great weight in London and Washington, and his part in implementing the 'New Deal' for Italy was an important one. But his influence, indeed power, extended much further: it covered every major political problem in Algeria, Yugoslavia and Greece. He had made himself indispensable to the conduct of the Mediterranean War. In 1944, four Ambassadors, though answerable to the Foreign Office, were in fact working under his control: they were Duff Cooper for France, Noel Charles for Italy, Adlai Stevenson for Yugoslavia and Rex Leeper for Greece. The envoys to Rumania and Bulgaria were soon to be included under his diplomatic umbrella. Macmillan attributed their co-operation to the fact that 'everyone relied upon what AFHQ would give them' and he added the understatement that 'I was supposed to have ... considerable influence with the various military, air and naval authorities.'[17]

Members of Macmillan's staff were equally enthusiastic in their tributes to him as their leader. His team in Italy was a small one, consisting of Roger Makins, Harold Caccia, Alaric Russell (who succeeded Tony Rumbold), Philip Broad and John Wyndham. He worked very quickly, listened to everyone, always took the blame if things went wrong and was inspiring and fun to work for. He was then, as always, a fascinating conversationalist and enjoyed good food, good wine, good company and giving informal parties, at which he sometimes had rather too much to drink. He also liked going for long walks and picnics in the country and, if his work allowed, he would shut himself up in his room without anything to eat or drink on one day in every month to read and sleep and recharge the batteries. The only occasions on which he ever appeared at all worried were when telegrams arrived from the Prime Minister, and there was an atmosphere of tension until they had been answered. He had a great admiration for Churchill but was also somewhat in awe of him.

At the end of September, to Macmillan's great regret, Roger Makins left for another post. He had been a most loyal support and was a great loss to the Mediterranean team. Macmillan recorded that Makins was 'never satisfied with the second best' and paid a well-deserved tribute to his 'rapier-like brain' and 'almost monastic devotion to duty'.[18]

During his time in Italy, Macmillan became involved with the Yugoslavian resistance movements and the political problems they created. King Peter had been in exile in England since his country's capitulation, but in 1941 two patriotic groups of guerrillas began to make trouble for the Germans in Yugoslavia. One group, known as the Chetniks, was led by Mihaelović and was loyal to the King. The other, commanded by Tito, consisted of Communists, but they were far more active against the Germans than the loyalists. The British Government therefore sent a Mission, skilfully and successfully led by Fitzroy Maclean, to Tito's headquarters in September 1943 and gave full support to his Partisans. It was Churchill's policy to sustain against Germany whatever local force seemed the most dynamic and effective. The Americans, who had a different point of view, did not fully understand this, so their approach to both the French and the Yugoslav situations sometimes diverged from Britain's.

It was clear by the end of the year that Tito, who already had nearly 250,000 men operating under him, would eventually be the most powerful man in Yugoslavia; but the Americans were more sympathetic to Mihaelović, and

King Peter was reluctant to disavow him. Britain had recognized the King's Government in exile and, although he no longer had any real authority in his own country, the position was a delicate one. General Wilson and Macmillan went to Bari in May 1944 to assess it. While they were there the news came through that the Germans had attacked Tito's Headquarters and that he and Randolph Churchill, who was with him, had narrowly escaped capture.

By this time King Peter had formed a new Government under the Croat leader, Dr Subašić, and was prepared to appoint Tito Supreme Military Commander in Yugoslavia. Subašić, convinced of Tito's strength, agreed to abandon Mihaelović, and Fitzroy Maclean and Randolph Churchill strongly advised the British Government to put its whole weight behind the Partisans. On 9 August, Tito went to Caserta to meet Macmillan and two days later they were joined there by Churchill; but the situation did not develop well and Tito rejected Subašić's suggestion of a united Yugoslav Government.

The claims of 'Operation Anvil' and the delay this operation entailed in Italy had prejudiced Allied prospects of influencing events in the Balkans, where Russia's military presence at the end of the war proved decisive. In November 1945, elections were held in Yugoslavia which resulted in an overwhelming victory for Tito's candidates. A Republic was proclaimed and another totalitarian state established. Macmillan noted later how different the story might have been if Alexander's strategic plan had been adopted in the summer of 1944.

At the end of November Macmillan went to London for a week, *en route*, as he thought, for Washington to resolve various financial and shipping problems which had arisen. In his absence a political crisis in Rome led to the emergence of De Gasperi, the leader of the Christian Democrats, and Togliatti as the most powerful figures. There was also a threat to arrest Badoglio and put him on trial, to which both Churchill and Macmillan objected strongly. Britain's whole position in Italy had been negotiated with him and her national honour was involved in protecting him. The State Department was less resolute, but Macmillan made it clear that he was ready to fly him to safety in Malta, and in the end Bonomi and Sforza gave guarantees that the Marshal would not be prosecuted.

In early December, just as Macmillan was about to leave for America, a new crisis arose, this time in Greece, which meant that he had to fly east to Athens instead of west to Washington.

Macmillan's new assignment was not his first wartime involvement in Greek affairs. During the summer of 1944 the Greek Government in exile had moved, at Churchill's suggestion, from Cairo to Italy, which brought it within Macmillan's orbit. The situation in Greece was much the same as in Yugoslavia. Soon after the German occupation in 1941, two partisan movements had come into existence – a Communist group called EAM and its republican counterpart, EDES – and a bitter internecine struggle had developed between the two.

The monarchy had little popular support and it seemed to Macmillan, though not at first to Churchill, that the best hope of a moderating influence in Greece, as in Italy and Yugoslavia, lay in the avoidance of too close an association with the royal cause. At a conference at Caserta early in October 1944, Churchill subjected the Greek Prime Minister, Papandreou, to a monologue on the merits of the monarchy; but Macmillan was right – the real issue was not between the King and a republic, but between evolutionary and revolutionary forces in the country.

It was clear that if civil was was to be averted, British troops would have to move into Athens and install a Greek Government as soon as the Germans withdrew. Failing that, EAM would seize power and a Communist regime would become established.

On the night of 13 October, Macmillan went on board HMS *Orion*, the flagship of the fleet which had been assembled for the liberation of Greece. Preceded by an airborne battalion and led by minesweepers, some of which were blown up, the expedition disembarked successfully and entered Athens on 18 October. Papandreou was well received by large crowds and the presence of the British troops prevented any attempted EAM *coup d'état*.

Macmillan saw the immediate needs as the urgent importation of relief supplies, the stabilization of the inflationary currency situation and the disarming of the Communist guerrillas in order to avert the danger of civil war. But it was easier to identify these priorities than to deal with them.

During this period Macmillan himself was commuting between Greece and Italy in order to cope with problems in both countries, but the arrival in Athens of a Treasury expert, Sir David Waley, was a great help in resolving the monetary difficulties; the return from Italy of the Greek 'Mountain Brigade' helped to restore confidence, and the prospects of achieving a peaceful demobilization of the partisans at first seemed hopeful. Unfortunately, his six Communist Ministers broke their agreement with Papandreou and resigned from the Government. Civil war broke out a few days later – provoked, it was alleged, by the Greek police firing into a civilian crowd; in fact, the Communist leaders had decided on the rebellion before this incident occurred.

Churchill at once pledged full support for Papandreou, but the State Department publicly criticized British policy, and the press in both countries, especially in the United States, was at first unfavourable. A debate took place in the House of Commons on 8 December. Macmillan, who was then still in London, described Churchill's speech as 'a superb Parliamentary performance' and Eden's as a 'brilliant wind-up', at the end of which only thirty Members voted against the Government.[19] Gradually, as the facts became known, the criticism died down. The situation in Athens, however, was a most serious one, and Churchill decided that General Alexander and Harold Macmillan should leave at once to take charge of it. He thought it 'a field of action incomparably superior to what was mapped out for you in Washington'.[20] And so it proved.

Alexander and Macmillan arrived in Athens on 11 December to find the Embassy and the British forces besieged in a small area of the city, the airfield insecure and the Greek ports already lost. The Communists held four-fifths of Athens, including the harbour and the power station, and the British troops had ammunition for only five days and food for eight. Macmillan recalled that 'there was a good deal of sniping and shelling. In the Ambassador's study the bullets came through the window, but there was a corner in which one could sit without undue risk.'[21] It would take a fortnight before military reinforcements could arrive from Italy, and in the confused and volatile situation, a political settlement was urgently needed. This was not made easier by American suspicions of Britain's role in Greece, which Churchill was determined to maintain. Macmillan worked hard and skilfully to achieve a solution. Reginald Leeper, the British Ambassador, wrote later that Macmillan 'was always looking ahead, foreseeing the next difficulty and taking steps to forestall it'.[22]

The moderate elements in the country were divided between monarchists and republicans, so the first task was to unite them against the Communist revolution which, if successful, would be irreversible. The key to a compromise seemed to be Archbishop Damaskinos, who had remained in Greece throughout the German occupation and had a high reputation among his compatriots. Macmillan recommended his immediate appointment as Regent, but King Paul of Greece objected and Churchill was reluctant to put undue pressure upon him.

When Alexander returned to Caserta, Macmillan remained in Athens in an effort to resolve these problems. Conditions at the Embassy, where he was living, were primitive. There was no heat or light, and very little water. Only Army rations were available and even those on a reduced scale. The rebels were two or three hundred yards away and snipers' bullets were a hazard if one ventured outside the house or stood too near a window. Most of the rooms were therefore evacuated and the beds put in the passages. Apart from the lack of a hot bath and a good meal, Macmillan rather enjoyed the siege. He was never averse to an element of danger, it suited his temperament; and the Embassy, painted pink, was a favourite target. Alexander commented, on his departure, 'You people are going to be very lucky if you don't have another Lucknow on your hands.'

Damaskinos was a man of moderation, good sense and courage, and Macmillan was delighted when he expressed his willingness to accept the Regency. Unfortunately Papandreou was against the appointment and so advised the King, whose own opposition to it was thereby strengthened. Endless negotiations ensued with the Greek politicians, who seldom agreed among themselves and, even when they did, changed their minds the next day. With the arrival of reinforcements they hoped for a complete victory over the Communists and this expectation increased their reluctance to accept a Regency. But Alexander could not spare sufficient forces for a long drawn-out Greek war.

It was decided to convene a conference representative of all Greek political opinion, including the Communists, with Damaskinos in the chair. At this point a message arrived from Churchill to say he and Eden would themselves visit Greece. They arrived on Christmas Day 1944 and met Papandreou and Damaskinos that evening. Fortunately, Churchill formed a good impression of the Archbishop and the final arrangements for the conference were speedily concluded. It assembled the following afternoon and included the Communist delegation. By this time Churchill had come round to the Regency proposal, in which the conference also concurred, and Macmillan was able to persuade Papandreou to report this unanimity to the King of the Hellenes, who at length agreed to the appointment of the Archbishop. It was a significant success and a fitting end to the period of exactly two years which Macmillan had by then spent in the Mediterranean.

Churchill's visit had been invaluable in converting him to Macmillan's regency policy and convincing him of the Archbishop's suitability for the post; but many peace-making problems remained. After the formation of a new Government under General Plastiras, truce terms were at length agreed with EAM. More permanent arrangements were still needed and Macmillan's next objective was a further conference between the Government and the Communists to negotiate a final settlement. Its composition proved difficult but, due mainly to his patient diplomacy, it eventually assembled and agreement on the main issues was achieved. Only the date on which martial law was to be lifted was still unresolved. After talking to both sides separately, Macmillan devised a compromise which he persuaded everyone to accept. Wisely, he would not allow the meeting to break up until a communiqué committing the participants had been agreed at 5.30 a.m. The Peace of Varkiza was formally signed the following day.

The timing was perfect because the Yalta Conference was just ending and this meant that Churchill and Eden could call again at Athens on their way home. They arrived on 14 February 1945, and Churchill and the Regent drove slowly in an open car through cheering crowds to the Old Palace, where at least 40,000 people were waiting to greet them. It was a triumphant moment for them both and Churchill made an inspiring extempore speech, calling for unity, which admirably suited the occasion.

The end of the rebellion relieved Macmillan of much of the work and anxiety which the Greek crisis had entailed and he only had to make two further visits to Athens in March and April to help Rex Leeper with some outstanding but relatively minor political problems. One of these was a further change of Government preparatory to the general elections to be held later in the year. General Plastiras had made some unwise appointments and was himself a rather reactionary figure. He was replaced by Admiral Voulgaris, a much more moderate man, clever and agreeable where Plastiras had been stupid and obstinate. Macmillan was fortunate in the loyalty and able assistance he received from Leeper, with whom his relations were always happy, and in the ready co-operation of Archbishop Damaskinos, who sent him a most generous letter in September 1946 when he retired from the Regency. In it he referred to Macmillan's 'penetrating intelligence' and to his unfailing tact and leadership. These were qualities he had indeed shown in his handling of the Greek situation.

With the New Year of 1945, the war in Italy had entered a static phase and there was no renewal of the offensive until the spring; but Macmillan had much to occupy his mind and his time. As President of the Allied Commission he now held an executive post, combined with his continuing role as political adviser to Field Marshal Alexander. Plans had to be prepared for the occupation of northern Italy when the Germans retired; the central area was administered under Allied control, and the Italian Government still needed help and advice in the south. Machinery and raw materials (as well as consumer goods) were required in order to provide employment. Lack of shipping, as always, was the limiting factor and every liberated country wanted more imports than the Allies could supply. The treatment of former Fascist collaborators was also controversial, especially if they possessed valuable technical skills in short supply; and it was important, as in Greece, to contain the Communist partisans.

In February Macmillan was able to announce the details of the 'New Deal' by which Bonomi's Government was given virtually full power in the territory under its own control, including the right to conduct its own foreign relations with Allied countries. British and American liaison officers were withdrawn and plans for economic reconstruction made known. Macmillan was anxious to enhance the prestige of the Italian Government and to strengthen its hand, when the time came, for dealing with the Communists.

At this period, North-East Italy was in danger of occupation by the Yugoslav Partisans, who hoped to occupy two of the provinces before Alexander could do so. The American State Department was determined to secure the return of the whole area to Italy, although no one would authorize Alexander to use force against Tito to achieve this. He and Macmillan decided that Trieste and its lines of communication must be seized, but that this was the best that could be done at this stage.

Although plans had been made to provide relief for the Balkan countries, the Russians were there first and Rumania, Bulgaria and Albania all fell under Communist control. The only country, apart from Germany itself, where authority was shared was Austria and, as Foreign Secretary, Macmillan was later able to sign a treaty finally freeing her from occupation.

The plight of Poland was the most tragic. Macmillan was not involved in her fate, but Britain had entered the war with a pledge to help her against Germany and, at the end of it, could do no more than conclude a sham formula at Yalta which obliged her to accept Russian domination instead of German. On 15 April came the news of the death of President Roosevelt. In the Mediterranean theatre he had not always been the easiest of allies, but he was a good friend to Britain in bad times and a great leader of his own people and of the whole free world.

The final offensive in Italy was launched on 9 April, and Macmillan was determined to see as much of it as possible. From Bologna, which had just been captured, he travelled by jeep to Modena. An American infantry battalion was advancing to attack the town, but he passed them on the road and got there first, to be greeted by a combination of German snipers' bullets and great rejoicing by the partisans when they realized that he was the famous 'Haroldo Macmillano – the ruler and father of the Italian people'.[23] He was kissed on both cheeks by their leader, presented with a partisan armlet and formally enrolled at the town hall. A spirited action followed, lasting two hours, against the remaining Germans, at the end of which he could claim, as the first of the Allies to arrive there, that he had 'liberated' Modena!

The Allied advance was moving fast and, after 100,000 prisoners had been taken and protracted negotiations concluded, the Germans signed a surrender agreement on 29 April. This event was announced by Churchill in the House of Commons on 1 May. It preceded by one week the general capitulation and was a considerable achievement by Field Marshal Alexander, who had been obliged to fight his final battle with insufficient ground forces. His partnership with Macmillan had been a happy and a successful one and the many tributes to him[24] are evidence of the admiration and affection Macmillan felt for him.

The respect was mutual and Macmillan's contribution in guiding him through many political and diplomatic minefields had been of inestimable value. There was only one matter, at the very end of the war, on which they disagreed. The incident concerned the forcible repatriation to Russia of – in Macmillan's words – 'about 40,000 Cossacks and White Russians with their wives and children',[25] who had been taken prisoner by the Germans earlier in the war.

On 13 May 1945, Macmillan flew to 5th Corps' Headquarters at Klagenfurt in Austria to confer with its commander, General Keightley, who reported to Alexander that the Minister-Resident had advised him to hand over the Cossacks to the Soviets 'at once'. He seems to have agreed with Macmillan, but felt he could not comply without Alexander's authority. The Field Marshal disliked the proposal and postponed his decision pending instructions from the Chiefs of Staff. Before these arrived, Nicholai Tolstoy suggests[26] that Macmillan had intervened to expedite the surrender of these people to the Russian authorities and, although there is no direct evidence of this, Macmillan's own words seem to confirm the possibility:

We had no alternative but to surrender them. Nor indeed had we any means of dealing with them had we refused to do so. But it was a great grief to me that there was no other course open. At least we obtained in exchange some 2,000 British prisoners and wounded who were in the area and had been in German hands.[27]

Tolstoy omitted to mention, or perhaps did not know, that a high-level agreement had been reached between the United States, the United Kingdom and the Soviet Government, to which Alexander and Macmillan were obliged to conform.[28]

The repatriated Russians were later hanged, massacred or sent to labour camps, where most of them died. In Krushchev's 1955 amnesty, fifteen of them were released. They arrived in Austria in 1957, ill and unable to work, but their plea for financial help was refused by the British Foreign Office in 1958. It was an unhappy episode, described by Lord Boothby as 'one of the most shocking things we have ever done';[29] but although Macmillan was in part to blame, the incident should be looked at in the wider context of his remarkable contribution to the war effort between January 1943 and May 1945. John Wyndham has described his qualities and achievements at that time:

He was Viceroy of the Mediterranean by stealth. [He] managed things ... modestly and obliquely.... He ran the whole show, but he was perfectly content to let the others think that they were doing so. ... Power for power's sake was what he enjoyed.[30]

Macmillan gave up his duties as Minister Resident on 26 May 1945. When he had received the appointment in December 1942, the assignment had seemed a secondary one. By the time he relinquished it twenty-nine months later, he had made himself indispensable to the conduct of the war in the Mediterranean. By a combination of tact, application and intellectual mastery he had acquired the substance of power without its trappings. The fact that this satisfied him is illustrative of his priorities and of his character. Successive Commanders-in-Chief – Eisenhower, Maitland Wilson and Alexander – had come to depend upon his advice, his judgement and his diplomatic skill.

When the war ended Macmillan was still largely unknown to the British people and was certainly eclipsed in the public estimation by the leading Ministers in 'The Great Coalition', but he had wielded greater influence and had exercised far more effective power than most of his Cabinet colleagues. In Churchill's mind and in the inner circle of Government, where it mattered most, his experience and authority had been immeasurably enhanced and he had emerged as a major figure with an assured future in the public life of Britain.

15

IN OPPOSITION

Although American Lend-Lease had saved Britain's wartime economy and Marshall Aid was to be given generously in the post-war period, the United Kingdom had sacrificed most of her foreign investments, direct taxation was high, and major social and economic changes were inevitable. These had begun after the First World War and were hastened by the high rates of taxation made necessary by the Second World War. The green baize door which had divided the house-owner and his family from their staff virtually disappeared. Far fewer people were content to enter domestic service and even if servants were obtainable, the upper classes could no longer afford to pay them the higher wages needed and demanded after the end of the war.

Technological progress was greatly accelerated by wartime inventions and industrial advance. Dramatic changes in the character and structure of the Commonwealth were also certain. India led the way. While the British Empire faced dissolution, the Russian Empire was being extended both by ruthless annexation and by the imposition of Communism on its weaker neighbours. Europe lay prostrate, her revival dependent upon the vision and generosity of the United States. Political change was almost as inevitable as the social, economic and colonial developments soon to take place.

Churchill, never a Party man, would have liked to have continued 'The Great Coalition' for a period of reconstruction at the end of hostilities or at least until the defeat of Japan, but Clement Attlee preferred an early General Election. The Labour Party was under-represented in a Parliament elected ten years earlier, the life of which had been prolonged only by the necessities of war. The Government resigned on 23 May 1945 and was succeeded by a predominantly Conservative 'caretaker' administration, pending arrangements for the Election.

Macmillan recorded Churchill's suggestion that he should become Minister of Labour 'but I said I thought I had been too much out of politics for the last two or three years for such a post'.[1] In the event he was made Secretary of State for Air. Although he had been offered the safe constituency of St George's, Westminster, he was unwilling to give up his Stockton seat without a fight. He had been away in the Mediterranean for two and a half years, his local Conservative organization had virtually ceased to exist and he did not expect to win. As the campaign developed, his misgivings grew. He was one of the few who foresaw the outcome of the election: 'As soon as electioneering began in earnest I knew what the result would be. ... We carried through the campaign as best we could, but I had little hope of success.'[2]

Churchill himself was rapturously received throughout the country, but this was misleading. Some people thought they could have a Labour Government and Churchill as well. Others turned out to greet him as a gesture of goodwill to their great wartime leader, but they never intended to vote for him. The Service vote was heavily for Labour and this was in fact decisive.

At Stockton Macmillan was defeated by 8,500 votes, and in the new House of Commons nearly 400 Labour Members faced a Conservative Opposition of only 213. It was a landslide to the Left. 'It may well be a blessing in disguise,' said Mrs Churchill. 'It seems quite effectively disguised,' replied Winston.[3]

The Tory Front Bench had been weakened by election losses and the leader of the Party was determined to secure the adoption of some of his senior colleagues as candidates in the series of safe Conservative by-elections which soon arose. He exercised his personal influence through Central Office to achieve this, but despite his great prestige this interference with the freedom of choice of constituency Associations was resented and has never been attempted since. It was effective in securing the early return to Parliament of Harold Macmillan, Brendan Bracken, Richard Law (later Lord Coleraine) and Peter (now Lord) Thorneycroft.

One of the vacancies was the Bromley division of North Kent, where the sitting Member had died suddenly. It was a solidly Conservative middle-class suburb of London. Randolph Churchill was a candidate for the nomination, but when he heard that Macmillan was also in the field, he wrote generously to the local Association: 'I think no one has a greater claim. Will you please, therefore, withdraw my name.' Harold Macmillan was duly adopted. The leader of the Party sent him a personal message:

The work you did ... during the war was important, difficult and delicate. It required qualities of an exceptional order. ... In the social field at home you are distinguished for your constructive and progressive outlook. We need you very much on the Opposition Front Bench in the Commons.[4]

No doubt to the surprise of some of his Conservative supporters, Macmillan fought the by-election that November on the philosophic platform of

'The Middle Way'. He was criticized for purveying pre-war theories and blueprints containing no new political inspiration 'as if nothing had happened in the meantime', but this was unfair. Macmillan understood the political importance of constant repetition; moreover no one had spoken on these lines for six years. He sincerely believed what he was saying and that it was the right philosophy for the modern Tory Party.

Macmillan was duly elected by a majority of 5,559. He was introduced into the House of Commons by his two old friends, Harry Crookshank and Henry Willink, who had both been his contemporaries in College at Eton.

In Opposition, Churchill avoided, as far as possible, appointing Shadow Ministers with exclusive departmental responsibilities. He preferred to give his colleagues the opportunity to attack the Government on a wide front. All Privy Councillors sat on the Front Bench and divided the work between them, often on an *ad hoc* basis. Eden was responsible for foreign affairs, and economic and financial questions were dealt with as they arose by a team of senior ex-Ministers, consisting of Oliver Stanley, Oliver Lyttelton, R.A. Butler and Harold Macmillan. Once a fortnight the fourteen members of the Shadow Cabinet, known then as the Consultative Committee, were given lunch by Churchill in a private room at the Savoy Hotel. On the broad foreign policy themes Churchill was magnificent, but he took relatively little interest in home issues and did not himself devise any new domestic policies.

Anthony Eden was the acknowledged second-in-command and Churchill's designated and unchallenged successor. Though not an orator, he was always sensible, moderate and persuasive, and was listened to sympathetically and with respect. He understood the House of Commons and was very effective when winding up important debates.

The best speaker on the Opposition side was Oliver Stanley. With his brilliant wit and dazzling epigrams he was always a joy to listen to, but he died unexpectedly in 1950 at the age of fifty-four. Had he lived longer, he would no doubt have been Chancellor in Churchill's 1951 Government and might well have succeeded Eden as Prime Minister in 1957. The other prominent Front Bench speakers in the 1945 Parliament were Harold Macmillan, R.A. Butler, Oliver Lyttelton, Harry Crookshank and David Maxwell-Fyfe, reinforced by Quintin Hogg, Peter Thorneycroft, Anthony Head and Selwyn Lloyd.

On the Labour side, Attlee, Morrison, Bevin, Cripps and Dalton were all Ministers of ability and experience, who had served in the wartime Coalition. Attlee was adroit and firm, a man of few words whose speeches were deliberately delivered in a low key. He was a very good chairman of the Cabinet. At a small lunch party at Hyde Park Gate during the 1950 Parliament, I remember Churchill saying of him: 'He was always very loyal to me in the war, but of course he has no ideas of his own.'

Harold Macmillan wrote short pen pictures of the Labour Ministers.[5] He described Herbert Morrison as a good administrator, a 'moderate', and a real London Cockney; he was a skilful Party manager, a good Home Secretary and a popular leader of the House of Commons, but was much less successful as Foreign Secretary after Bevin retired. Ernest Bevin was a powerful figure, a man of strong character and a great patriot; he was the outstanding trade-union leader of his own or any period. Dalton, too, was patriotic, but over-optimistic as Chancellor of the Exchequer; his booming voice and beaming smile exemplified his exuberant, indiscreet, extrovert personality. Stafford Cripps, who succeeded him at the Treasury, was a man of very different character, who seemed almost to delight in austerity; he was an eccentric, of upper-class background but sincere Socialist convictions, with an incisive mind and great powers of oratory. Aneurin Bevan, younger than the others and the only senior Minister who had not served in the Coalition, was described by Macmillan as the *enfant terrible* of the Labour Party, but an immensely attractive one; a good administrator and the architect of the National Health Service; a great orator in the Lloyd George tradition; and a man of real genius. He was perhaps the most brilliant and certainly the most exciting and most memorable of the Labour leaders.

This formidable array of Ministers began at once to introduce the Bills which they could fairly say they had been elected to pass. The nationalization of the Bank of England was followed swiftly by that of civil aviation, the coal industry and Cable & Wireless.

In his first speech in the new Parliament, Harold Macmillan said, 'I feel like a political Rip van Winkle. Everything is so changed ... on the benches opposite sit so many old colleagues.'[6] He spoke frequently for the Opposition and did his best to reconcile his attacks on the Government's legislation with the progressive policies he had himself advocated in pre-war days. This was not always easy and he was often taunted by Ministers with quotations from his earlier speeches. He adopted a light touch, using the rapier rather than the bludgeon, but in so doing made the error, in his own words, of 'attempting too many jokes'. His speaking style at this period was contrived and histrionic. Richard Crossman wrote later:

The studied Edwardian elegance of his despatch-box manner, the mannered witticisms and the whole style of professional Party polemics which he so consciously adopted – everything about him disconcerted me. ... I preferred to remember the man I knew for a few months in Algiers.[7]

Another Labour opponent, Emrys Hughes, was even more critical: 'He cultivated an oratorical style of the Gladstonian period.... His polished phrases reeked of midnight oil.... To those opposite he seemed the political actor and poseur, the cynic, the knock-about artiste of the Parliamentary stage.' Hughes thought Macmillan was 'flippant, superficial, supercilious and arrogant', but he conceded that to the Tories 'he was clever, hard-hitting, forceful, convincing, eloquent, one who knew all the tricks of the Parliamentary game'.[8] Typical of his technique at this time was his scornful description of the Festival of Britain as 'a little gem of mismanagement, a cameo of incompetence, a perfect little miniature of muddle'. Macmillan himself acknowledged that 'Opposition in Parliament cannot be said to be a very enthralling affair.... I did not much enjoy the work.'[9]

In contrast to his pre-war days when he was more likely to be cheered from the Labour benches than from his own side, Macmillan soon became the Front-Bench speaker who could most easily raise the temperature of the House. The *Observer* commented as early as January 1946 that he had set himself up as the scourge of the Socialists and, as a planner himself, continually attacked them for their lack of any real plan. He was caustic about the Socialist intellectuals like Harold Laski – 'those clever men who in every age were always wrong' and who were dragging their Party 'down the slippery slope to Communism'.[10] But the *Observer* also noted that since his return to Westminster he had increased in parliamentary stature and was qualifying for the leadership.

In the following few years road and rail transport and the electricity and gas industries passed into State ownership, and only steel remained in private hands by the time Parliament was dissolved. The Health Service, the jewel in Labour's crown, was brought into operation by Aneurin Bevan. The Government's legislative output was therefore considerable. Such was the need for goods and services throughout the world that the pre-war issue of unemployment was no longer relevant – the problem now was production. Macmillan persuaded his colleagues to initiate a debate on the Address in 1946 and himself moved the Opposition amendment: '... in this period on which we are now embarking, the problem of unemployment will be replaced by the problem of production.... By this measuring-rod Governments will be judged.' Under pre-war conditions, he said, monopoly selling methods and the restrictive practices of trade unions were justifiable but were now indefensible.[11]

Macmillan repeated these arguments in March 1947, based on his earlier advocacy of a partnership between Government and industry, the Government being responsible for economic strategy, the tactics being left to private initiative. This was the Middle Way over again, but it now commanded a consensus in Parliament; only the extreme right of the Conservative Party and the left of the Labour Party were fundamentally opposed to it. Even in those days Macmillan was thinking ahead to the need for a wages policy: '... we cannot close our eyes to the necessity of some form of voluntary self-discipline to replace the harsh and cruel discipline of the days of unemployment.'

For the present, however, the nation's financial and economic predicament was more immediate. A large loan of $3,750 million was accepted from the United States as the only alternative to bankruptcy; but it did not last long. By September 1947, only $400 million remained. Dalton minuted the Cabinet: seven-eighths of the dollars had gone 'to fill our own stomachs and to stock our own factories'. Crisis measures were required and were at hand. Sir Stafford Cripps succeeded Hugh Dalton as Chancellor of the Exchequer and proceeded to introduce austerity with as much enthusiasm as his predecessor had shown for good cheer and over-confidence. Direct and indirect taxes were raised steeply, with surtax payers as the main sufferers. Petrol-rationing was introduced and food-rationing remained rigid at wartime levels or lower. The meat ration was reduced to 1s per week. These measures helped to balance the budget and to reduce the adverse trade balance; but Britain's temporary salvation was mainly due to the generosity of Marshall Aid.

The improvement in the economic climate was not sustained. A run on the reserves developed from a trickle into a flood and, in September 1949, Cripps was obliged to announce the devaluation of the pound from $4.03 to $2.80.

Developments in international affairs had, in the meantime, been just as dramatic as those which had taken place in Britain itself. After the atom bomb was dropped on Hiroshima on 6 August 1945, Japan had surrendered on 14 August. But, despite her victories in war, Britain's peacetime position was weak, while Russia's had become relatively strong.

In opening a debate in the House of Commons on foreign affairs in February 1946, Harold Macmillan expressed the optimistic view that Soviet policy was aimed only at a defensive *cordon sanitaire*, but two weeks later Churchill took the opposite line. His 'Iron Curtain' speech at Fulton dramatized the Russian danger and shook American opinion, which had hitherto ignored it. Harold Macmillan, always much influenced by Churchill, quickly fell in line with his leader's views.

As time went on, and despite all Bevin's efforts for *détente* with the Soviet Union, Churchill's forebodings were proved all too accurate. They had one positive result, however, which Macmillan underlined in winding up another foreign affairs debate in May 1947 – the deteriorating situation had ranged the United States firmly on the side of Britain and Western Europe. Harry Truman defined the American position: there was to be no return to the

Monroe Doctrine and the pre-war policy of isolation. Marshall Aid, unprecedented in its generosity in time of peace, as Lend-Lease had been in time of war, was of immeasurable importance to the West. It was also offered to Russia, but she declined. Congress voted no less than $6,000 million for aid, of which $4,000 million was allocated to the European recovery programme.

As the partition of Germany was by this time a fact of life, Harold Macmillan urged the establishment of an effective economic administration in Western Germany, financed by American capital. With his Italian experience in mind, he was a strong advocate of self-government at every level and was critical that, as late as 1947, there were still 20,000 Allied administrators in West Germany.

For a year from June 1948, the Russian blockade of Berlin was a test of will, providing the occasion for a combined Anglo-American effort reminiscent of the wartime partnership. On 23 May 1949, the Federal Republic of Germany came formally into existence, with Bonn as its capital and Dr Adenauer as its first Chancellor.

Meanwhile, Czechoslovakia, like Poland, had fallen under Communist control. The Baltic States, East Germany, Bulgaria, Rumania, Hungary and Albania had all become satellites of Russia. But the North Atlantic Treaty was signed in April 1949, when the United States and Canada joined with the Western European countries in a defensive alliance to counter the threat of Soviet aggression. The world was divided but an uneasy peace prevailed, based on the mutual fear of their nuclear weapons which both America and Russia were developing.

The overriding objective of both the Government and the Opposition in the House of Commons was to strengthen Britain's influence abroad by demonstrating the unity and continuity of her foreign policy. Eden's task, admirably discharged, was to support and sustain Bevin against the pressures from the left wing of the Labour Party. The two men were on easy and informal personal terms and together they developed a bi-partisan approach to most international issues. Oliver Stanley congratulated Ernest Bevin in the House of Commons on his handling of foreign policy with the comment, 'It shows the importance of being . . . [pause] Anthony.' The trust and confidence which had grown during the war between these two men of widely different background stood them both, and the nation, in good stead in the post-war years.

Bevin died in April 1951. He had done much to educate the Labour Parliamentary Party and had conducted Britain's foreign policy with more national support than any Conservative Foreign Secretary, even Eden, could have commanded in the early post-war period.

During the years 1945-51, India, Pakistan and Ceylon had gained their independence as members of the Commonwealth, Burma had broken away, a guerrilla war was developing in Malaya, a Communist Government had gained power in China, the State of Israel had been established and an Arab-Israeli war had been waged with inconclusive results. The Prime Minister of Iran (General Razmara), King Abdullah of Jordan and Mahatma Gandhi had been assassinated and King Farouk of Egypt overthrown.

Parallel with the expansion of the Russian Empire by force of arms and an imposed ideology, the British Empire was facing dissolution by a voluntary transfer of power to its colonial territories. This process, which had conferred independence on the self-governing Dominions after the First World War, was continued after the Second in the Indian sub-continent and was to be largely completed for the Colonial territories by Macmillan himself a decade later.

The pattern had been set for India by the Montagu-Chelmsford proposals, followed by the India Act of 1935, which had been supported by Harold Macmillan, though strongly opposed by Churchill. When Attlee became Prime Minister in 1945, he was determined to devolve power to India's own elected Government. The difficulty in doing so was due to the bitter animosity between the Hindu and Moslem communities. The British Government was in the predicament of wanting to surrender responsibility, but being unable to do so without leaving anarchy in its wake.

Macmillan decided to visit India in the dual role of politician and publisher, to form his own assessment of this insoluble situation. The House of Macmillan had long been established in India and had a flourishing business there, so he was hospitably entertained by friends of the firm wherever he went. Accompanied by John Wyndham, he arrived in Bombay in January 1947. In addition to authors, teachers, educationalists and administrators, he met many of the leading politicians, both Moslem and Hindu, including Jinnah, Liaquat Ali Khan, Nehru, Moraiji Desai, Sarden Patel and Mrs Pandit. He visited Delhi, Lucknow, Calcutta, Madras and Karachi.

On the day of Macmillan's departure, Attlee announced in the House of Commons that Britain would leave India not later than June 1948, and that Lord Louis Mountbatten would replace Wavell as Viceroy, in order to preside over the transfer of power and the demise of the British Raj. In essence, the Government's argument was that Britain was going because she no longer had the power or the will to stay. Churchill complained with justice that, with the fourteen-month time limit, the Government had 'put an end to all prospect of Indian unity'. And so it proved.

Partition became inevitable and Mountbatten set to work to implement it. With a heavy heart Churchill accepted the implications on behalf of the

Conservative Party and agreed to support the necessary legislation. The Independence Bill followed, dividing the sub-continent between India and Pakistan, but not attempting to impose a Constitution upon either. In Churchill's absence through illness, Macmillan spoke for the Opposition in the Second Reading debate. The immediate sequel was predictable and tragic. Riots broke out in Lahore and Calcutta and mass murder and arson continued for months, during which millions lost their lives or their homes. At the end of it the problem of Kashmir was still unresolved and was to lead to war between India and Pakistan seventeen years later.

Moves towards self-government and eventual independence were also taking place in the Caribbean and in West Africa. Once granted in Asia, these changes were bound to follow throughout the Colonial Empire. Macmillan did not invent nationalism when he became Prime Minister; he responded to it and in so doing achieved with goodwill what he would otherwise have been forced to concede with bloodshed.

From 1947 onwards Macmillan was deeply involved in the movement for European unity, of which he was a protagonist. His work in this sphere, spread over many years, is collated in a later chapter.

The Conservative Party did not waste the years of Opposition. To anyone who had contested the 1945 election it was clear that the first priority must be to revive the moribund organization in the constituencies. Many members of the Tory Party were still involved in war work and only a few elderly supporters remained to form the nucleus of the new organization which had to be created after a heavy electoral defeat. The first essential was to find the right men for the top positions.

In the summer of 1946 Churchill persuaded Lord Woolton, the wartime Minister of Food, to become Chairman of the Party. This remarkable man, loved by all who came into contact with him, had only become a Conservative in 1945; he was first and foremost a business man of independent views and Liberal background, who had joined the Party on the day of its disaster in July 1945. He was a fine organizer, and the best Chairman the Party has ever had. He set to work at once to revive its fortunes and within less than four years had succeeded in this formidable task.

The Conservative Research Department was revived and enlarged under Rab Butler's leadership and the Conservative Political Centre was established. These changes cost money, so Woolton launched a national appeal for funds. With his psychological insight, he decided that the higher the target the better the chance of success. So he asked for £1 million and got it.

One of the most important reforms for the future of the Party was a change in the criteria for the selection of candidates. Too often in the past, rich men had been able to buy safe seats. They were not necessarily the most useful ministerial or even Back-Bench material and the younger men the Party needed could not afford to spend their meagre parliamentary salaries financing their local Associations.

New rules were introduced limiting the sum which any candidate or Member of Parliament might subscribe annually to his local Association and obliging the Association itself to raise the money required to fight elections. As a result, several young men, who could not previously have afforded to go into politics, entered the House of Commons at the next election in 1950 and constituted a more varied intake than ever before. Aneurin Bevan described this infusion as 'the finest Tory vintage in political history'.

Harold Macmillan whole-heartedly welcomed this reform. He knew it would attract a new and younger element into the Party's ranks in the House of Commons. At the same time he was working hard to promote the sort of progressive policies with which these new recruits could identify and which they would preach with conviction and enthusiasm.

For a time Macmillan believed that it would be beneficial to change the name of the Party. The word 'Conservative' lacked appeal for the modern electorate and did not reflect the Middle Way policies he was advocating. He even flirted with the possibility of a Conservative–Liberal merger. During the summer of 1946 he floated these ideas at Conservative rallies at Hatfield and Chatsworth, causing a considerable stir in the national press, and in a speech in September he referred to a 'new democratic Party'. In a later article in the *Daily Telegraph* under the title of 'The case for Alliance or Fusion', he developed his theme for the integration of the anti-Socialist Parties. Woolton was sympathetic, but felt that a Party could only change its name at a time of success and that to do so at a low ebb in its fortunes would seem defeatist and defensive. This view prevailed at the Party Conference that autumn and the idea was not pursued.

There was a general demand, however, for a new policy approach, particularly to industrial questions, and a small committee, on which Macmillan served, was appointed under Rab Butler's chairmanship. In May 1947 it published a document entitled *The Industrial Charter*, which became a landmark in post-war Conservative thinking and was the foundation for the thirteen years of Tory Government between 1951 and 1964. Macmillan claimed that it

... proved our determination to maintain full employment, to sustain and improve the social services and to continue the strategic control of the economy in the hands of the Government, while preserving wherever possible the tactical function of private enterprise. ... We also accepted as irreversible the nationalization of coal, the railways and the Bank of England.[12]

The document concluded by laying down three rights for manual workers: security of employment, incentives for their work and status as individuals, however large the firm. It was a final break with pre-war policies and a triumph for the philosophy Macmillan had long advocated but for which Butler was now accorded most of the credit. It was indeed the forerunner of the common ground between Conservatives and Socialists which came to be known as 'Butskellism', derived from the names of Butler and Gaitskell.

The Charter had a good public reception and a favourable press, except for the Beaverbrook newspapers on the Right and the Socialist *New Statesman* and *Tribune* publications on the Left. No longer could anyone portray the Party as reactionary. Macmillan was delighted: 'The Socialists are afraid of it and Lord Beaverbrook dislikes it. ... What more can one want? ... It is of course a challenge as well as a charter. It is the true doctrine of the Middle Way.'[13] He claimed with justification that 'Between the wars there was always a progressive element in the Party. Now it has seized control, not by force of palace revolution, but by the vigour of its intellectual and spiritual power.'

In the country, Macmillan was an ardent propagandist for the new policies. Only the *laissez-faire* Tories of the old school like Sir Waldron Smithers and Sir Herbert Williams objected to the theme of co-operation between Government and industry which Macmillan had asserted so assiduously from the Back Benches in the Thirties and which he could now proclaim from the Front Bench as the official policy of the Party. For his critics, he charged, 'time does not merely stand still, but runs backwards. ... I prefer to rest upon the tradition of Disraeli, fortified by the high authority of Churchill.'[14] He was delighted with a comment by 'Crossbencher' in the *Sunday Express*, who wrote that the Charter 'is a triumph for Mr Harold Macmillan. He once wrote a political treatise called *The Middle Way*. This is the second edition.'[15]

It gave Macmillan special pleasure to address a rally at Hawarden Castle, the holy soil of Liberalism, where he drew attention to the similarity in the aims and philosophy of the modern Conservative and Liberal Parties. The success of the Industrial Charter was followed by other policy documents, including *The Right Road for Britain*, which formed the basis of the Party Manifesto for the 1950 General Election. The end of Labour's first Government 'in power', as opposed to merely 'in Office', was now in sight, and Attlee dissolved the Parliament in February.

The election campaign was closely fought and resulted in 315 seats for Labour and 297 for the Conservatives and National Liberals. The Liberal Party, which had fielded 475 candidates, secured only 9 seats in the new House of Commons and the great Government majority of 166 in the 1945

Parliament was reduced to 6 in 1950. Macmillan was returned with a massive majority of 10,688 at Bromley.

The best hope of defeating the emasculated Labour Government appeared to lie in an alliance with the Liberal Party. This would have been easy to bring about had the Conservatives been willing to promise electoral reform. The first-past-the-post system of voting was manifestly unfair, especially to the Liberals, and Macmillan observed:

There is a great deal to be said, in principle, for an experiment in Proportional Representation. ... How else are the great Socialist 'blocks' to be eaten into? It seems absurd that an immense and dangerous change like steel nationalization should be made effective by a majority of six.[16]

He might have added that there was even less justification for such a measure on the basis of a minority of votes in the country.

Churchill was favourably disposed to electoral reform and made a moving appeal to the 1922 Committee to be allowed to make an arrangement with the Liberals on these lines. Despite his great authority and prestige, his suggestion was turned down in speech after speech by Members of the Parliamentary Party and nothing more was heard of it for a quarter of a century.

In the absence of any Conservative approach, the Liberals almost always voted with the Government. Without a formal pact, their role in the 1950 Parliament was comparable to the one they followed in 1929-31 and again in 1977-8. As Macmillan noted, 'their sole purpose seemed to be to prevent an early defeat of the Government'.[17] This no doubt had attractions as a means of short-term survival, but historically it has not been beneficial to the Liberal Party.

The next eighteen months in the House of Commons consisted of late hours, close divisions and constant harassment by the Opposition. In this hard-worked Parliament, with its strained atmosphere, three-line whips and all-night sessions, Churchill, at the age of seventy-six, set a fine example. He voted in every division and, as Harold Macmillan recalls, made many 'brilliant little speeches ... and crowned all by a remarkable breakfast at 7.30 a.m. of eggs, bacon, sausages and coffee, followed by a large whisky and soda and a huge cigar'.[18]

At the Conservative Party Conference in October 1950, a dramatic commitment to build 300,000 houses a year was demanded from the floor by Harmar Nicholls MP (now Lord Harmar Nicholls). The figure caught the imagination of the delegates, who insisted upon its inclusion in the next Tory Manifesto. Without research into its practicability, the platform was steamrollered into a hasty acceptance of this target. It chanced that Harold Macmillan was the only member of the Shadow Cabinet to congratulate Harmar Nicholls on the outcome of his speech. Macmillan had no idea then that he would be given the task of implementing the undertaking, but it was to become of great importance to his career.

Meanwhile, the Government was involved in the war in Korea, which added to its economic and Party difficulties at home. In June 1950 the North Koreans, supported by Russia and China, had attacked the southern part of the country across the 38th Parallel. The United Nations Security Council, hastily convened and in the temporary absence of Russia, demanded the withdrawal of the North Korean forces and called upon all UN members to support this. President Truman announced that America would go to the assistance of South Korea and, by the end of the year, fourteen nations, including Britain, had agreed to contribute. A powerful New Year offensive by the Chinese was held with difficulty and the line stabilized. In June, armistice terms were accepted in principle, though their negotiation proved protracted in practice and desultory fighting continued.

The Korean war induced the British Government to increase defence expenditure to £4,700 million over a period of three years. Service pay was improved and conscription extended from eighteen months to two years. These measures were supported by the Conservatives, but they constituted an unpalatable package for a Labour Government to propose, especially when cuts in domestic spending were an inevitable corollary.

To Aneurin Bevan the free Health Service was sacrosanct, and when the new Chancellor, Hugh Gaitskell, introduced charges for spectacles and dentures, Bevan resigned his office as Minister of Labour. He was critical of the whole scale of defence expenditure and was supported by Harold Wilson, the President of the Board of Trade, who also resigned from the Government. Churchill thought, wrongly, that Wilson would lose his seat at Huyton. 'I am sorry for Wilson and his little wife. He is finished. But Nye, with his big majority at Ebbw Vale, is a very different dish.'[19]

Soon after these resignations, the Anglo-Iranian Oil Company was nationalized by the fanatical Dr Mossadegh. Herbert Morrison, by then Foreign Secretary in succession to Bevin, was prepared to use force if necessary to save British lives, but not to safeguard British property. His handling of this crisis was unskilful and Macmillan thought he should either have taken a generous and co-operative line with Iran or landed troops to protect British interests.

Beset by these difficulties, the morale of the Labour Government was beginning to crumble. With such a small overall majority every vote counted; Conservative Members declined to pair and, owing to harassing tactics and some successful ambush operations, minor divisions were sometimes lost.

This would not have mattered much, but perhaps, after twelve gruelling years in office, Attlee was losing the will to govern under these conditions. Whatever the reason, he dissolved the Parliament for a General Election on 26 October.

Following Labour's restrictions, Churchill's slogan of 'Set the people free', combined with the dramatic Conservative undertaking to build 300,000 houses, had great popular impact and both these pledges proved potent vote-winners. To offset them, the Labour Party, bereft of any constructive appeal, campaigned on the charge that the Tories would have gone to war with Persia and Dalton even declared that under Churchill 'we shall be at war with Russia within twelve months'.[20] This wounding and rather disgraceful propaganda culminated in the infamous *Daily Mirror* banner headline, 'Whose finger on the trigger?' – which was thought to have swayed thousands of apprehensive voters. Nevertheless, the Conservatives gained twenty-three seats and an overall majority of seventeen in the House of Commons. Macmillan's majority at Bromley increased to 12,125.

There have been widely varying assessments of Harold Macmillan's political contribution and personal attitude of mind during the six years of Opposition. Emrys Hughes was, perhaps understandably, critical about the post-war Party leader as compared with the pre-war Party rebel, but his biography is too biased to carry conviction.[21]

Contemporary newspaper comment was generally complimentary. 'Every trace of his old diffidence and shyness has gone,' declared the *Observer* in October 1950, and the political correspondent of the *Liverpool Daily Post* wrote that 'the situation of the Conservative Party after the defeat of 1945 exactly suited his talents. It was not only that he himself had long been impatient with the old Conservatism, he also possesses a brilliantly speculative mind.' The *Sunday Times* of 22 January 1950 was even more eulogistic:

Harold Macmillan is a political philosopher as well as a practical statesman. And he is an able administrator ... he talks convincingly in the language of an intellectual, yet an intellectual with much practical experience of national and international affairs, of public and private commerce, and a sympathetic understanding of the life and difficulties of the ordinary man.

Macmillan was certainly a better (and more partisan) speaker after the war than before it. His wartime success had increased his self-confidence and made him contemptuous of the Socialist Ministers and of their ability to direct affairs. Anthony Sampson detected 'an almost Cassandra-like pessimism. He seemed to see little future for Britain or for Europe.'[22] In a talk with Hugh Dalton at Strasbourg in 1950, Macmillan expressed the view that 'Europe is finished. It is sinking. It is like Greece after the second Peloponnesian war ... If I were a younger man, I should emigrate from Europe to the United States.'[23]

L.A. Siedentrop adds to the evidence by recording that 'Macmillan became gloomy. His ambitions were thwarted and his skills largely unused.'[24] If indeed his pessimism was more than a passing mood, it may well have been due to a feeling of frustration that his talents and experience, at the height of his powers, were being wasted during the years in Opposition.

Macmillan is a very private man, who reveals little of himself either in the six somewhat colourless volumes of his memoirs or to his colleagues in Parliament. But to a newly-arrived Back-Bencher, he did not appear depressed or disillusioned. He was, on the contrary, a figure to whom one turned for inspiration and leadership. His drawl and the 'languor, irony and careless elegance' were part of a pose, like the well-cut but untidy clothes, to give the impression of a casual, gifted amateur. They did not, however, conceal the ambition, competence and sheer hard-working professionalism of this remarkable man.

Whatever the thoughts behind the façade, the election result of October 1951 and the new opportunities it brought were soon to transform Harold Macmillan once again into the effective man of action. His organizational skill and the personal success he achieved brought him, for the first time, into the public limelight and gave him a position in the Conservative hierarchy below only Churchill, Eden and R.A. Butler.

16
MINISTER OF HOUSING

In the new Government Eden went back to the Foreign Office and Rab Butler was made Chancellor of the Exchequer. After a short delay Macmillan was summoned to Chartwell and offered the post of Minister of Housing, with the task of building the 300,000 houses the Manifesto had promised. 'It is a gamble – it will make or mar your political career,' said Churchill, 'but every humble home will bless your name if you succeed.'[1] If he did not want this, the Prime Minister added, he could have the Board of Trade – but that was 'a mere matter of routine'.

Macmillan had hoped for a more senior position. He asked for time to consider, consulted Lady Dorothy – who advised him to accept – and then agreed to Churchill's proposal. It was a wise decision. He feared he might fail and if so that the appointment would kill him politically; in fact, it made him. He held the office for exactly three years, which 'proved in many ways the happiest and most rewarding of my time as a Minister'. 'It was a finite job, and every month there was a score of the number of houses built. It was also a practical job.'[2] Macmillan realized that, to achieve success, unorthodox methods would be needed, including 'improvisation and a certain ruthlessness ... there would be risks, but there would also be rewards'. He profited by the lessons he had learnt from Beaverbrook at the Ministry of Supply, and 'we ran it ... like a war department'.

The target of 300,000 houses was thought by many to be impossible and no one in the Department believed that more than 200,000 could be built in a year. Aneurin Bevan's last year as Minister had produced even fewer. In Opposition, the Conservative leaders had no idea of the gravity of the financial and economic situation which they were to inherit. With greater awareness of the difficulties they might never have assumed such an ambitious commitment.

By the end of 1951, the balance of payments was in serious deficit; imports had to be reduced, the Bank Rate raised and Government expenditure drastically curtailed. The sterling balances were a special problem and United States aid was by this time virtually at an end. Macmillan was obliged to wage continual war with the Treasury for more than his fair share of the national resources at a time when other Departments were being forced to accept cuts. Rab Butler was helpful, but the housing commitment made his own task more difficult and the aims of other colleagues were restricted in order to make way for Macmillan's success.

Building materials as well as money were in short supply. Lord Swinton, who was in charge of raw materials, and David Eccles at the Ministry of Works did all they could to help; but bricks, steel, cement and timber were not available in the quantities required and valuable dollars had to be spent to import additional supplies. Macmillan dealt with the brick shortage characteristically. He went to see (rather than sending for) the Chairman of the London Brick Company. 'Can you make more bricks?' he asked. 'Yes,' was the reply, 'if you give me more labour.'[3] So Harold Macmillan imported labour from Italy and brick production trebled in a short time.

There were other limiting factors: the Building Society movement was in relative decline; leading trade unionists had to be won over; production boards had to be established and priorities between house-building, repairs of existing housing-stock and school and factory construction had to be allocated by a newly-formed Building Committee of the Cabinet. Fortunately for Macmillan, Freddie (now Sir Frederick) Bishop was on hand to become secretary of this Committee. He is a man of exceptional tact and ability and was later to become Principal Private Secretary at Downing Street during Macmillan's premiership.

Macmillan was usually lucky in the men who worked for him – Roger Makins and Harold Caccia had been outstanding in his Mediterranean team – and he had good judgement in those he chose himself. This was especially so in the Ministry of Housing, where his task was made easier by the drive and zest of his Parliamentary Secretary, Ernest (later Lord) Marples, and the executive ability of Sir Percy (later Lord) Mills. At the age of forty-five, Marples had already made a fortune and gained valuable housing and engineering experience in the construction industry. 'Ernest Marples was one of the cleverest men I have ever met in a limited, practical field,' Macmillan said many years later.[4] Marples' grandfather had been the head gardener at Chatsworth and, as a boy, Ernest had sold newspapers and been a 'tic-tac man' to a bookmaker. He learnt engineering at night school and when he joined the army in the Second World War he was rapidly promoted to Sergeant-Major. He was ambitious, hard-working and full of ideas. Macmillan described him as 'a colleague of outstanding loyalty ... great ingenuity and untiring energy'.[5]

Percy Mills had been Machine-Tool Controller at the Ministry of Supply, where Macmillan had come to rely upon his down-to-earth common sense and business ability. Mills devised the Regional Housing Production Boards, which proved excellent vehicles for the task. 'What we should do without him, I shudder to think,' Macmillan remarked;[6] but his appointment caused suspicion and antagonism in the Department and even Sir Edward Bridges, the head of the Civil Service, became perturbed. The civil servants, led by the Permanent Secretary, Sir Thomas Sheepshanks (who 'knew nothing of the problems of industry or of production'[7]), wanted Mills to be advisory; Macmillan wanted him to be executive. 'Things are much changed since I was in office before,' Macmillan complained. 'The "trade union" of officials is back in power. The Treasury planners are supreme. Ministers are treated very politely, but with firmness, as temporary nuisances.'[8] He made one exception to this: among the senior civil servants, he formed the highest opinion of Dame Evelyn Sharp, at that time a Deputy Secretary and later to become Permanent Secretary in the Department, whom he considered 'the ablest woman I have ever known'.[9] She sometimes used strong language and on one occasion Mills remonstrated with her: 'Dame Evelyn, do remember there are gentlemen present.'

Macmillan exhibited the skill in planning and organization which had made him so effective in the war and gradually the civil servants came round. By March 1952 he was able to write, 'I really think they are beginning to enjoy the sort of modified "Beaverbrookism" which I am trying both to preach and to practise.'[10] They also came round to Percy Mills, 'a wise tycoon', as Macmillan described him, 'who soon charmed the senior civil servants, won their co-operation and always gave them all the credit for what the Department achieved'.[11]

Percy Mills had only been able to obtain one year's leave of absence from his business and, at the end of 1952, he returned to private industry. Macmillan wrote of him at the time: 'Sir Percy Mills, with his quiet but inflexible will, has really moulded the whole Ministry to our purpose. I could have done nothing without him.'[12] His contribution had been so notable that when Macmillan formed his own Government in 1957 he brought Mills back as a member of the Cabinet.

Even the hard work and initiative of Macmillan and his team might have been frustrated, owing to the financial and supply limitations, but for the unfailing sympathy and support of the Prime Minister. By the end of the first year 240,000 houses had been built. It was a good start.

The growing success of the housing programme was criticized by the Opposition on the grounds that it had only been made possible by neglecting school- and factory-building. Macmillan was able to discount this with the debating-point that, in both these categories, the construction figures were better than those achieved by the previous Government. The fact remains that industrial building was actually lower between 1952 and 1954 than in 1951, and that Britain's road-building programme lagged behind that of almost every other comparable country.

Macmillan owed one important new idea to his immediate predecessor, Hugh Dalton, from whom he took over plans for a simplified standard house, which could be built more quickly than the conventional construction and at a saving of £150 each. By May 1952, 60% of the new houses were of this type.

The Area Boards were working well and within his first year at the Ministry Macmillan was able to announce that 1,000 more houses were being built each week than under the Labour Government. He received a great ovation at the Party Conference at Scarborough in October when he re-affirmed the 300,000 pledge and claimed that he was making housing 'a great national crusade. . . . It is the first priority among the social services . . . for the home is the basis of the family, just as the family is the basis of the nation.'[13] 301,000 houses were built between 1 November 1952 and 31 October 1953, and over 318,000 in the calendar year 1953. The target had been achieved a year ahead of schedule.

No less than 350,000 houses were completed in 1954 and even larger numbers could have been built if Macmillan had not decided to switch some of his resources to slum clearance. The repair and improvement of old houses, to prevent the development of new slums, was equally urgent. An allied issue was rent control, which kept rents artificially low and made it impossible for landlords to keep their properties in good repair. Although Macmillan wrote a good Cabinet Paper on this subject, he was unable to raise the rent restrictions sufficiently to give the landlords enough help; but at least a start had been made in facing this continuing problem.

The Conservative housing-drive concentrated upon increased production by the private builders. In 1951, the proportion of private to local-authority building was only 12%. By 1954, it had risen to 26% and by 1959 to 56%. This was a conscious and integral part of the post-war Conservative policy to create a property-owning democracy. The aim was to give the people a stake in the country and a greater sense of personal pride and responsibility. It also had a political purpose – that home ownership inclined people to vote Conservative. Indeed, it must be acknowledged that Macmillan's house-building programme proved much more beneficial to the middle classes and the skilled working classes than to the majority of lower-paid and ill-housed manual workers.

Predictably, Emrys Hughes criticized Macmillan's housing legislation as giving 'every possible consideration and concession to the private vested interests' and the Rent Act as 'the greatest act of appeasement to the property-owning class that could have been devised'. He was on stronger ground in claiming that the slum clearance plans had little practical effect.[14] Other contemporaries were less critical and Hugh Dalton acknowledged that the Tory housing record was better than that of his own Party. Anthony Eden wrote that Harold Macmillan had 'brilliantly fulfilled a programme which I had considered over-ambitious when it was announced'.[15]

Reginald Bevins, his first Parliamentary Private Secretary, described life with Macmillan as an adventure. 'He exuded enthusiasm – his zeal was infectious ... he was really superb in handling people, tactful, courteous, never giving much away. ... He always seemed to be a patient listener, encouraging others to talk. ...' When Bevins became a junior Minister in 1953, he was succeeded as PPS by Sir Harwood Harrison, who quickly formed an equally high opinion of his chief. Macmillan was generous to subordinates and, when Harrison pointed out an important error in a departmental brief, Macmillan gave him the credit for having done so and did not pretend to officials, as some Ministers might have done, that he had himself noticed the mistake.

Macmillan never missed a political opportunity and dropped everything for an important speech, which he would prepare with meticulous care. He was equally good at replying to a debate and adopted the technique, followed by many Ministers, of preparing in advance the answers to every point which could conceivably be made by earlier speakers and then simply noting in the margin the name of the Member who had raised it. He was then able to reply, apparently spontaneously, to the argument by referring to 'the interesting point made by the Hon. Member for Blank'. But he was always in a state of acute nervous tension before making a speech of any importance. *The Economist* was critical of him for being too conscious of the political opportunity:

No one who sets about building 360,000 houses a year with such gusto and success, fully knowing ... what harm he was doing to the national economy, can be regarded as quite the ideal man to do the unpopular thing just because it is right.[16]

Macmillan was very ambitious and there may have been an element of truth in this assessment, but it is not altogether fair. He was given a difficult housing target which he succeeded in attaining, and he should not be criticized for the achievement.

Macmillan's three years at the Ministry of Housing established his reputation with the public as a man who could get things done. He was one of the outstanding successes of Churchill's second administration and was paid the compliment, in May 1953, of being invited to give the first-ever Party political broadcast on television. But by this time he was sixty years of age, three years older than Eden and eight years older than Butler, and he still seemed a long way from the top of the 'greasy pole'.

Although he had held Cabinet rank in the war, Macmillan had been abroad at the time and the Caretaker Government was short-lived, so this was his first real experience of work in Cabinet. There were only sixteen members of it, because Churchill was experimenting with the 'overlord' system, in which two or more Departments were controlled by a single senior Minister. This did not work well in peacetime and had to be abandoned.

Churchill treated the Cabinet with respect and used it as a genuine forum for discussion and decision. He liked his colleagues to 'fight their own corner', but he was not as good a chairman as Attlee, if speedy despatch of business is the criterion, and meetings would often continue till 1.30 or 1.45 p.m., to the inconvenience of Ministers with earlier luncheon engagements. He sometimes indulged in long monologues and on one such occasion, when he finally invited comments from his colleagues, no one responded until James Stuart (later Viscount Stuart of Findhorn) observed laconically: 'Prime Minister, it is time for lunch.' The only days when Cabinet meetings were certain to end punctually were those on which Churchill was going racing. He was by this time the owner of several horses, including a grey called Colonist II which won many good races.

The Prime Minister's main preoccupation was the international scene. Negotiations with Egypt over the Suez Canal and the Sudan were difficult and long-drawn-out and Churchill was also deeply concerned over East–West relations and the possibility of *détente* with Russia. It became obvious to Harold Macmillan that the Prime Minister had now abandoned or indefinitely postponed any serious attempt to implement his great European design. This was a severe disappointment to those like Macmillan, Maxwell-Fyfe and Duncan Sandys who had hoped for and expected a lead from Churchill when he returned to office in 1951.

In the spring of 1953, Eden became seriously ill. Two unsuccessful operations were performed in London and he had to go to Boston for a third. There, an obstruction to the bile duct was safely removed, but a long period of convalescence, first in the United States and later in the Mediterranean, was necessary and he did not return to Westminster until October.

In the meantime, at the end of June, Churchill suffered a severe stroke. A bulletin understating the gravity of his condition was issued, but the situation was most difficult. Eden was still in the Boston clinic and the country was without both a Prime Minister and a Foreign Secretary. Macmillan himself was due to go into hospital to have his gall bladder removed on 6 July.

Churchill did not want to retire, and it would in any case have been wrong for him to do so in circumstances which would have made it impossible for

Eden to succeed him. A compromise was agreed upon, with Salisbury in temporary charge of the Foreign Office and Rab Butler acting as head of the Government. This arrangement could not continue indefinitely, but the House of Commons would shortly be rising for the summer recess and thereafter there were two options: Churchill could hand over to Eden when Parliament re-assembled in October or, if he was sufficiently recovered by then, he could himself resume the reins of Government.

Macmillan noted in his diary on 2 July: 'Out of chivalry to Eden and in repayment of all he owes him, he must not hand over now to Butler ...' It is interesting to note that, at this time, Macmillan assumed Butler's position as next in line after Eden and did not consider himself as a contender. Yet, when the occasion arose four years later, he was to gain the prize at Butler's expense.

Churchill's own remarkable resilience resolved the immediate crisis. He was able to preside over the Cabinet at two of its meetings in August and, by September, although still unsteady on his feet, he felt fit to face the physical ordeal of a major speech at the Party Conference. He came through this magnificently and a little later spoke with great success in the debate on the Address in the House of Commons. His recovery was complete.

Sir John Colville, then the Prime Minister's Private Secretary, recalled that in August Churchill and Sir Norman Brook had discussed a reconstruction of the Cabinet with Eden becoming Leader of the House of Commons and Lord Salisbury or Harold Macmillan Foreign Secretary. Eden declined the proposal and Macmillan remained at the Ministry of Housing for another year.[17]

17

MINISTER OF DEFENCE

In October 1954 the Government was reorganized and Macmillan was offered the Ministry of Defence. He was not enthusiastic about the appointment, mainly because the whole defence programme for the following three years had just been agreed and he did not think there would be much constructive work for him to do. But technically it was promotion; he had achieved his main housing objective and was ready to move on and widen his experience. Three years is about the most productive length of time for a Minister to spend in any one Department.

From the outset, Macmillan doubted if his new duties would prove congenial. He found the Ministry of Defence 'a queer kind of affair. I have no power, yet I am responsible for everything -- especially if it goes wrong.'[1] The real difficulty lay in Churchill's personal involvement. The Defence Committee of the Cabinet often sat under the chairmanship of the Prime Minister, who was closely concerned with all the problems and took a large part in their solution. This restricted Macmillan's authority and did not suit his temperament. He was never satisfied with the trappings of office; it was the power of decision which was, for him, the purpose and fascination of politics. At the Ministry of Defence this was incompatible with Churchill's own overriding interest. Eden recalled that the Prime Minister 'never accepted in his heart the position of a Minister of Defence divorced from his own authority. In impatient moments he would sometimes murmur that the post did not exist.'[2]

During the Second World War, when he had been both Prime Minister and Minister of Defence, Churchill had acted through a small professional team consisting of the First Sea Lord, the Chief of the Imperial General Staff, the Chief of Air Staff and Lord Ismay. In those days this system had worked well; but in peacetime the organization had changed, and when Macmillan asked for a small meeting, he found that 'about forty or fifty people turn up'.

Peter Carrington, a young hereditary peer who was to become one of the leaders of the Conservative Party, was appointed as Parliamentary Secretary and it was at once clear to him that he was 'working for an unusual man, both in his quick grasp of problems and in his positive attitude towards them'. However, the Service Ministers regarded themselves as independent and the Minister of Defence had become a co-ordinator with overall responsibility and little real power. Macmillan's authority was ill-defined, and when he became Prime Minister he reorganized the whole structure of the Department, down-grading the Secretaries of State to virtually Minister of State level.

Just before Macmillan's appointment, Anthony Eden had scored a diplomatic triumph, as a result of which Britain became a full member of the European military alliance and Germany a full member of NATO. Paul-Henri Spaak considered that Eden's negotiations had saved the Atlantic Alliance and the Queen recognized his success by honouring him with a Knighthood of the Garter.

The only outstanding European issue was the future of the Saar and a Foreign Ministers' Conference, attended also by Defence Ministers, was convened in Paris, where the French and Germans eventually came to terms. Macmillan's own part was a minor one, but he recalls the signature of the NATO and other agreements as a proud moment for Britain, who had guided Europe through a 'maze of confusion'.

Outside Europe, the Government had been taken by surprise both in Malaya and Kenya, and Macmillan was conscious of the vulnerability of our Colonial Empire to Russian-inspired unrest and subversion under the guise of the growing spirit of nationalism. He judged that good prior intelligence was the key to security and he placed General Templar, an outstanding officer, in charge of this work. However, he was not happy about the lack of co-ordination in areas where the Ministry of Defence, the Colonial Office and the Foreign Office were all partially involved, but where no one was fully responsible; and he was concerned about the Cold War, 'for we are not really winning it'.[3]

During Macmillan's short tenure of the Ministry of Defence, it became clear that the real dilemma for the West was the use of nuclear power – the only effective deterrent against Russian aggression. It was generally felt that in a conventional war Western Europe would be crushed, yet in order to prevent this the Allies would have to *start* a nuclear war. There was no military alternative, but the political implications at home and abroad were and have remained a source of extreme embarrassment. Beyond this was the question of by whom and by what machinery the nuclear power would be released. This might have to be done at very short notice in the event of sudden attack, and the main responsibility would fall inevitably upon the United

States. Another awkward problem, of which the public was becoming aware, was the danger of nuclear 'fall-out', not only in war but also from the bomb-tests in time of peace.

A momentous Defence White Paper, announcing the Government's decision to produce the hydrogen bomb, was published in February 1955 and was followed by a two-day debate in the House of Commons, which Churchill decided to open himself. It was his last major speech and concluded with the peroration:

The day may dawn when fair play, love for one's fellow-men, respect for justice and freedom, will enable tormented generations to march forth serene and triumphant from the hideous epoch in which we have to dwell. Meanwhile, never flinch, never weary, never despair.[4]

The Opposition did not criticize the decision to manufacture the bomb, but Aneurin Bevan attacked Churchill with the charge that 'the magnificence of his language serves to conceal the mediocrity of his thought' and went on to say that he would support the use of the bomb if the Russians used it first but not if the British did.[5] This was embarrassing to Attlee because Bevan's line did not represent official Labour policy. It was left to Macmillan, who wound up the debate on the second day, to deal with, or rather to evade Bevan's point by saying it was impossible to give the precise circumstances in which the bomb would be used. He made the valid observation that it was important that an aggressor should know what he might *not* do, but equally important not to tell him what he could do with impunity.

Although convinced of the deterrent value of nuclear weapons, Macmillan does not seem to have fully appreciated the different but still important role of conventional forces and the need to maintain them. It is not perhaps surprising that, when he became Chancellor, he regarded money spent on normal defence equipment as being 'wasted' and as 'a great burden on industry as well as on the Exchequer';[6] but it is interesting that, even as Minister of Defence, he took the view that 'It is quite impossible to arm our forces with two sets of weapons – conventional and unconventional.'[7]

During the previous year Churchill's position had become a subject of speculation among his colleagues. He had no wish to retire, but he was nearly eighty and clearly could not lead the Party into another Election. Various dates were discussed, but as each drew nearer, there were reasons or excuses for remaining in office – as there always are – and no doubt Churchill genuinely believed them to be valid. The uncertainty led to an uneasy atmosphere in the Parliamentary Party; it was also unfair to Eden. Harold Macmillan observed: 'The Government had ceased to function with full efficiency ... no one co-ordinated policy; Cabinets were becoming long and wearisome as well as too frequent ... the whole Party machine was losing grip....'[8]

In June, Macmillan wrote to Churchill advising him to retire before the summer recess. He expected and received a curt acknowledgement and in July he asked to see Lady Churchill privately at 10 Downing Street. He told her that he was speaking on behalf of several colleagues in the Cabinet who thought, as he did, that the Prime Minister should retire in favour of Anthony Eden. She reported this conversation to Churchill, who sent for Macmillan that afternoon to discuss the matter.

Sir John Colville has commented on Churchill's successful tactics in dealing with this unwelcome suggestion.[9] In the course of a friendly talk, in which Macmillan reiterated his opinion that the Prime Minister should retire before the Party Conference in October, Churchill left him in no doubt that it was his intention to remain in office until 'either things become much better or I become much worse'.

After another talk on 1 October, Macmillan recorded that 'he is absolutely determined to go on and is not willing to contemplate any definite retirement date'.[10] The next day Macmillan sent a letter to Churchill, urging a clear and definite arrangement with Eden about a date for the hand-over. Other talks followed at intervals along the same lines, 'yet every visit to Churchill was still a delight'. Macmillan recalled being summoned one morning to find the Prime Minister in bed: 'With a little green budgerigar sitting on his head ... a cigar in his hand and a whisky & soda by his side, from which the little bird took sips from time to time ... while Gibbonesque sentences were rolling from the maestro's mouth about the Bomb. From time to time the bird said a few words in a husky kind of voice like an American actress. ... A bizarre but memorable scene.'[11]

On 24 January Lord Moran recorded: 'Plainly there is a growing feeling among Winston's friends that the time has come for him to go, but only Harold Macmillan has had the guts to say so.' At length the Prime Minister decided on the date of his resignation, which was fixed for 5 April. He invited Eden and Butler to the Cabinet room and said simply, 'I am going and Anthony will succeed me. We can discuss details later.'

Churchill's second Administration was at an end. In 1951 he had promised the people 'Work, Food and Homes' and these commitments had been kept. The Government had been a successful one and the prospects both for the economy and the preservation of peace seemed remarkably improved. In addition to Macmillan's housing achievement, the years 1953 and 1954 had seen stable prices, reduced taxation, the end of rationing, a balance of payments surplus and a marked rise in the rate of growth.

As a young Back-Bencher in the House of Commons, Harold Macmillan had been captivated by the charm and magnetism of David Lloyd George, but in the late 1930s, when his interest in defence and foreign policy was aroused by the German danger, he was increasingly drawn to the views and personality of Winston Churchill, who became his real hero in the older generation of contemporary politicians. As compared to de Gaulle, who looked backwards to the glory of France under Louis XIV and Napoleon, Churchill 'always looked forward to the next step'. Macmillan had a real affection, as well as a deep admiration for him, but, although never afraid of anyone, he stood in some awe of 'the greatest man I have ever known'.

Eden took over in an atmosphere of goodwill and optimism. He was trusted and respected in the country and was identified, with Butler and Macmillan, as representing the post-war progressive Conservatism. His inheritance appeared to be a good one. Abroad, there was a welcome thaw in East–West relations; at home, Butler had talked with confidence of doubling the standard of living in twenty-five years. But inflationary pressures were developing and it was unwise of the Chancellor to introduce a give-away Budget, which included cuts in income tax and purchase tax. Although this was supported by senior Treasury officials, there was also a strong political motivation – Eden's decision to go to the country in May made a popular Budget in April almost inevitable. Retribution was swift. By the autumn, Butler was obliged to bring in a deflationary second Budget, which made his spring tax reductions look like cynical electioneering. His reputation never fully recovered.

Henry Fairlie, a shrewd and perceptive observer of the political scene, thought that Butler lacked 'the toughness of fibre which gets a politician through scrape after scrape without his judgement or his courage being touched. Mr Macmillan, on the other hand, has always impressed me by his inner conviction and strength. ... It's just an idea, but in a year's time I may be writing about him as the most powerful man in the Government.'[12] The *New Statesman* was less prescient. While acknowledging that Macmillan 'is, in many ways, a formidable House of Commons man', its contributor commented that he 'kept the Tory conscience in the years the locusts ate and he has never entirely lost his vocation. ... Those who keep the Tory conscience are respected by their colleagues and praised by future generations, but they never head the Tory Party.'[13]

Sir John Colville noticed another side to Harold Macmillan and described him as 'a craftier politician than Churchill, as decisive but less impetuous and more ruthless in attaining his ends'.[14]

The Ministry of Defence under Churchill had been a frustrating experience and *The Economist* observed that Macmillan's performance had been 'rather disappointing. He ... gave the impression that his own undoubted capacity for imaginative running of his own show melted away when an august superior was breathing down his neck.'[15] Macmillan had held the office for less than six months and was himself dissatisfied with his service there.

18
FOREIGN SECRETARY

When Eden succeeded Churchill, Macmillan took his place as Foreign Secretary. He was not the new Prime Minister's first choice. Eden would have preferred Lord Salisbury, whom he considered 'exceptionally experienced and qualified for the post',[1] but he decided reluctantly that it was impossible for a Foreign Secretary to sit in the House of Lords – a view which both Macmillan and Margaret Thatcher were to disprove when they made the successful appointments of Lord Home in 1960 and Lord Carrington in 1979.

Harold Macmillan was delighted at the prospect of the Foreign Office, the fulfilment of a long-held ambition, and he hoped to remain there for some years. In fact, he was destined to be moved again within eight months.

Emrys Hughes noted with some acidity that 'he had presence, deportment and looked like a Foreign Secretary. He was Eton, Oxford and the Guards, exactly the kind of "old school tie" idea of what a Foreign Secretary ought to be.'[2] Most political commentators, however, welcomed Macmillan's new appointment, although some envisaged the possibility of conflict between him and Anthony Eden. The *Sunday Times* referred to this in an article in April 1955:

> He is not the man to submit to tutelage by a Prime Minister, however experienced, who differed from him. . . . He is the one top-level Conservative Minister with a touch of Churchillian brilliance. . . . If he can cultivate forbearance of criticism and avoid a certain Curzonesque superiority, his success is certain.

Henry Fairlie, writing in the *Spectator*, took much the same line:

> He is extremely able. Intellectually he can make even Mr Butler seem pedestrian, which perhaps accounts in part for Mr Butler's deep distrust of him. . . . Mr Macmillan has wanted a position of real authority – and preferably the Foreign Office. . . . He will develop a foreign policy of his own. . . . But whatever his attitude, the relationship between himself and Sir Anthony Eden is going to be of vital importance.[3]

In fact, as the months passed, it became clear that the direction of foreign policy was still in the hands of the Prime Minister. Macmillan seems to have accepted this and he did not press strongly enough for his own views, particularly for a more positive involvement in Europe. Indeed, in his book *Full Circle*, Eden scarcely mentions Macmillan and it is hard to tell from his account that any Foreign Secretary had been appointed. It was the Ministry of Defence over again with the substitution of Eden for Churchill as overlord. Macmillan did not care for this and there was inevitably some friction in their relationship.

Eden dissolved Parliament on 6 May for a General Election three weeks later. It was a quiet, uneventful campaign, skilfully timed and conducted, and resulted in an overall Conservative majority of fifty-eight in the new House of Commons. Macmillan was secure at Bromley and was overjoyed when his son, Maurice, won Halifax from Labour by 1,500 votes. He himself missed most of the election because he was negotiating the preparations for a four-power summit meeting between Britain, Russia, America and France, to be held in July. This was preceded by a formal treaty giving independence and neutrality to Austria, which was signed on 15 May. No doubt the treaty was helpful to the Government, although foreign affairs seldom loom large as an influence on votes at a British general election.

On his return from Vienna, Harold Macmillan took part in a television broadcast with four colleagues – Eden, Butler, Monckton and Macleod – which he described as 'amateurish'. Television was still a new medium of which politicians had not much experience, but he was certainly too modest when he wrote later 'I cannot claim ever to have mastered this art.'[4] In fact he became a talented and attractive performer, though it is true to say that his appearances after he left public life were more successful than when he was Prime Minister.

The Summit Conference at Geneva was the first meeting of its kind since the war and gave rise to high hopes and world-wide interest. Sir Ivone Kirkpatrick, the Permanent Secretary at the Foreign Office, thought insufficient time had been allowed to prepare for it and the formal speeches in plenary session were – as usual on such occasions – unproductive. The private talks were more business-like, but the Russians were unable to accept the reunification of Germany and no real progress was made. Bulganin and Khrushchev did not want the conference to fail and, in Macmillan's words, were playing for a draw. President Eisenhower, who was anxious to achieve something that looked like a success, proposed that nuclear armaments should be thrown open to full inspection by both sides, but the Russians rejected this suggestion and the conference ended after six days, having achieved an improvement in atmosphere but little of substance. Macmillan was very much the second string at Geneva and seems to have made only a minor contribution, although on their return to England he stole the headlines from the Prime Minister with the remark, 'There ain't gonna be no war.'

In a speech in the House of Commons at the end of July, he ruefully explained a Foreign Secretary's dilemma: 'Nothing he can say can do very much good and almost anything he may say may do a great deal of harm. Anything that he says that is not obvious is dangerous; whatever is not trite is risky. He is forever poised between the cliché and the indiscretion.'[5] The Geneva meeting was followed by a Foreign Ministers' conference there in November which resulted in complete failure and a general sense of disillusionment.

It had become apparent to Macmillan that Eisenhower was much under the influence of his Secretary of State, Foster Dulles (whose vanity, in Macmillan's view, more than equalled his talents), and he therefore did his best to establish a good working relationship and partially succeeded. Dulles was a complex character, often devious in method, possible to admire but difficult to like. He irritated and antagonized Eden and the two men never became friends. This was to have serious repercussions a year later.

In September 1955, the Egyptians concluded an arms deal with Russia, which altered the balance of power and jeopardized peace in the Middle East. It also caused some disagreement between Eden, who hoped to work with Russia on an agreed arms policy for the area, and Macmillan, who favoured a much harder line with the Soviet Government.

Meanwhile, the Baghdad Pact between Britain, Iraq, Iran, Pakistan and Turkey was formed as a defensive organization against the possibility of Russian aggression, but was weakened at the outset by lack of full support from the United States. Its first Ministerial meeting, held in November, was a success, and Macmillan was much impressed by the personality and statesmanship of Nuri Pasha, the Prime Minister of Iraq. The Pact was a useful link between Britain and the Muslim countries and a hopeful vehicle for resisting Communist incursions in the Middle East. An important objective was to detach as much as possible of the Arab world from the ambitions of the Egyptian dictator, Colonel Nasser, and to achieve a settlement with Israel; but these hopes were soon to be destroyed by the issue of the Aswan Dam, which was followed by Nasser's nationalization of the Suez Canal.

Another long and bitter conflict arose during Macmillan's short tenure of the Foreign Office. The government was amenable in Cyprus, as in other British Colonies, to the principle of self-government, but this was complicated by the additional Cypriot demand for self-determination, which in practice meant *Enosis* or union with Greece – a proposition to which Turkey could not agree. This, therefore, was an international rather than a colonial issue and in the face of increasing propaganda by Archbishop Makarios, followed by acts of terrorism, Macmillan convened a conference between Britain, Greece and Turkey. He summed up the position: 'The Turks are too tough, the Greeks are too weak, to make a concession. So poor old England will get the blame – and the bombs.'[6] EOKA, the terrorist organization, was banned, but Makarios did not control, still less put out, the fire he had started, and in March 1956 he was exiled to the Seychelles by the British Government.

One other difficulty arose in the last months of 1955 before Macmillan left the Foreign Office. The publication of the memoirs of a Russian agent revived public interest in the case of Burgess and Maclean, who had defected to Russia in May 1951, and the Government felt obliged to issue a White Paper. Herbert Morrison demanded a general enquiry into the Foreign Office and its system of security, which the Cabinet declined, but a debate took place in the House of Commons in November. While accepting Ministerial responsibility, Macmillan pointed out that, of those concerned, Bevin and Hector McNeil were dead and the blame must therefore be shared between those still alive – Eden, Morrison and himself. This had the effect of disarming Morrison's attack; but it was suggested that Kim Philby, a senior Foreign Office official who had resigned in July 1951, was the 'third man' who had warned Burgess and Maclean and thus facilitated their escape. Macmillan stated that, despite close investigation, no evidence had been found against Philby. This was the only answer he could have given at the time, although Philby's subsequent defection and confession inevitably led to later attacks upon Macmillan for his failure to discover the truth.

The Prime Minister's honeymoon period had been short-lived. As early as the autumn of 1955, even newspapers well disposed towards the Conservative Party and towards Eden personally were beginning to complain of indecision, changes of mind, and his habit of interfering in departmental affairs. Henry Fairlie referred to 'a terrifying lack of authority at the top'[7] and the *Daily Telegraph* called for 'the smack of firm Government'.[8] Eden was so unnerved by the criticism that, after only a few months as Prime Minister, he issued an extraordinary denial of any intention to resign.

Macmillan himself was not immune from unfavourable comment. The verdict of a periodical called the *National and English Review*, which described him as 'one of the worst Foreign Secretaries in our history', was clearly exaggerated and unfair, but the general consensus was that he was not a success at the Foreign Office, mainly because he failed to initiate policies of his own or influence Eden towards a greater appreciation of the importance of developments in Europe. Despite his own earlier (and later) enthusiasm for European unity, he did nothing as Foreign Secretary to promote a closer association with the Continent at a time when British support and leadership would have been warmly welcomed.

In an article entitled 'Stumbling Diplomacy', the *Spectator* severely criticized Government policy for lack of grip, skill and forethought, complaining that 'Cyprus has been badly bungled' and stating that Britain's diplomacy in the Middle East 'has failed lamentably for all the hopes pinned to the Baghdad Pact'.[9]

In September 1955, the Prime Minister invited Harold Macmillan to become Chancellor of the Exchequer as successor to Rab Butler, who was to become Lord Privy Seal and Leader of the House of Commons. The suggestion was a shock to Macmillan, who loved his work at the Foreign Office and had hoped to continue there for three or four years. He asked for the change to be delayed until the end of the year and this in fact became inevitable when inflationary pressures obliged Butler to bring in an autumn Budget.

In a letter to Eden, Macmillan made it clear that he did not wish to take third place behind Butler: 'If Rab becomes Leader of the House ... that will be fine. But I could not agree that he should be Deputy Prime Minister.'[10] When he came to write his memoirs, he may have thought that this would sound as though he was trying to supersede Butler and he corrected the impression with the words: 'It never occurred to me at that time that there could be any question of a choice between him and me as successor to the Prime Minister. ... Butler, who was five years younger than Eden and eight years younger than me, would be the natural successor.'[11] This was not how his colleagues saw it. David Kilmuir recorded that 'he accepted the Treasury on the strict understanding that this was to be regarded as a step towards, and not away from the Premiership'.[12]

The Government reconstruction took place just before Christmas. Selwyn Lloyd succeeded Macmillan as Foreign Secretary, Lord Woolton retired at his own request and Harry Crookshank, who had been a most successful Leader of the House, went to the Lords to make room for Butler. Iain Macleod entered the Cabinet as Minister of Labour, the first of the 1950 entry to do so, and Edward Heath became Chief Whip.

Butler was depressed following the death of his wife and tired after four gruelling years at the Treasury, so he may not have been reluctant to relinquish the Chancellorship; but it was assumed that the Prime Minister's real reason for the change was to regain greater personal control of foreign policy. He could achieve this by appointing a relatively inexperienced Secretary of State, who would follow his advice and guidance more readily than Harold Macmillan had been prepared to do. In view of Eden's special interest in foreign affairs this motive was understandable and Macmillan acknowledged that 'there had been a number of matters ... in which we had not seen altogether eye to eye....'[13] But as against the Prime Minister's wish for a more malleable Foreign Secretary must be set Eden's observation[16] that the choice for the Exchequer seemed to him to lie between Macmillan and Derick Heathcoat Amory, the Minister of Agriculture. Amory had only recently entered the Cabinet and was very junior to Macmillan in the Conservative hierarchy, so it was remarkable that he was seriously considered for so important an appointment.

Whatever the reason, the decision was a disappointing one for Macmillan, who only accepted the Chancellorship reluctantly and out of a sense of duty. He had enjoyed the Foreign Office, had only been there for nine months and was sad to leave the staff and the work he had found so congenial. In retrospect he thought he had made a mistake in agreeing to the change, but the Prime Minister disposes of offices as he thinks fit and in reality Macmillan had no choice.

19

CHANCELLOR OF THE EXCHEQUER

The Treasury is more likely to break than to make a leading politician's career. It is helpful, though by no means essential, for a Chancellor to have a good grasp of economics, but only three post-war holders of the office – Hugh Gaitskell, Reginald Maudling and Roy Jenkins – could claim this when they were appointed. Butler, who had held the post successfully for four years, acquired expertise during his time there, though his last budget marred his earlier record. Macmillan had studied some aspects of the economy between the wars, but the problems had changed in the intervening years and he had little up-to-date knowledge of this area of politics.

Following his brief tenure of the Foreign Office, Macmillan observed one evening to Harold Wilson: 'After a few months learning geography, now I've got to learn arithmetic.'[1] Wilson was appointed Shadow Chancellor at about the same time and, though opposed, their work brought them into close personal contact. 'It was a happy and stimulating relationship for us both,' Wilson said and, after attacking one another in the Chamber, they often had a drink together in the Smoking-Room.

As Prime Minister, Macmillan was an expansionist and there is no doubt that his policies were always influenced by his pre-war memories of mass unemployment at Stockton-on-Tees. He was entirely sincere in these views, which in the 1930s were fully justified in economic terms as well as on compassionate grounds, but they governed his thinking for longer than was appropriate. By the 1950s the situation had completely changed; with unemployment at $1\frac{1}{2}\%$ or 2%, expansion in the financial sense was no longer needed. It is arguable that the economist Roy Harrod encouraged Macmillan to be more Keynesian than Keynes himself would by then have been.

Samuel Brittan, a leading authority on economic policy, recalled that, when Macmillan was Chancellor, officials kept a mental tally of the number of times he mentioned Stockton in any one week; but Brittan added that 'cynics always underestimated Macmillan's economic understanding ... he had little intuitive feeling for economic timing. Yet he often had a better understanding of the logic of the really major issues than either his Treasury or his Bank advisers.'[2]

Macmillan was always pragmatic, never doctrinaire. By the time he became Chancellor, a deflationary emphasis, albeit temporary, was clearly required. He realized this and persuaded the Cabinet to accept it. He was also quite ready to put pressure on the Bank of England, which in those days was reluctant to adopt a strong monetary policy.

From the outset Macmillan made a favourable impression on his officials and Sir Robert Hall (later Lord Roberthall), head of the Economic Section, recalls that he was 'very satisfactory to deal with, as he comes quickly to the point and makes a decision'. Towards the end of the year 1956, Robert Hall noted in his diary: 'It seems to me that H.M. will be the man of the future. It will indeed be very unjust if he is not, for he has ideas and the courage to implement them.'

Macmillan wrote the drafts for most of his own speeches. As he was not an economist, the results were not always technically correct, but he enjoyed putting forward unorthodox views to see how his officials would react and he never pressed them if the counter-arguments were strongly and persuasively advanced. He was more critical of established institutions like the City and the Bank of England than most Conservative Chancellors, and he thought it important to keep on good terms with the Labour Party, leading trade unionists and the 'mass media'.

Press comment on his appointment varied. *The Economist*, always favourable to Butler, suggested that 'it is not the coming of Mr Macmillan that is disturbing so much as the going of Mr Butler'.[3] And it is true that, as Leader of the House of Commons, Rab Butler was no longer involved in major decisions affecting the economy, nor was he closely concerned with international issues, which may account for his virtual exclusion from the small inner circle of Ministers who directed the Suez policy.

Prices had risen 10% in less than two years and the *Spectator* carried an article at the end of December, entitled 'Strategy for Macmillan': 'The arrival of Mr Macmillan at the Treasury is welcome. .... The prospects for his Party and for his personal reputation now rest entirely on how he handles the inflation.' It went on to warn him that the country was entering 1956 with 'seriously reduced gold reserves to protect us against whatever hazards we shall meet in the New Year'.[4] Macmillan understood this and in his budget speech three months later he declared that the reserves were 'insufficient for their purpose' and must be increased. Yet, in backing military intervention at Suez, he ignored the danger, and it was the fall in the reserves which proved the main factor in forcing the Government, at his behest, to reverse the policy and withdraw from the Canal.

Further advice was forthcoming from the *Financial Times*, which suggested that a Chancellor should not consider himself as the captain of a liner, changing course only occasionally, but as the driver of a fast car on a greasy road – 'His speed of reaction is vital.'[5] Macmillan himself used this kind of metaphor in speeches, with frequent references to the brake and the accelerator, in order to simplify economic policy for his audiences, and this may have encouraged the 'stop-go' criticisms which commentators so often made.

Nevertheless, the Treasury tempo was less exacting than that of the Foreign Office and Macmillan was glad of the extra room for manœuvre which this allowed: 'I have often compared the Foreign Secretary to the editor of a daily newspaper,' he wrote. 'Telegrams come in announcing some unexpected turn of events . . . at all times of the day and night. The Chancellor of the Exchequer is more like the editor of a monthly, or at worst weekly, newspaper. He has a little more time.'[6] Macmillan would have liked to be a reforming Chancellor, but he realized that 'to reform the Treasury is like trying to reform the Kremlin or the Vatican'.[7] In the event there was no opportunity even to attempt any major changes during the critical year he spent as head of the Department.

As so often in the past, he was well served by his junior Ministers. The Financial Secretary, Henry (later Lord) Brooke, was an experienced administrator, 'sound rather than brilliant',[8] reliable and loyal; and Sir Edward Boyle (later Lord Boyle of Handsworth) was Economic Secretary. He was a better economist than Macmillan and although, at the age of thirty-three, young for such an appointment, he was knowledgeable, very clever, effective in debate and a man of charm and integrity, with progressive ideas well attuned to Macmillan's own. Andrew Shonfield wrote about 'this Macmillan–Boyle team at the Treasury'[9] and considered Boyle's influence important.

The Permanent Secretary, Sir Edward Bridges, was about to retire. As head of both the Civil Service and the Treasury he had had too much to do and the two posts were now divided. Sir Norman Brook took over the Civil Service and Macmillan persuaded the Prime Minister to allow him to appoint Sir Roger Makins, by then British Ambassador in Washington, to the Treasury. Such a move was a remarkable, indeed a unique innovation, but Macmillan always liked to be advised by people he knew and could rely upon, and it worked well while he was Chancellor. Although Sir Robert Hall thought highly of Makins, it is not surprising that the appointment was resented by some of the Treasury officials and there is little doubt that Makins would have been better as head of the Foreign Office, where all his experience lay, than in charge of a very different department. Before going to Washington, where he was a successful Ambassador, he had been head of the economic side of the Foreign Office, but Peter Thorneycroft, who followed Macmillan as Chancellor a year later, had no confidence in his advice. The other senior officials were Sir Leslie Rowan, in charge of overseas finance, and Sir Robert Hall, head of the Economic Section. This group of professional economists had been somewhat eclipsed during Butler's regime, but was revived with the help of Edward Boyle and did much to improve the statistical information upon which any Chancellor must depend and to remedy Macmillan's complaint that 'we are always ... looking up a train in last year's Bradshaw'.[10]

C.F. (later Lord) Cobbold was the Governor of the Bank of England. There was a tradition that the Bank and the Treasury should operate independently, which Macmillan thought unhelpful. He and Cobbold formed a firm friendship and were soon able to establish a much closer relationship than had hitherto existed.

The economic inheritance was worse than Macmillan had expected. Unemployment was only 1·1 per cent, but the reserves were falling and prices rising, so that, against all his instinctively expansionist inclinations, the new Chancellor felt obliged to take early and restrictive remedial action. On 16 February 1956, the Bank Rate was raised from $4\frac{1}{2}$ to $5\frac{1}{2}$ per cent, its highest level since the 1930s, and the following day Macmillan announced a series of measures he believed to be necessary: hire purchase was restricted, food subsidies cut, the investment allowance suspended (almost certainly a bad decision) and public expenditure, including the number of civil servants, reduced.

The most controversial of his proposals, to which Eden was strongly opposed, was the abolition of the subsidies on bread and milk. Any Chancellor needs the consistent support of the Prime Minister, which he is more likely to receive if the head of the Government has himself some knowledge of economics. Eden had none, but in this case his objection was political. He was adamant and Macmillan, equally unyielding, even contemplated resignation; he recorded:

Butler, Heathcoat Amory and Thorneycroft came to see me in my room to try and find a solution. They said the PM was determined not to give in on bread and milk. In that case, I replied, he must get another Chancellor.[11]

Eventually a compromise was reached, by which part of the bread subsidy was reduced and the milk subsidy left until July; but the episode sapped Macmillan's confidence in Eden. In retrospect it is difficult to understand why so much importance was attached to such a relatively minor matter.

Medicine seldom tastes nice and a good Chancellor is unlikely to be a popular one, but there was general approval of Macmillan's proposals. The verdict of *The Economist* was complimentary: 'A week's reflection on Mr Macmillan's maiden measures to stop over-spending has not subtracted from their virtues';[12] and the *Spectator* considered that 'the first round in the fight against inflation has gone to the Chancellor'.[13] In the same issue Henry Fairlie wrote: 'He has still . . . to be more severely tested – when he introduces his first budget – but no one now doubts he is this Government's potential leader, the best Prime Minister we don't have.' The experienced political journalist, Ian Waller, was even more explicit in suggesting, after a poor speech by Eden in March, that 'If the year goes on as it has begun, it will not be Sir Anthony Eden but Mr Harold Macmillan who reigns in Downing Street in 1957.' This prescient comment was remarkable not only for its prophetic warning of Eden's downfall, but for its public prediction that Macmillan, rather than Butler, would be his successor.

The new Chancellor would have liked to introduce a 'startling or revolutionary budget' including a capital gains tax, but this was firmly discouraged by the Inland Revenue and Macmillan's first and only budget was quiet, modest and marginally negative in its effect. Family allowances were raised and the stamp duty on house purchases reduced, but profits tax and the cigarette duty were increased. The theme of the budget, inspired by Anthony Eden, was 'savings', and it contained one imaginative innovation – the introduction of premium bonds.

At one time Macmillan had considered putting 6d on income tax, but the idea was abandoned and cuts of £100 million in public expenditure substituted. The Chancellor's Cabinet colleagues were 'more enthusiastic about the principle than the practice of public economy'[14] when it affected their own Departments, but he succeeded in obtaining immediate reductions of £76 million and a further £17 million by the end of the year. Despite his previous service as Minister of Defence, Macmillan allocated half the cuts to defence expenditure, justifying it on the grounds that Britain was devoting nine per cent of her gross national product to defence, whereas other European countries were spending only five per cent of theirs.

Press reactions to the budget speech were mixed. *The Times* liked Macmillan's 'agreeable presentation' and, writing in the *Observer*, Hugh Massingham thought it contained flashes of wit and 'some genuinely funny jokes'. Samuel Brittan described it as 'the most entertaining of the whole post-war series'. On the other hand, the *Spectator* considered it 'far from a personal triumph' and *The Economist* classed it as 'safety first and very little after'. The *Daily Telegraph* called it 'a budget for savers', but Jo Grimond decried it as 'the Monte Carlo budget'.[19] The *Guardian* entitled it 'small change' and reported next day that 'apart from the prospect of a little flutter on the Exchequer, most people seem to be forgetting about the budget already'.

The Government was still anxious about inflation, though its scale was minimal when compared to that of twenty years later. During the early summer of 1956, Macmillan, assisted by Iain Macleod, the Minister of Labour, held a series of private meetings with industrialists and trade-union leaders to urge restraint upon both sides of industry. The Federation of British Industry was critical of Government expenditure, which entailed a correspondingly high level of taxation, and argued that a reduction in spending would be the biggest single contribution the Government could make to curb inflation. The Trade Union Congress considered that the rise in prices made wage restraint impossible. Macmillan had agreed to reduce expenditure and he persuaded the boards of the nationalized industries not to increase the prices of their goods and services. The Federation of British Industries urged a corresponding restraint upon its members; but there was no response from the unions. In September the TUC rejected restraint by an overwhelming majority, and wage rates continued to rise. Nevertheless, savings were increasing as a result of the Budget and the balance of payments, helped by the sale of the Trinidad Oil Company, began to improve, so that by July Macmillan was able to announce a surplus of £144 million.

The problems of the economy were soon to be overshadowed by Colonel Nasser's seizure of the Suez Canal and the momentous events which ensued and which, in the end, destroyed Eden's Government.

20
SUEZ

British troops had occupied Egypt since 1882. They were withdrawn from Cairo in 1947, and from the Canal Zone during 1955 and in the early months of 1956, on the grounds that a military base could not be maintained in a hostile environment. This evacuation was carried out at Eden's instigation under a treaty concluded in 1954, to which Churchill had reluctantly agreed and which was strongly opposed by the right-wing Suez Group in the Conservative Party.

Eden continued to pursue a policy of conciliation towards Egypt, designed to keep Russia out of Africa, and this reached its zenith in December 1955 when the British and American Governments offered to help Nasser improve the irrigation of the Nile valley by building a new dam above Aswan. The World Bank agreed to provide additional finance for this grandiose project, but Anglo-American enthusiasm began to wane when Russia increased her sales of arms to Egypt and was rumoured to have offered an interest-free loan for the construction of the dam.

In March 1956, King Hussein of Jordan, no doubt under pressure from Nasser, summarily dismissed Glubb Pasha, the British creator and commander of the Jordanian army; and, although the Egyptian Government was still seeking financial aid from Britain and America, its radio relayed continuous anti-West propaganda from Cairo.

Disillusionment with the Egyptian dictator was mounting, but the seeds of the Suez conflict – ironically, in view of his subsequent attitude – were sown by Foster Dulles, the American Secretary of State. On 18 July, this gifted but obstinate statesman, brusquely and with minimal tact and finesse, withdrew his offer of the Aswan loan. The British Government was informed of this decision, though not consulted, and announced the withdrawal of its own offer two days later. On 26 July Nasser retaliated by nationalizing the Suez Canal Company, ostensibly as a means of financing the dam by appropriating the Canal dues, although there is evidence that he had decided to do so at an earlier date. His arbitrary action was in contravention not only of the 1888 Treaty of Constantinople but also of the Anglo-Egyptian Treaty of 1954.

British public and Parliamentary opinion was indignant and the pressures on Eden to take a firm line were not confined to the Conservative Party. In the House of Commons Hugh Gaitskell deplored 'this high-handed and totally unjustifiable step by the Egyptian Government'[1] and the whole of the British press, with the exception of the *Guardian*, argued for strong measures. These demands synchronized with Eden's own instinctive reactions. Almost a quarter of the United Kingdom's imports were transported through the Canal and a third of the ships which passed through it were British. The Prime Minister's first concern was the need to safeguard Britain's oil supplies, but the pre-war military adventures of the dictators in Abyssinia, Albania, the Rhineland, Austria and Czechoslovakia were also much in his mind: 'We were determined that the like should not come again. There might be other mistakes, there would not be that one.'[2] Macmillan shared this view and on 27 July described Nasser as 'an Asiatic Mussolini'. The flaw in the Eden–Macmillan comparison with the European dictators was the difference in scale. Nasser's style and language were the same as Hitler's; his military power was relatively insignificant.

The full Cabinet – apart from Butler, who was ill – met the same day and instructed the Chiefs of Staff to prepare a military contingency plan, later to be known as 'Operation Musketeer'. Eisenhower was informed of this by telegram and warned that the British Government was prepared 'in the last resort to use force to bring Nasser to his senses'.[3] Eden appointed a special Cabinet Committee under his own chairmanship to handle the situation. It consisted of Harold Macmillan; Selwyn Lloyd, the Foreign Secretary; Lord Salisbury, the Lord President of the Council; Lord Home, Secretary of State for the Commonwealth; and the Defence Minister, Sir Walter Monckton. The Lord Chancellor, Lord Kilmuir; Alan Lennox-Boyd, the Colonial Secretary; Peter Thorneycroft, the President of the Board of Trade; Anthony Head, Secretary of State for War; and Harold Watkinson, the Minister of Transport, attended from time to time. Rab Butler was not a member of the Committee, although he was present at some of its meetings; he was not in Eden's confidence during the Suez crisis – perhaps because of his lack of enthusiasm for the policy – and his position as the Prime Minister's probable successor was gradually eroded in the eyes of his colleagues. For the first time Macmillan looked like the second-in-command in the Cabinet.

The Foreign Office was cool about any course of action which might be out of line with the United States and the United Nations but, because of his great experience, Eden's word was law in foreign affairs and he dominated the Cabinet on any international issue.

The French reaction to the situation, mainly motivated by Nasser's support for the rebels in Algeria, was the same as the British, except that France was conscious of her close ties with Israel, whereas Britain had to consider her treaty engagements with Jordan. It was agreed, therefore, to treat the Arab–Israeli problem as quite distinct from the future of the Canal. Like Eden, Guy Mollet, the French Prime Minister, his Foreign Minister, Christian Pineau, and the French Defence Minister, Bourgès Maunoury, were in favour of military intervention; they believed that Nasser's destruction was the key to victory in Algeria.

The position of the United States was quite different. Her interests were far less affected by the seizure of the Canal than those of Britain and France. Moreover, Eisenhower was seeking a second term in the Presidential election due in November and believed that a belligerent policy would prejudice his prospects. He sent Robert Murphy, Macmillan's former colleague in Algiers, to London, to discourage impulsive armed action and to 'hold the fort . . . see what it's all about'.[4]

Murphy arrived late on 28 July, saw Selwyn Lloyd the following day and dined with Harold Macmillan at 11 Downing Street on 30 July. The only other guests were the American Chargé d'Affaires and Field Marshal Lord Alexander. Murphy was left in no doubt of the British Government's belief that 'Suez was a test which could be met only by the use of force' and he added, 'I was not surprised at this reaction because it seemed not unjustified.'[5] He was told that the French were prepared to join in a military operation which might start in August. In fact, the report of the Chiefs-of-Staff made it clear that no expedition could be mounted for at least six weeks, and Selwyn Lloyd believed that Macmillan had gone too far in his warning of early armed intervention.[6] He had done this deliberately in the hope of persuading the United States Government to bring pressure on Nasser and so achieve the Anglo-French objective *without* resorting to force, and he acknowledged that 'we certainly did our best to frighten' Murphy.[7] This was apparently successful because, when the American envoy left Downing Street at two a.m., he telegraphed 'a strictly factual account' of the conversation to Eisenhower, as a result of which the President sent Foster Dulles post-haste to London with instructions to prevent military intervention. Dulles arrived on the evening of 31 July, bringing with him a personal letter to Eden from Eisenhower, which stressed 'the unwisdom even of contemplating the use of force at this moment'.[8] Earlier that day Murphy had lunched with Eden, Macmillan, Selwyn Lloyd and Salisbury and had been told by Eden that Britain asked nothing of the United States except that they should 'take care of the Bear'.

Meanwhile, the Prime Minister had stated his position in the House of

Commons. 'No arrangements for the future of this great international water-way', he declared, 'could be acceptable to Her Majesty's Government which would leave it in the unfettered control of a single power which could, as recent events have shown, exploit it purely for purposes of national policy.'[9] No one dissented from this proposition and the Opposition Front Bench gave Eden almost unqualified support. *The Times* leader of 1 August asserted that there could be 'no stability or confidence in the world so long as agreements can be scrapped with impunity'.

Macmillan spent an hour with Dulles soon after his arrival in England and took the opportunity to underline the gravity of the situation from the British point of view. At a later meeting he warned the American Secretary of State that Britain and France would resort to force if diplomatic pressure failed and noted in his diary that 'Dulles had not seemed shocked by this statement'. In another diary entry he reiterated, 'We must keep the Americans really frightened ... then they will help us get what we want without the necessity for force.'[10]

Foster Dulles was a formidable figure, the undisputed arbiter of American foreign policy. He was also devious and disingenuous in the tactics he employed, saying one thing to British Ministers and almost the opposite in the United States. To Selwyn Lloyd he stated that a way had to be found 'to make Nasser disgorge what he is attempting to swallow', but he did not, in his own mind, include force as a method by which this could be achieved and he concealed this reservation from the British Government.[11]

One of the reasons for his attitude, shared to a lesser extent by President Eisenhower, was his intense dislike of colonialism, of which he appeared to think the Anglo-French Suez policy was a form. Another and more personal explanation for the continual misunderstandings which arose was the antipathy, almost animosity, between Dulles and Eden. If they had been friends, the Suez story might have developed differently. No doubt Macmillan, who had a much better relationship with Dulles and a close friendship with Eisenhower, believed that he could influence American policy more effectively than Eden and perhaps he would have been able to do so had he been Prime Minister; but without the main responsibility he could not overcome the different outlook and interests of the two Governments.

On 2 August the Cabinet took the decision, which governed all future policy, that a negotiated settlement should be sought but that, if this failed, force would be used. A debate followed in the House of Commons during which Gaitskell compared Nasser's ambitions with those of Hitler and Mussolini in the years before the war.

On the same day the American, British and French Governments invited the twenty-four principal users of the Canal to send representatives to a conference in London. Only Egypt and Greece declined to attend and the conference took place between 16 and 23 August. Dulles proposed an international board to manage the Canal, to which eighteen of the twenty-two nations agreed, and it was decided to send a mission to Cairo, led by Robert Menzies, the Prime Minister of Australia, and including an American representative, to put the Dulles plan to the Egyptian Government.

While Menzies was away, Macmillan gave the Cabinet an estimate of the modest cost of the precautionary military measures which had been put in hand. The indirect repercussions were more difficult to assess, but the Chancellor forecast that 'so long as America was firmly on our side on the main issue, there would be no flight from the pound'.[12] The proviso was important, but at this stage there seemed no reason to question the United States' financial support. The danger to Britain's oil supplies if Nasser controlled them appeared more serious and more expensive.

In the meantime, after a private interview with Nasser, Menzies – who handled the negotiation with exemplary skill – was making some progress towards a solution. On 5 September his position was fatally undermined as a result of a press statement by President Eisenhower which included the words: 'We are committed to a peaceful settlement of this dispute, nothing else.'[13] Not unnaturally, Nasser took this to mean that the use of force was excluded and that he could reject Menzies' terms with impunity. He promptly did so.

Following this reverse, the Cabinet considered referring the issue to the Security Council of the United Nations, but this was strongly discouraged by Dulles, who declined to support the draft resolution proposed by the British Government. Macmillan acknowledged later that he should have attached more importance to the State Department's attitude, but he still believed that in the long run Britain could rely upon American support. This was a serious miscalculation.

Instead of the reference to the Security Council, Dulles came forward with a new suggestion that a Suez Canal Users Association, known as SCUA, should be formed, which would control the Canal, engage pilots to take ships through it and receive payments for their passage, thus denying to Nasser the profits of his piracy. The British and French Governments agreed to this proposal with reluctance and only because of the importance they attached to close co-operation with the United States.

Parliament had been recalled on 12 September for a two-day debate on the Suez situation and Ministers had to put up with Labour demands that the matter should be taken to the United Nations – the very course they wished to follow and would have followed but for American opposition. Just as the Prime Minister was winding up the debate on the second day, the news came through on the House of Commons tape that, in answer to a question at a press conference, Dulles had said that if American ships were stopped, they would not shoot their way through the Canal but would go round the Cape. This did not augur well for the effectiveness of SCUA and was the second occasion on which American statesmen had torpedoed their own apparent policies.

The Canal Users Conference, which took place later in the month, ended indecisively and was notable only for the wit of a French delegate who, referring to Colonel Nasser, remarked: '*Il faut coloniser le canal ou canaliser le colonel.*' Harold Macmillan told Dulles that he would rather pawn the pictures in the National Gallery than accept humiliation at the hands of Nasser.

On 20 September, Macmillan left for the United States to attend a meeting of the International Monetary Fund. He had a cordial private talk with the President and a less agreeable meeting with Foster Dulles, who was indignant that the British and French Governments had by then announced their intention to take the Suez issue to the Security Council. Dulles expressed the hope that 'nothing serious would happen' until the Presidential election was over and Macmillan wrote later, 'Perhaps I should have attached greater weight' to this.[14]

On 1 October, SCUA re-assembled in London, only to be virtually destroyed by its originator at yet another American press conference on the same day. In answer to a question about whether the Users Association had any real strength, Dulles replied, 'I know of no teeth in it.'

By this time the basic differences in policy, although deliberately disguised by Dulles, should have been apparent. The British Government's wish to go to the Security Council was based upon the realization that Russia would veto the Anglo-French resolution and thus give Britain and France an excuse to use force. Dulles, on the other hand, was determined upon delay, at least until after the American election. His SCUA scheme, described by Paul Johnson as 'the Dulles Double-Cross', could only have been effective if supported by sanctions, which Dulles had no intention of imposing.

After the abortive meeting of the Users Association, Selwyn Lloyd and Pineau left for New York to present the Anglo-French case to the Security Council. A moderately-worded resolution was moved by Lloyd on 5 October and, although eventually passed by every member of the Council except Yugoslavia and Russia, it was vetoed by the Soviet representative on 13 October.

Events now began to move more swiftly to their climax, brought about by the involvement of Israel. She could not use the Canal or even her own port of Eilat and the economic pressures were reinforced by territorial attacks from the neighbouring Arab States. Fedayeen raids increased in scale and frequency during September and October, and Nasser spoke openly of his intention to mount a 'final assault'. To Ben Gurion, the Israeli Prime Minister, a preventive war seemed preferable to the alternative of tamely awaiting an Arab invasion, and this appeared inevitable when Egypt and Syria established a joint command, to which Jordan also adhered. Israel was already receiving substantial supplies of arms from France and by the beginning of September General Moshe Dayan, the Israeli Chief of Staff, was aware (from French sources) of 'Operation Musketeer', the Anglo-French military plan. This was important because only Britain had the bombers that were needed to destroy the Egyptian Air Force.

By this time collaboration between France and Israel was close, but Mollet would not act without Britain and he sent two emissaries, General Challe and Albert Gazier, to England to propose a plan, which was later adopted, for the Israeli offensive and the Anglo-French intervention. Anthony Nutting, then Minister of State at the Foreign Office, gives Sunday, 14 October, as the date of their talk with Eden,[15] and two days later there was a meeting of Ministers, at which Macmillan was present when the Mollet plan was discussed. It was supported by Macmillan and Kilmuir, though opposed by Monckton and Nutting. When Selwyn Lloyd arrived back from New York the same morning, he was at first doubtful about the wisdom of Mollet's proposal, but Eden's approval of it prevailed and he and Lloyd flew to Paris that afternoon to see Mollet and Pineau. On 22 October, Ben Gurion and General Dayan met the French Ministers at Sèvres near Paris, where they were joined later by Selwyn Lloyd.

Macmillan does not mention these meetings in his memoirs, although he was presumably aware of them, but Moshe Dayan gives an account of the Sèvres discussions in his own autobiography.[16] He records that the French Ministers were handed a memorandum signed by Eden and intended for the Israelis, which stated that after the Israeli advance into Sinai, Britain and France would demand the withdrawal of both Egypt and Israel from the Canal area. If Egypt refused, the Anglo-French forces would intervene to restore the free operation of the Canal. This would provide the legal and moral justification for the allied invasion. Britain would only join the enterprise if she could appear as an intermediary to restore peace. Selwyn Lloyd evidently found this meeting with the Israeli leaders distasteful and he did not stay long at Sèvres; he left Sir Patrick Dean to draw up and sign a document incorporating the agreement which had been reached.

It seems probable that the only civil servants who were fully informed of the Suez policy were Sir Ivone Kirkpatrick, the Permanent Secretary at the Foreign Office, Sir Norman Brook, the Secretary of the Cabinet, and Patrick

Dean. Sir Humphrey (now Lord) Trevelyan, the British Ambassador in Egypt, was not consulted and nor, apparently, was Sir Gladwyn Jebb (now Lord Gladwyn), the Ambassador in Paris. Lord Gore-Booth recorded that 'Just as Mr Chamberlain did not choose to have full advice from the Foreign Office in 1938, so did Sir Anthony Eden tragically avoid it in 1956 . . . [he] did not so much reject advice as decline to hear it.'[17]

The British Cabinet met on 24 and 25 October, and endorsed the arrangements which Eden and Lloyd had made. Only Monckton seems to have objected, although Macleod and Heathcoat Amory had misgivings and Butler was never fully in sympathy with Eden's policy. In fact, there were two strands of opinion in the Cabinet; both supported the Prime Minister's policy, but the aims of each were different. One section, led by Macmillan, concurred with Eden's anti-dictator line against Nasser, the other was anxious only to save the Canal and to internationalize it. At first these divergent attitudes were unobtrusive; they became more marked as events unfolded.

There is no doubt that, in the planning of the Suez campaign, collusion between France and Israel was complete. Britain and France were closely and openly allied from the first day of the crisis until the last; in the end overt co-operation with the French involved Britain in France's covert co-operation with Israel. In his last speech in the House of Commons, Eden denied any foreknowledge of the Israeli attack upon Egypt. This was no doubt true until October; it was not a candid account of later developments. It is certain that Macmillan, who always gave strong support to the Prime Minister's policy, was fully in his confidence; but collusion is not necessarily reprehensible if, as in this case, its perpetrators were acting in what they believed to be the national interest. There was nothing disreputable in the Government's plans or intentions, but there were mistakes in the handling of them.

Macmillan acknowledged one of these and accepted his full share of the responsibility for it:

The British Cabinet certainly made a profound miscalculation as to the likely reaction in Washington to the Franco-British intervention. . . . We altogether failed to appreciate the force of the resentment which would be directed against us. For this I carry a heavy responsibility. I knew Eisenhower well . . . and I thought I understood his character. I had also enjoyed . . . a close association with Dulles . . . I believed the Americans would issue a protest . . . in public; but that they would in their hearts be glad to see the matter brought to a conclusion.[18]

This was certainly the view of the Cabinet. United Nations and Commonwealth criticism was predictable, but Ministers did not expect the degree of American hostility they encountered. They hoped the United States would at least be neutral, if only because of the identity of interest in maintaining stability in the Middle East and protecting the flank which the Communists were always anxious to turn. As Chancellor of the Exchequer, Macmillan can, however, be criticized for not having realized that American support, or at least neutrality, was essential if an economic crisis was to be avoided. He of all people should have foreseen the financial danger.

Israel mobilized on 25 October and launched her Sinai offensive on 29 October. Identical notes were then sent to Egypt and Israel, demanding their withdrawal to ten miles on either side of the Canal. The United States Government was given no advance warning of the Anglo-French ultimatum, partly because an unwelcome attempt would certainly have been made to discourage its despatch, partly on security grounds, and partly because it was thought that to be informed but not consulted would be more embarrassing for the Americans than to know nothing.

The Security Council met on 30 October, and the American spokesman moved a resolution condemning the Israeli aggression and urging all members of the United Nations to refrain from force or the threat of force. The resolution received seven votes, with abstentions by Australia and Belgium. Britain and France voted against it and used the veto for the first time in the history of British membership of the United Nations.

On 31 October, Egypt rejected the Anglo-French note and the British Cabinet authorized 'Operation Musketeer'. Air bombing-attacks against military targets were launched from the British bases in Cyprus, Malta and Aden, and within twenty-four hours the Egyptian Air Force had been virtually destroyed; but the nearest deep-water port from which to embark the ground troops was Malta, nearly a thousand miles and six days' steaming from Port Said, and during the whole of this time international opinion was mounting against Britain and France.

Foster Dulles obtained an emergency meeting of the United Nations Assembly on 2 November and moved a resolution demanding a cease-fire which was passed by 64 votes to 5, with 6 abstentions. Only Britain, France, Israel, Australia and New Zealand voted against it.

Following the re-assembly of Parliament after the summer recess, the House of Commons was in almost continuous session. Opposition approval in July had turned to growing hostility by October and as the Government's support for the Israeli attack on Egypt became obvious, the anger of the Labour Party increased. Feeling on both sides ran high and the uproar was so strong and sustained that on one occasion the Speaker was obliged to suspend the sitting to allow tempers to cool. As Cabinet and Ministerial statements became increasingly frequent, the Government sometimes seemed to be only an hour or two ahead of the House of Commons.

On 4 November, Lester Pearson, the Foreign Minister of Canada, brought forward a new UN resolution which proposed the organization of an international force 'to secure and supervise the cessation of hostilities'. Meanwhile, the Israelis had won a series of brilliant victories in Sinai against better-equipped Egyptian troops, and had gained all their main objectives. On 5 November, British and French paratroops occupied the Gamil airfield and Port Fuad, and the next day the assault forces arrived from Malta. They took Port Said without difficulty and advanced twenty-three miles to El Cap. The Commander-in-Chief estimated that he could have occupied Ismailia by 8 November and Suez by 12 November, but fighting between Israel and Egypt had just ended and the Cabinet ordered a cease-fire at midnight on 6 November and British acceptance of the UN force.

The official explanation, put forward by Eden and endorsed by Macmillan, was: 'We had intervened to divide and above all to contain the conflict. The occasion for our intervention was over, the fire was out. Once the fighting had ceased, justification for intervention ceased with it.'[19] This was what Selwyn Lloyd rightly described as 'the ostensible reason'.[20] Had the motive for going in been simply to separate the combatants, this reason for ending the hostilities would have been plausible and would have been generally accepted, but Eden's real objectives were to topple Nasser and to secure the Canal, neither of which had been achieved. Having used the ostensible reason to defend the Government's action, it was difficult to continue down the Canal once the fighting had ceased. Some people supposed that Russian threats to intervene in support of Egypt had played a part in the Cabinet's decision, but there is no evidence that these were ever taken seriously.

The real reason for the cease-fire was the run on the pound. This had developed with increasing momentum over the previous three months, culminating in a fall in the reserves of over $270 million in the first few days of November. The United States Government now played the financial card and refused to help Britain in any way until an announcement had been made of her intention to withdraw from the Canal zone. The International Monetary Fund declined, under American influence, to grant Britain a loan or even to allow her to withdraw her own money from the Fund until a cease-fire had been agreed. It was Macmillan's duty as Chancellor of the Exchequer to warn his colleagues of this grievous situation and he did so on 6 November. Selwyn Lloyd recorded: 'Macmillan strongly advocated accepting the cease-fire both to me privately beforehand and at the Cabinet meeting';[21] and R.A. Butler recalled that the Chancellor had 'switched almost overnight from being the foremost protagonist of intervention to being the leading influence for disengagement'.[22] Disarmingly, Macmillan acknowledged:

I have often been reproached for having been at the same time one of the most keen supporters of strong action in the Middle East and one of the most rapid to withdraw when that policy met a serious check. 'First in, first out' was to be the elegant criticism of one of my chief Labour critics on many subsequent occasions.[23]

As Randolph Churchill asked in an article in the *Evening Standard* at the time: 'What was the difference between Rab Butler, who never wanted to go in, and Harold Macmillan, who took the Cabinet out?' The difference was to be one of the factors in the Party's choice of a successor when Eden retired two months later.

There was an excited meeting of the 1922 Committee in December, when the robust line taken by Macmillan was so much more in tune with the mood of the Parliamentary Party than Butler's more equivocal attitude. 'I held the Tory Party for the weekend. It was all I intended to do,' said Macmillan later that evening.[24] It sounded a somewhat cynical comment after the inspiring speech he had just made. In fact he had struck the right note at the right moment: the Members desperately wanted a touch of Palmerstonian language, if only to restore their pride and self-confidence. Timing is the essence of politics, as of so many other things in life, and Macmillan had sensed the need to restore the morale of the Party.

There were some Conservative opponents of the policy, like Nigel Nicolson, who never wanted to go into Suez, and several others who did not want to come out, but only eight Tories abstained when the House divided on 8 November and there were only two resignations from the Government – those of Anthony Nutting and Sir Edward Boyle.

The strain of Suez took a heavy toll of Eden's health. As early as 5 October, when preparations for the invasion were in progress, he suffered a severe attack of fever with a temperature of 105°F. He was not a good delegator, so was overworked and short of sleep and, as the crisis developed, he became mentally and physically exhausted. Clarissa Eden told her friends that it felt as though the Suez Canal was flowing through her drawing-room at Downing Street. During November, Eden's 1954 symptoms recurred. His doctors decided that he could no longer live on a diet of stimulants and tranquillizers and persuaded him to take a complete rest. He flew to Jamaica on 23 November, leaving Butler in charge of the Government; he always claimed, however, that his ill-health did not affect his policy and it is improbable that he would have acted differently if he had been well.

It cannot be denied that, due to the attitude of the United States Government, the Suez enterprise, though a tactical success, had proved a strategic failure. Control of the Canal reverted to Nasser, who soon refused passage to Israeli ships and cargoes; and the Arab–Israeli problem remained unsolved.

Perhaps the real criticism of Eden's policy is not that it was immoral, but that it was out of date. His thinking was conditioned by the events of the 1930s and he did not take fully into account the decline in Britain's economic, military and political power which followed the Second World War. His motives were patriotic and his actions courageous, but they were almost an anachronism by the 1950s.

Macmillan shared these views and strongly supported the policy which flowed from them, but he was quick to learn the lesson that, even in co-operation with a country the size of France, Britain could no longer take a major military initiative in defiance of world opinion and without the support or at least the neutral goodwill of the United States.

Throughout November and December there was a series of post-mortem debates in the House of Commons, in which Macmillan played his full part in defence of the Government's policy. The Opposition's attacks were led by Gaitskell and Aneurin Bevan and the barrage of noise and recrimination from the Back Benches was on a scale the House was not to see again until the ill-fated labour-relations legislation in the 1970 Parliament. During this and the earlier Suez period, the Chief Whip, Edward Heath, showed great skill in keeping the Parliamentary Party together and proved himself a most efficient Staff Officer. Eden went so far as to describe him as 'the best Chief Whip the Party has ever had'.[25]

A phased withdrawal from Suez of the British and French forces began early in December, and by the end of the month the last British troops had left Egyptian soil. Even before this, Dulles, who had done more than anyone to ensure the failure of the Anglo-French policy, told Lloyd and Pineau that they had been right and added: 'Why did you stop? Why didn't you go through with it and get Nasser down?'[26] As an example of nauseating hypocrisy this could scarcely have been bettered.

Eden returned to England on 14 December, apparently restored to health, but he was sleeping badly, and after Christmas suffered another bout of fever, which lingered on into the New Year. These attacks were debilitating and made it impossible for him to undertake a full day's work or the responsibility of running the Government and making important decisions. He was advised by his doctors that the fevers were likely to recur with increasing intensity. In view of this he felt he had no choice and must resign at once so that his successor could form a Government and be ready to face Parliament when it re-assembled after the Christmas recess.

On 8 January the Prime Minister telephoned Butler to tell him of this decision and then left for Sandringham to inform the Queen. The next day she returned to Buckingham Palace and Eden called there that evening to tender his resignation. Before doing so, he invited Macmillan to see him at

Downing Street and a Cabinet was called for five p.m. to inform his other colleagues. Briefly and with dignity he told them his decision. Salisbury spoke with some emotion of their long friendship and Butler and Macmillan said a few words. The short meeting ended with Eden bidding farewell to each of his Ministers individually.

Over twenty years before, Stanley Baldwin, who was then Prime Minister, had predicted to Duncan Sandys, 'Chamberlain will be your leader for a short time. Then Anthony will have a long reign.'[27] In fact, Eden was Prime Minister for only one year and nine months.

Despite Macmillan's many tributes to Eden in his memoirs, the two men were never close friends. Their characters were very different and they were temperamentally incompatible, so their relationship was often edgy and there was little real affinity between them. Eden's vanity grated on Macmillan – he thought Anthony emotional and self-centred and his reactions feminine, fussy and too intuitive.

Macmillan was three years older and may have been a little envious of Eden's rapid rise to Foreign Secretary in the pre-war decade when he was himself still a Back-Bencher. As Minister Resident in the Mediterranean during the Second World War, although nominally answerable to the Foreign Office, Macmillan reported directly to Churchill on any matter of importance. This arrangement was made to work without evident friction, but it was not always an easy partnership. When Macmillan became Foreign Secretary himself in 1955, he resented the new Prime Minister's interference in foreign policy and they did not work harmoniously together.

Their interests outside politics were also different. Macmillan's only recreations were reading and shooting. He enjoyed good conversation in the companionship of intelligent men in a club atmosphere. Both men were cultured and well read, but Eden seldom used clubs and did not care for shooting.

Each was a brilliant diplomatist, but by nature and training Eden was a conciliator, not a man of action. He was at his best as a second-in-command, Macmillan as a leader. It was unfortunate that, during Eden's premiership, their respective roles were inevitably the opposite of their natural qualities, so neither made his best contribution. Eden, whose charm and beautiful manners were proverbial and irresistible, was (at least outwardly) warmer and more extrovert. He inspired more personal affection, Macmillan more respect and admiration; and although I called Eden by his Christian name I would not have ventured to address Macmillan by his.

There were frequent and mutual surface irritations, but their shared experience of the First World War made a lasting bond between them. Macmillan always acknowledged Eden's skill and experience as a negotiator and respected his courage in the First World War and his resignation before the Second World War. In the later years, after Eden had retired from public life, their friendship was closer than when they had worked together in Government.

21

PRIME MINISTER:
THE FIRST YEAR

The succession lay between Harold Macmillan and Rab Butler. There were no other contenders for the Conservative crown and the issue was swiftly resolved by the initiative of Lord Salisbury and Lord Kilmuir, on which they had agreed before the meeting of Eden's last Cabinet. When Butler and Macmillan had withdrawn, the Lord President of the Council and the Lord Chancellor invited the other members of the Cabinet to wait behind for individual interviews. This seemed an appropriate procedure for ascertaining the views of their colleagues, since both were senior members of the Government and neither was a candidate for the leadership. Their concern was to obtain a speedy decision on which to base the Cabinet's advice to the Queen without infringing the exercise of her prerogative. Discretion was maintained by choosing Salisbury's room in the Privy Council offices as the venue, since this could be reached without leaving the building.

The story of the short interviews has often been told, but is perhaps worth repeating. Lord Kilmuir related later that almost every member of the Cabinet observed, as he entered the room, that it was 'like coming to the headmaster's study'.[1] The procedure was as simple as it was neutral and no attempt was made to influence anyone's opinion. Lord Salisbury found it difficult to pronounce the letter R, so his question to each Minister in turn was: 'Well, which is it to be, Wab or Hawold?' A large majority of the Cabinet favoured Macmillan.

Rab Butler was, perhaps understandably, a little critical of the method which had been adopted. He commented that 'Cabinet Ministers were "corralled" to give an immediate judgement . . .' and that 'Selwyn Lloyd objected to this procedure being carried out by two peers.'[2] It is not obvious who else could have discharged the task.

Before reporting to the Queen, Salisbury and Kilmuir saw Edward Heath, the Chief Whip, and Oliver Poole (later Lord Poole), the chairman of the Conservative Party Organization, in order to test the feeling in the Parliamentary Party and in the constituency Associations. John Morrison, the chairman of the 1922 Committee, telephoned his assessment from the Isle of Islay next morning. Back Bench opinion, as reported by Heath and Morrison, endorsed that of the Cabinet and no doubt it was representative even of those whose personal preference was neither volunteered nor invited.

The Queen's acceptance of Eden's resignation was announced that evening and Salisbury called at Buckingham Palace next morning to convey the collective advice of the Cabinet and the Parliamentary Party. The Queen also consulted both Sir Winston Churchill and Sir Anthony Eden before announcing a decision. Churchill was pleased to be summoned, and he advised the Queen to send for Macmillan. He told Rab Butler afterwards, 'I supported the older man.' [3] No doubt this was one of the reasons, but he must also have been influenced by the fact that he and Macmillan had been associated in friendship and policy since before the war while Butler was defending Chamberlain against Churchill's oratory. He had given Macmillan his first ministerial appointment and thought highly of his work in the Mediterranean and at the Ministry of Housing. When John Colville asked Churchill why he had recommended Macmillan, he replied: 'Harold is more decisive.' This was true and may have been the real reason for Churchill's advice.

Although Parliament was in recess at the time of Eden's resignation, anyone in close touch with Conservative opinion in the House of Commons should have known that Macmillan was the Party's probable choice as his successor. It is therefore surprising that on the morning of 10 January most of the newspapers made the wrong assessment. The *Daily Express*, the *Daily Mail*, the *Daily Herald*, the *Daily Mirror* and the *News Chronicle* all predicted that Butler would become Prime Minister; only Randolph Churchill in the *Evening Standard* suggested that Macmillan had the better prospects, and this was due to Beaverbrook's sources of information rather than his own. When he reported 'I think it's going to be Butler,' his employer replied, 'You said Macmillan, didn't you? That's right,' and put down the telephone.[4] Churchill took the tip and altered his article. *The Times* was ambivalent: its political correspondent doubted if Butler would be acceptable to the Right wing of the Party, but the leading article considered that, as 'the hope and leader of the younger Conservatives', he was the most likely choice. The *Manchester Guardian*, after weighing the pros and cons, came to the conclusion that 'Suez apart, it would be astounding if in present circumstances Mr Butler was not given the first invitation to form a Government.'

There is no doubt that his attitude over Suez depreciated Butler's standing both in the Cabinet and in the Parliamentary Party. This was especially true of the so-called Suez Group, who criticized his assumed opposition to the military intervention in Egypt and his reputedly lukewarm support of action after it had been taken. Even those MPs who agreed with him were critical, though to a lesser extent, of his apparent lack of resolution. They thought he should have carried his disapproval to the point of resignation. This was a misjudgement of his character. He is not always certain that he is right and his temperament is not that of a man who would be ready to resign if his counsel in Cabinet does not prevail. He believes in the need for compromise in politics and would never have divided the Party at so crucial a time.

Those best qualified to decide between two rival claimants to the leadership are undoubtedly their closest colleagues who have worked with them both for several years, and it is probable that Macmillan would have been the Cabinet's choice even if Suez had never happened. But it was certainly a weight in the scales against Butler and this was not only because of his ambiguous and non-committal support for Eden's policy. The Conservative Party was distressed and embarrassed by the Suez failure. One of the factors, therefore, in the choice of a new leader was the need to select the man most likely to heal the Party's wounded pride, to restore its self-confidence and to unite its membership. As the *Daily Telegraph* put it with hindsight, once the issue had been decided, 'Mr Macmillan is undoubtedly the best available choice when the first essential duty of the Party is to close its ranks.'

It would have been more difficult to reconcile the Right wing to Butler than for the Left wing to accept Macmillan, the author of *The Middle Way*. 'Butskellism', though agreeable to some, was disliked by others as an erosion of Conservative principles. In fact, as his premiership developed, Macmillan led the Party from a position which was well to the left of centre, but he knew instinctively when to make Right-wing speeches. Butler was far more suspect in the eyes of traditional Tories and, certainly in the aftermath of Suez, would have found it harder to hold the Party together.

It may not be out of place at this decisive moment in Macmillan's life to make an assessment of his personal and working relationship with Butler and of the different qualities and characters of the two men. Butler's early career, though less meteoric, was not unlike Eden's. He was ten years younger than Macmillan, but had several years' ministerial experience – at the India Office and at the Foreign Office – before Macmillian joined the Government for the first time in 1940.

Butler noted that Macmillan 'had spent much of his early life as a rebel, while I was a member of the . . . establishment'.[5] He believed, no doubt correctly, that this underlined a difference of temperament and may also have influenced their future relationship. 'In political philosophy', Butler wrote, 'we were not far apart. I admired, for the most part, the economic doctrines of *The Middle Way*, which he still espoused, and a great deal of the intellectual background of the Industrial Charter was due to him. Along with David

Eccles . . . he affected its positive content more than my other helpers on the Committee.' Macmillan paid a corresponding tribute to the chairman of this important policy group: 'I recall with admiration the skill with which Butler presided over our discussions and steered us through many difficulties.'[6]

Throughout the two post-war decades during which they worked together, sometimes in close co-operation, sometimes as rivals, there were seldom any serious differences of policy between them. There was, however, a total difference of style. Macmillan was more ambitious, more ruthless and more conscious of the political attitudes of the Parliamentary Party, which would influence his ascent of 'the greasy pole'. Butler's first wife, Sydney, might have pushed him to the top had she lived longer. She was a Courtauld by birth and, as Harold Macmillan commented, 'she was a brilliant woman of very strong character. If she had been a man, she would have run Courtauld's'[7] – he might have added 'or Downing Street'. Rab Butler's second wife, Mollie, a warmer personality of great charm, was perhaps as ambitious for him, but she lacked Sydney's political force and she loved him too deeply to drive him further or faster than he wanted to go.

By contrast, Macmillan did not need anyone's help. The steel was in himself and, once his success in North Africa and the Mediterranean had convinced him of his own potential, no one could have prevented its ultimate realization. He considered Butler an excellent colleague: 'Rab has a very good if somewhat academic mind', he once said, 'and he was more instrumental than anyone in creating the left-of-centre policy we both pursued.' [8]

Butler had greater intellectual subtlety, but whereas each could see both sides of a question, this tended to make Butler sound equivocal while Macmillan, a more determined character, was always able to choose the course which would suit him best. Macmillan never sacrificed principle or wavered in the sincerity of his convictions, but he knew when not to speak in a speculative way. Although they were both good administrators, Butler was a thinker rather than a doer. Macmillan combined the two; he spoke the language of an intellectual, but was more decisive in action and had an instinctive political flair which Butler sometimes seemed to lack. As a leader of Conservative thought in his generation, Butler was outstanding; but Macmillan was not only a leader of thought, he was a leader of men.

While his fate was being decided by his colleagues and his sovereign, Macmillan thought it wise to remain at 11 Downing Street, lest it should be imagined that he was canvassing for support. Instead of going to the Treasury, he passed the time re-reading *Pride and Prejudice*, which he described as 'very soothing'. He had a facility for switching his mind away from any problem he could not influence, and books were always his solace in times of stress. At noon on 10 January, Sir Michael (now Lord) Adeane, the Queen's Private

Secretary, telephoned to ask him to be at the Palace by two o'clock. Lady Dorothy was so worried about the illness of one of her grandchildren that she did not immediately appreciate the significance of the summons and, on being informed of it, her first reaction was to ask 'What do *they* want?'

Despite the Conservative majority of fifty-eight in the House of Commons, some people wondered if, faced with the serious post-Suez situation, the new Government could last long, and Harold Macmillan, only half in jest, warned the Queen during an audience with her that he could not guarantee that it would survive for more than six weeks. She reminded him of this remark at an audience six years later. It is of interest that it was not until he had been Prime Minister for four months that Macmillan asked John Wyndham, who had retired a year earlier, to rejoin his staff. In a letter dated 27 May 1957 he wrote: 'The fact is that I did not really think my Administration could last more than a few weeks.'[9] He would have invited Wyndham sooner and would certainly not have written in this way to such a close friend if he had not himself believed that his Government was at risk in the early months. In fact, the degree of the Conservative depression was an advantage to the new leader; things could hardly get worse and the state of disarray was itself a unifying influence in the Parliamentary Party.

On his return to Downing Street, Macmillan at once went to work on the formation of his Government. He well understood how disappointed Butler must be and realized the importance of co-operation between them in uniting the Party. In his own account, he wrote that Rab had 'the right to whatever post he might choose, in addition to the leadership of the House of Commons'.[10] It is clear, however, that Butler would have liked to go to the Foreign Office, where he thought he could be useful in mending the many ruptured friendships in the aftermath of the Suez adventure.[11] Understandably, Macmillan did not feel able to replace Selwyn Lloyd, since to have done so would have given the impression that the Eden–Lloyd policy had been a mistake. Instead, he offered Butler the Home Office and was relieved when he accepted it.

To facilitate this, Gwilym Lloyd George, the former Home Secretary, retired to the House of Lords, as did Walter Monckton and Macmillan's brother-in-law, James Stuart, who had been Secretary of State for Scotland. Peter Thorneycroft became Chancellor of the Exchequer and was succeeded at the Board of Trade by Sir David (now Viscount) Eccles. Lord Hailsham was the new Minister of Education and, on the retirement of Anthony Head, Duncan Sandys became Minister of Defence. Henry Brooke followed Sandys at Housing, and Jack Maclay, Harold Watkinson and Charles Hill all entered the Cabinet. The only other new addition to it was Macmillan's old friend, Sir Percy Mills, who was not a Member of Parliament and was therefore given a peerage and made Minister of Power. The list was complete by 13 January and the Prime Minister's next task was the appointment of Ministers outside the Cabinet, including Ernest Marples as Postmaster-General and Edward Boyle, whom Macmillan had persuaded to return to the Government, as Parliamentary Secretary to the Ministry of Education.

On the evening of his appointment, the new Prime Minister took his Chief Whip, Edward Heath, out to dinner at the Turf Club, where they ate game pie and drank a bottle of champagne. In recounting the episode, Macmillan wrote: 'Some of the critics suggested that a fatal choice had been made between the rival candidates. In Smith Square – the Butler home – there would have been plain living and high thinking.'[12]

The ritual Party meeting to elect the new leader was held in Church Hall, Westminster, on 22 January. It was attended by the Conservative hierarchy of about a thousand people, drawn from those taking the whip in the Lords and Commons, the Executive Committee of the National Union and the adopted Conservative candidates. Lord Salisbury presided and moved a resolution to accept with regret the resignation of Anthony Eden. This was seconded by Walter Elliot, the senior Privy Councillor present in the absence of Winston Churchill. Harold Macmillan's election as leader of the Party was proposed by Salisbury, seconded by Butler and supported by Sir Eric Errington, the chairman of the Executive of the National Union. It was passed unanimously.

Macmillan then addressed the meeting. After a tribute to Eden's courage and integrity and a well-known quotation from Disraeli, he said that 'We have never been, and I trust that while I am your leader we never will be, a Party of any class or sectional interest. . . . We believe that unless we give opportunity to the strong and able we shall never have the means to provide real protection for the weak and old.'[13] The same afternoon he spoke in the House of Commons for the first time as Prime Minister. His leadership of the nation, which was to last for six years and nine months, had begun.

No description of the way in which Macmillan worked would be complete without an account of the Private Office, its occupants and its atmosphere. The team at 10 Downing Street was a small one in those days and consisted of only four Private Secretaries. They were hand-picked for their intelligence and they respected Macmillan's. They also liked him and enjoyed working for him. He was quick, decisive and, unlike Anthony Eden, a good delegator, who told them clearly what he wanted done; their job was to find the best way of doing it. Macmillan took a little time to get used to any new arrival in the office, but once he had confidence in members of his staff, he disliked them leaving to be promoted. This was especially so in the case of his first Principal Private Secretary, Freddie Bishop, who, after two years with the

Prime Minister, became Deputy Secretary of the Cabinet. He was an able and efficient adjutant and it was almost a year before Macmillan fully accepted his admirable successor, Tim Bligh, on whom, however, he thereafter greatly relied.

Philip de Zulueta, who was the Foreign Affairs Private Secretary, remained at Downing Street for the whole duration of Macmillan's premiership and served him superbly well. On the home affairs side, Neil Cairncross was there for the first eighteen months and was then succeeded by Anthony Phelps and later by Philip Woodfield. It was an effective and harmonious team.

Apart from de Zulueta, the only Private Secretary who was with the Prime Minister throughout was John Wyndham. He had worked for Macmillan at the Ministry of Supply, the Colonial Office, in the Mediterranean and at the Foreign Office, but had retired when his chief became Chancellor of the Exchequer because he was in negotiation with the Treasury at the time over the payment of family death duties and thought it improper to be working for the head of the Department, lest it should be thought that he was being given unduly favourable treatment. Wyndham's position was a rather special one. He was, in a sense, an amateur, and neither needed nor accepted any remuneration, though he did his full share of the work and was regarded by the Civil Service secretaries as an asset to and a most helpful member of the Private Office. He was amusing and agreeable, sharing Macmillan's sense of humour, and they enjoyed each other's company, but it is improbable that he had, or even sought, any influence on higher policy.

One of the most valuable members of Macmillan's staff was his Press Officer, Harold Evans, who was with him for the whole period of the premiership. The Prime Minister had appointed Charles Hill (now Lord Hill of Luton) as Chancellor of the Duchy of Lancaster with special responsibility for co-ordinating the Government's public relations, and Evans acted as adviser to them both. He was a most fortunate choice because, although Macmillan appreciated the importance of good public relations, he did not like dealing with journalists, and found press conferences crude and somewhat distasteful. He therefore left this side of the work to Evans and the arrangement worked well and suited them both.

Harold Evans was a remarkably effective Press Officer, perhaps the most successful who has ever held this position. He was in daily contact with the Lobby, gave the political correspondents a quick and straightforward answer to their questions and never told them an untruth. This soon became known and was relied upon and appreciated. He knew the background and always had the fullest information at his fingertips, although he seldom received a formal briefing unless he deliberately sought the Prime Minister's guidance; they simply had a gossip from time to time. This was typical of Macmillan's

Daniel Macmillan (1813–1852), Harold
Macmillan's grandfather.

Harold at the age of eleven.

Lady Dorothy and Harold Macmillan leaving St Margaret's, Westminster, after
their wedding in April 1920.

Lady Dorothy and Harold Macmillan in the early 1920s.

Anthony Eden, Winston Churchill and Harold Macmillan in North Africa, 1943.

Macmillan at Birch Grove House when he was Foreign Secretary.

Selwyn Lloyd, President Eisenhower, Harold Macmillan and Foster Dulles, Bermuda Conference, 1957.

Macmillan and Khrushchev in Moscow, 1959.

The Prime Minister at his desk in
10 Downing Street.

Harold Macmillan's Cabinet in October 1959. Left to right, sitting: John Maclay, Lord Home, Selwyn Lloyd, R.A. Butler, Harold Macmillan, Lord Kilmuir, Derick Heathcote Amory, Alan Lennox-Boyd and Lord Hailsham. Standing: Dr Charles Hill, Geoffrey Lloyd, Lord Mills, Henry Brooke, Iain Macleod, Duncan Sandys, Sir David Eccles, Harold Watkinson, John Hare, Reginald Maudling and Sir Norman Brook, Secretary of the Cabinet.

ABOVE: Macmillan and Duncan Sandys in June 1963.

LEFT: The 1959 General Election.

As Chancellor of Oxford University receiving Her Majesty The Queen.

Harold with his son Maurice at Birch Grove.

At a pheasant shoot during the
winter of 1969–70.

Harold Macmillan and Margaret
Thatcher at the Carlton Club in
1979.

method of working. He liked talking informally to people he knew well and could trust, and he was always accessible. He wanted his staff to know his mind, so that he did not have to explain his thoughts in detail on specific subjects. It was one of the reasons for his reluctance to part with a Private Secretary and start anew with someone he had scarcely met.

During his time as Prime Minister, Macmillan had three Parliamentary Private Secretaries. Bobby (later Lord) Allan was with him for the first year and Tony (later Lord) Barber for the next. Both were good, especially Barber, but they were also qualified for and received promotion, so Macmillan next looked for someone older who would not expect political preferment. His choice fell on Knox Cunningham, an Ulster Unionist Member, who served him loyally for four years. When Barber was recommended for Ministerial office as Economic Secretary to the Treasuary, he offered to stay on as Parliamentary Private Secretary because he enjoyed it so much. For a politician on the way up, this genuine reaction was a remarkable tribute to Macmillan personally and to the happy atmosphere in the Private Office.

Macmillan relied greatly on this small entourage of personal assistants, trusted them implicitly and was closer to them than to most of his Cabinet colleagues. They were serviced by the duty clerks, and the occupants of the 'Garden Room' (so called because it faced the garden of No. 10), a team of efficient young women who worked as shorthand-typists on a twenty-four-hour rota for the Prime Minister and his private secretaries.

There were few rules or directives, except that work coming into the office had to be dealt with on the same day unless there was a very good reason for delay. At the initial interview after his appointment, a new arrival was almost made to feel that he was doing the Prime Minister a favour by accepting the post and the only admonition he was likely to receive was 'I hate long sentences'.

As far as his staff were concerned, Harold Macmillan, unlike Churchill and Eden, kept office hours – perhaps because of his earlier business training. He was personally conscientious and worked late, or woke early in the morning to deal with his boxes, but he did not expect anyone to stay and go through them with him. The boxes were open for submissions throughout the day and were closed at night by the private secretary on late duty, who gave them to a messenger to put in the Prime Minister's bedroom. Macmillan read and absorbed documents quickly, and annotated each as briefly as possible, sometimes with a simple 'Yes' or 'No'. The boxes were always ready when the staff arrived in the office next morning; but, like Churchill, Macmillan stayed in bed as long as he could, drafting instructions or in discussion with his secretaries. He often held morning meetings, lasting about half an hour, with the Chief Whip, the principal Private Secretary, the Parliamentary

Private Secretary, and sometimes with the Secretary of the Cabinet. He had a sure instinct for what should be dealt with immediately and what it would be wiser to postpone.

In addition to the official boxes, there were two other receptacles in the office. One was called 'the Dip' and contained copies of all the letters and minutes written the day before, so that each Private Secretary could dip in to see what his colleagues had done about matters in which he was not himself directly involved. The other container was described as the 'Bits and Pieces' or 'Discard' box, into which were put any unused or unreported passages from the Prime Minister's previous speeches or any new ideas for future speeches. Over a drink in the Members' Smoking-Room one evening, Macmillan surprised Harold Wilson by enquiring 'Do you have a discard box?'

The prevailing atmosphere at 10 Downing Street, established by the Prime Minister himself, was one of complete calm. He wrote out and hung on the door between the Cabinet room and the Private Secretaries' room the quotation, 'Quiet, calm deliberation disentangles every knot.' This was the attitude he wished to inculcate in his colleagues and staff and, in its striking contrast to the regime of his predecessor, it had a good effect. It quickly became known to a wider circle and was no doubt the foundation of the reputation for being 'unflappable' which he soon acquired. In fact, his own precept may sometimes have been more difficult for Macmillan himself to follow than for those who worked with him. Whatever the outward appearance, he was nervous and on edge over a major speech and, if he had to eat before making it, he preferred a ham sandwich and a whisky and soda to a proper meal. He worried more than he seemed to and although he made a conscious effort to appear calm, this was not always how he felt and was achieved by self-control and self-discipline. Once he had made a decision he never brooded over it; he simply retired to his study and read a book.

Macmillan thought ahead more than most Ministers and made time to do so. He talked frankly and freely to his Private Secretaries, not merely about immediate issues but about the possible consequences of new policies, and he often asked their advice. He was adventurous in conversation and used them as a sounding-board for ideas, half-fantasy, half-serious, which had just come into his head. He enjoyed thinking and talking in a broad, historical context, often till late at night, and was always fascinating to listen to. There are few better conversationalists, but the quality of expression is less evident in the written word, and his memoirs, in this respect, are disappointing.

There was one small mannerism, noticed by everyone who worked with him. Whenever he was bored, irritated or annoyed, he drummed his right foot on the floor, and a Private Secretary, who was uncertain about the reception of a suggestion or submission, had only to look under the table to see if the Prime Minister's foot was tapping.

Macmillan was approachable and kind to those who worked for him; John Wyndham wrote of his 'gentleness'. To people who knew him less well, however, he could be awe-inspiring, but he was equable in manner, appreciative of the help he received and considerate about the impact of the work on the personal lives of his staff. They all loved working for him. No one wanted to leave and they have said that they found nothing so satisfying afterwards. In the Private Office he was always known affectionately as 'Uncle Harold'.

The atmosphere at 10 Downing Street was relaxed and friendly, and this was due largely to Lady Dorothy. She loved having her grandchildren with her and John Wyndham recalled that a visitor might easily encounter a small child playing with a toy motor-car in the hall. A notice was drafted for the children: 'Roller-skating not allowed on Cabinet days.' No. 10 was very much a family home as well as a centre of Government.

Dorothy Macmillan was a delightful hostess, whose welcoming and entirely natural manner made her guests feel happy and at ease. Her influence in the house was a helpful and calming one and her political judgement was instinctively good, so that the Private Secretaries felt they could talk to her as a friend. She was invariably late for any social commitment, whereas the Prime Minister was meticulously punctual; so he formed the habit of telling her that a dinner engagement was a quarter of an hour earlier than it actually was. By this device he had the satisfaction of being on time and Lady Dorothy of being unpunctual.

The Macmillans had an exceptionally good cook called Mrs Bell, of whom the Prime Minister spoke admiringly: 'Under-Secretaries are two-a-penny; Mrs Bell is much more important.'[14] She was a great asset at Downing Street, where there was inevitably entertaining to be done, even in the private part of the house, though Macmillan was not much interested in food and preferred cold meat and champagne to anything more elaborate. When he was alone he seldom even drank wine and was more likely to have a whisky and soda at dinner.

Life in Sussex was even simpler, with no luxury or ostentation of any kind. The household at Birch Grove was a modest one and, apart from Mrs Bell and an excellent housemaid called Edith, there was only daily help from the village. When there were visitors, Macmillan was always a good host, but they did not have many close friends outside the family and entertained very little. This was no doubt partly because the Prime Minister always had papers to work through and time was therefore precious, but it was also because Lady Dorothy was not at all 'grand' by nature and, despite her family background, preferred as simple a life as possible. She was a domesticated person, whose interest centred round her garden and her grandchildren. She was a wonderful grandmother until the children reached the age of ten or twelve, when she seemed to lose interest and transferred her affections to a younger brother or sister. By contrast, Harold Macmillan took more interest as they grew older. He was undemonstrative and was perhaps closer to his grandchildren – especially Maurice's eldest son, Alexander – than to his own children. Lady Dorothy was a dedicated and enthusiastic, though occasionally eccentric gardener, who was sometimes seen tying up roses at night with the aid of a torch and with hot-water bottles strapped to her legs to enable her to kneel without damp or discomfort. In the summer she would often have her bed taken into the garden, where she liked to sleep if the weather was good.

Lady Dorothy was a woman of strong likes and dislikes. The latter included her mother-in-law in the early days of her marriage and her cousin, Lady Salisbury, also a Cavendish, who was unkind to her and bullied her as a child. Nor did she have a good relationship with her daughter-in-law. Katie Macmillan is an attractive and popular lady, but they were both strong characters and they did not like each other. Relations between them were not made easier by the feud between the Cavendish and Cecil families, which could almost be compared with that of the Montagues and Capulets. Of Macmillan's colleagues, Lady Dorothy did not care for Rab Butler, but this was political rather than personal, because she was loyal to Harold and, until he became Prime Minister, she regarded Rab as a rival who might deprive him of the prize. Her likes were as positive as her dislikes and she was a good friend, warm and kind to those she loved.

Dorothy's clothes, especially in the country, were always untidy, but she admired physical beauty in other people. She was immensely energetic and could often be seen running rather than walking in the house or garden. She had a quick temper and was apt to throw things when she lost it; she was once known to have ripped the telephone out of the wall after a conversation which had angered her. In this she was the opposite of Harold Macmillan, who was always restrained and controlled even under great stress.

Dorothy had no intellectual pretensions, seldom read a book and was a little nervous of talking to very intelligent people. There was, therefore, little communication between her and Harold, and when others were present there tended to be two conversations, with Macmillan discussing politics or books, while she preferred to talk about her grandchildren. She often said she thought she was marrying a publisher, not a politican, and she might have preferred him to remain one; but she was much loved by his constituents, both at Stockton and Bromley, because she liked them and was genuinely interested in their lives and problems. She had a warm nature and a wonderful sense of humour. Part of her charm was her directness: she had an attractively natural, down-to-earth manner which won the affection of all who were fortunate enough to enjoy her friendship. Harold Macmillan was always both courteous to her and complimentary about her – almost consciously so – and he respected her judgement, especially about people. She was a source of strength and support to him throughout the premiership.

In addition to his own staff at Downing Street, the Prime Minister had at his disposal the advice of the Cabinet Office, which exists to serve all members of the Cabinet, but is of particular value to the head of the Government. It is presided over by the Secretary to the Cabinet and Macmillan was fortunate that, in his time, the post was held by two men of distinguished public service and quite exceptional ability – Sir Norman Brook until his retirement in 1962 and thereafter Sir Burke Trend.

Throughout his premiership, Harold Macmillan dominated the Cabinet, not by overriding his colleagues, but by sheer intellectual superiority and good judgement. He was older and more experienced than most of them and controlled their discussions with inimitable style and dexterity. He was firm, business-like and methodical, and was usually able to ensure a rational conclusion, though the subsequent minutes sometimes bore little relation to the arguments and on occasion even appeared to have been written before the meeting took place!

Macmillan has been criticized[15] for his Presidential style, especially in the later years of his Administration; and it is true that he often decided an issue with a few colleagues closely concerned in it, before the Cabinet met. This practice is, however, a normal one in any Government; most problems are resolved by the appropriate Cabinet committee and do not even come before the full Cabinet, except for more or less formal ratification, unless there are major or controversial matters at stake.

Macmillan always allowed, indeed encouraged, discussion, provided Ministers kept to the point, but there was also a glint of steel. Like Churchill, but unlike Attlee, he was prepared to gamble if it seemed a reasonable risk. He was good at summing up the points of agreement and of difference and was able to present them in an objective way, while at the same time achieving the outcome he wanted. If there was a substantial body of opinion differing from his own, he either conceded gracefully or deferred a decision till a later meeting and talked to recalcitrant colleagues privately and individually before it took place. He enjoyed and was skilful at manœuvring Ministers in order to secure his objective – often a relatively unimportant one – and he loved the whole game of politics. This does not imply insincerity, but his idealism was tempered by realism, a good combination for any statesman.

Macmillan's handling of the Cabinet was helped by having few close friends among its members. Charles Hill considered that the Prime Minister 'took an objective view of his colleagues, seldom getting so close to them (or allowing them to get so close to him) that his judgement became complicated by personal relationships'.[16] As far as their departmental work was concerned, he liked to know what was going on, but seldom interfered.

Macmillan enjoyed launching a major new initiative, but after a time he became bored with its detailed implementation. This was especially true of the Colonial policy: having appointed Iain Macleod to accelerate the advance to self-government and independence in Africa, he was irritated by the continual arguments which developed between Macleod and Duncan Sandys, the Secretary of State for Commonwealth Relations, each of whom represented not only his own departmental interest, but two sincere though differing schools of thought in the Conservative Party and whose approach to the problems was therefore often opposed. In this, as in other matters, Macmillan held the balance and, if this became too difficult, he simply moved one or other of the Ministers concerned to a new department. Few former colleagues would disagree with Charles Hill's assessment that Macmillan's chairmanship of the Cabinet was 'superb by any standards'.[17] Yet it was from within the Cabinet that his first difficulty as Prime Minister arose.

Lord Salisbury, head of the house of Cecil and hailed (erroneously) by the press as the 'king-maker' who had put Macmillan in power, was the representative of what might loosely be described as the Right wing of the Conservative Party. He was out of sympathy with the majority of the Cabinet and with the Prime Minister himself over the way in which the post-Suez problems were being handled; but developments in Cyprus were the immediate cause of the disagreement which culminated in his resignation.

For some months terrorism had been increasing in the island and the Prime Minister, supported by the Colonial Secretary and by the Governor, Sir John Harding, believed that the situation would be eased if Archbishop Makarios was released from detention in the Seychelles. A dissentient view was expressed by Lord Salisbury. Macmillan recorded, 'He came to see me after dinner ... I felt that he was determined to resign about something. He seemed in one of his resigning moods.'[18] No doubt to Salisbury's surprise, the Prime Minister accepted his decision with alacrity and adopted the technique, to be used again later, of treating the matter as trivial. The resignation of so senior a Minister caused far less sensation than might have been expected and within a week was almost forgotten. Lord Kilmuir commented that the Lord President's departure 'removed a probable source of considerable strain from our councils'.[19] Soon afterwards Salisbury publicly criticized the Government's announcement that ship-owners would no longer be discouraged from using the Suez Canal and Macmillan noted in his diary: 'What a blessing he went over Makarios!'[20]

The after-effects of Suez were not, in fact, as serious or as lasting as had at first seemed likely. Macmillan was the first to understand and adjust to Britain's reduced role in world affairs and the Anglo-American alliance survived the shock, mainly because of his old friendship with Eisenhower and his own diplomatic skill in substituting influence for the use of force. The Prime Minister did not wish to appear as a suppliant and he was therefore delighted when the initiative came from the President, in the form of a message suggesting a personal meeting in Bermuda. It was also helpful that this was to take place on British territory; 21–24 March were agreed as convenient dates.

The British team consisted of Selwyn Lloyd, Sir Norman Brook, Freddie Bishop and Patrick Dean, and Macmillan was glad to find that the American delegation included his old friend, Bob Murphy. On the night of their arrival, Eisenhower, Foster Dulles, Macmillan and Lloyd dined alone together, without officials. The atmosphere was good, with no reproaches on either side, although the President recalled that 'Foster and I at first found it difficult to talk constructively with our British colleagues about Suez.'[21]

The conference began next morning with an opening statement by the Prime Minister. It is clear from his speech notes[22] that he said all the right things in the right way. This set the tone for the meeting and during the next three days he and Eisenhower had several private talks, in addition to the more formal sessions.

No final conclusions were reached over Egypt and Israel and no agreement was yet possible about trade with China; but the United States proved willing to join the Military Committee of the Baghdad Pact – for which Macmillan had been hoping since his time as Foreign Secretary; to supply Britain with guided missiles; and to concur in the continuation of British nuclear tests, one of which was shortly to take place, in conjunction with the Americans, on Christmas Island.

The President had hitherto appeared to regard faith in the United Nations as a substitute for a foreign policy, but Macmillan was able to influence his thinking along more realistic lines and it was agreed that the two countries should work together much more closely at the UN and co-ordinate their policies in advance. Eisenhower and Macmillan also arranged to write regularly, frankly and privately to each other whenever an exchange of views seemed useful.

The real importance of the conference lay in the successful restoration of Anglo-American relations, which had been its main objective. No doubt this was partly due to an unexpressed guilt the President and Dulles may have felt for their attitude over Suez, for which they were anxious to make amends; but the purpose of the meeting could hardly have been achieved as quickly and completely if Anthony Eden had still been Prime Minister. Macmillan's personal friendship with Eisenhower and his relatively good relations with Dulles were important factors, as well as his own talent for diplomacy, which had been so evident fifteen years earlier in North Africa.

President Eisenhower regarded the meeting as:

. . . by far the most successful international conference that I had attended since the close of World War II . . . there was a noticeable atmosphere of frankness and confidence. . . . Our determination to rebuild our close understanding was aided . . . by the fact that Harold and I were old comrades.[23]

One of the first problems which had faced Macmillan when he became Prime Minister, the need to re-establish the alliance 'which I knew to be essential in the modern world',[24] had been overcome within three months of his accession to power.

A short communiqué was drafted and Eisenhower returned to the United States on 25 March, leaving Macmillan to hold the usual press conference. Later that day, Louis St Laurent, the Canadian Prime Minister, and his Foreign Secretary, Lester Pearson, arrived in Bermuda for a useful discussion before Macmillan flew back to England on 27 March.

A debate followed in the House of Commons and Harold Macmillan noted in his diary that he had never felt so strained and nervous before a speech. Press comment contended that the continuance of the Government and the unity of the Conservative Party depended on his performance and one news-paper carried an article which read:

Suez and its aftermath, abstentions by Conservative voters at by-elections, the contin-uance . . . of the ship-building and engineering strikes, Lord Salisbury's week-end resignation – in Labour eyes the Prime Minister must have looked like a man about to be 'butchered to make a Roman holiday'. . . . What happened in the first part of the debate destroyed all such notions. By the time that Mr Gaitskell resumed his seat . . . the tables had been turned. . . .[25]

Macmillan had indeed enjoyed a considerable success. Wisely, he devoted most of his speech to the agreement on nuclear tests. This both diverted attention from the Canal, on which there was little to say, and exploited the division of opinion in the Labour Party. Gaitskell was unable to answer a direct question as to whether the Opposition would cancel the Christmas Island tests and the Conservative Back Benches were delighted and united in acclaiming the Prime Minister's performance. The 'Canal turn' had still to be negotiated, but meanwhile the Government had surmounted a formidable fence and was still in the race.

The next hurdle was the Defence White Paper, on which Duncan Sandys had been working with his usual assiduity and application. The claims of defence on the nation's resources had been rising, but Britain's economic ability to support them had declined. Nuclear deterrence instead of conventional defence, prevention rather than cure, seemed the only solution. Sandys' proposals were published on 4 April and, in Harold Macmillan's words, 'constituted the biggest change in military policy ever made in normal times'.[26]

The Prime Minister's brief had been to prepare a new defence organization, based on the need to reduce expenditure and manpower. Subject to this directive and to the final approval of the Cabinet, Sandys' authority was absolute. This was facilitated by Macmillan's own experience as Minister of Defence and his determination to give his successor real freedom of action. When appointing the new Service Ministers, who were no longer to be members of the Cabinet, he had made it clear to them that their autonomy was to be curtailed and that any proposals they wished to make would in future be submitted through the Minister of Defence. It was the sort of authority Duncan Sandys enjoyed and he exercised it to the full. As Field Marshal Montgomery wrote in a letter to the Prime Minister: 'Hurrah! Duncan Sandys now has the power given him by you to give orders; and being the man he is, he will see his orders are carried out.'[27] President Eisenhower helped by agreeing to deploy a number of intermediate-range ballistic missiles in Britain, which gave the United Kingdom a rocket deterrent long before it could otherwise have been produced. The overriding principle was to be dependence on the nuclear deterrent, with a corresponding reduction in conventional forces; and this enabled Britain to abolish conscription and return to voluntary recruitment by the end of 1960.

The White Paper achieved its objectives of saving money and manpower, but its reliance on nuclear deterrence carried its own dangers. Nigel Birch (later Lord Rhyl) described it as 'the hydrogen atomic ace, unplayed and unplayable'; and George Wigg, speaking in the debate on the White Paper, said: 'We can have defence on the cheap if we concentrate on weapons which we cannot possibly use.'[28] It was a valid point which went to the heart of the objections to the new defence strategy.

The residual repercussions of the Suez failure were a continuing anxiety for Macmillan. On 29 March, Nasser sent the United Nations his terms for a final settlement. While guaranteeing freedom of passage, he insisted that the Canal dues should be paid to the Egyptian authorities. By early April, the waterway was clear for shipping and the Government had to decide whether to boycott the Canal – which would have been damaging to British commercial interests – or accept the terms. There was no real choice; Macmillan had to acknowledge defeat with the least possible loss of face. As this became clear, criticism mounted from the Right wing of the Conservative Party and a motion appeared on the House of Commons Order Paper, supported by fifteen Tory signatures, which soon rose to thirty. Lord Salisbury sided with the rebels and the scene was set for a major two-day debate.

The official Opposition motion was skilfully worded to attract both opponents and supporters of the Suez operation and Macmillan rightly treated it as a vote of censure. He opened for the Government on the first day amid disconcerting jeers and laughter from the Labour benches and the speech was not a success. That morning, the end of petrol-rationing – which had been imposed in December – was announced, but this did not allay the criticism. By a lucky chance, however, the newspapers the following day were full of the successful explosion of the nuclear bomb, which helped to divert public attention from Suez. Harold Macmillan wound up the debate on the night of 16 May. He was able to drive a wedge between Gaitskell and Bevan, and his speech was as great a success as the previous day's had been a failure. When the vote was taken there were fourteen Tory abstentions, but the Opposition motion was defeated by a majority of 49 and the Conservative Party stood up and cheered the Prime Minister as he left the Chamber. He commented in his diary: 'How odd the English are! They rather like a gallant failure. Suez has become a sort of Mons retreat.'[29]

Although Macmillan had been forced to admit defeat in his attempt to obtain better terms than Nasser had offered, he had contrived to disguise Britain's humiliation. The Tory Party, and indeed the people as a whole, wanted it disguised; so they accepted the deception, made plausible by Macmillan's style and skill, and forgot the Suez episode as quickly as they could. It played no part in the General Election two years later. John Wyndham noted that, in the early months of the Government, Macmillan 'because everything seemed loaded against him . . . was at his very best. His friends found him full of fight and spirit and fun and gaiety. He thrived in adversity.'[30] Lord Hailsham, one of those who had privately questioned the Government's prospects of survival for longer than six months, wrote later that 'the credit . . . must undoubtedly go to the virtuosity of Harold Macmillan as Prime Minister'.[31]

Despite this Parliamentary success and the *rapprochement* with the United States, sterling was still under pressure and Macmillan was anxious to avoid any crisis at home which might worsen Britain's credit overseas; but within a few weeks of forming the Government, he was faced with a series of disputes and threatened strikes in the motor-car, railway, engineering and ship-building industries. The first of these, which arose at Briggs Motors in Dagenham, a part of the Ford Group, was handled with skill and resolution by Iain Macleod, the Minister of Labour, and strike action was averted. It was typical of Macmillan's style that, at the height of it, he telephoned

Macleod with the suggestion, 'Iain, there's a very good film on tonight. Dorothy and I would like you to come.'[32]

In the following month, when Macmillan was about to depart for the Bermuda Conference, a more serious danger developed of simultaneous strikes in the other three industries – a combination which would have been calamitous for the economy. It was essential to separate the issues and avoid fighting on all three of them at the same time. Fortunately, the rail dispute was soon settled and the Prime Minister cabled Macleod from Bermuda to congratulate him on having managed it with calmness and courage. But a strike had begun in all the shipyards on 16 March and the engineering unions joined it a week later. By 1 April, more than 780,000 men were idle. It was the largest stoppage in Britain since the General Strike over thirty years earlier. Following the appointment of a Court of Enquiry, a compromise settlement was reached and the strikes were called off, but it had been a worrying time because, in the spring of 1957, the Government was in no position to face a trial of strength with the unions in a key sector of the economy.

One outcome of the Court's report was the establishment by the Chancellor of the Exchequer of a Council on Prices, Productivity and Incomes, whose members soon became known as the 'Three Wise Men'. This was the first of many attempts to achieve 'restraint without tears' – a brake upon inflation without recourse to statutory powers.

At first Macmillan seems to have been favourably impressed with the Chancellor's performance: 'I found Thorneycroft an admirable partner, full of resolve and contrivance,' and 'firm but understanding'[33] in steering a compromise course through the annual Farm Price Review. The April budget reduced taxation by £100 million, divided equally between help for overseas trading companies, surtax relief, higher children's allowances and cuts in the purchase tax. Although Thorneycroft's speech was admirable and his proposals well received by the Press, the improving morale in the Parliamentary Party was not yet reflected in the country as a whole.

A series of by-elections in February and March had resulted in strong swings against the Conservatives, with the North Lewisham seat falling to Labour, and even Warwick and Leamington, Eden's former stronghold, showing an adverse swing of over 12%. This trend continued in May, when the Socialists captured eleven Councils in the local elections and the Tory majority fell from nearly 13,000 to 3,000 in a by-election at Hornsey.

In spite of these set-backs, Macmillan had already established an ascendancy in Parliament and Hugh Massingham was able to report in the *Observer* on 12 May that Conservative Back Benchers had 'absolute trust in their beloved leader. . . . At the moment there is nothing the Prime Minister cannot do with his followers.' This was true and is well summarized by Laddie

Lucas: 'He lifted us up by the boot-straps, welded the various factions together and by sheer intellectual quality came to dominate the House of
Commons.'[34]

Macmillan understood that a political leader must control the House before
he can inspire his own Party in the country or effectively attract and influence
the wider electorate. He was determined to achieve this when he became
Prime Minister and triumphantly succeeded. Very few in the Opposition
cared to take him on in debate and, when they did, they usually failed. This
was partly due to the content of his speeches and his answers at Question
Time, but mainly to the style of their delivery and his own personality. The
tide of parliamentary enthusiasm for his leadership soon spread outwards in
the weekend constituency speeches of Conservative MPs, and led gradually to
a growing appreciation of his qualities, first by the Party faithful and, within
about eighteen months, by the public as a whole.

In July, Macmillan made a speech at Bedford in which he included a phrase
later to become notorious:

Let's be frank about it, most of our people have never had it so good. Go around the
country, go to the industrial towns, go to the farms, and you will see a state of
prosperity such as we have never had in my life-time – nor indeed ever in the history
of this country.

On this occasion the words were not quoted out of context, as they were later,
and excited no adverse comment. They were simply a statement of fact and
were accompanied by the warning that this state of affairs could not be
sustained if prices continued to rise: 'Our constant concern to-day', he went
on, 'is, can prices be steadied while at the same time we maintain full employment in an expanding economy? Can we control inflation? This is the problem
of our time.' It has certainly been Britain's principal problem, and in an
increasingly acute form, for more than two decades since Macmillan's Bedford speech.

It was apparent to the Prime Minister that, although strong and united in
Parliament, the Conservative Party's position in the country was far less
satisfactory. A more inspiring and dramatic projection of the Government's
achievements and what it stood for was clearly needed and Macmillan
thought that a change in the Chairmanship at Central Office would be the
best way to bring this about.

When Lord Woolton resigned in 1955, Eden had appointed Oliver (later
Lord) Poole to succeed him and there was no better organizer of the Party
machine. But Poole was not an an exciting speaker and was unable to rouse
the large audiences which the Chairman was expected to address throughout
the country. He was admirable in the office but less fitted for the hustings.

Macmillan believed that the right man for this role was Lord Hailsham, and with selfless loyalty Poole agreed to serve as his deputy and continue the day-to-day management of the machine. In a diary entry in August Macmillan noted that, 'Poole will do organization; Hailsham political leadership and ideas. This should make a very good combination.'[35] It was a shrewd judgement, well justified in the event.

The choice of Quintin Hailsham was indeed an inspired one and he did more than anyone, except the Prime Minister himself, to revive the fortunes and popularity of the Conservative Party. He toured the country arousing the enthusiam of the faithful, explaining Government policy in the constituencies and acting to some extent as if he was the leader, while leaving the decisions to the real leader and not exciting his jealousy:

I deliberately studied Harold Macmillan's character and set myself to do for him exactly the things which he was occupationally or temperamentally incapable of doing himself. I acted as his professional advocate, making myself as much a contrast to him as I possibly could: Where he would understate, I would be strident, where he would be serious, I would be humorous. . . . Where he would play the Duke's son-in-law . . . I would be eloquent and ostentatious to the point of vulgarity . . . where he was devious, I would be plainspoken.[36]

During the month of July, a new if minor problem arose in the Middle East. A revolt broke out against the Sultan of Muscat and Oman, whose state Britain had supported for over a hundred years and who now appealed for help against the rebels. Although there was no formal obligation, it seemed to Macmillan that a failure by the Government to send assistance might be interpreted as reluctance or inability to help a friend in time of trouble. The House of Commons accepted this view and the Royal Air Force carried out a number of rocket attacks against military targets in Oman. A small British force was despatched and the Sultan's authority re-established. The Prime Minister then sent his son-in-law, Julian Amery, who was Under-Secretary for War, to negotiate a more formal agreement for the future, which was successfully concluded. The operation in Oman was on a small scale; but, without the need for any American assistance, it had restored confidence in the Gulf and Macmillan recorded that, so soon after Suez, 'it was at least some encouragement to feel that we had not lost our nerve'.[37]

Towards the end of August a potentially more serious situation developed in the Levant, due to Communist infiltration in Syria. The neighbouring Arab States were uneasy and Turkey was subjected to indirect Russian threats. Great concern was felt in Washington about the possibility of Soviet penetration into the eastern Mediterranean and Dulles was almost over-enthusiastic in his anxiety to co-operate with Britain in a joint policy for the area.

Throughout September there was a daily exchange of telegrams between Washington and London, and contingency planning was carefully co-ordinated. Macmillan recalls that 'charges and counter-charges were made not only between Turkey and Syria but between the American and Russian Governments', in what he described as 'this war of nerves';[38] and Dulles declared that if the Soviet Union attacked Turkey, the United States would not restrict itself to a 'purely defensive operation'. At the end of October, Khrushchev suddenly called off the crisis with a bland statement that the whole affair had been misunderstood.

This episode and the Oman rebellion had occupied an immense amount of Macmillan's time and had deprived him of all but a few days' holiday in Scotland at the end of August. It had shown, however, that the Anglo-American relationship, renewed in Bermuda, could stand the test of later problems in which their mutual interests were involved.

Following the brutal suppression of Hungary in the previous autumn, Russia was anxious to regain her moral position in the world and, in April 1957, Bulganin wrote a 10,000-word letter to Macmillan advocating nuclear, but not conventional, disarmament. In Britain the Aldermaston marches were gaining support and the hydrogen bomb was causing genuine public apprehension, which was exploited by Aneurin Bevan in a debate in the House of Commons. Subject to adequate safeguards, Macmillan himself wanted to work for the limitation of nuclear tests, but from his point of view, the Soviet initiative was premature because the British tests were by no means complete.

Governor Harold Stassen, the leader of the American delegation to a disarmament conference at Lancaster House, now dropped his private bomb by advocating an unofficial personal plan, known as the 'cut-off', which would have entailed the abandonment of Britain's nuclear programme. To Macmillan's embarrassment, Stassen presented the text of this proposal to the Russians before the British Government had even been provided with a copy. Thereafter Soviet propaganda was predictably concentrated on the suspension of nuclear tests to the exclusion of all other aspects of disarmament. In the end the Western powers put forward package proposals, which included the cessation of tests for one year. These were rejected by the Russians and the disarmament talks were adjourned.

In October, Macmillan flew to Washington, a week after the Queen had visited America for the 350th anniversary of the founding of Virginia. This had been an immense success and the British Ambassador, Sir Harold Caccia, reported 'she has buried George III for good and all'. The timing was therefore fortunate and Macmillan wrote that 'both in official and unofficial circles I sensed a friendly and even enthusiastic mood'.[39] The Prime Minister's main purpose was to persuade the President to repeal the McMahon Act. This was agreed with far less difficulty than had been expected and arrangements were made for the exchange of nuclear information between the two Governments.

From Washington Macmillan went on to Ottawa for talks with the new Canadian Prime Minister, John Diefenbaker. He stayed, nostalgically, at Government House for the first time since, as a young ADC, he had become engaged to Dorothy Cavendish.

The last international conference in the year 1957 was the NATO meeting in Paris in December, which was attended by the heads of Governments, including Eisenhower, as well as by their Foreign Ministers. Long-range intercontinental weapons had not yet been perfected, so it was important to obtain agreement for the stationing of shorter range American rockets in the various allied countries. This was achieved and Macmillan was well satisfied with the outcome not only of the conference, but of the other diplomatic efforts during the first year of his premiership. Suez was forgiven and almost forgotten; close friendship with the United States had been re-established; the NATO powers were united; relations with the French and German Governments were good; and Commonwealth confidence had been restored. From the low point of Britain's international relations at the beginning of the year, these were considerable achievements.

At home the position was less favourable: wages were rising without a corresponding increase in productivity, which inevitably resulted in higher prices. Yet a motion rejecting wage restraint in any form was passed enthusiastically at the TUC Conference in September.

The devaluation of the French franc and a rumoured revaluation of the German mark combined to cause a run on the pound and Harold Macmillan noted in his diary:

The collapse of the franc and the tremendous rise in the mark has meant a very bad month for us on the exchanges – the worst since Suez. But the actual balance of payments position is good and so is the trade balance. So we must hold on.[40]

The September prospects for sterling were poor and corrective action was clearly required. Peter Thorneycroft was convinced that a spectacular rise in the bank rate was the only way to deal with the run on the reserves. Roy Harrod argued against a deflationary policy and Macmillan, who instinctively sympathized with this view, was unhappy about the Chancellor's demand for an almost unprecedented increase in the bank rate from five to seven per cent; but, after lengthy discussion, he bowed to Treasury advice and the new measures were announced on 19 September. They included not only the two per cent rise in the bank rate, but reductions in public investment and an intensified 'credit squeeze'. Macmillan recorded: 'I deeply regret that I did not stick to my point. . . . Nevertheless, I stored up the incident in my mind and was determined not to yield indefinitely to pressure.'[41]

By October the pound was beginning to stabilize, but the British public were more concerned about high prices than about the strength of sterling and the Government's standing in the country remained low. A Gallup poll published on 1 October showed the Conservatives trailing Labour by over eighteen per cent and another poll four weeks later placed Macmillan as the most unpopular Prime Minister since Neville Chamberlain. When contrasted with his great personal prestige and the massive Conservative victory in the General Election two years later, this illustrates the volatility of British public opinion.

In a speech in the House of Commons on 5 November Macmillan made it clear that, while the Government would accept arbitration awards to public employees, the extra money would have to be found from total current expenditure, and he expressed the hope that in private industry the credit squeeze would 'exert a healthy check on unreasonable wage demands. . . . Increases of wages must come from greater productivity, but not from increased supplies of money.' The Government's own spending was an important contributor to inflation and Thorneycroft argued strongly for cuts of £153 million in the civil estimates. In a diary note on 22 December, Macmillan observed: 'The Chancellor wants some swingeing cuts in the Welfare State expenditure – more, I fear, than is feasible politically.'[42]

The Cabinet objected to Thorneycroft's main proposal, which was to abolish the children's allowance for the second child – equivalent to a ten per cent wage cut for over three million low-paid families; but he was determined to keep down the estimates to the previous year's figure and, after prolonged discussions, his colleagues agreed to economies of £100 million. Although a gap of £50 million still remained, this was in fact less than 1% of total Government expenditure. Nevertheless, as Macmillan noted, 'the Chancellor of the Exchequer held to his view with almost fanatical rigidity',[43] arguing that as capital investment and bank advances had been pegged to 1957 levels, the Government must take its own medicine. This was no doubt logical, if somewhat dogmatic, but the Prime Minister did not think 'a precise arithmetical equilibrium could be achieved' and he feared that if Thorneycroft's policy prevailed, other Ministers might resign in protest against further cuts in their Departments and the survival of the Government might be at risk.

The Cabinet crisis was complicated by the circumstance that the Prime Minister and Lady Dorothy were about to leave England for an important tour, which had been arranged during the Prime Minister's Commonwealth Conference the previous summer and which was to include visits to India, Pakistan, Ceylon, Singapore, New Zealand and Australia. Clearly this could not be cancelled or even postponed and the departure date had been fixed for 7 January.

On Sunday, 5 January 1958, Macmillan saw Thorneycroft and appealed to him to accept the collective view of his colleagues, 'but I got the impression that he had made up his mind to resign unless he got his full demand'. [44] The Cabinet met at 6.30 p.m. and again at 10.30. In the interval Butler, Sandys, Macleod and Heath dined at Downing Street. It seemed foolish to be fighting such a major battle over £50 million when Treasury figures were often inaccurate and the margin of error alone could make the calculations invalid. Macleod expressed the view, which Macmillan was inclined to share, that the Chancellor was 'obsessed and dominated by Powell'.

At 10.30 the following morning the Prime Minister received letters of resignation from Thorneycroft, Birch and Enoch Powell. The abrupt departure of the entire team of Treasury Ministers was without precedent, but Macmillan behaved with studied calm. John Wyndham described his entry into the Private Office, with an agreeable word to everyone, a joke or two, then he rapidly drafted acceptances of the resignations.[45] After a meeting of the Cabinet at eleven o'clock, he invited Derick Heathcoat Amory (later Viscount Amory), the Minister of Agriculture, to succeed Thorneycroft as Chancellor. This was an admirable choice. Amory was loyal, liberal-minded, a good administrator and one of the best-liked men in the House of Commons. When appointing him, Macmillan said typically: 'They tell me you can telephone to Australia, but don't bother. Do as you like at the Treasury and tell me about it all when I get home.'[46]

The consequential ministerial vacancies were quickly filled, and the next morning the Prime Minister and Lady Dorothy left London Airport on schedule, with almost every member of the Cabinet there to bid them farewell. In a statement to the press and the BBC, Macmillan deliberately dismissed the episode by referring to 'these little local difficulties' as compared to 'the wider vision of the Commonwealth'. This was a very good way of dealing with the matter; it amused the British people and effectively defused the crisis.

A few days later, Sir David Eccles, the President of the Board of Trade, who was away in the United States, sent Macmillan a message: 'You may like to know that your decision not to delay your departure greatly impressed the American bankers and held their confidence in sterling'[47]; and in lighter vein Randolph Churchill cabled characteristically to Macleod: 'YOU AND HAROLD WOULD BE GRATIFIED BY TOTAL LACK OF INTEREST IN WASHINGTON ABOUT RECENT RESIGNATIONS STOP MY SECRETARY DOES NOT KNOW WHO THORNEYCROFT IS OR WAS OR WILL BE.'[48]

It was a year, almost to the day, since Anthony Eden's resignation and Harold Macmillan's accession as Prime Minister.

22
THE COMMONWEALTH
TOUR 1958

The Commonwealth Prime Minister's Conference, over which Harold Macmillan presided, had met in London in the summer of 1957 and had welcomed Dr Nkrumah of Ghana as the first African Prime Minister to attend. *The Times* reported that 'the Conference has been a personal success for Mr Macmillan',[1] but he was conscious that the Commonwealth was in a period of transition, when the gathering momentum of independence would soon increase its membership and change its character. Invitations from Nehru to visit India and from Menzies to go to Australia prompted him to decide upon a Far East tour, in order to see for himself what role Britain could most usefully play in this evolving situation. There was an obvious opportunity for mediation between India and Pakistan in their bitter quarrel over Kashmir and the waters of the Indus river; more widely, the older Dominions must learn to accept the new nations of different races and cultures which would soon join them in the Commonwealth association. Macmillan's modest purpose in undertaking the tour – the first by a British Prime Minister in office – was to look, listen and learn, and to carry messages of goodwill and friendship to the countries he was to visit.

The Prime Minister took with him Sir Norman Brook, Sir Morrice James, Harold Evans, Neil Cairncross and John Wyndham. On an expedition lasting over five weeks, they covered 33,000 miles by air and 1,500 miles by road, with New Delhi as the first stop.

Nehru, whom Macmillan described later as 'able, full of charm, cultivated and ruthless',[2] dominated the Indian scene. He invited the Prime Minister and Lady Dorothy to stay at his own home, an unusual compliment, and showed them 'exquisite courtesy' throughout the visit. Tens of thousands of people greeted them enthusiastically at the Red Fort, and they dined one evening at the Viceroy's House, unchanged in pomp and ceremonial from the days of the British Raj – indeed, Dorothy sat opposite a portrait of her grandfather, Lord Lansdowne, who had been Viceroy of India more than half a century before. Nehru pleased the Prime Minister by saying, 'I wonder if the Romans ever went back to visit Britain.'³ In private talks, the two leaders discussed China, the possibility of negotiations with Russia, and India's economic problems and her Five-Year Plan; but no progress was made over Kashmir.

On visits to villages near Delhi, Macmillan was accorded a moving welcome, with the people dancing, singing and cheering wherever he appeared. Malcolm Macdonald, then British High Commissioner at Delhi, described the visit as an outstanding success, of great value to Anglo-Indian relations, and said that Macmillan had made a marked personal impression on the leaders and people alike.⁴ This was high praise from a man whose own diplomacy under successive Governments for over thrity years was a unique contribution to the New Commonwealth.

On 12 January Macmillan arrived at Karachi for talks with President Iskander Mirza and the Prime Minister, Sir Malik Firoz Khan Noon, which centred largely on the Indo-Pakistan dispute and a request for supplies of arms from Britain. Pakistan was politically unstable and only a few months later the Government and the Parliamentary system were to be overthrown and a military regime established under Mohammed Ayub Khan.

Macmillan took the opportunity to drive through the Khyber Pass to the Afghanistan frontier before leaving for Ceylon, where he was received by cheering crowds in what almost amounted to a royal progress through the island. After talks with the Oxford-educated Prime Minister, Mr Bandaranaike, which covered China, the situation in Indonesia and the economy of Ceylon, Macmillan received an Honorary Degree at the University and departed on 18 January for Singapore. There, he attended a session of the Annual Conference of senior civil and military leaders which was meeting under the chairmanship of Sir Robert Scott, the Commissioner-General for South-East Asia, whom Macmillan had appointed to the post when he was Foreign Secretary. At that time Scott had been a relatively junior diplomat, who had been suggested by Malcolm Macdonald as his own successor when he transferred to India – a recommendation which, rather to Macdonald's surprise, Macmillan had readily accepted. He was never disposed to bow to the Civil Service bias for 'Buggin's turn' next.

Singapore was moving towards independence and the Prime Minister was glad to have the Chief Minister, Lim Yew Hock, to dinner for a private talk; but the visit was a short one and the following afternoon Macmillan flew on to New Zealand. He had contracted a severe chill and, when his airplane stopped to refuel at Darwin, he was unable to leave it to greet a reception committee; this gave rise to some undeserved criticism in the Australian press.

Macmillan had a temperature and was tired by the time he arrived in

Auckland. The High Commissioner, Sir George Mallaby, thought he should have been sent straight to bed; but he survived an initially awkward dinner with the Prime Minister, Walter Nash, and the two men sat up together late into the night. The elegant British Conservative statesman and the talkative old New Zealand radical soon became friends, and at Nash's invitation Macmillan attended a two-hour meeting of the Cabinet on 23 January. Large civic receptions and a Maori gathering were included in a busy programme and in Wellington he and Lady Dorothy stayed with the popular Governor-General, Lord Cobham. After being warmly welcomed at Dunedin, they drove, to Christchurch, where the Prime Minister made a speech to the Chamber of Commerce before leaving for Australia on 28 January.

The Macmillans loved New Zealand, so far away, yet, in the character of its people, so like Britain. The scenery in the South Island reminded them of Scotland with the rivers full of trout and so many deer that, in contrast to the high cost of stalking in the Scottish Highlands, the New Zealanders were paid to shoot them. The country seemed like 'an oasis set in the cruel desert of modern life'.[5]

In Canberra they were met by Robert Menzies and the British High Commissioner, Lord Carrington, and stayed with the Governor-General, Field Marshal Sir William Slim. A Parliamentary dinner was held the following evening, although both Houses were in recess and many members had to travel long distances to attend it. Macmillan had lengthy discussions with Menzies, mainly about defence and European integration, and with the Leader of the Opposition, Dr Evatt. He received an Honorary Degree at the National University and attended a Cabinet, at which he spoke with great effect.

Visits to Brisbane, Sydney, Melbourne and Tasmania followed in quick succession, with the requisite number of luncheons, receptions and dinners in each. The weather was hot and the exhausting schedule included press conferences, factory visits and innumerable speeches, some of them impromptu, over a period of a fortnight; but Macmillan never flagged and indeed seemed to thrive on this arduous programme. Throughout the tour, he received many messages and telegrams from Rab Butler – who was acting as head of the Government – all of which had to be dealt with, usually late at night at the end of a long day of engagements. On 10 February, his sixty-fourth birthday, Macmillan returned to Canberra for the last two days in Australia before leaving for a second visit to Singapore. There were further talks with Menzies, and Lord Carrington gave a final dinner-party in his honour.

There was no doubt about the success of the visit. In Peter Carrington's words: 'To his genuine surprise, he took Australia by storm and got better and better as the tour progressed. He is rather a shy man, but the success greatly increased his self-confidence.'[6] The Prime Minister was equally impressed by Carrington, whom he has described as 'perhaps the best envoy that we have ever sent'[7] to Australia.

John Wyndham confirmed Macmillan's 'mixture of shyness and zest' and wrote that 'he found himself . . . by walking about in crowds and realizing that he could dominate them quite naturally, always making the apposite remark, saying the right thing'.[8] Even Emrys Hughes, a stern Socialist critic, acknowledged that he made 'just the right speeches in all the capitals of the Commonwealth he visited'.[9]

Macmillan paid generous tributes to all those, especially Lady Dorothy, who had helped and supported him on the tour.[10] Field Marshall Slim and Lord Cobham were outstanding Governors-General and Britain was well served by her High Commissioners, Malcolm Macdonald, George Mallaby and Peter Carrington, each perceptively chosen for the particular country to which he was accredited. Everyone had played a part, but the real credit must go to the Prime Minister himself. His personal success gave him a new confidence and authority and was recognized in every section of the British and Commonwealth press.

23
HOME AFFAIRS 1958-9

Macmillan returned to England to both good news and bad. He was relieved to hear that a Judicial Enquiry into an alleged 'bank rate leak' had completely exonerated Peter Thorneycroft, the Chancellor of the Exchequer at the time, and Oliver Poole, the Deputy Chairman of the Conservative Party, who had both been publicly accused by Harold Wilson of divulging advance information about the rise in the Bank Rate the previous autumn. On the other hand, the Government candidate had not only lost a by-election at Rochdale on 12 February, but had taken third place to the Liberal in a seat hitherto held by the Conservatives. This set-back was followed in March by the loss of Kelvingrove to Labour and Torrington to the Liberals.

At the beginning of 1958, sterling was at its highest point for over eighteen months, the gold and dollar reserves were rising and the balance of payments seemed likely to improve. An impending recession was rumoured in the United States and Macmillan noted in his diary: 'I wish I could persuade the American administration that the Free World cannot be defended by H-bombs if it is allowed to fall into trade collapse and large-scale unemployment.'[1] He felt that a plan for steady economic expansion could be made to work if proper international machinery could be devised. All the resources in raw materials, manpower and demand were at hand and only failure to organize them prevented success. Unemployment was rising and Roy Harrod suggested that an expansionist policy might soon become appropriate. This advice synchronized with the Prime Minister's own inclinations and, although Amory introduced a stand-still budget, the Bank Rate was reduced in two stages from 7% to 5% and, at Macmillan's insistence, the Treasury prepared plans to expand the economy if and when it seemed right to do so.

Although progressive and liberal-minded on social questions, the new Chancellor was by nature cautious and almost as conservative as his predecessor in his handling of the economy. He was careful not to expand too soon, lest another wage-price spiral should develop or foreign confidence be disturbed and, during his two and a half years at the Treasury, retail prices rose by less than 1%. Though helped by a steep fall in import prices, this was a remarkable achievement and, looked at twenty years later, seems little short of miraculous.

Even in 1958, the perennial problem was to avoid another onset of inflation, while preventing too great a deflation. The Treasury thought Britain was still in a period of boom and that caution was needed. Macmillan, Butler and Mills had doubts about this diagnosis; they were determined to restrain incomes unless rises were matched by higher productivity, but once the wages war was won, the Prime Minister favoured an expansionist policy.

The test was soon to come in the transport sector, where strikes on the railways, buses, and in the road haulage and docks industries were all threatened at the same time. The meat-lorry drivers at Smithfield were the first to come out and their action soon spread to the whole market and later to the docks. It was two months before this strike petered out; but Macmillan was much more concerned about the rail dispute. He had some sympathy with the railway workers and was especially anxious to avoid a strike which would cause serious dislocation throughout industry.

On 22 April, supported by Iain Macleod, the Minister of Labour, and Sir Brian Robertson, the Chairman of the British Transport Commission, Macmillan saw the union leaders at 10 Downing Street. He proposed an extension of the modernization programme in return for the acceptance of some redundancies, the elimination of restrictive practices and the closure of some of the uneconomic branch-lines in order to save manpower. The discussion was amicable and the consumption of whisky considerable.

The union demand was for a 4% pay rise. The Government's position was a maximum increase of 2%. In fact Macmillan and Sidney Greene, the General Secretary of the National Union of Railwaymen, had already arranged a compromise settlement at 3%, to which the Cabinet grudgingly agreed. The argument with the union representatives went on for most of the day, and Macmillan, apparently very reluctantly, at last offered 3%. After more talk and a great deal more whisky this was accepted. As he left No. 10 Downing Street, Greene gave a press interview on the doorstep, claiming a great victory; wisely, Macmillan made no such assertion. It had all been an elaborate charade, but that is the way in which these negotiations have to be conducted. By contrast, in 1973, Sir Derek Ezra made the miners his maximum offer at the outset. This left no room for manoeuvre and was one of the factors in Joe Gormley's failure to persuade his union colleagues to agree to the private arrangement he had made with Edward Heath, the then Prime Minister.

The first and most formidable hurdle had been surmounted and Macmillan was now prepared to face the bus strike, which began on 5 May. Although this was supported by the Labour Party in Parliament, it was a good issue on which to confront the growing power of the trade unions, because a busmen's strike does not harm production or disrupt the economy, but it does annoy and inconvenience the public, who tend, therefore, to support the Government. Moreover, Frank Cousins, the new secretary of the Transport & General Workers Union, was the ideal opponent. As a trenchant Left-wing critic of the Administration, he was already anathema to most Conservatives, and his militant attitude alienated the sympathy of the public. The Cabinet was not looking for a fight, but this was a battle in which the Ministers were not reluctant to engage.

Nevertheless, Macleod's position was a difficult one. In a curious way the union leaders did not, at that time, think of the Ministry of Labour as an ordinary Department of Government. They felt they could go to St James's Square for advice and that the Minister would hold the ring impartially between them and the employers. Macleod would like to have preserved this special relationship, but a unanimous decision of the Cabinet instructed him to resist the busmen's claim and, having accepted this, he fought the issue with brilliance and tenacity. As Harold Macmillan noted, the role of the Minister of Labour as a conciliator 'is something of a farce when one of the parties is a nationalized industry in which the Government is both equity-holder and banker'.[2] He added that this was one of the insoluble problems arising from nationalization.

The Opposition initiated a motion of censure against Macleod on 8 May. He replied so effectively, without the aid of a single note, that Alfred (now Lord) Robens, then Shadow Minister of Labour, congratulated him afterwards with the words 'Iain, that was a bloody fine speech'[3] and Macmillan described his attack on Gaitskell as 'a fine bit of invective'.[4]

Frank Cousins tried to involve the railway unions, the power workers and the drivers of petrol-lorries in support of the busmen, but a TUC deputation saw Macmillan on 30 May and again on 4 June, and its members were clearly against any extension of the strike; so the attempt to widen it failed and the bus workers were isolated. Negotiations were resumed and a settlement was reached on 21 June, after the strike had lasted for seven weeks.

The public were pleased that the wages front had been held, and politically the Prime Minister regarded the failure of the strike as a turning-point in the popularity of the Government. It had been a relatively easy ball to hit, but Macleod had clouted it to the boundary and his reputation stood high as the man who had stood up to the unions and defeated Frank Cousins.

The outcome of this dispute was a contributory factor in the Conservative election victory the following year. Another was a remarkably successful television discussion between Macmillan and Ed Murrow, the experienced

American interviewer. This was a communication triumph and, almost for the first time, the British public understood and began to appreciate the Prime Minister's leadership qualities, which Members of Parliament had recognized at least a year earlier.

Five by-elections were held on 12 June, resulting in good majorities in the three Conservative seats, with the Liberals no longer a real danger. Historically, Liberal revivals are always ephemeral and occur only during a period when a Conservative Government is unpopular. By the beginning of July, Macmillan felt that the political as well as the economic tide had turned and when two favourable public opinion polls in August seemed to confirm this, the newspapers began to speculate about the possibility of an early General Election. The Prime Minister's instinct was against this; he thought 'the people would regard it as rather unfair and slick'[5] and on 12 September he announced that there would be no election during the winter.

Despite this decision, he was always looking ahead and, as early as 1957, had set up a Steering Committee, under his own chairmanship, which consisted of Rab Butler, Iain Macleod, Lord Hailsham, Alec Home and the Chief Whip, Edward Heath, with Michael Fraser (now Lord Fraser of Kilmorack) as Secretary. The Committee met seventeen times and invited the attendance of other Ministers when their departmental subjects were under discussion. Fraser thought this was the most effective Committee of senior Ministers that he encountered during his thirty years at the centre of Conservative politics. In December 1958, Macmillan appointed a study group to do detailed policy work for the Steering Committee. This was presided over by Macleod and included Reggie Maudling, David Ormsby-Gore (later Lord Harlech), Jack Simon (later Lord Simon of Glaisdale), Enoch Powell and Peter Goldman. Michael Fraser, who again acted as its secretary, noted the care the Prime Minister properly took to keep separate the Civil Service and Party advice he received, and his efficiency in getting the best out of both.

In the late summer of 1958, the banks were given freedom to lend as much money as they liked and in the autumn hire-purchase controls were removed. By October the Conservative Party, which had been 18% behind Labour a year before, had achieved a lead of 3% in the opinion polls. The bank rate was reduced to 4% in November. At the end of the year, the economic prospects looked good enough to justify the bold step of making sterling convertible and this was announced on 27 December. It was a fitting end to the second year of Macmillan's Premiership and, in January 1959, he and Lady Dorothy set out on a tour of the North-East, which they knew so well from the pre-war days at Stockton. The Prime Minister was concerned about the future of the heavy industries in the area and about the unemployment figures, which were higher than for many years past – indeed, by January the overall national total had risen to 621,000. The Conservatives were always sensitive to the Socialist charge that they were 'the Party of unemployment' and if there was a fly in the pre-election Government ointment it was the level of unemployment, which had not been as high since 1947.

The Prime Minister was involved in another long-standing problem which came to a head in 1959. For some time, and especially throughout the previous year, the arrival of cheap cotton goods from India, Pakistan and Hong Kong had been causing considerable concern to the Lancashire textile industry, and repeated attempts had been made to secure a voluntary limitation on these Commonwealth imports. With the patient help of Lord Rochdale, the Chairman of the British Cotton Board, this was at last achieved in September 1959. It was accompanied by the passage of the Cotton Industry Bill, the purpose of which was to reconstruct and modernize the industry and reduce its excess capacity, at a cost to the Government of £30 million.

Another important measure passed in this last session of the Parliament was the Pensions Bill, promoted by John (now Lord) Boyd-Carpenter, which was followed in June by his statement in the House that National Assistance was to be increased by £32 million.

In an election year there is always a strong temptation to present a popular budget, but in 1959 this natural bias was supported by the economic facts and by expert opinion. Britain had the biggest balance of payments for many years and senior Treasury officials assured Derick Heathcoat Amory that expansion was not only safe but necessary. Under their and the Prime Minister's influence the Chancellor was persuaded to introduce one of the most generous budgets ever proposed in peacetime.

Purchase tax was cut, 2d was taken off the price of beer, post-war credits and investment allowances were restored, and income tax was reduced by 9d in the £. Initially this cut was to have been 6d, but the Prime Minister personally insisted on the larger remission, with the result that the total tax reductions amounted to £360 million in a full year. Macmillan described the Budget as 'simple and attractive'[6] and noted that it 'was well received in the country and by the press' – which was not surprising.

In contrast to the concessions, the budget speech itself was cautiously phrased. Heathcoat Amory said he was encouraging 'a steady but not excessive expansion in production' and he added that the Budget signalled not 'full-steam ahead, but steady ahead with confidence. This is no spending-spree Budget.'[7] But that is exactly what it was. The Chancellor had given added impetus to a boom already in existence, with the result that industrial production rose by over 10% in the year, far too rapid a rate to be maintained for long.

Most economists have criticized the Budget for giving away too much, but a more justified complaint is not that it went too far, but that it was introduced too late and that a smoother advance could have been achieved if some of the measures had been brought in, as Macmillan would himself have preferred, a year earlier. Whatever the economic criticisms, there was no doubt about the political effect. Iain Macleod often said, 'You can't have full employment, stable prices and a strong balance of payments.'[8] In fact all three coincided at the time of the 1959 election and virtually ensured its successful outcome.

24
FOREIGN AFFAIRS 1958–9

Macmillan was well supported at this period by his Cabinet colleagues. Rab Butler – who held simultaneously the offices of Home Secretary, Lord Privy Seal and Leader of the House of Commons – always presided over the Cabinet during the Prime Minister's many absences abroad and was universally accepted as his deputy. His words of advice on any problem although 'sometimes Delphic ... were none the less profound'.[1] Macmillan also greatly depended on the common sense and good humour of the Chancellor, Derick Heathcoat Amory, and upon the quick and brilliant minds of Iain Macleod, Reggie Maudling and David Eccles. Lord Kilmuir and Lord Mills added wisdom and experience to this able and talented team.

Throughout his premiership, the conduct of foreign policy claimed a high proportion of Macmillan's time. Although he had strong views on the economy, foreign affairs were his great interest and economics, by comparison, were of secondary concern. On external matters he was ably assisted by the Foreign Secretary, Selwyn Lloyd; by Alan Lennox-Boyd (now Viscount Boyd of Merton) and Alec Home, in charge respectively of the Colonial and Commonwealth Departments, and by Duncan Sandys, who was a strong and capable Minister of Defence. This was fortunate because foreign, Commonwealth and defence issues dominated the political scene during 1958 and 1959.

For the first six months of 1958, foreign policy centred mainly upon the problem of nuclear tests and the possibility of arranging a Summit Conference between the United States, Britain, France and the Soviet Union. The Prime Minister's position was that any agreement to suspend tests must be subject to an effective system of inspection and control, and accompanied by a parallel reduction in conventional arms. He remembered the abortive Geneva meeting in 1955, which had failed because the ground had not been properly prepared beforehand, and he insisted upon adequate preparation and an agreed agenda before any Summit Conference could take place.

Macmillan was interested in the possibility of a non-aggression pact with Russia, but his preliminary correspondence with Bulganin on this subject was inevitably protracted because, though taking the initiative, he was bound to consult and agree his replies with the Allied Governments in order to preserve a united Western position. President Eisenhower and Foster Dulles were at first lukewarm and felt that Macmillan was going too far in proposing a non-aggression pact and too fast in his plans for a Summit Conference. His efforts were well received, however, by the British press: *The Times* and the *Guardian* were complimentary, and the *Daily Express* commented that Britain's role as an intermediary had never been more vital.

In a House of Commons debate, Gaitskell's attitude was statesmanlike, but Aneurin Bevan's less helpful, despite his earlier observation that a British Foreign Secretary could not go 'naked' into an international conference. Selwyn Lloyd's speech on this occasion was a failure and led to some press demands for his replacement. He offered his resignation, which the Prime Minister declined to accept.

At the end of March 1958, Bulganin resigned and thereafter Khrushchev's power in Russia was supreme. Within days he had stolen a march on the West by announcing the unilateral suspension of nuclear tests. The Soviet Government had just completed a major series of tests, so Russia's own position was not prejudiced and Khrushchev's initiative was enthusiastically received by the Socialist Left in Britain, though Gaitskell was too public-spirited to join in the clamour. Successful United Kingdom tests took place at the end of April, but the programme could not be completed until September.

In June, Macmillan made another journey to the United States, the official purpose of which was to receive an honorary degree at his American grandfather's university of De Pauw in Indiana. He was accompanied by Lady Dorothy and took with him Sir Norman Brook, Freddie Bishop and Philip de Zulueta. He was warmly welcomed in the Middle West, where opinion was no longer as isolationist as it had been in the past. After a talk at the White House on 9 June, Macmillan and the President went by helicopter to Baltimore, where they both received honorary degrees at John Hopkins University. Back in Washington, the Prime Minister visited Capitol Hill and addressed the Senate of the United States, tactfully recalling that his mother had once told him that to be an American Senator was the height of human endeavour.

After further talks with Eisenhower and Dulles, Macmillan left for Canada, where he and Lady Dorothy stayed with the Governor-General, Vincent Massey. It was their first joint visit to Government House since they had become engaged to be married there nearly forty years earlier. Macmillan made a good speech, partly in French, to the Canadian House of Commons and, after returning to England, paid a short visit to Paris to apprise de Gaulle of his talks in Washington.

At the beginning of July came the welcome news of the repeal of the McMahon Act, followed by Congressional approval of the Atomic Bilateral Agreement; from then on the exchange of information between the two Governments was constant and complete. Eighteen months after Suez, Anglo-American relations were not only fully restored but had seldom been closer.

This was just as well, because the summer of 1958 was to see further critical events in the Middle East, with the fortunate difference that the United States and the United Kingdom were now working together with the same objectives. The trouble began with the formation by Egypt and Syria of the United Arab Republic, in which they were joined a month later by the Yemen. In the Aden Protectorate, the Sultan of Lahej defected to Cairo and a wave of unrest, inspired by Nasser, began to spread through Lebanon. The pro-Western President was obliged to ask for British and American help to prevent his country joining the UAR.

Worse news followed in July, when a revolutionary *coup* in Baghdad resulted in the brutal murders of the King, the Crown Prince and Nuri Pasha, and brought to an end the Hashemite monarchy, which had done so much for Iraq. This was a serious blow to the whole system of security so laboriously built up by Britain, and made Lebanon's position even more precarious. President Eisenhower decided to send the Sixth Fleet to land troops at Beirut in support of the Lebanese Government.

After a debate in the House of Commons on the United States' intervention, Selwyn Lloyd left for Washington to co-ordinate policy with Foster Dulles, and the same night a telegram arrived from King Hussein asking for British help in sustaining his regime in Jordan. Macmillan held an immediate Cabinet meeting, which unanimously authorized the despatch of two paratroop battalions from Cyprus to hold the airfield at Amman. This was an honourable response to King Hussein's plea, but the operation was a hazardous one and could only be launched if Israel agreed to the planes overflying her territory. Macmillan went to bed at 3.30 a.m., leaving it to Norman Brook to make the detailed arrangements. Unfortunately the flights from Cyprus were begun without first having obtained Israeli permission to overfly, and the airplanes had to return. Next morning, Macmillan, supported by the United States Government, sent an urgent personal request to Ben Gurion; at length a favourable reply was received and the troops were despatched.

A second debate followed in the House of Commons, opened and wound up by the Prime Minister. On this occasion the Labour Party voted against the Government, although they had not divided the House the night before.

Macmillan could not resist the reasonable rebuke: 'If it was not right to vote against America yesterday, why is it right to vote against Britain today?'[2]

Two days later Khrushchev demanded Summit talks on the Middle East situation and, partly due to Russian pressure, the Israelis withdrew the over-flying rights for both British and American reinforcements. A third battalion was therefore sent to Amman from Aden. In the end Khrushchev opted for a special session of the United Nations Assembly instead of a Summit meeting and this was held during August. Gradually the situation improved and by the beginning of November all the British and American troops had been withdrawn form the Middle East. The Allied intervention had preserved stability in the area for a decade and only Iraq remained a problem. She withdrew from the Baghdad Pact and repudiated her military arrangements with Britain; but this loss of an ally was offset by America's accession to the Pact as a full member, for which Macmillan had hoped and worked since 1955.

The troubles in the Middle East had barely been resolved when a new problem arose in the Far East. At the end of August, the Communist Government of mainland China began a bombardment of the off-shore island of Quemoy. This, with its sister-island of Matsu, was held by Chiang Kai-shek's Nationalist forces which, after their defeat by Mao Tse-tung, had occupied Formosa, now known as Taiwan. The United States had always supported General Chiang's Government and had refused to give even *de facto* recognition to the new rulers of China. Indeed, America, who at that time could still control the United Nations, had insisted that the Nationalists, though they consisted of ten million people as compared to the 600 million in mainland China, should retain their place on the Security Council, the permanent members of which were therefore the United States, the Soviet Union, Britain, France – and Formosa. It was unrealistic and absurd, but America's pride and prestige were involved in loyal if emotional support of her Nationalist friends, and her reaction to the Communist threats against the two islands was a strong one. Foster Dulles took a tough line, with a warning of military aid to Chiang Kai-shek if the integrity of Formosa was endangered. He believed that, unless the anti-Communist line was held, the whole of South-East Asia would eventually fall to the Chinese.

The position was a difficult one for both the United States and the United Kingdom. Britain had recognized Chou En-lai's Government in 1950 and considered that the off-shore islands should properly be included in mainland China; but Macmillan was anxious not to prejudice the Anglo-American relationship he had worked so hard to rebuild. He suggested to Eisenhower that any attempt to change the *status quo* by force should be denounced by the United States and by her friends and that the islands should be demilitarized; but the President felt, no doubt correctly, that Chiang, who had 80,000 troops in Quemoy, would never agree to abandon any part of his defence perimeter.

In a television programme Eisenhower declared that the bombardment of Quemoy was an act of aggression, but that his Government was ready to negotiate a solution. Macmillan was prepared to give moral support to the United States, but made it clear that he had not offered or been asked for military support. At that time Russia was on China's side, and Khrushchev sent such a rudely-worded letter to Washington that it was rejected as diplomatically unacceptable. So the matter continued throughout September, and for the second year in succession Macmillan's hopes of a holiday in Scotland receded. He did get a few days in Caithness, though he was pursued by telegrams even there.

There was never a formal settlement of the Quemoy episode, but the bombardment was suspended for a fortnight in October and, although resumed in a bizarre compromise on 'the odd days of each month' till the end of the year, the dispute gradually faded out. The 'brinkmanship' practised by Foster Dulles had paid a handsome dividend in avoiding both war with China and humiliation for the United States.

For some time Harold Macmillan had been concerned about the deterioration in Western relations with the Soviet Union and his anxieties were heightened in November 1958 by a public Russian demand for the withdrawal of the Allied forces from West Berlin within six months. He wrote to Khrushchev: 'I cannot imagine anything more calculated to increase tension ... than the kind of action which your statements appear to foreshadow.'[3] A prolonged exchange of diplomatic notes achieved nothing, and in January 1959 Macmillan conceived the idea of a personal visit to Russia. In Churchill's tradition, he always liked to take the role of mediator between East and West.

After clearing the project with the United States, he instructed Sir Patrick Reilly, the British Ambassador in Moscow, to enquire if the visit would be acceptable to the Soviet Government. After an embarrassing delay of more than a week, a favourable reply was at length received and messages were sent to the German, French and Commonwealth leaders to inform them of the proposed visit. Its purpose was not to negotiate on behalf of the West, which Macmillan had no authority to do, but to ascertain Russia's real intentions and establish a better understanding. It was a reconnaissance rather than a negotiation and would be followed by visits to Paris, Bonn and Washington.

The Prime Minister's party consisted of Selwyn Lloyd, Sir Norman Brook, Freddie Bishop, Philip de Zulueta, Tony Barber, Harold Evans and a number of Foreign Office officials. It was the first time any Western leader had visited Russia since the Second World War.

For his arrival on 21 February at Moscow Airport, where he was met by Khrushchev, Macmillan wore the white fur hat, twelve inches high, that he had last used on his expedition to Finland in 1940. It had been found in a toy cupboard at Birch Grove. He knew that this sort of hat was never worn in Russia and that his hosts would realize its Finnish origin, so he thought it would be fun to wear it on this visit. It was the cynosure of all eyes.

Days of discussion and evenings of banquets – which included a liberal supply of vodka and speeches – followed, with Khrushchev unyielding over Berlin but more encouraging about disarmament. The talks were in general terms, but the atmosphere was friendly, presents were exchanged and Khrushchev spoke of a 'thaw' in East–West relations. He went out of his way to be attentive and courteous to his guests and at one dinner proposed the health of the Queen. The impression formed by the British and foreign journalists in Russia to report on the meetings was that these were going well and until 24 February this was certainly true; but on that day, while Macmillan and Selwyn Lloyd were inspecting a nuclear research station 120 miles from Moscow, Khrushchev made a prearranged public speech, in which he criticized Eisenhower and Dulles and made violent attacks on Adenauer, the Shah of Iran and the capitalist systems in Britain, France and the United States. Surprisingly, in view of its general tone, the speech also contained the offer of a non-aggression pact with Britain.

A report of Khrushchev's attack on the West was at once made to Macmillan, but the programme for the visit had to continue and, at a British Embassy reception that evening, no reference was made to the Soviet leader's speech. Macmillan and Lloyd then left for a *dacha* outside Moscow, which had been put at their disposal by the Russian Government. Although an agreeable retreat, this guest-house was certainly 'wired for sound', so the following morning the Prime Minister was obliged to venture outside in the snow to consult his advisers about the line he should take. Khrushchev arrived for luncheon and Macmillan made it clear that by offering Britain a non-aggression pact but at the same time abusing her allies Khrushchev could not succeed in separating Britain from her friends. Macmillan stressed the danger of the German situation and an acrimonious conversation developed about the future of Berlin.

Later that evening, Khrushchev went out of his way to be publicly friendly at a performance of *Romeo and Juliet* at the Bolshoi theatre and Macmillan's appearance with him in the State box was greeted with great applause by the audience.

The official talks continued the following day in a better atmosphere, and progress was made in discussions about the less controversial matters such as increased trade, a reciprocal air service and better 'cultural relations'; but when the proposed peace treaty between Russia and East Germany was again discussed, Khrushchev reverted to a hostile, rather offensive manner, with irrelevant attacks upon Eden and the Suez episode. He was to have accompanied Macmillan on a visit to Kiev next day, but announced that he could not do so because he had to see his dentist to have a tooth filled. Such a transparent excuse was bound to excite press comment and every newspaper featured 'the tooth-ache insult', saying that 'Mr Khrushchev snubs the Premier and wrecks the talks'. However, Macmillan showed no sign of irritation and came out of the incident with dignity. The Kiev expedition went well. Macmillan had learned a few words of Russian and was able to shout to the crowds who greeted him: 'I wish you success. I wish you success.' He also knew the Russian for 'good-day', which sounded like 'double gin' in English and which he therefore used repeatedly and to good effect with the Russians and to his own enjoyment. Kiev was followed by a short visit to Leningrad, where Mikoyan and Gromyko did their best to make amends for Khrushchev's discourtesy.

On his return to Moscow, Macmillan was able to resume his discussions with the Russian leader on a more amicable basis. Khrushchev's Berlin ultimatum was in effect withdrawn and Macmillan's suggestion of a meeting of Allied and Russian Foreign Ministers, leading to one between heads of Governments, was accepted. The Prime Minister's only remaining task was a television broadcast, which he was allowed to make from an uncensored text. This was a unique concession, which he was careful not to abuse, but he felt able, in the course of it, to give Britain's industrial and scientific achievements some public recognition and to draw attention to her standard of living, at that time the highest in Europe.

A communiqué was prepared which envisaged an agreement to stop nuclear tests, but which frankly acknowledged the lack of accord over the German peace treaty and the problem of Berlin. A press conference followed and, amid airport speeches, bands and guards of honour, Macmillan was given a splendid send-off by Khrushchev at the end of eleven gruelling days, during which, despite difficulties, he had achieved what can best be described as a limited success.

On his return to England the Prime Minister reported to the Queen, the Cabinet and the House of Commons, and sent messages to the Commonwealth Prime Ministers and to President Eisenhower. On 9 March, he and Selwyn Lloyd flew to Paris for talks with de Gaulle, followed a few days later by a visit to Bonn to see Adenauer. After a brief call at Ottawa to secure Diefenbaker's support, they proceeded to Washington on 19 March, and the following day Macmillan accompanied the President to the Walter Reed Hospital to see Foster Dulles, who was dying of cancer. Dulles was rigidly opposed to any new initiative over Berlin, where he thought the Allies could 'stick it out' without risking any interference from Russia. Eisenhower wrote:

I thought again of how good it was to have as the leader of our closest and strongest ally a man with whom my acquaintance had been cordial and intimate since the days when we were together in North Africa. True, we had a troubling difference of opinion on Berlin policy, but he was a statesman upon whose integrity and friendship I could depend.[4]

The President was grateful for the care Macmillan had taken to keep him informed 'on a day-by-day basis' of his Russian visit and he recorded that 'Harold was a solid ally. I admired him the more for the frankness with which he always presented his views.'

Eisenhower took Macmillan and Lloyd to stay at Camp David, where it soon became clear that the most important decision they had to make was whether to hold a Summit meeting. The President was unenthusiastic about this proposal, on which there was a clear difference of opinion between the two men. Eventually a compromise was reached and a message was sent to the Russians suggesting a Foreign Minsiters' meeting to 'narrow the differences . . . and prepare constructive proposals for . . . a Conference of Heads of Government later in the summer'.[5] This proposition was accepted by Paris and Bonn and was agreed by the Soviet Government on 30 March.

Macmillan and Eisenhower went on to discuss Berlin, 'the limitation and inspection of forces in an agreed area' and the abolition or restriction of atomic tests. Talks followed on the Middle East, where a large measure of agreement was confirmed, and on economic issues of difficulty such as the liberalization of trade between the two countries, to which Congress was often hostile. Before leaving the United States, Macmillan again visited Foster Dulles, who seemed better and less intransigent, and who was fighting his fatal illness with immense courage and tenacity; but it was to be their last meeting because Dulles resigned on 15 April and died on 24 May. His strong personality had overshadowed American foreign policy and his death left a large gap in Eisenhower's Administration. Macmillan recorded in his diary: 'With all his faults, he had an element of greatness – a strange and essentially lonely man.'[6]

The Prime Minister reached home on 24 March, and made the usual reports on the Washington visit to his colleagues, the House of Commons, the Commonwealth Prime Ministers, President de Gaulle and Chancellor Adenauer. There was now nothing further to be done except to await the meeting of Foreign Ministers, which took place at Geneva on 11 May 1959. Little progress was made and the conference was adjourned when it was announced in August that Khrushchev and Eisenhower had agreed to exchange personal visits.

The Russian leader arrived in Washington on 15 September. He was clearly impressed by the industrial success achieved by the United States and by the high standard of living of her workers. His own ebullient personality appealed to the American people and the visit was a success. Khrushchev spoke of the President's 'far-sightedness' and said that 'the ice of the Cold War has not only cracked, but begun to melt'. He withdrew his Berlin ultimatum and an era of *détente* seemed possible between Russia and the West.

Eisenhower and Macmillan were optimistic about the prospects for the Summit meeting, though de Gaulle did not expect much to come of it. He saw no hope of concessions by either side over Berlin and Adenauer shared his pessimism. Nevertheless, it was agreed that the conference should begin in Paris on 16 May 1960.

In the meantime the problem of Cyprus, though of less importance world-wide, had continued to occupy much of Macmillan's time. Although pilloried in the United Nations as colonialism, Britain's interests in the island were simple and straightforward – to preserve peace between Greece and Turkey and to maintain the British bases against the possibility of Communist aggression in the area.

In the autumn of 1957, Field Marshal Sir John Harding had retired as Governor and been succeeded by Sir Hugh Foot (now Lord Caradon). The British Government's plan, supported by the United States, was to partition the island between the Greek and Turkish communities, with powers reserved to the Governor for external defence and internal security. Through their separate legislatures the Greek and Turkish Cypriots would control their own communal affairs. Macmillan's objective was, in his own words, to make Cyprus 'a symbol of co-operation instead of a cause of conflict'[7] between Britain, Greece and Turkey.

Owing to the firm and patriotic line taken by Hugh Gaitskell, the Labour Party did not divide the House after a debate in June 1958 and, as a result, Macmillan's plan got off to a good start, with appeals by the local leaders to their own communities to end the violence on the island. By July, the Turkish Government had agreed to Macmillan's solution and in August he visited Athens, Ankara and Cyprus for further discussions. The plan was announced to and favourably received by the British press on 15 August, but unfortunately it was rejected by Greece a week later and terrorism on the island increased.

Just before Christmas, however, there was a most hopeful development, which was to form the basis of a final settlement. The Greek and Turkish

Foreign Ministers devised a solution by which the two communities would enjoy autonomy in an independent Cyprus, with the military base areas still held under full British sovereignty. Macmillan encouraged this unexpected initiative and a preliminary agreement was negotiated at Zurich, quickly followed by a conference at Lancaster House where the three Governments endorsed the final arrangements: Cyprus was to be an independent Republic with a Greek President and a Turkish Vice-President, a Council of seven Greek and three Turkish Ministers and a House of Representatives consisting of 70% Greek and 30% Turkish Members. The Civil Service was to be staffed in the same proportions. Archbishop Makarios and Dr Kutchuk were present at the conference, representing their respective Cypriot populations, and both accepted its conclusions.

The claims for *Enosis* on the Greek side and partitioning on the Turkish side had been abandoned, and the leaders of both countries – Karamanlis and Averoff for Greece, and Menderes and Zorlu for Turkey – had shown real statesmanship in reaching a compromise on this long-standing problem. Much credit was also due to the patience and perseverance of Harold Macmillan, Selwyn Lloyd, Alan Lennox-Boyd and Sir Hugh Foot. Archbishop Makarios, who had been living in Athens since his release from the Seychelles, now returned to Cyprus.

It was not quite the end of the story because negotiations about the size of the base areas continued for many months. Macmillan entrusted these to Julian Amery, who conducted them with skill and determination, and power was eventually transferred to the independent Commonwealth country of Cyprus on 16 August 1960, with Archbishop Makarios as its first President.

In the spring of 1959, two other Colonial issues arose, this time in East Africa, which caused the Government much concern and were a source of considerable criticism by the Opposition. In March, eleven 'hard-core' Mau Mau rebels died at the Hola detention camp in Kenya and the subsequent inquest revealed that their deaths were due to 'multiple bruising' owing to a combination of ignorance and brutality on the part of the prison guards.

A full enquiry was held, which largely exonerated both the Governor, Sir Evelyn Baring (later Lord Howick of Glendale), and the Colonial Secretary of any personal responsibility. It was followed by two debates in the House of Commons in June and July; but the Cabinet as well as Parliament were shocked by the incident and Alan Lennox-Boyd felt bound to offer his resignation. Macmillan had great difficulty in dissuading him, on the grounds that it would be a blow to the Government on the eve of a General Election, a sad end to his distinguished and hitherto successful career, and that it would inevitably involve the Governor's resignation as well as his own for mistakes made by relatively minor officials.

At almost the same time, fifty-two Africans were killed by the security forces during a state of emergency in Nyasaland. Mr Justice Devlin was invited to conduct a formal enquiry and his critical report became available in July. No doubt this was somewhat over-written and did less than justice to the difficulties of the Governor and his small staff in trying to cope with a planned uprising, but the description of a British colony as a 'police state' was a shock to public opinion. As at Hola, no personal blame attached to the Secretary of State, but he was ultimately responsible for all the Colonial territories and was again anxious to resign. On this occasion the Prime Minister left the decision to his colleagues, who decided unanimously and without hesitation to reject Lennox-Boyd's offer. When every member of the Cabinet had expressed this view, Macmillan, who spoke last, revealed that, had the verdict been otherwise, he would himself not have continued as Prime Minister. A debate took place in the House of Commons, at the end of which Lennox-Boyd made a fine defence of his administration and the Government secured a good majority of sixty-three in the division lobby.

It is of note that at this period Harold Macmillan was not much interested in Colonial affairs, which he regarded as an irritating distraction from more important matters. All sentiment was excluded and on one occasion he asked Alan Lennox-Boyd for a profit and loss account to show what each Colony cost and what Britain got out of it; but he was always understanding of the problems which arose and he had a high opinion of Lennox-Boyd's ability in handling them and of his personal charm and popularity with Colonial leaders, which did much to minimize the difficulties.

In the Parliament elected after the 1959 election, Macmillan was to be involved to a far greater extent in Colonial policy and the rapid advance to self-government and independence over which he presided will no doubt be regarded by historians as one of the most significant achievements of his whole Administration.

25

THE 1959 GENERAL ELECTION

The 1959 election campaign had been in course of preparation almost from the time Harold Macmillan became Prime Minister. This was based on the premise that good public relations can best be built up over a long period and with the help of professional experts.

The firm of Colman, Prentis and Varley was in charge of Conservative publicity and in the twenty-seven months between June 1957 and September 1959 the Party spent nearly half a million pounds on advertising. The emphasis of this effort was on positive achievements. Little reference was made to the Labour Party or to negative issues like nationalization; and in the earlier stages even the name and photograph of the Prime Minister were scarcely used. Much of the press advertising was designed to correct the picture of the Party as representing a privileged minority and this was remarkably successful: whereas in 1955, 27% of the public had identified the Conservatives with wealth and privilege, by 1959 this had fallen to 17%.

The theme of the election was to be prosperity at home and peace abroad, and in January 1959 a national poster campaign was launched, which was concentrated in the marginal constituencies. One of these posters depicted a family sitting round a table well laden with food and with a television set in the background; another showed the new family car being washed by its proud owners. The accompanying slogan was 'Life's better with the Conservatives. Don't let Labour ruin it.'

Although the Steering Committee and Iain Macleod's study group had been preparing the ground for some time, it was not until the spring of 1959 that the election date was seriously discussed. On 10 April, Macmillan invited Butler, Amory, Hailsham, Poole, Macleod and Heath to a three-hour working luncheon, at which 11 June was considered and rejected and Hailsham, as Party Chairman, advised against an early election. Nevertheless, the Parliament was now in its fifth year and it was apparent that an election must be held either in the autumn of 1959 or in the spring of 1960.

The Prime Minister himself had been held in reserve until his personal popularity began to rise and he was able to undertake a series of short tours, mainly in the marginal areas, to 'meet the people and dispel the notion that he was aloof'. Macmillan's visit to Russia and his well-publicized part in promoting the Summit project were a helpful prelude to the General Election, since they gave to the Conservative leader the aura of a world statesman, working to reduce international tension and striving sincerely and successfully for peace.

In August 1959 President Eisenhower paid a five-day visit to Britain, in the course of which the two leaders appeared together in a twenty-minute television discussion. It was a natural conversation between two friends and exactly suited Macmillan's style. Though it was not deliberately political, it highlighted Macmillan's apparent influence and importance in world affairs and added to his prestige; indeed critics of the Government described it as 'the first of the campaign broadcasts'. But the decisive election influence was no doubt the prevailing sense of prosperity at home, engendered by stable prices, low unemployment, a popular budget and the people's realization that their living-standards were rising and that they could afford the holidays abroad, the cars, the television sets and the washing-machines which would have been far beyond their reach only a few years earlier.

An appeal to the country could scarcely have been made at a more propitious moment and Macmillan decided to wait no longer. He visited Balmoral on 7 September to ask the Queen for a dissolution. Polling Day was arranged for 8 October. In announcing the dissolution, the Prime Minister drew attention to the important international negotiations which lay ahead and added that it was 'clearly right that the people should have the opportunity of deciding ... who are to represent them in these negotiations'.

The purpose of the Steering Committee had been to produce the Election Manifesto. Thirty-six policy papers had been prepared, on which seven draft Manifestos had been based. The eighth draft was approved at a final meeting of the Committee on 8 September and the Manifesto was published on 11 September, under the title of 'The Next Five Years', which Macmillan had himself proposed. It was well received by the press and summarized the key issues briefly and in simple terms:

Do you want to go ahead on the lines which have brought prosperity at home?
Do you want your present leaders to represent you abroad?

The Labour Party's programme was more ambitious and contained extensive and expensive schemes for social reform, including an undertaking to increase retirement pensions immediately by an extra ten shillings a week. Macmillan replied that he would not enter into a public auction over pensions, but the promise made an impact and Labour's first television broadcast was better than its Conservative counterpart, so that after ten days the Government appeared to have lost ground and the opinion polls showed the Conservative lead down to 2%.

Hugh Gaitskell then made a fatal error by declaring that his Party's pension promise and the other increases in social expenditure could be paid for without raising income tax. This claim was ridiculed by Rab Butler, who said that Labour's slogan seemed to be 'a bribe a day keeps the Tories away', and Macmillan commented that 'Mr Gaitskell has managed to destroy in a week a reputation he had built up over a number of years.'[1] As this Conservative counter-attack was pressed home, Gaitskell's promises lost credibility in the eyes of the electorate and in the last ten days of the campaign the tide began to turn against him.

Meanwhile Macmillan had undertaken a heavy schedule of meetings, large and small, throughout the country. He travelled 2,500 miles and made 74 speeches, reiterating prosperity and peace as his election theme: 'I do not remember any period in my lifetime', he claimed, 'when the economy has been so sound and the prosperity of our people ... so widely spread. ...'[2]

It was his tenth election and the pressures of the campaign, superimposed on his continuing work as Prime Minister, were an exhausting experience. He returned to London on 5 October to make a final television appearance the following day. For this he wisely put himself in the hands of the novelist and television expert Norman Collins, who took the trouble to journey to Nottingham a few days before the broadcast to meet Macmillan and hear him speak. In his hotel, the Prime Minister was slumped in a chair, looking old and tired but later, in the hall, he seemed transformed, the model of a Guards officer in his prime, and Collins at once decided that he should do his television broadcast standing and moving about. This technique had never been attempted before and Collins was strongly advised against the experiment, but it was successful.

When the broadcast began, Macmillan was seen seated at a desk, which has been described by John Wyndham: 'Uncle Harold thinks the desk used to belong to William Pitt. Uncle Harold is the only one who thinks that.'[3] Rehearsed by Collins, Macmillan then rose and walked to a table, then to a globe and finally to a book-case. The thirteen-minute performance was thus divided into four-minute pieces, with notes left round the room in case he wanted to refresh his memory. On Collins's advice he had had his moustache clipped and was persuaded not to do up his three-button jacket by the top button, which was his usual inelegant custom.

The practice broadcast was made at a small recording-studio in Foley Street and before the last run-through, said to be merely for timing, Collins gave Macmillan a glass of vintage port, which is thought to be good for the vocal chords. This time the practice was perfect and Collins confessed that the whole thing had been recorded and there was nothing further to do. 'You wonderful fellow,' exclaimed Macmillan, 'do you mean that I have had my tooth out and not felt it?'[4] He was much relieved to have been saved the strain of a 'live' performance and the risks it involved. The BBC was less enthusiastic because the recording had not been made by its own engineers, but John Wyndham was able to arrange a compromise, by which Macmillan went personally to Lime Grove to take over if the recording broke down, which of course it did not, and the broadcast was generally acclaimed as a great personal success for the Prime Minister.

Apart from an eve-of-poll meeting at Bromley and the usual constituency tour on Polling Day, the campaign was now over and Macmillan spent the evening of 8 October at Downing Street. By one a.m. it was clear that the Conservatives had won and Gaitskell conceded the election. Harold Macmillan's own majority rose to over 15,000 and the Government's majority in the House of Commons was exactly 100 over all Parties.

For the next two years Macmillan was at the height of his power and prestige. The cartoonist Vicky portrayed him as 'Supermac' and there were accusations that he was 'being sold to the country as though he were a detergent'. Even after the collapse of the 1960 Summit, he had a 79% popularity rating in the country.

Press comment on the result of the election varied: *The Times* considered that 'a prosperous, mainly middle-class Britain cannot be stampeded by the crude old cries of under-privilege'; the *Daily Telegraph* cautioned the Conservatives that opinion was 'only predominantly, not universally, in their favour'; the *News Chronicle* observed that 'most electors did indeed believe that they had never had it so good'; and the *Daily Express* saw the outcome as 'an immense personal tribute to Mr Macmillan'.

Stock Exchange prices rocketed when the result of the election was known and *The Times*'s City correspondent reported that 'men with forty years experience had never before witnessed such scenes ... as a veritable flood of buying orders broke all records'.[5]

For the fourth time in succession the Conservatives had increased their representation in the House of Commons and, as Butler and Rose noted, 'for the first time in a century, the longer a Government has stayed in office the more established it has become'.[6] In a typical understatement, the Prime Minister's own comment was 'it has gone off rather well', and he added two days later: 'The great thing now is to keep the Tory Party on modern and progressive lines.'[7] It is often more difficult to ensure this with a large majority than with a small one.

26
THE PRIME MINISTER AND THE NEW GOVERNMENT

The Labour Party was disappointed and for a time demoralized by the scale of its defeat, especially as it was in the twenty to thirty age-group that it had lost most heavily. Articles appeared in the press speculating on the possibility of one-Party Government, with the Conservatives permanently in power. Anthony Crosland asked 'Can Labour Win?' and Gaitskell took the defeat so seriously that he embarked on a bitter battle to change the constitution of his Party.

Mary Proudfoot wrote that the next two years 'saw Mr Macmillan at the top of his form. He was popular, confident, relaxed and very much in control ... a first-class asset to his Party.'

Humphry Berkeley, then a Conservative Member of Parliament, thought:

He seemed a younger man than when I first saw him eleven years earlier, although he retained his exaggerated manner and shuffling walk. I remember him addressing the new MPs and telling us that the House of Commons was rather like a school. He cautioned us against too servile an attitude towards the whips and referred lightly to his own distinctly rebellious past.[1]

In the new Administration, Macmillan made a number of changes. Rab Butler became Chairman of the Party Organization, in addition to his appointments as Home Secretary and Leader of the House of Commons. Even for someone with as quick a mind and as great a capacity for work as Butler, this was a heavy burden and it was perhaps unwise of Macmillan to place three such major responsibilities in the hands of one man.

Another important position was vacant through the departure of Alan Lennox-Boyd, who had retired from the Government and from the House of Commons in order to devote his time to the Guinness family business. He had been an outstanding Colonial Secretary and the Prime Minister was grieved to see him go. The post was to be a most sensitive one for the next few years and would, in Macmillan's words, 'need a Minister of great imagination, even genius.... There was one man who seemed to me to possess the obvious qualities ... it was without hesitation, therefore, that I selected Iain Macleod. To my great satisfaction, he accepted with enthusiasm.'[2] Heath followed Macleod as Minister of Labour, Marples became Minister of Transport, Duncan Sandys took over Supply in order to dissolve it and create out of it a new Ministry of Aviation; and Maudling was promoted to become President of the Board of Trade.

One difficult appointment remained. Speaker Morrison had retired at the end of the previous Parliament, so a new Speaker had to be elected. Macmillan thought it was time to choose a Labour Member for this high office and suggested Sir Frank Soskice (later Lord Stow-Hill), but Gaitskell would not spare him from the Opposition Front Bench and instead put forward some other less suitable names, to which the Prime Minister felt unable to agree. Eventually, the Solicitor-General, Sir Harry Hylton-Foster, was chosen and elected unanimously.

Writing many years later Harold Macmillan paid a well-justified tribute to the Queen, whose duties were always most scrupulously performed and who gradually 'accumulated more political experience and knowledge than most of her advisers'.[3] He saw her in almost every week of his Premiership, usually on Tuesdays, and was always allowed to sit in her presence, which made their talks easier and more informal. In addition to the weekly audiences, he paid periodic visits to Windsor, Sandringham and Balmoral when the Queen was away from London.

One of the Prime Minister's duties, often involving considerable care and concern, is the submission of honours and appointments. These included life peerages, knighthoods, Regius professorships and ecclesiastical patronage in the form of the selection of bishops and deans. In Macmillan's time he had to recommend the appointment of an Archbishop of Canterbury and of an Archbishop of York. In such cases, where advice was difficult to obtain, this was often an onerous responsibility. Most ecclesiastical appointments are now no longer recommended by Downing Street but by the Crown Appointments Commission.

Macmillan noted in his memoirs[4] that the power of the Prime Minister had grown gradually over the centuries, but he acknowledged certain practical limitations upon it, including the need for constant contact and discussion with two of his principal colleagues, the Foreign Secretary and the Chancellor of the Exchequer. And he was careful with the House of Commons; apart from conversation with individual Members in the Smoking Room, which were usually Macmillan monologues and which he and they enjoyed, he always took trouble over his answers to Prime Minister's Questions on Tuesdays and Thursdays and over his speeches from the Despatch Box. He had no 'Court' or 'Kitchen Cabinet', apart from his Private Secretaries, but he sometimes consulted personal friends like James Stuart and Lord Mills, in whose judgement he had confidence.

Macmillan believed that Cabinet meetings should not be too solemn and that a little humour could relieve a tense situation. David Harlech, who as Minister of State at the Foreign Office sometimes attended Cabinets if the Foreign Secretary was away, recalled[5] that in the difficult months after Suez, the Prime Minister provided 'relaxer tablets' for the use of his colleagues. On one occasion Harlech took his tablet, though no one else did, and at the next meeting Macmillan remarked that the Foreign Office representative was the only Minister who had needed its tranquillizing effect.

Throughout his life, Macmillan was a member of many London clubs, most of which he used. During the period of his Premiership and after his retirement these included the Carlton, of which he later became Chairman, the Athenaeum, the Turf, Bucks, the Beefsteak and Pratts. He is a fascinating conversationalist and club life provided the opportunity for indulging this pleasure with an intelligent, appreciative audience who listened enthralled to his wide-ranging political and philosophical disquisitions, well laced with historical and literary allusions. He thought good conversation was fun, though not always to be taken seriously, and he enjoyed floating ideas which did not necessarily reflect his real views. He would talk for hours on a wide variety of subjects and his son-in-law, Julian Amery, recalls one occasion on which he arrived to lunch at Eaton Square at 1.00 p.m. and did not leave till 1.00 a.m. that night. Argument was a favourite way of bringing out the points of a discussion and when they first met at Caserta during the war, Macmillan spent an hour disputing a report Amery was making and then concluded their conversation with the words, 'Of course I agree with all you've said.'[6]

The physical as well as the mental strain of office, including much travelling overseas, was a burden to a man of Macmillan's age; but however long and tiring the day had been, he made it a rule to read in bed for an hour before going to sleep. The authors he preferred and re-read again and again were Jane Austen, Dickens, Thackeray and Trollope. He thought *David Copperfield* 'a noble and wonderful book' and Boswell's *Life of Johnson* was another favourite.

A twentieth-century Prime Minister has little or no privacy and can take virtually no holidays. During even the few hours Macmillan was able to spend on the golf course or grouse moor in August, he was often pursued by press photographers and there was always work to be done every evening with the Private Secretaries and on his Government boxes.

One event of importance to Harold Macmillan occurred during this period. Following the death of Lord Halifax in 1959, the Chancellorship of Oxford

University had fallen vacant and the Prime Minister was persuaded to let his name go forward for this coveted appointment. Sir Oliver (later Lord) Franks had already been nominated and the contest aroused considerable public interest.

The electors were confined to Oxford graduates in possession of MA degrees, so that many would-be voters who had not troubled to convert their BAS had to pay the additional fees to qualify. They also had to be present at the University in academic dress and on election day the trains were full and cars streamed down from London to Oxford. Derick Heathcoat Amory, then Chancellor of the Exchequer, travelled from London by train, but had no gown, so Roy Harrod arranged for him to borrow one. A.P. Herbert was another old colleague who voted for the Prime Minister.

Macmillan thought it an advantage that *The Times* printed 'a somewhat pontifical leading article'[7] attacking his candidature:

To be either Prime Minister of England or Chancellor of Oxford University is sufficient for any one man ... a single holder of two such posts may face a conflict of claims on time, on attention, on influence. ... As for the argument that now Mr Macmillan has entered the lists he cannot, because he is Prime Minister, be allowed to lose, that underlines ... the undesirability of his victory. We hope the majority of Oxford MAS ... will elect Sir Oliver Franks.

The hope was disappointed. About half those entitled to vote fulfilled the conditions and, with the loyal help of many friends, led by Hugh Trevor-Roper, Macmillan was elected by a majority of 279 votes. He was delighted to receive this honour and carried out his duties as Chancellor conscientiously and with great personal interest and enjoyment.

Macmillan was installed on 1 May, wearing the Chancellor's gown of brocaded black silk trimmed with gold lace and with his mortar-board back-to-front. His speech of acceptance, half in English, half in Latin, affirmed his affection for Oxford, and the debt he owed to his college and to the University, which he said he could never repay. He recalled with nostalgia the days before Morris motor-cars, when Oxford's only industry was a factory which made marmalade.

In June he was able to dispense the patronage which was a perquisite of the post by nominating fourteen honorary doctors of law, including Alec Home, Selwyn Lloyd, Harry Crookshank and Dame Evelyn Sharp, who had been his Permanent Secretary at the Ministry of Housing.

Macmillan had always enjoyed his visits to Oxford, but after becoming Chancellor he spent much more time there, either in his official capacity or in visiting his grandson at Balliol; and occasionally he would call in at Summer-fields, the preparatory school of his boyhood. He was interested to find so many female undergraduates in residence at the University. 'It's all very different now,' he observed. 'In my day, there were chaps' sisters and cousins in eight weeks, and then there were Gaiety Girls.'[8] When he spoke to the Oxford Society in July 1960, he said that those who had not known Oxford before the wars were like people who had never experienced *la douceur de la vie* before the French Revolution. He often seemed prouder of being Chancellor of the University than of being Prime Minister of England.

By the early months of 1960, the Chancellor of the Exchequer and the Governor of the Bank of England were growing anxious about the economy and believed that a measure of deflation was becoming necessary. The Conservative victory had been followed by an investment boom, imports were increasing rapidly and it was clear that Britain was heading for a large overseas trade deficit. In these circumstances it was decided that all Ministers should make speeches on the need for exports and Harold Macmillan agreed to make the last of the series at Church House in the summer of 1960. Freddie Erroll (now Lord Erroll of Hale), who was then Minister of State at the Board of Trade, sent him a draft beforehand which stressed the advantages of an export drive which included the phrase 'exporting is fun'. At the last minute the Prime Minister's political instinct warned him to omit this, but the press had been given an advance hand-out, so it was included in reports of the speech, although Macmillan had never said it. It caused the derisory comment he had anticipated, but he never reproached Erroll for having suggested it and indeed promoted him to the post of President of the Board of Trade in the next Government re-shuffle a year later.

The Chancellor's wish to deflate the economy was vigorously opposed by the Prime Minister. After much discussion a compromise was reached and the April Budget was broadly neutral, with a small increase in the tobacco and profits taxes. Owing to the widening trade gap, the Bank Rate was increased to 6% in June.

For some time Derick Heathcoat Amory had been anxious to give up the Chancellorship and retire from the House of Commons. He had agreed to stay for the Budget and the Finance Bill, but with these safely over he was replaced at the Treasury by Selwyn Lloyd, who had been Foreign Secretary for over four years and was due for a change of Department. Macmillan was genuinely sorry to lose Heathcoat Amory, whom he described as 'a sweet man – a really charming character'.[9] They had worked harmoniously together and Amory had proved an able and conscientious Chancellor.

Alec Home had been a success as Commonwealth Secretary and Macmillan believed, rightly, that he had all the qualities of judgement, tact and integrity needed at the Foreign Office. Nevertheless, Kenneth Young suggests that the

Prime Minister's first choice as Foreign Secretary was Butler and adds: '...
but Rab didn't want it. He was in the middle of some interesting work at the
Home Office, so he was quite unexpectedly not interested.'[10] Macmillan
confirmed that Butler had no wish either to return to the Treasury or to take
the Foreign Office.[11] The Prime Minister's next thought was to offer him
Commonwealth Affairs, in order to place in safe and experienced hands the
difficult problem of Rhodesia; but, as he noted in his diary: 'Rab does not
want anything but his present position.' Duncan Sandys, therefore, replaced
Home as Commonwealth Secretary. Thorneycroft and Powell returned to the
Government as Ministers for Aviation and Health respectively.

The Opposition were strongly critical of a peer as Foreign Secretary and
demanded a debate. The difficulty of Foreign Office representation in the
House of Commons was resolved by the appointment of Edward Heath as
Lord Privy Seal with the duty of answering for the Foreign Secretary in the
lower House. This worked well in practice. Alec Home was a great success at
the Foreign Office, where a peer has the advantage of being free to travel
without constituency commitments or House of Common whips. The
arrangement has been repeated with equally happy results by the choice of
Lord Carrington as Foreign Secretary in the present Government.

Although it caused no complaint at the time, Selwyn Lloyd's appointment
as Chancellor of the Exchequer was, in retrospect, less successful. Lord
Kilmuir considered it a mistake and L. A. Siedentrop went so far as to describe
it as a disastrous move, which 'marked the beginning of the end for Macmillan'.[12] This was unfair to Selwyn Lloyd, whose Treasury policies, though
badly presented and politically inept, were economically correct.

It is certainly true, however, that the year 1960 was the zenith of Macmillan's Government. The first three and a half years of the Premiership were a
period of almost unalloyed success, the last three of gradual decline.

27

THE AFRICAN TOUR

It is as difficult to dissolve an Empire as to create one and the deliberate acceleration of decolonization, especially in Africa, will be assessed by history as one of the most significant contributions of Harold Macmillan's entire Administration. The transfer of power between the years 1959 and 1963 was achieved without bitterness or loss of life and it ensured that the former Colonial territories in the African continent would remain members of the Commonwealth.

The key to the new approach was the Prime Minister's appointment of Iain Macleod as Secretary of State for the Colonies. Alan Lennox-Boyd, who now became Viscount Boyd of Merton, had been Colonial Secretary for five years and Minister of State at an earlier period. His whole interest in public life had been centred in colonial affairs. He was an able, popular and very knowledgeable Minister, and to most of the colonial political leaders he was a friend whom they liked, admired and totally trusted. But the nationalist wind was beginning to blow and the warm personality, wide experience and complete dedication of one man could no longer divert it.

Once independence had been granted to the Indian sub-continent, Africa was bound to follow. Ghana, soon to be joined by Nigeria, had begun the process in West Africa and this trend, although complicated by their white settler communities, was certain to continue throughout the East and Central African colonies.

After two World Wars Britain no longer had the military or economic strength to hold down her African colonies by force, even if that had been her intention. If General de Gaulle could not contain Algeria, Macmillan could not have hoped to sustain British domination over a third of the continent; in any case he had no wish to do so. Britain's policy had always been to lead her dependent territories to self-government within the Commonwealth and, in appointing Macleod as Colonial Secretary, the Prime Minister was in effect issuing a directive to quicken the pace of British withdrawal from Africa.

Theoretically Government policy remained unaltered, but the change of timing was so radical that it amounted in practice to a change of policy.

In an editorial in the *Spectator* some years later, Iain Macleod wrote:

It has been said that after I became Colonial Secretary there was a deliberate speeding-up of the movement towards independence. I agree. There was. And in my view any other policy would have led to terrible bloodshed in Africa.... Were the countries fully ready for independence? Of course not. Nor was India. ... Yet the decision of the Attlee Government was the only realistic one. ... The march of men towards their freedom can be guided, but not halted.[1]

In January 1959, Alan Lennox-Boyd had presided over a conference attended by the Governors of the three East African colonies, at which it was tentatively decided that Tanganyika might achieve independence by 1970 and Kenya by 1975, with Uganda somewhere between the two. In fact, Tanganyika became independent in 1961, Uganda in 1962 and Kenya in 1963.

There can be no doubt that the devolution of power would have been better effected if the extra decade envisaged by Lennox-Boyd had been adhered to. More African magistrates, administrators and technicians could have been trained to succeed Britain's overseas civil servants and expatriate experts. But in Africa in the 1960s, delay would probably have been fatal. Although it was dangerous to go too fast, it would have been still more dangerous to go too slowly. It was the doctrine of the lesser risk. As it was, the Government devolved power too quickly but they did so with goodwill.

In justification of this policy, Macmillan recalled the words of Thomas Babington Macaulay, written over one hundred years ago:

Many politicians of our time are in the habit of laying it down as a self-evident proposition that no people ought to be free till they are fit to use their freedom. The maxim is worthy of the fool in the old story, who resolved not to go into the water till he had learnt to swim. If men are to wait for liberty till they become wise and good in slavery, they may indeed wait for ever.[2]

The Prime Minister had also sought the advice of an experienced colonial Governor who, while admitting that his people would not be ready for independence for fifteen or twenty years, nevertheless advised that it be granted immediately. Macmillan quoted him as saying: 'If the fifteen years were to be applied in learning the job ... I would be all for it. But that is not what will happen. All the most intelligent men capable of Government will be in rebellion. I will have to put them in prison. There they will learn nothing about administration, only about hatred and revenge ... so I say give them independence now.'[3] It was a convincing argument and the premise on which colonial policy was now to be based.

The new philosophy was vigorously opposed from the outset by the Empire traditionalists in the Tory Party, led by Lord Salisbury and Lord Lloyd of Dolobran in the House of Lords and by Lord Hinchingbrooke, Lord Lambton, Patrick Wall, John Biggs-Davison, Paul Williams and Anthony Fell in the House of Commons. It was supported with equal enthusiasm by Sir Godfrey Nicholson, Hugh Molson, Richard Hornby and myself, now reinforced by a group of young Members who had entered Parliament at the 1959 General Election. These included Christopher Chataway, Charles Longbottom, Peter Tapsell and Humphry Berkeley.

Macmillan's own sympathies were, of course, with this section, but he well understood the need to keep the Parliamentary Party together and, as Humphry Berkeley relates,[4] 'he was a genius in disguising from the Right Wing his intention to disengage from Africa as rapidly as possible'. One evening Berkeley overheard him say to some of them: 'It's awfully good of Simon Dalhousie [then Governor-General of the Central African Federation] to have taken out the vice-regal gold plate which was presented to his ancestor. It's so good for morale.' On other occasions, when the disturbing news of the release from gaol of Dr Banda or Jomo Kenyatta was being discussed disapprovingly, Macmillan would flit from group to group in the Smoking-Room with chatty observations that X's son had been commissioned in the Coldstream Guards, had he, how splendid! or that Y had become Lord Lieutenant of Leicestershire, how well deserved! or that they say there are plenty of grouse at Swinton this year. Berkeley adds that the Conservative Members could then go home to dinner in the comfortable knowledge that their world had not really been disturbed.

Macmillan was much concerned about the future of the Central African Federation and he decided to send out a Commission, headed by Lord Monckton, to take evidence in the three component territories and to make recommendations to the Government. Its terms of reference, purposely wide, led later to some acrimonious comment by Sir Roy Welensky, the Prime Minister of the Federation, who had only accepted the Commission on condition that secession was ruled out; whereas Lord Shawcross, a former Labour Cabinet Minister, had only agreed to serve on condition that secession was not excluded as a solution. To Macmillan's disappointment, the Labour Party declined to nominate representatives on the Commission.

Harold Macmillan was conscious of 'dangers and storms ahead'[5] in colonial Africa and was determined to visit the continent in order to see for himself how and where the next stages of constitutional advance could best be made and to focus public opinion on the problems and thus lift them above the level of Party politics in Britain.

Whereas the Far Eastern tour two years earlier had been designed mainly to strengthen already established links, the African visit involved more complex issues, especially race relations, and Macmillan found it 'mentally and morally more testing'. He and Lady Dorothy set out on 5 January 1960, accompanied by Sir Norman Brook, Tim Bligh, who was now Principal Private Secretary, Harold Evans, John Wyndham and two officials from the Commonwealth and Colonial Departments. They were received with warmth and enthusiasm by the people of every country they visited.

The first stop was Ghana, where the Premier, Dr Kwame Nkrumah, was already moving towards the dictatorship rule he later achieved. His immediate aim was to become President of a one-Party republican state, which would, however, retain its membership of the Commonwealth. Macmillan liked him as a man and found him charming and courteous in their personal relations. At a State banquet in Accra the Prime Minister used a phrase, unremarked at the time but to receive much publicity later: 'The wind of change is blowing through Africa.' This truism had in fact been coined some months before by Alec Home.

After six days in Ghana the Macmillans left for Nigeria – the largest country in British Colonial Africa – which was divided into Northern, Western and Eastern regions and was soon to become independent as a Federation of these areas. Every federal state in the New Commonwealth, though soundly based in economic terms, has run into ruinous political problems and, in retrospect, the Nigerian Federation was doomed to disruption from its inception. Its first Prime Minister, Sir Abubakar Tafawa Balewa, later murdered by his opponents, was making a valiant attempt to instil a sense of Nigerian national unity into an essentially tribal society, which was composed of the Hausas in the North, the Yorubas in the West and the Ibos in the East. Although hopes were high in 1960, it was not long before political assassinations and then civil war destroyed this African democracy in its infancy. Parliamentary government was not restored until 1979.

On 12 January 1960, Macmillan, after discussions with Abubakar, addressed the Nigerian Cabinet, talked to Chief Awolowo, the Leader of the Opposition, and received the Premier of the Southern Cameroons, who had journeyed to Lagos to meet him. On the following day, the Senate and the House of Representatives met in joint session to hear the British Prime Minister and he spent the next four days visiting the capitals of each region.

From Nigeria, Macmillan's party flew across the continent to the self-governing colony of Southern Rhodesia, with its ruling white minority and large but unfranchised African majority. They stayed with the Governor-General, Lord Dalhousie, in Salisbury, the capital of another ill-fated Federation, beset by racial instead of tribal tribulations. Here again, the economic advantages of the Federation were immense for all the three territories which composed it, but the political problems were formidable and in the end fatal.

Northern Rhodesia (since renamed Zambia) and Nyasaland (now called Malawi) were dependencies under Colonial Office rule, but Southern Rhodesia was autonomous, governed by its European settlers and without a single British civil servant in its administration. Its Prime Minister was Sir Edgar Whitehead, and the Federation as a whole was presided over by the redoubtable Sir Roy Welensky. After discussions with these two leaders, Macmillan made a major speech on 19 January, designed to clarify the position of the British Government and to allay some anxieties which had arisen as a result of a speech he had made in Lagos. He repeated that, whatever the outcome of the Monckton Commission, the United Kingdom would not withdraw its protection from the people of Northern Rhodesia or Nyasaland 'until it is clear that the expressed wish of these people is to enter into a full and independent Federation'. He was explicit about future constitutional developments:

In all parts of this continent the tide of nationalism is flowing fast. Fifteen years ago, at the end of the war, we saw something very similar in Asia. ... As a result, India, Pakistan, Ceylon, Malaya all stand with us to-day as free and equal partners in the Commonwealth. Now we are faced with a similar growth of national consciousness in Africa. This is one of the facts of the African situation to-day. We must accept it as a fact and take it into account in forming our policies.[6]

This was an even plainer statement than the 'wind of change' warning he was later to deliver in Capetown, because it lacked the softening reference to Afrikaner nationalism and linked more clearly the achievement of independence in Asia with the prospect of it in Africa.

From Salisbury, Macmillan flew to Lusaka, where he met representatives of the various political parties, toured the Copper Belt and visited the Kariba Dam and the Victoria Falls. The next stop was Nyasaland, where feeling was noticeably hostile to the Federation. The African leader, Dr Banda, was in gaol in Southern Rhodesia and there was an atmosphere of suspense and uncertainty which could only be allayed by his release. Sir Roy Welensky was strongly opposed to this and Sir Malcolm Barrow, one of his Cabinet colleagues and a leading authority on Nyasaland, went so far as to assert that ten thousand Africans would be killed in riots if Banda was freed. The Governor, Sir Robert Armitage, thought it unwise, as did the Governor-General of the Federation; and several members of the British Cabinet were also against it. Even the Prime Minister was at first undecided. Only Iain Macleod, the new Colonial Secretary, was insistent upon release. He based his judgement on the fact that Dr Banda was the acknowledged leader of a country of four million people, only seven or eight thousand of whom were Europeans, and if the British Government was to deal at all with the majority race in Nyasaland, it must be through Banda. Macleod took the view that as long as the African leader was in gaol he was a myth, but that as soon as he came out he would be a man, and the man would be easier to cope with than the myth. And so it proved.

Banda was released on 1 April and flown immediately to Blantyre for a private talk with the Secretary of State. They got on well and, at Macleod's suggestion, Banda broadcast to the people to tell them he was free and that the future of Nyasaland could safely be entrusted to the British Government. This worked like a charm. It was as though a boil had been lanced and the tension evaporated overnight. Despite all the sombre warnings, Macleod's judgement had been vindicated and no security problems arose. The first and most difficult hurdle had been cleared and from then on the Nyasaland question was soluble.

Dr Banda's own magnanimity contributed to the new atmosphere. Soon after his release he told a cheering crowd at Blantyre: 'I am here because we have a great man at the Colonial Office. ... It took courage to do what he did – to bring me back to you.'[7]

Roy Welensky's reaction to these events was predictably unenthusiastic. The whole future of the Central African Federation and his own position as its Prime Minister were threatened by the development of Macleod's policies. With his usual clarity of thought, Macleod realized that Welensky's white-dominated, multi-racial concept, well intentioned though it undoubtedly was, could not satisfy either the determination of the European settlers to retain authority or the ambitions of the Africans to acquire it. Political power was the prize. It could be held by a black majority or by a white minority through force of arms, as in South Africa. It could not be shared for long, so the compromise was ephemeral, based on a chimera which could not endure.

Macleod thought Welensky's talk of partnership between the races was disingenuous – that it was only the partnership between the rider and the horse. This may have been true, but Welensky was fighting his own corner and no one can be blamed for doing that. His censure was not confined to the Colonial Secretary. As far back as April 1959 he had recorded the receipt of a personal letter from Harold Macmillan, 'as soothing as cream and as sharp as a razor';[8] and his distrust was reinforced by the Prime Minister's reluctance, which Welensky regarded as deliberate evasion, to tell him whether Dr Banda was to be released or not. In fact, the opposing views of those most directly concerned had first to be reconciled and Macmillan wrote: 'Accordingly I informed Welensky that I would consult further with my colleagues and would wait for communication with London. He would very shortly receive a message from Lord Home.'[9] On this ambivalent and somewhat sour note, the visit to the Federation ended; but the last and most difficult stage of the African journey still lay ahead.

On 29 January 1960 the Prime Minister arrived in Johannesburg. Several days of sight-seeing followed, which also included talks with Sir de Villiers Graaff, the leader of the United Party, Patrick Duncan of the Liberal Party, Dr Joost de Blank, the Archbishop of Cape Town, and some leading industrialists like Harry Oppenheimer; but Macmillan, who was accompanied throughout by the Foreign Minister, Eric Louw, was not permitted to meet members of the African National Congress.

The serious business of the visit did not begin till 2 February, when the Macmillans reached Cape Town. They stayed at Groote Schuur, the home of the Prime Minister, Dr Verwoerd, which provided the opportunity for long discussions between the two men. Macmillan made an interesting assessment of the character and convictions of his host.[10] He described 'the degree of obstinacy, amounting really to fanaticism' which inspired Verwoerd's policies. 'Apartheid to him was more than a political philosophy, it was a religion; a religion based on the Old Testament rather than on the New.' This was reflected even in small domestic matters. He refused to have a single African in his house, preferring the services of an old and incompetent Dutch butler. He was almost pathetically anxious for his policies to be understood by the outside world and showed a naive sense of grievance that they were not. No argument had the smallest effect upon him and, although there is normally some give and take in politics, Macmillan recorded that 'Here it was a blank wall. His charming smile, his courtesy, his readiness to expound his views without any concealment ... were in a sense impressive. But they filled me with gloom.'

Dr Verwoerd had already announced that he would hold a referendum to decide whether South Africa should become a republic, but he surprised Macmillan by saying that there was strong feeling in the Union not only against continuing as a monarchy, but also against recognizing the Queen as Head of the Commonwealth. This attitude, in contrast to that of India and Pakistan and clearly inimical to the views of the South Africans of British descent who formed nearly half the European population, seemed to Macmillan 'not merely illiberal but definitely shabby'.[11] Dr Verwoerd asked for the Prime Minister's advice as to whether, at the meeting of the Commonwealth leaders in May, he should raise the hypothetical question of South Africa's retention of Commonwealth membership if she became a republic. Macmillan expressed the view that there would be advantages in doing so.

On 3 February, the date which marked the fiftieth anniversary of the Union Parliament, the Prime Minister addressed a joint meeting of both Houses. It was the most important speech of the African tour and he was well aware that much of it would not be agreeable to his audience. After tactful tributes to South Africa's great achievements, to her wartime contribution and to the strength of her economy, including references to Britain's help through capital investment and mutual trade, Macmillan turned to the growing spirit of nationalism throughout the world. He reminded his listeners of the evidence of this in Asia and more recently in Africa itself. He repeated:

The wind of change is blowing through this continent, and whether we like it or not this growth of national consciousness is a political fact. We must all accept it as a fact and our national policies must take account of it.

He softened the impact of this statement by the disarming addendum:

Of course you understand this better than anyone. You are sprung from Europe, the home of nationalism, and here in Africa you have yourselves created a new nation. Indeed, in the history of our times yours will be recorded as the first of the African nationalisms.

He went on, however, to spell out Britain's position:

It has been our aim in the countries for which we have borne responsibility ... to create a society which respects the rights of individuals, a society in which men are given the opportunity to grow to their full stature – and that must in our view include the opportunity to have an increasing share in political power and responsibility, a society in which ... individual merit alone is the criterion for a man's advancement.

He reinforced this message by quoting from a speech made by Selwyn Lloyd at the United Nations Assembly some months earlier:

We reject the idea of any inherent superiority of one race over another. Our policy therefore is non-racial. It offers a future in which ... all play their full part as citizens ... and in which feelings of race will be submerged in loyalty to new nations.

Macmillan continued with the warning that Britain could not support 'some aspects of your policies ... without being false to our own deep convictions about the political destinies of free men, to which in our own territories we are trying to give effect'. He concluded with the words: 'Let us resolve to build, not to destroy, and let us remember always that weakness comes from division, strength from unity.'[12]

Dr Verwoerd had not seen the speech before, although he had been told the gist of it, and in his vote of thanks he felt obliged to make an impromptu defence of his policies; but local press reactions were much less hostile than Macmillan had expected and, in Bernard Levin's words, he had 'managed to spread the speech, unambiguous as it was, with so much butter that he fairly hypnotized the joint assembly ... into believing that it implied support for them and he was cheered when it was over'.[13] It was only when the British and world press highlighted the more controversial passages that criticism and resentment began to grow in the Union.

Many Europeans in Africa and their supporters in Britain were shocked by Macmillan's pronouncement. They reacted as though he had invented nationalism instead of merely pointing out its existence. At home, Right-wing Conservatives formed the Monday Club to commemorate as 'Black Monday' the day on which the speech was delivered and to condemn its contents.

During dinner that night at Groote Schuur, Verwoerd made little direct reference to the speech, but he acknowledged 'the strength of the prejudices held in Westminster and by world opinion at large against the internal policies of the Union Government'.[14] This was said more in sorrow than in anger. A month later, confidence recovered, he accused Macmillan of 'appeasement of the black man'.

The last few days of the visit were spent in sight-seeing and attending various formal functions. Whenever the Prime Minister and Lady Dorothy appeared in public, they were greeted with great enthusiasm by the people of British descent; and at a luncheon in Cape Town on the day of their departure, the Mayor proposed the loyal toast, which was followed, unusually in the Union, by the National Anthem. Cheering crowds saw them off at the docks with spontaneous renderings of *Auld Lang Syne* and *God Save the Queen*.

The return journey was by sea as far as Las Palmas, which enabled Macmillan to deal with a number of matters sent to him by Butler for decision. These included a rise from 4% to 5% in the Bank rate and a 5% pay increase for the railwaymen. Cyprus was another source of anxiety, with a complete deadlock in the negotiations between Archbishop Makarios and Julian Amery, who had been sent to the island to conduct them. Amery's skill and patience were eventually rewarded when, later in the year, Cyprus gained independence as a member of the Commonwealth.

The Prime Minister's African tour had taken six weeks and covered nearly 20,000 miles. Comment in the British press had been favourable and his speech in South Africa was well received throughout the Western world. He was gratified to receive a warm letter of congratulation from President Eisenhower, who had been much impressed by 'your masterful address in Cape Town and your analysis of the forces of nationalism in Africa'.[15] Macmillan was well aware, however, that his visit had been the beginning, not the end, of his involvement in the problems of both Central Africa and the Union.

28
AFRICA 1960–3

Events in South Africa took a turn for the worse shortly after the Prime Minister's return to London. On the morning of 21 March 1960, a crowd of several thousand Africans gathered at the township of Sharpeville, near Vereeniging, to protest against the laws which require non-whites to carry passes. The police fired on the demonstrators, killing 67 and wounding 180 in what became known as the 'Sharpeville massacre'. There was an immediate outcry and a renewal of anti-South African feeling throughout the world, which gave rise to the danger of a major split in the Commonwealth on the issue of condemning South Africa in the United Nations Security Council. A resolution deploring apartheid was introduced, which the older Commonwealth countries thought Britain should veto, but for which the New Commonwealth demanded support. The Government took the sensible if unheroic decision to abstain.

There seemed no end to the troubles in Africa and on 9 April news reached Macmillan that an attempt had been made to assassinate Dr Verwoerd. He had been shot in the face and neck by a madman – fortunately white – but made a remarkable recovery from the wound.

Soon afterwards, the Commonwealth Prime Ministers' Conference assembled in London. It began auspiciously with a splendid dinner-party given by the Queen in the Waterloo Room at Windsor, but it was inevitable that the South African issue would dominate the discussions and it was duly raised, though in very moderate terms, by Tunku Abdul Rahman, the Prime Minister of Malaya. It was agreed that the matter should be debated 'upstairs' with only the Prime Ministers present and Mr Louw, who was representing his country in the absence of Dr Verwoerd.

The first of these informal sessions went badly and Macmillan noted that 'the feeling against South Africa is swelling to really dangerous proportions'.[1] The developments the following day, 5 May, are best described in the Prime Minister's own diary entry:

Eric Louw gave a Press Conference yesterday – bitter, unyielding – but very well done. ... The Tunku has replied by issuing an offensive (and inaccurate) attack ... at the end of the afternoon session there was a row between them. Nkrumah of Ghana, who 'joined' last year and is behaving with great restraint, is said to regard the Tunku's performance with disfavour. ... Field Marshal Ayub of Pakistan, who is like an old Indian Army colonel, thinks that 'none of them come out of the top drawer anyway'. Diefenbaker – who is ... deaf and very sensitive – joined in.[2]

After an appeal for reflection over the weekend, Macmillan adjourned the meeting, but the prospects were unpromising: 'If we do nothing, the Commonwealth will seem to have no faith and no purpose. If we do too much, South Africa will secede and this may mean the beginning of a general break-up.'

The diary notes continue:

When we met on Monday morning ... Louw spoke – too long but ably.... Then everyone spoke, every single one of them – I wound up at 12.30 p.m. ... every aspect – internal and external – of South African policy was fully debated.

Macmillan added some further comments on his Commonwealth colleagues:

Dr Nkrumah has been sensible and moderate ... Menzies has been a tower of strength ... Nash is a nice, good-natured, well-intentioned, old fashioned Liberal – a bore, but sincere. ... I found Diefenbaker more difficult to understand. ...

The work of the Conference was concluded on 12 May; but the final communiqué, always the most difficult part of any conference, was not completed till midnight. Although the next day was Friday the 13th, the text was unanimously agreed by noon and the unity of the Commonwealth, albeit precariously, had been preserved. This had been Macmillan's main preoccupation throughout the Conference. He had written to the Queen: 'My supreme task is to try to steer the Commonwealth through this crisis and to avoid anything in the nature of disintegration.'[3] Disaster had been averted, but the problem of South Africa had been postponed, not resolved.

Verwoerd was still determined to press his application to remain in the Commonwealth though declaring South Africa a republic. His position was a logical one, because most of the New Commonwealth countries had opted for a republican form of government, while retaining their association with the Commonwealth and acknowledging the Queen as its Head. But Verwoerd underestimated the strength of feeling which his apartheid policy and the Sharpeville tragedy had generated, and Macmillan felt bound to warn him that South Africa's continued membership would probably be opposed unless her racial policies were modified. He therefore urged postponement of the constitutional change.

Verwoerd persisted in the view that apartheid was an internal matter in which other countries had no right to interfere and on 5 October 1960 he held a referendum in South Africa, which resulted in a majority in favour of a republic. Citizens of the Union who were of British descent voted solidly for remaining a monarchy, but Verwoerd was not to be deflected and he restated his resolve in a long letter to Macmillan. In order to decide the matter, another meeting of the Commonwealth Prime Ministers became inevitable and this was arranged for the Spring of 1961.

During the intervening months, Macmillan did all he could to keep South Africa in the Commonwealth and he was hopeful of success when both Nkrumah and Tunku indicated that they would not force the issue. Opposition then arose from an unexpected quarter in the form of a letter from Diefenbaker warning that Canada could not be counted upon to support South Africa's application. This was a severe disappointment. As Harold Macmillan noted in his diary: 'If the Whites take an anti-South African line, how can we expect the Browns and the Blacks to be more tolerant?'[4] He argued the matter by telephone and in an eloquent and persuasive letter to Diefenbaker, urging him to come to the Prime Ministers' meeting with an open mind, and also wrote on the same lines to Nehru.

The Conference assembled at Lancaster House on 8 March 1961. Due partly to press agitation against South Africa, partly to Nehru's decision to oppose the application and partly to the rigid attitude adopted by Dr Verwoerd, the discussions went badly and feeling ran so high that Macmillan was often obliged to adjourn the sessions. The balance was finally tipped against South Africa by Verwoerd himself, who refused to accord the normal diplomatic courtesies to representatives of African Commonwealth countries. This petty discrimination was the last straw. It seemed absurd for South Africa to remain in the Commonwealth and for Verwoerd to meet his fellow Prime Ministers at Marlborough House, yet decline to grant the usual civilities to their ambassadors in the Union.

When it was clear that no compromise could be devised, Macmillan persuaded Verwoerd to withdraw his application rather than take the matter to a vote, which could have led to the dissolution of the Commonwealth and would certainly have been highly embarrassing to Britain. A communiqué was issued accordingly and the Prime Minister made a short statement in the House of Commons the following day. He was deeply depressed to have presided over such a distressing event and conscious that the Conference had served to embitter, rather than soothe, the feelings of the participants. It was a sad end to Britain's long association with South Africa and an unhappy breach in the British Commonwealth of Nations.

While the future of South Africa was being decided, other constitutional issues in East and Central Africa were also causing concern. The first of these arose in Kenya. The Colony's original white settlers, before and after the 1914 war, had been aristocratic and upper-class landowners. They had developed large, lucrative estates in the Highlands and their children, educated in Britain, were often liberal-minded men who realized that eventually the Africans were bound to rule in Kenya and who regarded this prospect without despair. They were in a minority. The second and numerically larger category of Europeans had emigrated from Britain either just before or soon after the Second World War. Their skill, enterprise and capital investment had, as in Southern Rhodesia, made an important contribution to the economy of the colony and they expected it to be governed in their interests more or less indefinitely. This may have been myopic but it was understandable. The impetus towards nationalism had been unrecognized by these privileged paternalists, who slowly realized that their way of life was being threatened and who resented what they regarded as a betrayal of all they had created in Kenya. There had also been a large influx of immigrants from India, who were later to cause problems of a different kind when African jealousy of their commercial success led to their expulsion from the country.

The Mau-Mau rebellion between 1952 and 1956 had retarded progress, but the emergency powers, which had lasted for seven years, were lifted in November 1959 and a Kenya constitutional conference was convened two months later. It was a long and difficult one and Macmillan commented in his diary on 21 February that its satisfactory conclusion 'is certainly a great triumph for the Colonial Secretary'.[5] Macleod had been able to enlist the support of the moderate Europeans led by Michael Blundell, to whom much of the credit for the success of the conference was due. 'You can't compel people to be moderate,' Macleod observed, 'but you can so draft the constitutions that the moderate is encouraged.'[6] Blundell was the bridge between white rule and black and without his help the transition would certainly have been delayed.

By the summer of 1961, it was possible for Macleod to release Jomo Kenyatta from detention and two years later he became Prime Minister of an independent Kenya. The man who in 1960 had been described by the then Governor of the colony, Sir Patrick Renison, as 'the leader to darkness and death' was soon being praised by Europeans as 'the great stabilizing influence in East Africa' and by 1964 Duncan Sandys could remark with complete sincerity: 'If every Commonwealth statesman was as wise, as co-operative and as helpful as Jomo Kenyatta, there would be no problems in the Commonwealth.'[7]

The corresponding conference for Tanganyika was a much easier one. It was held in Dar-es-Salaam early in 1961 and resulted in full and speedy agreement. The African leader, Julius Nyerere, is an intellectual who also has a peculiarly English sense of humour and Macleod liked him at once. They were able to draw up and agree all the main constitutional points on the back of a postcard before the conference even met.

The Uganda Conference followed in September of the same year, but was more difficult because Macleod never established a good relationship with the Kabaka, whom he thought obstinate and obsessed with minor points of precedence. Dr Obote, then leader of the Opposition, was, however, a helpful influence and the Conference eventually came to a successful conclusion. Uganda became independent in October 1962.

Meanwhile, a constitutional conference for Nyasaland had been held in London in July 1960 and had agreed on an African majority in the Legislative Council. Macmillan again described this result in his diary as 'a great triumph for the Colonial Secretary'.[8] In isolation this was true, but it presaged wider problems for the Federation, since Banda was determined to secede as soon as Nyasaland became independent. Welensky might reluctantly have accepted this because the colony's overwhelming black population reduced the relative strength of whites in the Federation as a whole. Indeed, many Europeans preferred the line-of-rail policy for Northern and Southern Rhodesia. But independence and secession for Nyasaland would be the precursor for the same demands in Northern Rhodesia, whose economic potential and large mineral resources were essential to the Federation; so these interrelated issues could no longer be shelved.

The Central African Federation had brought great gains to the three territories it comprised: a common market, the development of industry and ambitious projects such as the Kariba dam had resulted in a remarkable rise in the standard of living for all sections of the population. The Monckton Commission report, published in October 1960, gave full endorsement to these economic advantages; but it also recognized that African opinion was strongly opposed to the continuance of the Federation on the grounds that it was impeding political advance for the African people.

The report recommended changes in the Federal constitution which would give greater African representation in the Assembly; constitutional advance in Northern Rhodesia including an African majority in the Legislature of the colony; and the repeal of discriminatory legislation in Southern Rhodesia. It advised that the British Government should be prepared to consider requests from any of the three territories to secede from the Federation. These recommendations, especially the last, gave rise to prolonged argument with Sir Roy Welensky, who maintained, with some justification, that the Commission had exceeded its terms of reference; but the report was well received in the British press and the stage was now set for the Review Conference on the future of the Federation, to which everyone had agreed and which opened at Lancaster House on 5 December.

When Macmillan invited the chief participants to Chequers for the weekend, he was amazed to discover that Welensky was meeting Banda and Kenneth Kaunda for the first time, in England. Although they were the acknowledged leaders of majority opinion in two out of the three territories in the Federation of which Welensky was Prime Minister, he had not thought it necessary to meet them in Africa. This failure of communication exemplified much that was at fault in the way the Federation had been governed.

The discussions were prejudiced by the frequent press conferences in which all the delegates indulged and by periodic walk-outs by the Africans. Nothing was achieved and Macmillan adjourned the Review Conference *sine die* on 17 December. The two territorial conferences were also postponed until the New Year. Duncan Sandys managed the Southern Rhodesia negotiations with great skill and the new constitution which emerged from them was endorsed by a local referendum in July 1961 and enacted by the British Parliament in November.

The Northern Rhodesia Conference was more controversial. Whatever the European view about Nyasaland, there could be no doubt in anyone's mind that Northern Rhodesia was crucial to the survival of the Federation. Macleod's ultimate objective of independence for the colony was therefore bitterly opposed by Sir Roy Welensky and the negotiations were complicated, almost continuous and usually acrimonious.

When the Conference reconvened in February 1961, it was boycotted by Welensky's United Federal Party, but not by the European Liberal Party led by Sir John Moffat. Macleod's aim was parity for one Northern Rhodesia Parliament, to be followed by an African majority in the next. Welensky might not have opposed parity in perpetuity; he could not tolerate the prospect of an African majority which would lead inevitably to independence and secession. His decision to boycott was a mistake, as it almost always is – one cannot influence the outcome of a conference of which one is not a member. Nevertheless, he exerted great pressure upon the British Government and was supported throughout by the Right wing of the Conservative Parliamentary Party. This tended to weaken the resolve of the Cabinet, whose attempts to mollify Welensky created distrust among the Africans. It was a vicious circle.

Since the Northern Rhodesia negotiations affected the Federation, Welensky claimed and was accorded the right to be consulted. The word 'consult' is ambiguous and was interpreted in Salisbury as a right of veto. Although this was refuted by the British Government, the consultative process led to concessions which not only aroused African suspicions, but also misled Welensky. He imagined he could alter basic policy, which he could not. The result was what Macleod described as 'parity of abuse'. He did not mind this, because if both Welensky and Kaunda criticized his proposals, neither could claim that he had sold out to the other. His aim was to persuade both sides to take part in a general election. In this he was eventually successful, but he had to tack and turn to get there.

Macleod's position was complicated by the Cabinet's compromise in allowing parallel talks to proceed between Salisbury and the Commonwealth Relations Office. In an attempt to reconcile these two separate negotiations, the Prime Minister set up a Cabinet committee, over which he himself presided, to co-ordinate the work of the Colonial and Commonwealth Ministers. It was a cumbersome procedure, involving the discussion of endless formulae and long hours of often abortive work, but it had become necessary because of the conflicting views of Sandys and Macleod.

The differences between the two Ministers were of timing and emphasis, not of principle; but they were never friends. Almost their only common characteristics were courage and determination. Their relationship was once described by Hugh Fraser as being as cold and bleak and silent as that between the Matterhorn and Mont Blanc. Macmillan made this comparison:

The Colonial Secretary (although a brilliant and most likeable man) is not an easy colleague. He is a Highlander – which means that he is easily worked up into an emotional mood; it also means that he is proud and ambitious. But he has great qualities – a soaring spirit and a real mastery of Parliamentary speaking. Sandys is a great contrast. ... As cool as a cucumber; methodical; very strong in character ... tremendously hard-working; not easily shaken from his course.[9]

The Prime Minister's reference to Macleod's Highland characteristics recalls a comment on Harold Macmillan himself, which was made by another Ministerial colleague, also a Highlander, who thought Macmillan's own ancestry was an important element in his personality. He paid tribute to the Prime Minister's imagination and vision, but added that he was sometimes devious. 'Anglicized crofters', he remarked, 'have not got the same sense of honesty as the English.'

Duncan Sandys was one of the strongest and most experienced Ministers in Macmillan's Government. He worked extremely hard and his thoroughness and attention to detail were proverbial. When he had been in a department for a few months, he knew more about its main areas of responsibility than most of the officials who had worked there for twenty years. He is essentially a doer rather than a thinker, more concerned to resolve practical problems than to evolve theories or philosophies. His contribution to public life has been second to none and those who believe that Britain is ruled by its civil servants can never have worked for Duncan Sandys.

The disagreements between the two Secretaries of State took up too much of Macmillan's time and energy. He wanted to get Northern Rhodesia off the Cabinet agenda and he became impatient with Macleod's persistent arguments and complicated proposals. A rift developed in their hitherto close relationship. Sir Reginald Bennett, then Macleod's Parliamentary Private Secretary, recalls that, when there was a division in the House of Commons, Macmillan and Macleod would often come swinging into the lobby together, the Prime Minister's arm round Iain's shoulder and the two men clearly in the closest accord. But one evening, early in the year 1961, as Macleod entered the lobby with Bennett, Macmillan, who was sitting on a bench opposite, caught Iain's gaze and his eyes flickered away. At that moment it was plain to Bennett that Macleod no longer had the Prime Minister's full confidence and support.

After the February conference on Northern Rhodesia, the Government published a White Paper outlining Macleod's proposals, as a result of which the five United Federal Party Ministers in the colony resigned their offices and withdrew from the Executive Council. This enabled Sir John Moffat to form a transitional government. He filled the same thankless but essential role that Michael Blundell was already discharging in Kenya.

Many of the Government's Back Bench supporters were critical of Macleod's policies and a motion signed by ninety Conservative Members appeared on the Order Paper. Its significance lay in the fact that it attracted support from the centre of the Party as well as from known Right-wingers. There was corresponding criticism in the House of Lords, which culminated in Lord Salisbury's denunciation of Macleod as 'too clever by half'. Salisbury said he spoke for the white communities in Africa, who felt they could not trust the Colonial Secretary, and added that he thought Macleod was 'rather unscrupulous'. This was a personal attack upon the man as well as upon his policies and was strongly refuted by Lord Hailsham and Lord Perth, but the damage had been done. Macleod had alienated an important section of the Conservative Party and this prejudiced his prospects of ever becoming its leader.

During his frequent visits to London, Sir Roy Welensky not only wearied Macmillan with endless discussions about the Northern Rhodesian constitution and the future of the Federation, but was often invited to address the Conservative Commonwealth Affairs Committee. He always took these opportunities to rally Back Bench support for his views and in this climate of political pressure many modifications were made to Macleod's earlier proposals. These concessions to Welensky were incorporated in another White Paper published in June, which aroused the suspicion and mistrust of the Africans. After further discussion with the Secretary of State, Kaunda, who is a man of character and strong Christian faith, agreed to try and sell the new White Paper to his followers. Despite his attempts to do so, there was some violence and sabotage in Northern Rhodesia during the summer and, although Macmillan rightly rejected any concessions to violence, he agreed to receive representations from Kaunda if order was restored.

At the beginning of October, the Prime Minister decided upon a Cabinet re-shuffle. He had become irritated by Macleod's emotional involvement in the problems of Northern Rhodesia and by his intolerance of any views which differed from his own; but Macmillan had a high opinion of the intellectual brilliance of the Colonial Secretary, whom he described later as 'the last of the orators in the Tory Party',[10] and he showed his continued confidence by awarding Macleod promotion as Leader of the House of Commons and Chairman of the Party Organization. Reggie Maudling, who succeeded Macleod at the the Colonial Office, had the same liberal outlook and pursued the same policies, but without the same passion. Macleod's initiative and determination had been needed to launch and sustain the new momentum in Africa, but Maudling's milder technique smoothed many ruffled feathers and the Prime Minister showed good judgement in making the change when he did. Nevertheless, he commented ruefully:

Had I thought that there would be some relief in the pressures from the Colonial Office, I was doomed to disappointment – I soon found that Maudling was quite as 'progressive' as Macleod. Indeed, in some respects he seemed *plus royaliste que le roi*.[11]

The new Secretary of State made a number of concessions to the Africans and finally, though not without difficulty, brought the matter to a conclusion in February 1962 on much the same basis as Macleod had recommended a year before. The delay had achieved nothing for anyone. It had annoyed the Africans without pacifying the Europeans and the often ambivalent attitude of the British Government had given substance to Welensky's charge of equivocation. The Northern Rhodesian constitution, as it finally emerged after the long, intricate and often tortuous negotiations, could be shot full of holes. It was far too complicated and the technical criticisms of it were certainly valid, but it set the colony on the road to independence and this spelt the doom of the Federation.

Two years' experience had convinced Macmillan that the divided control by which Southern Rhodesia came under the Commonwealth Secretary, and Northern Rhodesia and Nyasaland under the Colonial Office, was an unworkable system. He therefore decided to give responsibility for the whole area to one Minister and persuaded his most senior colleague, Rab Butler, to accept this onerous and thankless task. In October, the Prime Minister gratefully recorded that Butler

... has certainly succeeded in giving us a quiet six months. ... It was an enormous relief to me to be spared the almost daily flow of telegrams in and out and the continual and divergent pressures which had operated under the old system.[12]

It had become clear by this time that, even outside the African continent, Commonwealth and colonial problems were overlapping in so many areas that it would be sensible to combine their direction under one Minister and in July 1962 Macmillan invited Duncan Sandys to assume responsibility for both Departments.

Following elections under the new constitution in December 1962, an African Government took office in Northern Rhodesia and in the same month Sir Edgar Whitehead's Party was defeated in Southern Rhodesia. This was a disappointment to Macmillan, who wrote him a personal letter of appreciation for 'the moderation and understanding which you have always brought to discussions with us here'.[13] Whitehead was succeeded by Winston Field, the leader of the victorious Rhodesian Front, whose objective was independence for Southern Rhodesia. As Macmillan commented, the change 'may really simplify the situation for Butler, since none of the three Provisional Governments is now in favour of Federation'.[14] It was important, however, to maintain the economic links between the territories, which were beneficial to them all.

Butler convened a conference at the Victoria Falls in June 1963 and conducted this with such tact and skill that agreement was reached within a week. The Federation was dissolved on the last day of the year, by which time Macmillan had retired from the Premiership. The story of Central and South Africa in the last three years of his Government had not been a happy one and the amount of time and trouble the problems there had taken was disproportionate to the results the Prime Minister and his colleagues had been able to achieve.

29
THE 1960 SUMMIT

Harold Macmillan always believed in the efficacy of Summit meetings as the best way of working towards world peace. He thought the only hope of making progress with the Soviet Union was through face-to-face talks with Khrushchev and he saw such meetings as a continuing process, a series of Summits, slowly surmounting each of the major problems in turn, until an atmosphere of peaceful co-existence had become firmly established. No one could have worked harder to reach this objective than Macmillan.

A Foreign Ministers' Conference had been held in May 1959, the purpose of which was to make enough progress to justify a later meeting between Eisenhower, Khrushchev, Macmillan and de Gaulle. Little was achieved and President Eisenhower wrote firmly to Macmillan in June reiterating his view that 'a Summit meeting based on nothing more than wishful thinking would be a disaster'; and in July, without consulting his allies, he suddenly issued an invitation to Khrushchev to visit the United States. This important event took place in September and proved successful. It was to be followed by a return visit to Russia by Eisenhower and, as a result of it, the President issued a public statement that his talks with Khrushchev had removed many of the objections to a Summit which he had hitherto felt.

A pre-Summit meeting of the four Western leaders was held in Paris in December 1959, at which it was agreed that Paris should also be the setting for the Summit itself. The date was arranged with Khrushchev for 16 May 1960. De Gaulle made the imaginative suggestion that joint agricultural and social plans for the underdeveloped countries should be discussed with the Soviet leader and such a partnership between the Communist and the non-Communist world would clearly have been a dramatic advance in East/West relations if it could have been achieved; but the main subjects for the Summit agenda were bound to be Berlin and disarmament. It was agreed that the Allied meeting in Paris should only be the first of several, perhaps annual, conferences, the others to be held successively in the capital cities of the countries concerned. De Gaulle also secured assent to his proposal for regular tripartite discussions between France, the United States and the United Kingdom.

The whole atmosphere of the Western Conference was one of friendship and confidence. In an informal talk with de Gaulle after the President and Adenauer had departed, Macmillan felt that their relationship was more cordial and relaxed than ever before. De Gaulle considered it important that France and West Germany should be close economically and said it was for this reason that he had approved the Common Market, though he had no real liking for it. Macmillan believed that it would now be possible 'to get much nearer to the French without in any way upsetting the Americans'[1] and, in a note to the Foreign Secretary, he wrote that his purpose was 'to support de Gaulle on the political front ...'[2] in return for French help for British trade interests.

In March, Macmillan again flew to Paris for two days of informal talks, conducted entirely in French, with de Gaulle and his Prime Minister, Michel Debré. He recorded that the President of France 'does *not* want political integration'[3] in Europe and had only accepted economic integration with regret, but believed it had had a useful effect in making French industry more competitive and in keeping Germany orientated to the West. De Gaulle did not care for the NATO command structure, which he thought 'demoralized' the French Army: and he was frank about the defects of French agriculture, due to the small units which had resulted from the partition of land under the Code Napoléon. Although he resented his exclusion from Anglo-American discussions and seemed jealous of Macmillan's close personal association with Eisenhower, the Prime Minister noted that he had mellowed with the years: 'Now that he is old ... his charm is great.'

A few days later the Russians made an unexpected move towards a moratorium on nuclear tests and Macmillan decided upon a quick visit to Washington to persuade President Eisenhower to respond positively to the Soviet proposal. He informed de Gaulle, Adenauer and the Commonwealth Prime Ministers of his intention and at the same time received a friendly letter from Khrushchev expressing optimism about the Summit meeting in May. Eisenhower, supported by Christian Herter, the new American Secretary of State, accepted the principle of a moratorium, despite the strenuous opposition of the Pentagon and the Atomic Energy Commission, which both believed the Russians would cheat and which in any case wished to continue America's own experiments. After spending the weekend at Camp David, Macmillan returned to Washington for a lunch with Senator Fulbright, followed by an extempore speech to the Senate of the United States, and flew back to London on the night of 30 March.

Lord Kilmuir paid tribute to the Prime Minister's pre-Summit success:

Macmillan had held an initiative in foreign affairs which was quite remarkable. He had led an uneasy Eisenhower carefully and skilfully along the road to Paris. He had persuaded the chronically suspicious Russians that there was a genuine desire on the part of the West for a *rapprochement*.[4]

De Gaulle stayed at Buckingham Palace during a successful visit to England in April and was received with enthusiasm by large crowds in the streets. This was the final prelude to the Summit meeting, for which the Prime Minister had worked so hard; but almost on the eve of the Conference an unexpected event destroyed all his hopes.

On 5 May Khrushchev announced that an American U2 airplane had been shot down over Soviet territory four days before. The pilot, who had parachuted to safety, admitted that he had been engaged on an espionage flight. His cameras and photographs were captured by the Russians and official denials that he had been spying were plainly untrue. Despite this, Khrushchev did not threaten to cancel the Conference. He wrote a relatively mild letter of complaint to Macmillan, to which the Prime Minister and Philip de Zulueta drafted a tactful and constructive reply; and on 9 May Christian Herter issued a statement admitting the use by the United States of 'extensive aerial surveillance', but claiming that these missions 'have not been subject to presidential authorization'. The situation might still have been retrieved if nothing further had been said, but unfortunately President Eisenhower stated at a press conference on 11 May that the U2 flights had been made with his knowledge and approval. He did not even explain until later that he had ordered the flights to cease at the end of April and that this was, in fact, the last one to have been despatched. His unnecessary admission of personal responsibility had the inevitable effect of hardening the Russian reaction and, when Macmillan arrived in Paris on 15 May, Khrushchev at once called to see him with demands that Eisenhower should apologize for the U2 incident, undertake never to repeat it and punish the offenders.

The French, cynically but shrewdly, thought the Conference was over before it had begun. The British and Americans were more optimistic; but at the first plenary session the following morning Khrushchev delivered a vitriolic personal attack on Eisenhower. In addition to the demands he had made to Macmillan, he added that the President's proposed visit to Russia must now be cancelled and that the Conference should be postponed for eight months until Eisenhower was no longer the Head of the United States Administration. After a short and restrained reply by the President, Macmillan pointed out that over-flying was not to be resumed and appealed for time for reflection, followed, hopefully, by a resumption of the Conference on the grounds that *ce qui est déferré est perdu*. Although de Gaulle realized the talks were doomed, he made an effective and helpful contribution and, after a long argument, the meeting was adjourned. In an attempt to save the Conference, Macmillan saw each of the other leaders separately between six p.m. and midnight, but Khrushchev was immovable; he would not attend another session unless his demands were first fully met.

De Gaulle described the meeting next morning as 'mere formalities'. Effectively, the Conference was over. It had failed disastrously, leaving the East/West atmosphere far worse than if it had never been attempted. This was no fault of Macmillan's, but so important was the Anglo-American relationship to Britain that he never reproached Eisenhower by private word or even inference for the calamitous error of judgement he had made through over-honesty at his press conference. After returning to Washington the President sent him a warm letter of appreciation: '... No one could have tried harder. I applaud your efforts; no one could have done more.'[5] De Gaulle also wrote to say that he believed recent events had strengthened the alliance.

Macmillan recorded his realization that

Khrushchev had risked much by ... trying to achieve co-existence and even some degree of co-operation between the Communist and the non-Communist world. It was, of course, doctrinally dangerous. ... The U2 incident was a blow to the image which he had built up and the inept American handling of the affair ... must have given him genuine offence. ... He may have acted partly under pressure and partly under a real sense of indignation. ... A greater man would have made all the capital he could by his protests, but would have seized the opportunity to rise above his feelings of injury and thus shown himself the dominant figure in world politics. By his actual handling of the affair he lost a great opportunity – but so, alas, did the whole world.[6]

On his return from Paris, Macmillan made a short and sombre statement to the House of Commons, which was sympathetically received by Parliament and in the press:

I cannot conceal from the House that there may be grave implications in what has happened. ... We must be prepared for the international outlook to be more stern.[7]

And so it proved, as crisis followed crisis over the Congo, Berlin and Cuba.

Although Macmillan was bitterly disappointed by the collapse of all his hopes for a genuine *détente*, his efforts as an honest broker between the United States and the Soviet Union ensured that his own and Britain's reputation did not suffer from the breakdown. Indeed, the 1960 *Survey of International Affairs* commented that:

It was the peculiar service of the British Prime Minister to have stepped into the breach and restored some element of balance, coherence and sang-froid to the badly rattled Western alliance.

Despite the blow to his Summit policy, Macmillan's standing as a world statesman in the summer of 1960 was high and a Gallup poll at the time showed a popularity rating of 79%, the highest ever recorded for a peacetime Prime Minister. Such are the vicissitudes of public life that less than three years later his rating was lower than that of any Prime Minister since Neville Chamberlain.

The first consequence of the Summit failure was a Russian walk-out from the Disarmament Conference at Geneva. This was quickly followed by another aircraft incident. An American RB 47 airplane from a British base disappeared in the course of an Arctic Ocean survey. Although it was not flying over Russian territorial waters, as the Soviet Government claimed, it was chased and shot down by Russian fighters. Protests followed to the American and British Governments, to which Macmillan replied with an open letter to Khrushchev, phrased in temperate terms. The only answer took the form of an attack on Western depravity, with no further reference to the RB 47, so it seemed that the whole episode had been deliberately staged by Russia in order to make trouble.

Meanwhile, Macmillan, who was anxious to improve co-operation between the British, French and American Governments, wrote to Eisenhower and de Gaulle setting out a possible mechanism for tripartite consultation, as a result of which the three Foreign Ministers met in Washington. Eisenhower sent a favourable reply to Macmillan's initiative and de Gaulle suggested an extension of the arrangements to include political co-operation between the Ministers of Defence or the Chiefs-of-Staff. Eisenhower accepted this in principle but added, in his reply to de Gaulle, that liaison on military matters would best be achieved through NATO. This was unacceptable to the General, who believed it would prejudice the tripartite system and would in any case confine co-operation within too narrow a compass to fulfil the global objective he had in mind. He suggested a meeting between the three Heads of State in Bermuda and, although Eisenhower wished to postpone this till the end of the year, de Gaulle was grateful for the support Macmillan gave him.

Since 1958, the design and development of increasingly sophisticated and expensive new weapons had taxed the minds and money of the British Government and Macmillan acknowledged, 'I must bear the full responsibility for many costly decisions and mistakes.'[8] At first a rocket known as Blue Steel, to be projected from a bomber in flight, was thought to be the right solution. This was replaced by Blue Streak, a ground-to-ground ballistic rocket upon which the Minister of Defence, Duncan Sandys, worked with great assiduity. Against his advice, however, it was abandoned in 1960, partly because of the cost, but mainly because a fixed-site missile was clearly more vulnerable than one operated from a mobile firing-point, such as a submarine.

Meanwhile, an interim air-to-ground weapon called Skybolt was being developed in the United States, which could serve American and British needs until Polaris submarines became available.

Macmillan reported to the Queen in April that he had been able:

... to get an assurance from the President that we shall be able to obtain either Skybolt or Polaris when we need them. This will enable us ... to put an end to Blue Streak, a weapon which the Chiefs of Staff now feel to be obsolescent.[9]

In the debate in the House of Commons which followed, the Opposition played into the Prime Minister's hands. Instead of uniting to criticize the Government for the delays and waste of public money in deciding upon the most suitable deterrent, the Labour Party was divided as to whether Britain should have a nuclear weapon at all.

Harold Watkinson, who had succeeded Sandys as Minister of Defence, was able to conclude a formal agreement for Skybolt, and in September the Cabinet consented to a nuclear submarine base in Britain in return for the right to buy or build Polaris. When Macmillan announced this arrangement, there were violent objections, demonstrations and protest marches against the dangers to the population which a base was thought to entail; but in the defence debate in the House of Commons, seventy-three Labour Members abstained, due to the internal disagreements in the Party, and the public gradually came to accept the prospect of a Polaris base in Scotland. There were rumours at this time that the Americans might not be able to develop Skybolt satisfactorily, but Eisenhower reassured Macmillan that these doubts could be discounted and in any case the Prime Minister was convinced that the United States was so committed to support a British deterrent that either Skybolt or Polaris could be counted upon with confidence.

The closer liaison between Britain, France and the United States and the development of the Anglo-American nuclear missiles would have taken place in any event, but they were given added urgency by the failure of the Summit Conference and all that that implied. As it happened, however, the next international crisis arose not in Europe but in Africa.

By the middle of 1960, the Belgian Congo had, rather hurriedly, become independent; but a conflict on constitutional policy at once arose between those, led by Patrice Lumumba, who favoured a unitary State and others who preferred a federal structure. No Party achieved a clear majority in the first election and it was evident that the issue would be settled by the bullet rather than the ballot-box.

The mineral wealth of the Congo was concentrated in the province of Katanga, the leader of which, Moise Tshombe, soon proclaimed its independence. Sir Roy Welensky, in the neighbouring Central African Federation, supported Tshombe, while Russia began to meddle in these muddy waters by siding with Lumumba. Belgium sent in reinforcements to protect her civilians in the former Belgian colony and there were clashes between these troops and the Congolese soldiers. Russia launched a massive propaganda offensive against the West and was said to be sending technicians and equipment to assist Lumumba. The stage seemed set for a catastrophe in the Congo, which might widen into a world conflict.

In these circumstances the British Government acquiesced in a Security Council Resolution requesting Belgium to withdraw her troops and supported the introduction of a United Nations force, which was speedily organized by the Secretary-General, Dag Hammarskjöld, and was able to occupy all the important towns except in Katanga, where Tshombe would not admit the UN soldiers and did not in fact need them because the province was quiet and was being administered in an orderly way. Nkrumah showed signs of leading some of the new African States in support of Lumumba, and Harold Macmillan sent Duncan Sandys, by then Commonwealth Secretary, to Accra to exercise a moderating influence upon the Ghanaian Premier, which he was successful in doing. The situation changed from day to day – President Kasavubu dismissed his Prime Minister and in return Lumumba declared that Kasavubu was no longer President.

A meeting of the United Nations Assembly was to be held in September and Khrushchev had already announced that he would lead the Russian delegation. Macmillan decided to go to New York himself in an attempt to counter, if necessary, any propaganda advantage Khrushchev might seek to extract from the situation.

The Russian leader pulled out every publicity stop in his personal appearances in New York City and in the Assembly, but he made the mistake of attacking the United Nations and its Secretary-General in a three-hour speech designed to win Afro-Asian support. In his reply Macmillan was deliberately moderate and his speech, delivered in parliamentary style, was a successful contrast to Khrushchev's. He defended Hammerskjöld's efforts in the Congo, Britain's record in decolonization and Adenauer's leadership of Western Germany, and he put forward some constructive suggestions for further progress on disarmament. Khrushchev made frequent interruptions – including banging on the desk with his shoe – which were helpful to Macmillan because it seemed to other delegates to be discourteous and the Prime Minister's calm moderation was acclaimed when compared with the Russian leader's rudeness and excitability. Macmillan's speech was well received by both the Assembly and the world press and his visit to New York was an undoubted success.

The troubles of the Congo were by no means resolved. Lumumba was killed in Katanga, but was replaced by a man called Gizenga, who, though sustained by aid from Russia, was later included as Vice-Premier in a new central Government led by the non-Communist Adoula. During this period Macmillan was much concerned about the effect of events in the Congo upon the unity of the Commonwealth. The African States, supported by Nehru, were ardent supporters of Lumumba, while the white Commonwealth countries took sides with President Kasavubu. There was thus a danger of a division on racial and ideological lines, which happily did not materialize.

There remained the problem of Katanga. It was important to integrate the province, about the size of Spain, into the Congo, because its rich copper-mining areas provided two-thirds of the national revenue, and without it the country's economy was not viable. To achieve this re-unification, President Kasavubu was working loyally with the United Nations, but Tshombe declared his total opposition to the policy and in April 1961 he was arrested as an insuperable obstacle to Congolese unity. He was freed in June and signed an agreement under which Katanga would be re-united with the rest of the country, but the relief was short-lived and within four days he repudiated the settlement he had just signed.

The United Nations Command then decided to move against Katanga, but its troops were led by men without political or military experience in this sort of operation and Hammarskjöld could not control them from New York. Many atrocities were committed and Sir Roy Welensky, supported by the Right wing of the Conservative Parliamentary Party in Britain, became critical of the United Nations intervention. Under these circumstances, Macmillan sent out Lord Lansdowne, an Under-Secretary of State at the Foreign Office, to report and advise on the situation. He informed the Prime Minister that the actions of the United Nations officials were due to folly and inexperience rather than malice, and that Adoula, though under some pressure from Gizenga, was himself a reasonable man and certainly not a Communist. George Lansdowne, who speaks good French, explained clearly the views of the British Government and it was arranged that Hammarskjöld should fly from America for talks with him at Ndola in Northern Rhodesia. Tragedy supervened. The plane crashed four miles from Ndola airport and the Secretary-General was killed.

Tshombe refused to negotiate with Adoula and the situation remained unaltered until, in December, the British Cabinet authorized the supply of twenty-four 1,000 lb bombs to the United Nations forces for use against air attacks from Katanga. This caused an outcry in the Conservative press and in the section of the Parliamentary Party which was in sympathy with Tshombe's wish to secede. A debate took place in the House of Commons on 14 December in which three different points of view were advanced: the

Labour Opposition advocated the defeat of Katanga and its forced absorption into the Congo; the Right wing of the Conservative Party spoke for an independent Katanga; the Government supported the aim of the United Nations, which was to prevent civil war, and to negotiate a cease-fire and a peaceful solution on a federal basis. The Prime Minister, who wound up for the Government, recounted the Congo story, justified the British policy of a cease-fire and a negotiated settlement and pointed out that, although Russia voted on and often vetoed United Nations resolutions, she had not in fact paid a penny towards the cost of the UN forces, almost all of which was defrayed by Britain and the United States. There were ten Conservative abstentions when the vote was taken, but the Government secured a majority of ninety-four.

On 20 December a meeting between Adoula and Tshombe was finally arranged and resulted in an agreement to end the secession of Katanga. Although the Congo's troubles continued for a further two years, the crisis had passed and conditions in the country had become nearly normal by the end of 1961. Throughout, the British Government had been a conciliatory influence in a difficult situation and the Prime Minister had no reason to regret the part he and his colleagues had played in its solution.

30
PRESIDENT KENNEDY

In November 1960 the American Presidential election resulted in the narrow victory of John F. Kennedy over the Republican Vice-President, Richard Nixon. President Eisenhower retired quietly from public life; he had had a successful first term as the holder of the most important office in the Free World, but an unlucky second term, at the end of which the U2 incident had revealed a lack of flexibility and improvisation in his make-up as a statesman. He was a man of great integrity, who was described by Harold Macmillan as 'a sort of Duke of Wellington of America'.[1] Their personal friendship had been close and sincere since their wartime association in Algiers and when he retired it seemed that the 'special relationship', of value to both countries but especially to Britain, was unlikely to continue. In fact it was to prove even closer under his successor.

Macmillan had never met Kennedy, although there was a family link because the new President's elder sister, 'Kick', had married Lady Dorothy's nephew, Lord Hartington. This young man had been killed a few weeks later in Normandy and Kick's life was cut short in an airplane crash in 1948, but the connection was a help to Macmillan in his early contacts with Kennedy. The young President was reputedly an attractive man of great personal charm, but much would depend on whether the generation gap could be bridged by the ideas and policies which the Prime Minister hoped to share with the new leader of the United States. Macmillan did not hurry a personal meeting. His first move was to send Kennedy a carefully drafted letter, setting out his views on the more important issues of the day.

At the end of November the Prime Minister entertained two Senators, Lyndon Johnson and William Fulbright, to dinner at Downing Street. He had a high opinion of Fulbright's ability and influence in foreign affairs, but his diary note about Johnson was less enthusiastic. He described the Vice-President Elect as 'an acute and ruthless politician, but not ... a man of any intellectual power'.[2]

During the Christmas recess, Macmillan worked on a paper dealing with the international problems of the coming year, which came to be known in the Private Office as the 'Grand Design'. This assessment of the main economic, political and defence issues to be faced by the Free World was intended as the basis for his future discussions with Jack Kennedy. The Prime Minister was apprehensive about their first meeting and somewhat depressed to hear from Jock Whitney that the President's appointments were 'conservative'. This seemed to bode ill for Macmillan's hopes, outlined in the 'Grand Design', for a more flexible monetary system and the expansion of credit to finance the growing volume of world trade. Lord Longford recalled the Prime Minister's remark to a friend: 'How am I ever going to get along with that cocky young Irishman?'[3]

While the 'Grand Design' was being studied and amended by his staff and some of his colleagues, Macmillan himself faced a heavy schedule of commitments, including a visit to de Gaulle in January 1961, followed by one from Adenauer in February. He was also planning a trip to the West Indies in March and, as matters turned out, this was to give him the opportunity to meet President Kennedy for the first time, because no sooner had he arrived in Trinidad than he received a message inviting him to Key West in Florida for an urgent talk with the President about Laos, where a new crisis had erupted.

As soon as the morning session of their conference was over, the President and the Prime Minister lunched together alone, without advisers. Macmillan claimed that the rapport between them was almost instantaneous:

Before our conversation had gone on for many minutes I felt a deep sense of relief. Although we had never met and belonged to such different generations, he was just forty and I was nearly seventy, we seemed immediately to talk as old friends.[4]

This was no doubt true, and important, at a personal level, but the American and British Laos policies were not identical, and it has been suggested[5] that the Key West conference was not therefore as unqualified a success as Macmillan maintained.

Kennedy was under considerable pressure from the Pentagon to support a large-scale military intervention by SEATO, which the Prime Minister and the British Chiefs-of-Staff thought unrealistic and dangerous. Although stating that 'Kennedy seemed to share my doubts', Macmilan admitted that the President 'pressed me very hard on this'. They discussed an alternative plan put forward by the American experts involving 31,000 troops, to be supported by air, which Macmillan described as 'a ruinous undertaking'. Kennedy then suggested an intervention by four or five battalions which would hold an enclave in Laos, but the Prime Minister was doubtful even about this more modest proposal, as it meant 'the danger of sliding into unlimited commitments'. He agreed that 'it might be politically necessary to do something' in order to forestall the Russians and noted that he would join in

... the appearance of resistance and in the necessary military planning. But I must reserve to Cabinet the ultimate decision. President quite understood this.[6]

Kennedy may have understood it, but he did not want the United States to have to act alone and had hoped for more than merely moral support from Britain. He regarded Macmillan's reference to the need for Cabinet approval as an excuse, which it clearly was, and he came away from their first meeting disappointed by the Prime Minister's response.

For his part, Macmillan was faced with the dilemma that his overriding purpose, to retain the special relationship with the United States so laboriously re-established after Suez, conflicted with his reluctance to agree to any British military commitment and his disapproval of American involvement in South-East Asia, especially if it diverted attention from Europe and the Atlantic alliance. The British policy was to try and persuade the Russians to agree to a cease-fire and a conference.

With speed and efficiency the Prime Minister's small staff, which consisted of Tim Bligh and two secretaries, assisted by Harold Caccia, the British Ambassador, produced a record of the talks and a communiqué before leaving Key West, to both of which the President agreed. Macmillan commented characteristically: 'It is always more important at these international conferences to have good shorthand girls than to have generals and admirals.'[7]

Before returning to Trinidad, the Prime Minister had an opportunity to discuss the appointment of a successor to Harold Caccia, whose term in Washington was drawing to a close. The President strongly urged that David Ormsby-Gore (later Lord Harlech), then a Minister of State in the Foreign Office, should be the selection. 'He is my brother's most intimate friend,' Kennedy averred.[8] Macmillan agreed to the suggestion and, when the time came, this proved a brilliant choice: 'no ambassador has ever served us so well in Washington,' the Prime Minister wrote later. Due mainly to his close friendship with the Kennedy family, Ormsby Gore 'had access to the White House such as no ambassador has had before or since'[9] and was able to play a unique role of great value to both countries.

In Trinidad the Macmillans were splendidly entertained by the Governor-General, Lord Hailes, and his wife, Diana. As Patrick Buchan-Hepburn, Hailes had been Government Chief Whip in the House of Commons and his advice, based on long political experience reinforced by recent local knowledge, was valuable to the Prime Minister.

Outside Africa, the Caribbean was the most important remaining area of

British colonial responsibility and it was Macmillan's first visit to this part of the world. The West Indies were genuinely multi-racial, relatively sophisticated and more ready for political advance than the African colonies; but, judged by the standards of the early 1960s, most of the territories were too small for independence as separate units and their best prospect seemed to lie in a Federation. This had first been suggested by Oliver Stanley, then Colonial Secretary, in 1945, and was finally approved in 1956. Two years later Princess Margaret opened the first, and last, Federal Parliament; but the obstacles to success were formidable and in the end fatal.

Federations consisting of a solid land mass are difficult enough; a nation every unit of which is separated by sea was correspondingly even less cohesive. It is a thousand miles from Kingston in Jamaica to Port of Spain in Trinidad. At that time there was little inter-island communication and even the leading politicians were more likely to meet each other at conferences in London than in the Caribbean. Although an island patriotism existed, there was no real sense of West Indian nationhood and cricket was almost the only unifying influence.

Discord soon developed between divergent territorial interests. Jamaica and Trinidad did not wish to subsidize the economies of the smaller, less viable units, while the Eastern Caribbean disliked the prospect of political domination by Jamaica. The new Federal Government had too little central power and too little money to be effective, and this made the strongest political leadership essential. Unfortunately, the two most able men, who were also the Premiers of the two most important islands – Norman Manley of Jamaica and Eric Williams of Trinidad – chose to remain as local leaders and the Federation was run by a second XI from the small islands. The Prime Minister, Sir Grantley Adams, had been a wise and respected Premier of Barbados and Robert Bradshaw of St Kitts was an able and hard-working Finance Minister, but they lacked the authority in the larger territories to popularize the Federation and make it a success.

Norman Manley and Eric Williams were themselves supporters of the federal idea, but in September 1961 Manley made the mistake of putting its endorsement to the people of Jamaica in the form of a referendum and, in the face of defections in his own Cabinet and Sir Alexander Bustamante's rip-roaring campaign against it, the vote was lost. The future of the Federation was already in doubt at the time of Macmillan's visit in March and he noted: 'I am not too happy about the prospects and I tried to bring some pressure on the island politicians to take a wider view.'[10]

Jamaica's rejection of the Federation was a shock to the British Government, which had done no contingency planning. Dr Eric Williams had already announced that Trinidad would not stay in if Jamaica went out. 'In this kind of arithmetic,' he remarked, 'I from 10 doesn't leave 9; it leaves 0.' As a result the Federation disintegrated and, ironically, 31 May 1962, the date which had been agreed for the independence of the Federation, became the day of its dissolution.

After two days in Trinidad, Macmillan made short visits to Barbados and Antigua before flying to Jamaica on 29 March. He had a talk with and was much impressed by Norman Manley, but Bustamante refused to meet him because he considered a speech by the Prime Minister in Trinidad had been 'an intervention by HMG in local affairs'.[11]

On 4 April the Macmillans left the Caribbean for Washington, where the President and Prime Minister were able to have full-scale talks on all the main issues of the day covered by the 'Grand Design'. Alec Home arrived from London to join the discussions, in which the new Secretary of State, Dean Rusk, Chester Bowles and Dean Acheson took part for the United States, and Sir Frederick Hoyer Millar, Sir Norman Brook and Sir Harold Caccia for Britain.

Macmillan wrote:

The President impressed us all, not only by his quiet confidence but by his great courtesy. He listened well, did not talk too much, and encouraged others on both sides to speak.[12]

Of an hour alone with Kennedy next day, the Prime Minister recorded in his diary, 'It was really most satisfactory – far better than I could have hoped. ...'[13] But Arthur Schlesinger had reservations: he expressed the view that Macmillan was worried that 'Dean Acheson had been permitted to dominate the proceedings with hard talk about showdowns over Berlin and the President had seemed excessively diffident'.[4]

Whatever the difference of emphasis in their working relations, Macmillan was clearly intrigued and charmed by Kennedy's personality; he is quoted as saying:

There is something very eighteenth century about this young man. ... He is always on his toes during our discussions. But in the evening there will be music and wine and pretty women.[15]

James Reston gives the same impression in reporting that:

In the past the visit of a British Prime Minister to Washington was usually a solemn procession, full of hands-across-the-sea clichés, formal meetings and dinners and vapid communiqués. Harold Macmillan's visit here this time, in contrast, was like a house-party and at times almost like a spree.[16]

Their talks continued during a cruise on the *Potomac* as far as Mount Vernon; and the next day the Prime Minister went to Boston to address a large audience at the Massachusetts Institute of Technology, before returning to Washington to bid farewell to the President.

Macmillan was pleased with the relationship which was developing between Jack Kennedy and himself. He was gratified when the President sought his advice on a number of matters, including meetings with de Gaulle and Khrushchev, which had been planned for the end of May and the beginning of June, and which were to be followed by a visit to London. It is possible that the Prime Minister may have rather resented his exclusion from the Khrushchev encounter, since this indicated that he was no longer to act as an intermediary between the United States and the Soviet Union; and Lord Home was concerned that Kennedy had arranged the meeting before allowing enough time to 'play himself in' on major international issues.

In their talk about de Gaulle, however, Macmillan was surprised and pleased that the President did not think the tripartite discussions, agreed with Eisenhower, would present much difficulty; he had realized that de Gaulle was more anxious for the appearance of close co-operation than for the reality. Kennedy was anxious that Britain should join the EEC because it would be easier economically for America to deal with one large group than with two smaller ones, and because he hoped that the United Kingdom would have greater political influence in Europe if she was a member of the Community. The Prime Minister suggested the possibility of making available an independent deterrent for France, with Britain supplying either warheads or nuclear information, and Kennedy agreed that this could be studied. Macmillan commented:

All this was satisfactory, and yet I could not help feeling that he spoke about all these things in a rather detached way. Perhaps because it is his character to be ready to listen to anything. What he decides is another matter.[17]

Before leaving for a short visit to Canada, a long communiqué was issued which showed that the two leaders intended to maintain the close co-operation they had established and there was favourable comment in the American press on their clearly congenial relationship.

In a letter to the Queen, Macmillan reported that President Kennedy had 'surrounded himself with a large retinue of highly intelligent men', including Averell Harriman, Adlai Stevenson and Dean Acheson of the older generation, with Dillon to reassure Conservative opinion, to whom he had added representatives of 'progressive thought', collected from the universities and foundations, and several negroes. Macmillan observed that the President 'has great charm . . . and a light touch. Since so many Americans are so ponderous, this is a welcome change.'[18]

When he arrived in Ottawa, the Prime Minister had talks with Diefenbaker, alone, and with the Cabinet, and although 'the political business done was rather perfunctory ... they like one to go to Ottawa after Washington.... It may help if and when we have to undertake a serious negotiation over Europe.'[19] At the end of April, the British and Russian Governments appealed jointly for a cease-fire in Laos and for the reconvention of the Fourteen Power Conference in Geneva. There were the usual delays and difficulties in achieving these objectives, but a major war had at least been averted.

Shortly after Macmillan's return to England, news reached him of the Bay of Pigs débâcle in Cuba. He wrote: 'My only anxiety was lest the failure of the covert action in Cuba might lead to the Americans insisting upon overt action in Laos.'[20] British intelligence reports had concluded that there was no likelihood of a general uprising against Castro and it is surprising that the CIA took a completely contrary view. The fiasco was a severe blow to the President, but – in Macmillan's words – 'although naturally shaken, [he] was by nature brave and resilient' and soon recovered from the reverse. David Nunnerley suggests a more lasting effect:

... by exposing his inexperience in foreign affairs, it made him much more receptive ... to advice, particularly from outside his Administration. Macmillan in consequence assumed his rightful place as an older and wiser counsellor.[21]

By the end of April the collapse of the French army revolt in Algeria left de Gaulle triumphant and all-powerful. At Kennedy's request Macmillan prepared a memorandum for his guidance designed to create a sympathetic atmosphere for his meeting with the General. This took place in Paris a month later, but was unproductive. The President told Macmillan afterwards that de Gaulle had been gracious and avuncular but unyielding. He accepted everything that Kennedy was able to offer, but gave nothing in return and on the subject of Britain's entry into Europe 'was in his most austere mood'.[22]

The President's meeting with Khrushchev in Vienna was even less successful. Kennedy was impressed by the Russian leader, but shocked by his almost brutal frankness and his aggressive confidence in the nuclear power and potential prosperity of the Soviet Union. Macmillan noted that it must have been 'rather like somebody meeting Napoleon (at the height of his power) for the first time'. No progress was made on any issue and the President was baffled and disappointed by the failure of a meeting by which he had set great store.

The reception given to Jack Kennedy and his wife in London must have been a welcome contrast. Enthusiastic crowds cheered them as they drove with Harold and Dorothy Macmillan from London Airport to Buckingham Place on 4 June, where they were staying privately with Jacqueline Kennedy's sister, Princess Lee Radziwill. A formal meeting with ambassadors and Civil

Service advisers had been arranged for the following day, but Macmillan was pleased to find that the President, tense and tired after his grim encounter with Khrushchev, preferred a private talk and their discussion lasted from 10.30 in the morning till 1.00 p.m. Schlesinger considered this meeting a great success and that 'their talk ... marked the real beginning of what became Kennedy's closest personal relationship with a foreign leader'.[23] The social side of the visit was equally harmonious, including a relaxed, mainly family lunch party at Admiralty House and a small dinner-party at Buckingham Palace.

Macmillan was delighted that his personal accord with Kennedy was growing as close as it had been with Eisenhower after a few months in Algiers. Indeed, he noted in his diary that their

... intellectual relationship is of course much easier. Eisenhower was ... trained as a soldier and talking that language.... Kennedy, with an entirely different mental background, is quiet, well-informed, subtle, but proceeds more by asking questions than answering them.[24]

The two men had now met and talked on three occasions, at Key West, in Washington and in London, for a total of less than a week in terms of the amount of time they had spent together; but with each meeting their friendship grew firmer and this was to continue until the day of Kennedy's death.

31

THE PAY PAUSE

In the autumn of 1960 Harold Macmillan was beginning to feel the strain of the previous nine years of high office, for nearly four of which he had carried the responsibility of the Premiership. It had been a difficult period in foreign relations and Britain's changing and gradually diminishing role in world affairs had brought added anxiety. For the time being, however, the Government's domestic problems seemed relatively simple. John Hare (later Lord Blakenham) was proving a successful Minister of Labour, and strikes were either averted or short-lived. The principal and perennial fly in the economic ointment was the balance of payments and the need to reduce imports and improve overseas earnings. The Prime Minister therefore issued a directive to his colleagues, instructing them to give this objective priority over domestic and political considerations.

At the end of October, Macmillan made some minor changes in the Administration. There were good-natured jibes about nepotism when he appointed his son-in-law, Julian Amery, as Secretary of State for Air, and Dorothy's nephew, Andrew Devonshire, as Under-Secretary for Commonwealth Relations. In a jocular justification for this choice, Macmillan was heard to say: 'Andrew is awfully good with the natives. The Devonshires have always been good with the natives.'[1] When Maurice Macmillan was chosen to move the Address at the opening of the new session, he disarmed criticism by beginning his speech: 'As the only Back-Bench member of my family . . .'

It had gradually become evident that the Labour Government's 1947 plan to combine the railways, docks, inland waterways and London Transport in one giant Transport Commission was inefficient and indeed almost unworkable; in December 1960 it was decided to create four separate Boards for these public undertakings. Doctor (later Lord) Beeching was persuaded to preside over the transition and then to become head of British Railways. The capital liabilities and annual deficits of the railways were very large and Beeching set about improving matters with characteristic energy and determination. His plan was to modernize equipment, reduce the number of employees and eliminate uneconomic stations and branch-lines. These measures, which included the introduction of 'liner trains', were not announced until March 1963 and were naturally unpopular with the National Union of Railwaymen, the travelling public and with Members of Parliament whose constituencies, especially in Scotland and Wales, were adversely affected; but Beeching carried them through with great resolution and some success.

Macmillan was becoming interested in modernization within Britain, and at about this time a number of enquiries were initiated, the reports of which, when they became available, were intended to provide the basis for a forward-looking domestic programme. In addition to transport, these studies included the ports, traffic in towns, consumer protection, broadcasting, company law, and secondary and higher education. Newspaper mergers were also giving rise to anxiety, and in February 1961 the Prime Minister announced the appointment of a Royal Commission on the press under the chairmanship of Lord Shawcross. Regrettably, its report, though much praised, was largely disregarded.

In March 1961, there was a serious 'bear' attack on sterling, occasioned mainly by the upward revaluation of the Deutschmark. 'Hot' money was withdrawn from London in order to buy marks and the reserves lost £187 million. The Central Banks helped with large credits, but discouraging balance-of-payment figures precluded the possibility of a popular budget. Despite this, Selwyn Lloyd responded to pressure from the Prime Minister to raise the starting point for surtax on earned income to £4,000. Some people thought this concession tactlessly timed, but it was certainly overdue and if it had not been made in 1961, it would have been politically impossible to introduce it any later in the life of the 1959 Parliament.

There were innovations in the form of two so-called 'regulators'. The first was a useful measure which allowed the Chancellor to vary the purchase tax and the duties on tobacco, alcohol and petrol by 10%, up or down, without the need to bring in a budget. The wisdom of the second was more questionable. It enabled up to 4s od per week to be added to the employer's national insurance stamp for every employee on his staff. If this regulator had been on the *employees'* contributions, it would have been effective in increasing purchasing power in a slump or reducing it in a boom, but an increase in *employers'* costs was slow-acting and could only affect consumer spending to the extent that it was eventually passed on in the form of higher prices; it would also increase industrial costs, including export costs, so was indirectly harmful to the balance-of-payments. The reason for introducing this tax in the wrong way was presumably that it was politically easier to levy it on industry than on those employed in industry.

The summer months showed no improvement in the economy. The June trade figures were again bad, with a deficit of £80 million, and money continued to flow out of the reserves. The pattern, repeated so often before and since, was familiar: rising personal demand was not being matched by any compensating improvement in productivity. In 1960-1 wages and salaries had increased by 8% and production by only 3%, so Britain was becoming increasingly uncompetitive and it was essential to reduce Government expenditure and restrain wage demands. Samuel Brittan asserts that 'the fact that wages were rising with alarming rapidity was obvious well before the April budget' and that Selwyn Lloyd should have acted much sooner than he did.[2] Kilmuir complained that the economic crisis was 'utterly unexpected' and came as a shock to other Ministers.[3] It gave rise to an interim budget which raised the Bank Rate to 7%, curbed Government spending and increased indirect taxation by the full 10% of the new consumer regulator, although the payroll regulator was not used and hire-purchase terms remained unaltered.

The Parliamentary Party took this July budget well and, in the debate which followed the Chancellor's statement, Harold Macmillan was given a standing ovation by the Conservative benches and a majority of 110 after his winding-up speech. He was very tired and even contemplated resigning rather than having to face another exhausting session of Parliament; but the trade gap narrowed in July, sterling recovered, and he felt that the economic situation was on the mend. Before the House of Commons rose for the summer recess, he addressed the 1922 Committee and made a successful broadcast to the nation.

In August, Macmillan and Selwyn Lloyd drafted a letter to both sides of industry proposing the creation of the National Economic Development Council, nicknamed Neddy, on which representatives of management, trade unions and the Government would work together to analyse and advise on the problems of the economy. This proved a valuable forum for discussion and gave rise to smaller bodies, known as 'little Neddys', which performed the same function for individual industries and have done something to improve productivity and labour relations in Britain. NEDC was an imaginative and constructive concept, described a little uncharitably by David Kilmuir as 'the one achievement to Lloyd's credit while he was at the Treasury'.[4]

The most controversial outcome of the economic crisis was the introduction of the 'pay pause', which was felt to be unfair to nurses, teachers, civil servants and other public sector employees, whose wages the Government could directly control. Although unpopular, the pause was justified and the public reaction to it need not have been so hostile if it had been better presented; the art of public relations was not Selwyn Lloyd's long suit. The Prime Minister was well aware that pay restraint was bound to lead to industrial disputes with the more militant trade-union leaders. The first of these arose in November, unluckily in the power industry, where, due to the complexity of the plant and the country's dependence on electricity, the Government was particularly vulnerable to the demands of organized labour.

In this first trial of strength, the Electricity Board and the Minister of Power capitulated almost at once and weakly agreed to a large wage increase, without even seeking the advice of the Prime Minister or the Chancellor of the Exchequer before doing so. The press was contemptuously critical, from the *Daily Mirror*'s dismissive comment that within four months the 'wages pause is bust wide open' to *The Economist*'s more solemn reproach that 'the Government deserves the deepest censure for its contribution to the electricity wages surrender'.[5]

By the turn of the year the Cabinet was faced with pay demands from the coal-miners and railwaymen, but both disputes were settled by compromise offers of 4% and 3% respectively and Macmillan was amused to note that, in place of attacks on 'the ageing and feeble Premier', the headlines had become 'Mac's triumph'. Though precarious, the pay pause was still in operation, but it was due to end on 31 March 1962, when it would have to be replaced by a new and more flexible system. The Chancellor's attempt to devise one was based on keeping pay in line with the rise in productivity, estimated by the Treasury at $2\frac{1}{2}\%$ for the year 1962, and this became known as 'the guiding light'. It was not a convincing long-term solution of the problem and did not satisfy the Prime Minister.

Macmillan was an instinctive expansionist and by the end of 1961 strong political considerations were reinforcing his economic thinking. During the year there had been a gradual change in the Party balance, both in Parliament and in the country as a whole. The Opposition were becoming more united, Labour morale in the House of Commons was reviving and Hugh Gaitskell's star was rising. He had earned the respect of the House, whereas the Prime Minister was beginning to lose his former command of it, mainly through lack of practice. He seldom spoke and even a good speech on South Africa was more acceptable to the Labour Party than to his own Back Benchers.

Outside Parliament, Britain's worsening economic problems were eroding the Government's popularity and Labour was moving ahead of the Conservatives in the opinion polls. This was mainly because the momentum of rising prosperity, which had been broadly consistent over a whole decade, had checked at the very time when a more affluent society was becoming increasingly materialist in outlook and more expectant of a continuous improvement in its standard of living.

Economic policy was clearly the key. The public wanted expansion and were being given restraint. The pay pause for people like the hospital nurses was plainly unfair and it was difficult, in the face of it, to project the image that 'Conservatives care'. A long series of by-election reverses reflected the public discontent. The Conservative poll fell, often by 20% or more, in a succession of bad results at Moss Side, Oswestry, East Fife, Bridgetown, Lincoln and, sensationally, in the traditionally Tory stronghold of Orpington, where the Liberals were the beneficiaries. It was a far cry from Macmillan's triumph in the General Election only two years earlier.

Against a background of rising inflation and balance-of-payment difficulties, the Chancellor had been forced to adopt a policy of restraint which, although correct, indeed necessary, for the economy, was not a recipe for electoral success. Selwyn Lloyd's 'guiding light' did not give people much encouragement and by the spring the Labour Party was beginning to benefit, with good by-election results at Pontefract and North Derby, and at Stockton-on-Tees, where only the Prime Minister's personal (and in those days unusual) intervention in his old constituency just secured second place for the Conservative candidate by a narrow margin over the Liberal.

The budget, which imposed purchase tax on sweets and ice cream, was criticized as an attack on the children and dubbed by Jo Grimond 'a mouse of a budget'. It introduced a new tax on speculative capital gains, but was deliberately neutral in its overall effect. Official advice was cautious. The Treasury expected an investment boom to follow Britain's entry into the EEC and in the meantime premature reflationary measures were considered dangerous. Selwyn Lloyd made no attempt to respond to the Prime Minister's constant pressure to reflate and there was therefore no easing in the Government's unpopularity. The local elections in May resulted in heavy Conservative losses and Labour gained the seat in a Parliamentary by-election at Middlesborough. In another, at West Lothian, the Conservative candidate lost his deposit.

Macmillan recorded in his diary that the pay pause had been successful in keeping rises lower than they would otherwise have been and the wage structure nearer to that of France and Germany; but he was dismayed at the absence of any imaginative ideas coming forward from the Treasury and disappointed that 'the Chancellor of the Exchequer gave no real lead to the Cabinet'.[6] The burden of devising a new incomes policy seemed to be devolving on him and his small Downing Street staff, and he resented this.

Throughout the first six months of 1962, there had been a political hiatus with no positive policies and the public mood was becoming increasingly introspective and satirical. *Beyond the Fringe* played to packed houses, *Private Eye* began its stormy and sometimes libellous career and *That Was the Week*

That Was commanded huge television audiences every Saturday night. The people were bored with a Government which had been in power for eleven years and the slogan 'It's time for a change' was gaining circulation. A sense of frustration was also evident on the Tory benches. Morale was low and Conservative Members were demanding reflation as the only way of restoring the Government's reputation. Macmillan agreed. He regarded the Chancellor's approach as politically unacceptable and far too cautious; and he was becoming impatient with Lloyd's reluctance to reflate. He was also aware of an anti-Macmillan faction in the Parliamentary Party and he began to think in terms of a Ministerial re-shuffle to restore confidence in the Administration.

The immediate task, however, was to decide what form the next phase of the incomes policy should take. With no constructive advice available from the Treasury and after long but unproductive discussions in Cabinet, the Prime Minister by-passed Selwyn Lloyd and took the unusual initiative of getting to work himself with the help of his Private Secretaries and two officials from the Cabinet Office. After further talks with Hailsham, Macleod, Lloyd and Michael Fraser, he was able to produce the draft of a new policy, the centrepiece of which was the establishment of a National Incomes Commission. This permanent body would examine and report upon the relative merits and priorities of the more important pay claims, in the light of the national interest, and its conclusions would be made public. It was to be presented not as an instrument of deflation, but as a springboard for growth. The proposals were completed by 19 June and, before submitting them to the whole Cabinet, Macmillan put them to selected Ministers for their approval: 'I thought the Chancellor of the Exchequer rather chilly. The others seemed strongly in favour.'[7]

Lloyd's inability to devise a more viable and productive policy than the 'guiding light' of January had transformed it, by June, into a warning light for his own future, but the Prime Minister gave no sign of his dissatisfaction and Lloyd was unaware of the danger he was in.

32

THE JULY MASSACRE

The pay pause had been in operation for exactly a year, but in that time Selwyn Lloyd had not come forward with any more permanent policy to replace this temporary expedient and a whole year had been wasted. This delay and lack of initiative had led to the Prime Minister's gradually growing sense of irritation, almost disillusion, with his Chancellor.

Butler lunched with him on 21 June and expressed the view that the Party's difficult political position in the country was due to Lloyd's inept handling and presentation of the economic problem. He wrote later that:

In the Prime Minister's view, shared by several of us in the Cabinet, both the working out of a longer-term incomes policy and the modification of the rigours of deflation had been unduly delayed. Macmillan was particularly sensitive about the latter.[1]

The Prime Minister was beginning to feel that new men as well as new measures would soon be needed and the Chancellor's future was clearly in question.

The Wall Street collapse in May had revived Macmillan's concern over liquidity and he wanted a Chancellor who would force the Treasury and the Bank of England to take an initiative about the amount of gold needed to finance world trade. The main reason, however, for his increasing lack of confidence in Lloyd was the inaction over an incomes policy, which had compelled Macmillan himself to take the lead in working out a solution.

Rab Butler met with him again on 6 July and was asked what he would do if he was Prime Minister and forming a new government, because, said Macmillan, 'that is virtually what I want to do now'. Butler replied that he would make a change at the Treasury and they discussed Maudling's qualifications as a possible Chancellor. In the course of conversation it became clear that the Prime Minister was contemplating a major reorganization and the names of David Kilmuir, Percy Mills, Harold Watkinson, Jack Maclay, David Eccles and Charles Hill were mentioned as those likely to retire. Butler questioned whether Eccles, 'whose intellect was valuable in any Cabinet', could be spared and he was distressed about the departure of Kilmuir, who represented, with himself and the Prime Minister, the last remaining link with the Churchill era.[2]

On 10 July, Butler and Macleod saw the Prime Minister. They argued strongly for reflation and although they made no specific attack on Selwyn Lloyd, it was apparent that he was the target and that their demand for a more positive direction of the economy could only be met if the Treasury was placed in different hands. Macmillan had already reached the same conclusion.

The next day, Macleod, as Chairman of the Party, sent a note to the Prime Minister warning him that the result of the East Leicester by-election, where the poll was to be declared two days later, would show a serious drop in the Conservative vote, which would put the Party's candidate in third place. He added: 'I feel I should urge upon you that if you are contemplating making changes in the Government, these should be made before we rise for the recess.'[3] The Chief Whip tendered the same advice.

Selwyn Lloyd himself had no inkling that the Prime Minister viewed his performance unfavourably, still less that his days as Chancellor were numbered. On the evening before his peremptory dismissal, he and Macmillan had been the chief guests at a dinner organized by the Methodists at the Reform Club and had returned to Admiralty House for a drink together afterwards. The Prime Minister was most cordial and never uttered a word of criticism, yet his diary note for 8 July included the entry: 'I am to talk with Lloyd on Thursday [July 12th] and try to give him forewarning.'[4] Selwyn Lloyd was hurt when he realized next day that, after all their years of working together, Macmillan was not closer to him. In fact, the Prime Minister was fond of Lloyd and could not bring himself to face, before he had to, the ordeal of asking him to resign. Despite the bloodbath soon to take place, he was not a good butcher.

Lloyd had been a Minister for eleven years and for nearly seven of them had held the arduous offices of Foreign Secretary and Chancellor of the Exchequer. He was tired and no doubt drained of original political thought and initiative, but he had served Macmillan loyally and could not have expected such an abrupt and humiliating termination of a distinguished career.

Selwyn Lloyd's policy as Chancellor was economically sound, but although courageous in pursuing it, he was a bad communicator and his presentation of an inevitably unpopular policy was unskilful. He was trying to do the right thing, but he handled his publicity badly and when the Party's political prospects were adversely affected, the Prime Minister withdrew his support. In retrospect, one can see the point of view of both men. Selwyn Lloyd thought Macmillan was too unconcerned about inflation, admittedly a much less serious issue then than it has since become.[5] No doubt the Prime Minister believed that a little inflation was not a bad thing and he may well have been right; it certainly oiled the electoral wheels. But a small dose can lead to a larger one, and to Selwyn the Prime Minister did not seem sufficiently aware of its dangers. Lord Robbins thought his dismissal was a mistake; it is equally arguable that his original appointment to the post was an even worse mistake, as Kilmuir considered at the time. As a former Chancellor, who had faced the same problems in a less acute form, Lord Amory took the view that, in the economic circumstances of 1961–2, Lloyd had to damp down the fire a little, or at least not stoke it up, and he has said that he would have done the same if he had still been Chancellor.[6]

Macmillan, on the other hand, was the leader of a great political Party, which would have to face a General Election within a year or two from a low base of popular support. He needed a boom to coincide with an appeal to the country; he had stage-managed this successfully in 1959 and was anxious to repeat the performance. He tried hard to persuade Lloyd to expand the economy but failed – so the Chancellor, who had become a political liability, had to go.

In the battle for votes at election time, there is a great temptation for Party leaders to try and outbid each other by bribing the people with their own money, and for Prime Ministers to create an atmosphere of prosperity to suit the date of an election. Macmillan understood and practised with skill the art of manipulating the economy to gain the electoral prize. Harold Wilson was good at this too. It is interesting, though not surprising, that leading economists and senior Treasury officials – Lord Robbins, Lord Kaldor, Lord Roberthall, Lord Armstrong and Sir Alec Cairncross – and former Ministers with Treasury experience like Lord Amory, all thought that Lloyd was right to refuse to reflate; but the politicians who were consulted supported Macmillan's decision. The truth is that in a conflict between political and economic priorities, politics usually prevail, if only because a Cabinet is composed of politicians, not economists.

Rab Butler, a most sophisticated practitioner of the art of politics, as well as the most successful post-war Chancellor of the Exchequer, could see both sides of the slate and although he had had a hand in Lloyd's downfall, paid him an agreeable tribute when he wrote:

The man Selwyn is probity and sense itself and this is of great capital value. His success has been in the proud role of service. His future may now be re-elevated into spheres unknown and by him uncharted.[7]

Written before Lloyd's selection as Speaker of the House of Commons, this was a prescient observation. In fact, he charted the Speakership with great skill, popularity and success and was certainly happier in this role than he had been as Chancellor of the Exchequer.

On Thursday morning, 12 July, an article by Walter Terry appeared in the *Daily Mail*. It predicted major Cabinet changes, including the resignation of Selwyn Lloyd. Few people knew of the Prime Minister's intentions and as Butler was notoriously and often deliberately indiscreet, he was immediately suspected as the source of the story.

Macmillan had not planned an announcement until the following week, but to avoid further speculation in the weekend newspapers, he decided to act at once. That evening Selwyn Lloyd was summoned to Admiralty House and relieved of his appointment. It was a painful interview which lasted three-quarters of a hour. The Prime Minister had hoped that Lloyd would leave politics and embark on a new career in the City. He was taken aback when Lloyd refused a peerage and said he would stay in the House of Commons. He insisted on a public exchange of letters and, not surprisingly, his own was somewhat stiff and formal in tone. He expressed his anxiety that 'the growth of public expenditure, so much of it highly desirable in itself, should not outstrip our resources'.[8] The Prime Minister had dreaded their interview and the blow he knew his decision would be to such an old friend. Indeed, it was this personal aspect which led him to make a grave political error.

In an attempt to mask the damage which the dismissal would do to Lloyd's reputation, Macmillan decided to combine it with the general reconstruction of the Government, upon which he was already determined, but which would have been better left till later. At seven p.m. on Friday the 13th, an unlucky day for those concerned, the changes were announced. No less than seven senior Ministers – a third of the Cabinet – were requested to resign at a few hours' notice. Only Butler, Macleod and the Chief Whip, Martin Redmayne, seem to have known of this in advance, and even Macleod was unaware of its extent. He had helped to sow the seed but was unprepared for the whirlwind.

The episode disturbed rather than reassured the Parliamentary Party and if Macmillan hoped that the changes would give his Administration a look of renewed vitality, he was disappointed. Instead, the public regarded the whole operation as an unattractive display of panic or ruthlessness, or both, and it did nothing to enhance his reputation, rather the reverse. But the people who accused him of disloyalty to those who worked with him must have forgotten that exactly the opposite charge had been made against him only two years before. An article in the *Spectator* dated 28 August 1959 was typical and included this criticism:

His loyalty to his colleagues, which ought to be a watchword, has become a byword; he has stuck to incompetents through thick and thicker, giving the impression that he is concerned not so much with their reputation as with his own – to sack them could be construed as a confession of incompetence on his part for having appointed them.

Various suggestions have been advanced to explain both the timing and the extent of the reconstruction. In a letter to the Queen, Macmillan wrote that it seemed best that the new incomes policy, to be announced before the House rose at the end of July, should be in the hands of the new Chancellor. He was also influenced by the consideration that he was planning to carry the European project through the Conservative Party Conference in October and did not want the public to form the impression that Ministers had resigned because of disagreement over Europe. It was, therefore, preferable to get the Government reorganization out of the way and hopefully half-forgotten by the time the Party representatives met at Llandudno.

The Chief Whip may have had some influence if, as was thought, he advised the Prime Minister that the Parliamentary Party was restless and would not be placated by the sacrifice of only one Minister or patient about the postponement of the wider purge until the autumn. This was bad advice, but Redmayne was not always a reliable barometer of Conservative Parliamentary opinion and was not as good a Chief Whip as the others who have occupied that position since the Second World War. Derek Marks, the usually well-informed Lobby correspondent of the *Daily Express*, wrote on 20 July that Macmillan had told one of the departing Ministers that Redmayne had reported grave unrest among the Back Benchers and that the consequences of sending them away dissatisfied to their constituencies for the long summer recess would be serious.

Whatever the reasons for it, the 'July massacre' or the 'Night of the long knives', as it was variously described, was a mistake – perhaps the first serious mistake Macmillan had made during his Premiership. He, too, had been a senior Minister for eleven years and Prime Minister for half that period and the strain and fatigue of high office may well have impaired his hitherto almost impeccable political judgement. Such, at any rate, is the opinion of Lord Fraser of Kilmorack, the ablest and most experienced of the Conservative Party Secretariat, who greatly admired Macmillan and was critical of only this and two other matters, all three of which occurred during the last fifteen months of the Premiership.

Macmillan himself acknowledged, in retrospect,[9] the 'serious error' he had made in combining the change at the Treasury with the other relegations; but, curiously, he did not apparently appreciate at the time that, in trying to soften the blow for Selwyn Lloyd, he was in fact being unfair to some of the other Ministers dropped in the reconstruction. It is true that almost all of them had indicated their wish or willingness to retire at the end of the Parliament or at an earlier convenient date, but none can have expected to be removed without warning in a single day of unprecedented abasement. Publicly and most loyally they all accepted the Prime Minister's decision without protest and in some cases even without resentment. Privately, feelings were hurt by such a sudden, undignified end to their careers, with scarcely an acknowledgement of the long service they had rendered to the Party and the State. Only the Minister of Education, David Eccles, was offered another appointment as President of the Board of Trade, but he declined it. One former Minister told a friend that his dismissal was 'the most brutal humiliation of my life'.[10] It must have seemed so to the victims, but a Minister is either in charge of a Department or he is not. The news of his retirement cannot be prepared in advance, so it has to be announced in an abrupt and apparently callous way.

The departure of David Kilmuir, described by Macmillan as 'one of my oldest and dearest friends',[11] was surprising to many others as well as to himself. Kilmuir recalled that on the evening of 11 July, as a Committee of the Cabinet was ending, the Prime Minister took him aside and said, 'The Government is breaking up ... you don't mind going?' Kilmuir recorded that he was startled, but merely replied, 'You know my views.'[12] He had told Macmillan that he realized the Government must be reconstructed before the next General Election and that he would understand if a new Lord Chancellor was wanted; but he had made his plans on the assumption that this would not be before early in 1963. Indeed, when he had asked the Prime Minister only a month before whether he might accept two engagements abroad in September and in the following January, he was refused permission because he would be required for the Commonwealth Prime Ministers' Conference in September and for the then expected Common Market legislation early in 1963. The sudden demand for his resignation was, therefore, a shock. Macmillan excused it on the grounds that it would be fair to give the Attorney-General the chance to succeed to the Woolsack before the Parliament ended, but the Government was certainly not strengthened by the change, because Sir Reginald Manningham-Buller (later Lord Dilhorne), who was described by a former colleague as 'impartially truculent', was not only a less agreeable personality but also a far less distinguished lawyer.

Nevertheless, Kilmuir had had a long innings and more sympathy was felt by most Conservative MPs for Charles Hill, who was a good speaker and administrator, and who had only been Minister of Housing for a year. There seemed to be no reason for the dismissal of this effective, likeable Minister and Macmillan gave none in his memoirs. It is true that, like Kilmuir, he had told the Prime Minister that he wished to retire at the end of the Parliament, but no one expected this before 1963 or 1964, whereas on 13 July his resignation was demanded at once – 'tonight'. It was callous to disregard the sensibilities of colleagues in this way and to remove them, as one discarded

Minister remarked bitterly, 'with no more notice than you would give to an office boy caught robbing the till'.[13] It was also unlike Macmillan, who was usually considerate in his dealings with other people.

By ten minutes past six on 13 July, the list of resignations and new appointments had been submitted to the Queen as soon as she re-entered Buckingham Palace after presiding at a royal garden party. With Maudling's move from the Colonial Office to the Treasury, Macmillan was able, as he had long wished, to amalgamate the Commonwealth and Colonial Offices under Duncan Sandys. Peter Thorneycroft succeeded Watkinson as Minister of Defence, Edward Boyle took over Education from David Eccles, and Keith Joseph became Minister of Housing and Local Government in place of Charles Hill. William Deedes (now editor of the *Daily Telegraph*) followed Mills as Minister without Portfolio. Rab Butler, by this time fully occupied with his responsibility for Central Africa, preferred to leave the Home Office, to which Henry Brooke, formerly Chief Secretary to the Treasury, was promoted. With an earldom for Kilmuir, a viscountcy for Mills and Companions of Honour for Lloyd, Watkinson and Maclay, the deed was done. The comment was still to come.

The press could not be expected to treat these sensational developments with much restraint and 'Mac the Knife' and 'Panic in Whitehall' were typical of the headlines in the popular newspapers. In private, the Conservative Parliamentary reaction was at first almost equally scathing, with Back Bench attacks on Macmillan for his 'brutal treatment' of Selwyn Lloyd and a caustic complaint from Gerald Nabarro that Westminster had been made to 'look like an abattoir'.

It was freely, though quite incorrectly, rumoured that Macmillan had sacked his colleagues to save himself, and Jeremy Thorpe could not resist the witty if mordant comment: 'Greater love hath no man than this – that he lay down his friends for his life.'[14] Nigel Birch, one of Macmillan's most constant and corrosive critics, wrote acidly to *The Times*: 'For the second time, the Prime Minister has got rid of a Chancellor of the Exchequer who tried to get expenditure under control. Once is more than enough.'[15] Even Anthony Eden (by then Lord Avon), in a speech at Leamington Spa on 21 July, said 'I feel that Mr Selwyn Lloyd has been harshly treated.' This was, indeed, the general view both in and outside Parliament and when Macmillan took his seat for Prime Minister's Questions on 17 July, he was received in dead silence by the benches behind him. Next morning the *Daily Telegraph* reported:

The disapproval was almost palpable. . . . What made this inglorious entry even harder to bear was the contrast with the cordial reception which Mr Selwyn Lloyd had enjoyed twenty minutes earlier . . .

Question time was an ordeal and, in an answer about nuclear tests, some of Macmillan's unfortunate references to seismic techniques, earthquake records and underground explosions were bound to be greeted with ironic laughter. Sir Gilbert Longden must have had his tongue well in his cheek when he solemnly quoted Kipling in congratulating the Prime Minister on 'keeping his head while all about him were losing theirs'.

Gradually the political climate improved. Question time on 19 July was much quieter and, when Macmillan addressed the 1922 Committee the same evening, he formed the impression that 'feeling was now moving definitely towards me and my action'.[16] The *Daily Telegraph* summed up the meeting in its report that

... hopes of the reconstruction turning out for the best were more prevalent at the end than at the beginning .... The duration of the meeting was in itself an indication that things had gone pretty well. It lasted only about half an hour.

There was not and had never been any real threat to Macmillan's position. As Henry Fairlie noted in the *Spectator*: 'On the whole, the voluble Conservative critics are the eccentrics and the marginally loyal.' On this as on most occasions, the Conservative Party accorded its leader greater support than a Labour leader would normally have commanded in the same circumstances; but in the event of failure the Tories are ultimately more ruthless. This combination of loyalty up to a point, but merciless rejection beyond that, has usually been an advantage to the Party.

The Prime Minister took the opportunity of the Cabinet changes to make an almost equally draconian purge of the junior Ministers. I have always remembered one of his remarks when he appointed me Under-Secretary of State for the Colonies, because it was typical of an aspect of his personality. Perhaps due to his own humble ancestry and upper-middle-class upbringing, he always had an almost exaggerated respect for the aristocracy. It so happened that Lord Lansdowne was Minister of State at the Colonial Office and, after discussing the promotions of Julian Amery, Hugh Fraser and others for about ten minutes, Macmillan finally came to the point: 'I have a proposal to make to you which I hope you will find agreeable. I would like you to go to the Colonial Office.' Then, almost abruptly: 'Do you know George Lansdowne?' I replied that he was an old friend; indeed we had been at school together. 'That is splendid,' said the Prime Minister. 'You will work well together.' Then he added reflectively: 'George will never set the Thames on fire, but he is very good and they like him in the Lords, because of course he is a *real* Marquess, none of your jumped-up stuff.'

Shortly afterwards, Macmillan addressed the new Ministers: 'I do not ask of you gentlemen great oratorical brilliance in the House of Commons,' he said, 'or great administrative ability in your Departments. All I ask of you is sheer physical endurance.'

On 26 July, a full-dress censure debate took place in the House of Commons on a motion of no confidence in the Government and an Opposition demand for the dissolution of Parliament and a General Election. Gaitskell opened with a strong attack on the unprecedented removal of a third of the Cabinet and eight other Ministers and the curt dismissal of the Chancellor of the Exchequer, which he described as 'the act of a desperate man in a desperate situation, following the steady, remorseless and steep decline in the Conservative Party's fortunes in by-election after by-election'. He charged the Prime Minister with sacrificing men and measures in order to retain power.

After a brief defence of his own record and a tribute to 'the courage, single-mindedness and patriotism' of Selwyn Lloyd, Macmillan devoted the rest of his speech to the economic situation. He claimed that a respite had been gained by the pay pause, but acknowledged that new machinery was now needed; and he outlined the purpose and functions of the new Incomes Commission which, he explained, would not have statutory power to compel compliance, but would rely on the support of public opinion for the observance of its recommendations. He went on to refer to other reforms, such as the Shops and Offices Bill and the need for consumer protection, retraining and proper contracts of service. His most important statement was a declaration that an incomes policy was necessary as a 'permanent feature of our economic life'.[17]

At the cost of some damage to his personal reputation, the Prime Minister had achieved his political objective. He had eliminated, in Selwyn Lloyd, the obstacle to reflation and had appointed a Chancellor whose views were in tune with his own. It is at least questionable whether these views and their implementation over the following two years were in the national interest. They were certainly in the Conservative interest, because they produced the pre-election improvement in the Party's political prospects which the Prime Minister required. After the run of disastrous by-elections in 1961 and 1962, the Government's position gradually recovered, to the extent that when the General Election was eventually held in October 1964, the Conservatives lost by only four seats and might well have won their fourth victory in succession if Macmillan, with his magician's touch, had still been leader of the Party.

The benefit to the British people, except in the short term, was dubious. Inflation was already becoming a problem and would clearly only be encouraged by an expansion of the economy. Lord Kaldor believed that the damage had been done earlier, but that the Prime Minister could have corrected it had he taken a longer and less political view. It was not only Socialist economists who held this opinion. A more charitable analysis of Macmillan's motives was suggested by Reggie Maudling, who wrote later that the Prime Minister genuinely believed that economic orthodoxy had caused an unnecessary waste of resources and that his simple objective was to expand the economy in order to make people better off, so that they could lead fuller and happier lives. No one could quarrel with the sentiment. The method was more doubtful and was certainly diametrically opposed to the policy now being pursued by a very different Conservative Government.

33

PROBLEMS AT HOME AND
ABROAD

During the summer of 1961, President de Gaulle indicated through his Ambassador in London that he would welcome an invitation to pay a private visit to Macmillan and this was eventually arranged for a weekend in November at Birch Grove House.

De Gaulle had been elected President of France three years earlier. He was a strange man – proud, remote, dignified and brave, with an overriding sense of patriotism and national duty. Although he was affable, charming and always courteous (Macmillan described him as 'a man who was never rude by mistake'[1]), he was also autocratic, inflexible in his views and impervious to advice or argument. From their wartime days together in Algeria, he had retained a feeling of affection for Harold Macmillan, despite a strong dislike and distrust of 'Anglo-Americans', whom he thought had treated him badly in the war. He was suspicious of the United States and resentful of the British, and his personal friendship with Macmillan could not overcome this prejudice, so he was always an uneasy partner in the Western alliance. When he talked of Europe, he meant France and, in Macmillan's words, 'his sense of history only worked backwards',[2] so that he saw his country as the France of Louis XIV and Napoleon and regarded himself as their natural heir.

De Gaulle's arrival at Gatwick airport was preceded by a bizarre telephone call from the Foreign Office, enquiring what was to be done about the General's blood. It seemed that fear of an attempted assassination and the possible need for an immediate blood transfusion made it necessary to store a special supply of an unusual category in a refrigerator or deep-freeze. Mrs Bell, the admirable cook at Birch Grove, objected on the grounds that both these appliances were already full with provisions for the weekend, so a new refrigerator had to be installed in the coach-house to accommodate the Presidential blood plasma. The car cavalcade from Gatwick included an ambulance, and several doctors and surgeons prepared for all eventualities.

On the Saturday morning when the Prime Minister, Alec Home, Couve de

Murville, the French Foreign Secretary, two Ambassadors and two Private Secretaries were gathered in the library listening to a lengthy discourse by de Gaulle on the world situation, loud knocks on the door suddenly interrupted the proceedings. Macmillan went out to find his head keeper in a high state of indignation, complaining bitterly that the woods were full of Alsatian dogs and policemen on security duty and that there would be no birds left on Monday, when a shoot had been planned. 'This has got to stop,' was the keeper's ultimatum, 'either he goes or I go.' When Macmillan told de Gaulle the story that evening, he did not seem amused. A sense of humour was not among his many attributes.

The Birch Grove talks, though apparently cordial, were in fact unproductive. The President's attitude to the Anglo-American wish for negotiations with Russia over Berlin was negative. He thought the time inopportune and even if Germany was willing to participate, France would not do so. He saw himself as the protector of German interests and when Macmillan suggested 'You would be *plus royaliste que le roi?*' he replied 'Certainly. Then the Germans of the future will know that France was true.'[3]

On the prospect of Britain joining the Common Market, de Gaulle was equally cool. Macmillan recorded:

His views are inward, not outward-looking. I fear he has decided to oppose us – yet, in a way, he wants us in Europe.... The tragedy is that we agree ... on almost everything. We like the ... *union des patries* that de Gaulle likes. We are anti-federalists; so is he ... but his pride, his inherited hatred of England (since Joan of Arc) ... above all, his intense 'vanity' for France – she must dominate – make him half welcome, half repel us, with a strange love–hate complex.... I still feel that he has not absolutely decided about our admission ... he will be more likely to yield to pressure than persuasion.[4]

They discussed the matter at some length and de Gaulle claimed that the French were not against Britain's entry, but were concerned about 'the flock of British connections', by which he apparently meant the United States, the Commonwealth countries and the colonial dependencies, many of which might sooner or later wish to join, 'thus swamping the very Europe that the Six were determined to preserve'. Macmillan pointed out that the French had made very good arrangements for the countries of the old French Empire and that, if Britain abandoned the Commonwealth, Canada, Australia and New Zealand would drift into the American orbit and many of the remaining countries into the Russian.

The Prime Minister formed the impression that de Gaulle was reluctant to oppose overtly Britain's accession to the EEC and would prefer to rely upon her hoped-for inability to overcome Commonwealth objections to the project. He also affected to believe that Macmillan would be unable to carry the Conservative Party, so traditionally orientated to the Commonwealth, in support of the European association.

While the Prime Minister was anxious for a quick conclusion of the issue, he feared that de Gaulle's tactics would be to delay the negotiations by a minute examination of every detail in the hope that the whole concept would collapse under the weight of unimportant objections and the endless procrastination of peripheral points of difference. This was precisely what the French approach to the British application proved to be. Two weeks later, after a meeting with Adenauer, de Gaulle sent Macmillan an enigmatic message:

... *nous avons réaffirmé notre intention de faire avancer les choses, en souhaitant tous les deux que la Grande-Bretagne puisse se joindre un jour à notre organisation dans les mêmes conditions où nous nous y trouvons nous-mêmes.*[5]

This was not perhaps a very positive outcome of the Birch Grove weekend, but Macmillan chose to draw a little encouragement from it for the Christmas season.

A more gratifying gift came his way during December when he was given the Freedom of the City of London. Except for Churchill, this honour had not been accorded to a Prime Minister in office for a long time and Macmillan prized it, next to the Chancellorship of Oxford University, 'above any which I have ever received'.

Another matter which caused the Prime Minister much anxiety during November 1961 concerned the Queen in her important role as Head of the Commonwealth. This concept, which did so much to keep the New Commonwealth together, could scarcely have been sustained but for the character, grace and personality of the Queen herself, and the tireless visits she and her family paid to every Commonwealth country. One of these, to the newly-independent State of Ghana, had been arranged for November and was a source of concern to the Prime Minister as the date of her departure drew near.

The large financial surplus President Nkrumah had inherited at independence had been dissipated, and an unpopular budget in the summer of 1961 led to strikes and widespread unrest. The country seemed to be developing into a police state and Nkrumah himself was becoming increasingly unpopular. He had recently made an extensive tour of Eastern Europe, Russia and China and, on his return to Accra, he dismissed the British officer, General Alexander, who had built up and hitherto commanded the Ghanaian army. It looked as though he was moving more and more towards the Eastern bloc and although he disclaimed this in a friendly letter to Macmillan, the British press was hostile to his regime and the Prime Minister decided to send

Duncan Sandys, the Commonwealth Secretary, to Ghana to reconnoitre the situation before the Queen's visit.

In early October, Nkrumah dismissed some of his leading colleagues and imprisoned about fifty of his political opponents; but his talks with Sandys were satisfactory and Macmillan advised the Queen that the visit should take place unless the position in Ghana grew worse. Both Churchill and Eden privately expressed their concern about the possible risk to the Queen, and during the course of a House of Commons debate some Members demanded the cancellation of the visit as a mark of political disapproval. The Prime Minister rightly rejected such a gesture, which might have led to Ghana's withdrawal from the Commonwealth and to her closer alignment with Russia. His only reservation was over the personal safety of the Sovereign. The security assessments concluded that there was no danger of a deliberate attack on the Queen herself, but there was still the possibility of an attempt to kill Nkrumah while she was with him. His public appearances were rare and it was thought that someone might try to assassinate him while they were driving together in a car cavalcade or on some similar occasion.

On 4 November there was a serious bomb explosion in Accra and the Prime Minister felt that Duncan Sandys should go there again before a final Cabinet decision could be taken. Ostensibly in order to test the timing and crowd control, Sandys, who is quite without fear, persuaded a reluctant President to drive with him in an open car along the whole of the royal route. This passed off without incident, but a number of respected Conservative Members – including John Morrison, the Chairman of the 1922 Committee – were still anxious about the Queen's safety and there was the possibility of a revolt in the Tory Party against Macmillan's advice to her that the visit could proceed. He told a number of colleagues over a drink in the Smoking-Room that, in fact, he had very little option, as the Queen herself was determined to go and, short of an official Cabinet prohibition, intended to do so.

It was an anxious week for the Prime Minister, who would have been held responsible for any misadventure; but in the event the people of Ghana were most enthusiastic in their welcome, the whole tour was an outstanding success and the Queen's courage and sense of duty won world acclamation.

At home, another contentious issue concerning the Commonwealth had arisen. Immigration was becoming a major problem for Macmillan's Government. This arose initially from legislation passed by the American Congress in 1952, which virtually ended emigration from the Caribbean to the United States and left Britain as the only country with an open door policy for Commonwealth immigrants. The comparatively low living standards and the high level of unemployment in the West Indies made England a magnet for the more enterprising. At first this was helpful to the British economy, because workers were needed to fill employment vacancies, especially in public transport and the National Health Service. Indeed, Enoch Powell, later to become the leading spokesman against coloured immigration was – as Minister of Health – actually advertising in Barbados for nurses and ward maids to staff British hospitals.

Between 1955 and 1961 the number of immigrants, mainly from the West Indies, rose dramatically. Problems of housing and integration gradually became serious and in 1958 the race riots at Nottingham and Notting Hill, London, focused public attention on the need to limit the influx. Macmillan was reluctant to impose this by law because restrictions on admission would clearly breach the traditional right of every Commonwealth citizen to come to Britain. He knew this would cause repercussions throughout the New Commonwealth and that any legislation would be criticized as racial. This was not, of course, the intention, but it would be the effect because the rapid rise in immigration was entirely due to the entry from the poorer Commonwealth countries.

By 1961, the annual number of arrivals had risen from 21,000 (in 1959) to 136,000 and the Cabinet decided that some limitation had to be imposed. The Commonwealth Immigrants Bill was published that November and passed its Third Reading the following February. It was skilfully conducted by Rab Butler as Home Secretary, but vigorously opposed by the Labour Party led by Hugh Gaitskell, who attacked it with furious indignation as a 'miserable, shameful and shabby Bill'. Nevertheless the Labour Government, elected two years later, retained the new immigration controls and in fact intensified the restrictions which Butler had introduced. Since that time public criticism of the measure has been not of its harshness but of its leniency.

As the year 1961 drew to its close, trouble again developed in the Middle East. For the last two years of Macmillan's premiership, the problem of Aden, South Arabia and the Yemen was a continuing source of anxiety affecting Britain's power and prestige throughout the Arab world and her strategic security over an even wider area.

Aden was at that time a colony, comprising a port, docks and an air base vital to Britain's defence interests and an essential staging and communication link with the Far East. It was surrounded by the sheikdoms of South Arabia, which were friendly to Britain and which had been formed into a Federation under British protection in 1959. Conditions in these Emirates, though feudal and primitive, were politically stable; in Aden colony this was less so, because the Arab Trade Union Congress was a continual source of agitation, fostered by the Egyptian Government. Macmillan's plan, evolved after consultation with the Colonial Secretary, Duncan Sandys, and Sir Charles Johnston, the able Governor of Aden, was to merge the colony with the Protectorate States in order to ensure its greater stability through the influence of the federal rulers.

The situation was complicated by developments in the Yemen, which bordered on South Arabia. Imam Ahmed, the reactionary royal ruler who died in September 1962, had been despotic and medieval in the methods by which he had successfully controlled his country for fourteen years. His son and successor attempted some overdue reforms but was soon overthrown as a result of an Army *coup* headed by Colonel el Sallal, who declared himself President of a republican Yemen and was supported by troops sent from Egypt by Colonel Nasser. Civil war followed, with Sallal in occupation of the main towns and royalist tribes in control of the mountainous areas beyond. The federal rulers in South Arabia sided with the Yemeni royalists, while the working-class Arabs in Aden colony were sympathetic to, and likely to be subverted by, Colonel Sallal. Under these circumstances the merger between the colony and the protectorate states became increasingly difficult and it was much to Duncan Sandys' credit that it was eventually achieved.

A further complication arose from a difference of policy between the United States and the United Kingdom over the recognition of the new republican regime in the Yemen. America wished to recognize Sallal's Government; Britain took the opposite view and counselled delay. Even in Whitehall there were conflicting views, the Foreign Office favouring recognition while the Colonial Office and the Ministry of Defence were strongly against it. Many messages were exchanged between Macmillan and President Kennedy before the issue was eventually settled by Sallal himself, who asked for the withdrawal of the British Legation.

The purpose of the Government's policy was to retain and secure the Aden base; but all the skill, patience and hard work devoted by Duncan Sandys to this objective came to nothing in the end because the Labour Government, elected in 1964, proceeded to evacuate Aden. To Britain's shame, the federal rulers, who were our friends, were cynically abandoned and this vital defence post was lost to the West.

34

THE NUCLEAR ARMS RACE

East/West relations deteriorated during the second half of 1961, with a continued failure to reach any agreement on the problem of Berlin or on the banning of nuclear tests. The flood of refugees from East Germany made it difficult even to begin negotiations over Berlin and caused the Russians to build a massive concrete wall to prevent further movements of population to the Western zone of the city.

The weakness of the Allied position on this issue was the initial difference of emphasis between Britain and the United States over the best way to deal with Khrushchev. The American Administration was at first inclined to agree with France that the West should take no initiative and enter no negotiations with the Soviet Government. Many Americans believed that Macmillan was too conciliatory, and he certainly disapproved of a tank confrontation on the border which was engineered by General Clay in October 1961, and which he thought would only escalate an already dangerous situation. But although his approach was always flexible, the Prime Minister was never, in fact, as keen to grant concessions to Khrushchev as was suggested. In any event, 'before the close of the year the Americans had moved towards the British position in respect of Berlin'; and a diary note for 23 December is emphatic that the President 'does not intend to risk war about Berlin, although outwardly and publicly he talks big'.[1] Kennedy commented later that '... if ... the Germans think we are rushing into a war over Berlin, except as a last desperate move to save the NATO alliance, they've got another think coming'.[2]

In the autumn, Khrushchev had resumed the Soviet H-bomb tests and President Kennedy thereupon announced his decision to begin a new series of underground, though not atmospheric, American explosions. In Britain the Opposition demanded the immediate recall of Parliament from the summer recess, but Macmillan rightly refused this request, as such a move would merely have magnified the importance of these developments. The House reassembled a month later with a two-day debate on foreign affairs, which was concluded without a division after a quiet non-Party speech by the Prime Minister. Soon afterwards the Russians exploded first a thirty- then a fifty-megaton bomb and President Kennedy asked Macmillan for permission to use Christmas Island for an American test.

Throughout these anxious weeks, the President and the Prime Minister were in continuous contact by message and telephone. Kennedy constantly sought Macmillan's advice and their personal relations became closer and more intimate as a result; but it was clear to both of them that a meeting was becoming necessary, indeed urgent, and on 19 December Macmillan left for Bermuda, where the President was to join him. The British team for this conference consisted of Sir Norman Brook, Sir Evelyn Shuckburgh, Philip de Zulueta and the Government's chief scientific adviser, Sir William Penney. Macmillan arrived first and after a good lunch at Government House and several glasses of port, greeted the Americans with the words 'What do you bloody people want?', which surprised some of them, but which the President enjoyed.

The talks lasted for two days without interruption, although not without some moments of light relief. Schlesinger recalls that when someone asked Penney, an Australian by birth, how many bombs would be needed to destroy his country, he replied: 'If you are talking about Australia, it would take twelve. If you are talking about Britain, it would take five or six, but to be on the safe side, let us say seven or eight and' – without the slightest pause or change in tone – 'I'll have another gin and tonic, if you would be so kind.'[3]

It was agreed that the tests at Christmas Island should be postponed for a few months in the hope of progress on Berlin and disarmament, but that preparations for them should be made by putting the installations in a state of readiness, pending the decision of both Governments to use them. The talks were wide-ranging and covered, in addition to Berlin and nuclear tests, several other subjects such as the EEC, the Congo, Laos and the Far and Middle East.

On his return to England, the Prime Minister made his usual report to the Queen and included in his letter a reference to the pain the President suffered from his back trouble and some interesting sidelights on his character:

He is ... a very sensitive man, very easily pleased and very easily offended. He likes presents.... He likes letters, he likes attention.... I thought he was more interested in short-term than in large and distant problems.... [He] carries the weight of his great office with simplicity and dignity.

Macmillan had noticed that on a specific matter like the Congo, Kennedy was 'an extraordinarily quick and effective operator', but on the wider nuclear issues between East and West 'he seems rather lost'. The Prime Minister mentioned in his letter that Kennedy had spoken of the Queen with much interest and great admiration for her gallantry in going to Ghana; and he added the unusual suggestion that she might send the President 'an occasional letter', which he thought would be much welcomed.[4]

David Ormsby-Gore considered that the relationship between the two leaders had 'blossomed very considerably' at Bermuda and 'after that it was almost like a family discussion when we all met'.[5] Macmillan, too, felt that 'Kennedy and I had become even closer friends than before.'[6] Longford attributes the affection Kennedy was coming to feel for Macmillan to the Prime Minister's 'combination of deeply serious and knowledgeable statesmanship with rather elaborate jokiness',[7] and Schlesinger agrees that

they found the same things funny and the same things serious. . . . They soon discovered that they could match each other's transitions from gravity to mischief and communicate as in shorthand. It was as if they had known each other all their lives.

Despite the difference in age, Schlesinger noted a temperamental rapport between them. Kennedy was impressed and intrigued by Macmillan's style and admired his

. . . patrician approach to politics, his impatience with official ritual, his insouciance about the professionals, his pose of nonchalance, even when most deeply committed. Macmillan, for his part, responded to Kennedy's courage, his ability to see events unfolding against the vast canvas of history, his contempt for cliché, his unfailing sense of the ridiculous.[8]

The role of David Ormsby-Gore was of importance in the relationship. The Prime Minister enjoyed talking to him and they met 'out of school' at Birch Grove and at Pratt's Club, so that before he went to Washington Ormsby-Gore already knew the Prime Minister's mind and whenever he returned to England, they had long private sessions together. Ormsby-Gore also knew the President and the whole Kennedy family well, and this was the purpose and the special value of his appointment as Ambassador. His friendships with both the President and the Prime Minister were a unique advantage which made his position a different and more important one than any professional diplomat could have achieved. 'I trust David as I would my own Cabinet,' Kennedy declared.[9]

Ormsby-Gore often stayed with the Kennedy family at Hyannisport, which enabled him to meet the President in a relaxed atmosphere. He also had an almost open invitation to the White House and could slip in unofficially and unobserved whenever this seemed necessary. It was a convenient arrangement, as otherwise their frequent meetings might have been resented by Dean Rusk and the State Department and by other less favoured members of the

Diplomatic Corps. If there was a drawback in this close relationship, it was that, after a time, Ormsby-Gore became 'Kennedy's man' and was much under his influence; but Macmillan understood and could discount this, and it suited him to have a far closer personal link with the White House than any other Western leader enjoyed.

The Cabinet confirmed Macmillan's undertaking to make Christmas Island available to the Americans for the defensive anti-missile missile atmospheric tests, but Ministers were anxious that when the announcement of these was made, it should be accompanied by a new disarmament initiative which would make its reception more acceptable to British public opinion.

Macmillan did not wish to make this a condition for granting the test facilities, but he hoped the President would agree and wrote him a long letter at the beginning of January 1962 suggesting that the timing of the tests should depend to some extent on the Soviet reaction to any Allied proposals for disarmament. He was afraid that the American tests would lead to a further series of Russian tests and to a future in which, at enormous expense, each side would continue its attempts to obtain a nuclear lead over the other. Apart from scientific doubts as to whether an effective anti-missile system was possible, Macmillan was also concerned about the proliferation of nuclear weapons by other countries if the Great Powers continued the arms race.

An unwieldy eighteen-Power Disarmament Conference was to meet in March and, in order to make this productive, the Prime Minister proposed a preliminary meeting of the American, British and Russian Foreign Ministers. Before any public announcement, he suggested that a private approach should be made to Khrushchev, in which the French might be invited to join. He hoped it might even be possible to link the disarmament initiative with negotiations over Berlin.

Adlai Stevenson wrote promptly to the President to say: 'It would be unfortunate ... if we were to give the Prime Minister a dusty answer' to his letter,[10] but Arthur Schlesinger gives this account of the State Department's reaction:

On 12 January, Bundy and I went over to Rusk's office to examine State's draft reply. The answer could hardly have been dustier. It was an evasive bureaucratic screed, falling so far below Macmillan in style and tone as to be unresponsive. One high State Department officer said contemptuously about the Macmillan letter: 'Why are we taking so much trouble over this hysterical document? We can't let Macmillan practice this emotional blackmail on us.'[11]

In fact, there was much constructive thought and no element of hysteria in Macmillan's letter. Rusk agreed that the answer to it should not be perfunctory and set out some guidelines, on which Bundy prepared a reasonable reply.

A joint appeal from the President and the Prime Minister was sent to Khruschchev on 7 February, and the following day Macmillan announced the proposed Christmas Island tests and the invitation to the Soviet Foreign Minister to join a preliminary tripartite meeting on disarmament. This 'two-pronged' approach made all the difference to the reception of the Prime Minister's statement in the House of Commons. Khrushchev countered with a more spectacular, but much less realistic, proposal for a Summit meeting of eighteen heads of government at Geneva without even any previous preparation; but a month later he finally agreed to the meeting of Foreign Ministers and this acceptance, by disarming the Left wing in the Labour Party, was helpful to Macmillan when, at the same time, he informed the House that the American bomb tests would take place towards the end of April.

Theodore Sorensen has suggested that Kennedy's timing of the tests and of his announcement owed something to advice he had received from Hugh Gaitskell, 'whom the President liked immensely'.[12] Harold Macmillan did not share this high opinion of the Labour leader. Although he made several references in his memoirs to Gaitskell's often helpful attitude as Leader of the Opposition, he regarded him privately as a 'sanctimonious Wykehamist' and once said to Kennedy, 'I think you will find him very conservative compared to me.' It has been suggested that one reason for his disapproval was the fact that Gaitskell had not served in the war and it is true that Macmillan had a certain contempt for men of military age who had not done so; but it is hard to reconcile this with his good opinion of Harold Wilson, who had also seen no wartime service in the forces, but whom he liked personally, if not politically. He commented on one occasion that Wilson '... has beautiful manners and he has always been very agreeable to me'.[13] The regard was mutual, as Wilson has shown in his book *A Prime Minister on Prime Ministers*.

Macmillan had asked Kennedy for a postponement of the nuclear test announcement, but the President would only delay it for twenty-four hours, which saddened the Prime Minister, because the news 'would shatter the hopes of millions of people across the earth'.[14] In order to secure an abatement of the nuclear race, Macmillan was prepared to abandon the Allied insistence on listening stations to detect underground tests on Soviet soil and would have been content with occasional visits to Russia by neutral scientific teams to look at unexplained seismic events; yet even this modest requirement was rejected by the Russians, although Khrushchev had himself agreed to it at the time of Macmillan's visit to the USSR in 1959. Three years later the Russian position had hardened to the extent that any method of international control was regarded as a form of espionage.

The American tests began on 25 April and on 5 August the Prime Minister received news of a further series of Russian tests, which must have been in preparation for many months and no doubt accounted for the intransigent Soviet attitude to inspection. In the end, however, there was some reward for Macmillan's persistence. Without his earlier initiatives, the 1963 Test Ban Treaty might never have been signed.

35
THE CUBAN CRISIS

In 1959, a revolution led by Fidel Castro had overthrown Battista's Right-wing but corrupt regime in Cuba and it soon became clear that Castro, who was a Communist, was completely committed to the Russian bloc. Subsequently he had shaken Kennedy's confidence and prestige over the unfortunate incident at the Bay of Pigs and this influenced the President to take an interest in British Guiana, which was moving towards independence. He did not care for the prospect of a Castro-type government led by Cheddi Jagan on the South American mainland, and told Iain Macleod, then Colonial Secretary, that he hoped Britain would not proceed too quickly to independence for the colony. 'Do I understand, Mr President,' Macleod replied, 'that you want us to decolonize as fast as possible all over the world except on your own doorstep?' Kennedy laughed and said: 'Well, that's probably just about it.'[1]

The American attitude did not slow down Macleod's approach to the problem and on a later occasion his Under-Secretary, Hugh Fraser, asked the President, whom he knew well, not to press it too hard; but in a world context the Anglo-American relationship was of much more importance to Macmillan than the future of British Guiana and when the independence negotiations were coming to a head, the Prime Minister made this quite clear to Duncan Sandys, by then Secretary of State for the Colonies.[2]

If British Guiana was a sensitive subject, Cuba was an even greater source of anxiety in the State Department. Towards the end of June 1962, Macmillan dined with the Foreign Secretary to meet Dean Rusk. The Prime Minister reproached the American Secretary of State about a recent description by the President of Archbishop Makarios as a 'famous fighter for Freedom' and remarked that he would take an opportunity to refer to Castro in the same terms. To Macmillan's amusement, Rusk took this quite seriously and begged him not to do so. But four months later Cuba was no longer a laughing matter; a grave new crisis confronted the President.

On Sunday evening, 21 October 1962, the duty clerk at Admiralty House handed the Prime Minister a message from Kennedy, informing him that a serious situation was developing in the Caribbean between the United States and the Soviet Union. In fact, Macmillan had had advance warning of this two days before from David Ormsby-Gore. Nunnerley has revealed[3] how the Ambassador was alerted, without at that stage being officially informed of the impending crisis. Two British intelligence officers were in Washington at the time for a conference with the CIA and 'their suspicions were aroused by the diminishing attendance of key American officials at their joint meetings and by the movement of beds inside the Pentagon'. They informed Ormsby-Gore that something was afoot and, by a process of elimination, he came to the conclusion that an international crisis, probably concerning Cuba, was imminent. He sent a speculative telegram to this effect on Friday, 19 October, so that, by chance and good detective work, Macmillan was prepared for the news two days before he or any other foreign leader actually received it. He was also the first of America's allies to be told officially.

Kennedy's message informed the Prime Minister that, during the previous week, photographic intelligence had established beyond doubt that medium-range missile installations were being erected in Cuba. Six sites had already been identified. A build-up of Soviet arms and technicians had been observed during the summer, and in September Kennedy had issued a warning that if offensive missiles were introduced, America would take appropriate action to protect her own security. He now told Macmillan of his decision to prevent any further importation of missiles by sea and to demand the removal of those already there. He added, almost apologetically:

I have found it absolutely essential, in the interest of security and speed, to make my first decision on my own responsibility, but from now on I expect that we can and should be in the closest touch and I know that, together with our other friends, we will resolutely meet this challenge.[4]

He was determined not to show any weakness in the face of the Soviet threat, but he wisely resisted the pressure put upon him by most of his advisers to invade and occupy Cuba immediately. Influenced largely by his brother, Robert, he was anxious to find a way in which Khrushchev could retreat without too much loss of face.

The next morning the American Ambassador, David Bruce, called to see the Prime Minister. If Britain was fortunate to have David Ormsby-Gore at Washington at this time, the United States was also well represented at the Court of St James. Bruce was a quiet, cultured, elegant man, who had the detached air of an amateur, but was in fact one of the ablest and most experienced ambassadors in the American Service. He produced the evidence of the short- and medium- (2,000 miles) range missiles pointed at the heart of America and Canada, and described the 'quarantine' which the President had ordered against all ships carrying arms to Cuba. He and the Prime Minister discussed the danger that Khrushchev might try to trade Cuba for Berlin and answer Kennedy's blockade in the Caribbean by one of his own against the Western zone of the German city. Initially, Macmillan was worried about European opinion, especially in the context of the possible danger to Berlin, but after he had talked to the President, Schlesinger testifies that 'Macmillan did not falter and his counsel and support proved constant through the week'.[5]

Kennedy had already asked for a meeting of the Security Council of the United Nations, where the American representative would move a resolution calling for the withdrawal of the missile bases, to be supervised by UN observers. He requested British support for this, to which the Prime Minister readily responded.

Later that day Macmillan received a copy of the public statement the President was about to make and a long report from David Ormsby-Gore, who had been summoned to go 'unseen' to the White House the previous day for a private talk with Kennedy. At this stage no one else outside the United States Government had been informed of what was happening. The President put two alternative courses to the British Ambassador – an all-out, immediate air strike on the missile sites, involving many casualties, or an arms blockade of Cuba – and asked him which he preferred. Ormsby-Gore recommended the second and the President said he had come to the same conclusion. That night Kennedy telephoned Macmillan on their private line. This was the first of many such conversations, which were to become the regular method of communication throughout the week, with sometimes as many as three calls a day and even one at five o'clock in the morning, because the President had forgotten the time difference in the two countries. Next morning the Prime Minister explained the situation to the Cabinet and later to Gaitskell, George Brown and Harold Wilson, who called to see him. In the evening he reported the position to the Queen at his usual Tuesday audience.

Some people thought Britain's support for Kennedy's action should have been quicker and more categoric and one Minister was reported as saying '... the French – the "disloyal" anti-NATO French – beat us by several hours'.[6] Unlike France, however, the Minister of Defence did place Bomber Command in a state of readiness, should any help be required, although this was not of course known to the public at the time. In fact, military support was never offered by Macmillan or requested by Kennedy.

Press reaction in Britain was at first mixed. Although the *Daily Express* predicted that there would be full understanding and full backing for Kennedy, the *Daily Herald* saw 'no valid reason for going it alone and imperilling peace' and the *Daily Worker* condemned 'the crazy action of the wild men of Washington'. Even the *Daily Telegraph* wondered whether it would not have been wiser for the President to state his case to the United Nations before rather than after announcing the action he had decided to take. The *Guardian* took the line that if Khrushchev had in fact brought in nuclear missiles, 'he had done so primarily to demonstrate to the United States and the world the meaning of American bases close to the Soviet frontier', and suggested that Britain should vote against America in the United Nations. *The Economist* warned against 'forcing a showdown over the shipment of Russian arms to Cuba'.

Trade-union opinion was hostile and in the House of Commons thirty-seven Left-wing Labour MPs signed a motion demanding increased trade with Cuba and Britain's resistance to any shipping boycott. CND sympathizers demonstrated outside the American Embassy with cries of 'Viva Fidel, Kennedy to hell'. The Oxford Union passed a motion of protest against the American action and the Cambridge Union declined to support 'the present powers assumed by America'. Cuba committees were formed at both these Universities and at others, including Leeds and Liverpool; and the Socialist Society at the University of London called for a one-day strike as a protest against United States policy.

A group of well-known intellectuals attacked the quarantine and advocated British neutrality, and Bertrand Russell went so far as to describe Kennedy as 'much more wicked than Hitler' and sent messages to Khrushchev appealing humbly for his help in lowering the temperature. Many people in Britain questioned whether there really were any missiles in Cuba and wondered if this was all a pretext to justify an American invasion. Even Hugh Gaitskell doubted the legality of the quarantine and thought Kennedy should first have gone to the United Nations.

In view of this reaction, it was perhaps not surprising that Macmillan was concerned to placate public opinion and he soon had help in doing so from an unexpected quarter. At the meeting of the Security Council on 23 October, the Soviet representative had the effrontery to deny that there were any missiles in Cuba, but Adlai Stevenson was able to produce enlarged photographs which were incontrovertible proof of their existence. This evidence both of the facts and of Russian duplicity was widely reported and had a significant effect on world opinion. Macmillan was delighted. He had been anxious that the photographs should be published and David Ormsby-Gore had helped the President to select the most suitable ones at dinner the previous evening; he had also suggested that an explanatory note should be attached to each, as without this it was difficult for a layman to interpret them correctly.

Some of the resentment in Britain no doubt derived from the feeling that

Kennedy had taken a momentous decision which affected his allies without consulting them before doing so. Richard Crossman referred to this in an article in the *Guardian* on 26 October: 'We are told that Britain's nuclear weapons do give us a place in the councils of the nations. And in particular make sure that the Americans will listen to us ... that little myth is exploded.' Macmillan was sensitive to this criticism and believed that if he could have informed Parliament of Kennedy's constant telephone calls, it would have dispelled the accusation that there was no special relationship between London and Washington. In fact, there was: Britain was kept fully informed and to a much greater extent than the other Allied Powers, although Macmillan was not consulted about the actual policy decisions before they were taken. Kennedy's conversation with Ormsby-Gore on 21 October was characteristic of the President's technique. He appeared to be seeking advice, but in fact he had already decided upon his own course of action. On the one occasion when he did genuinely ask the Prime Minister for his opinion on an aspect of the problem as it affected Berlin, Macmillan replied cautiously: 'Well, I should like to think about that.'[7]

Although American policy was not greatly influenced by Britain, David Ormsby-Gore was able to make one important suggestion, which was at once adopted. He was dining privately with Jack and Bobby Kennedy and made the point that if the objective was to give Khrushchev the time and opportunity to reconsider and get himself off the Cuban hook before there was an actual incident at sea, every additional hour might help. He thought, therefore, that it would be advisable to reduce the interception line from 800 miles away from Cuba to 500 miles, and to ensure that orders to stop Soviet ships should not be automatic within the interception line, but should be referred for decision to the President and Robert McNamara. Despite United States Navy protests, this idea was accepted. It was a valuable contribution in postponing the moment of irreversible action and its adoption was a relief to Macmillan, who was worried that the Americans might overreach themselves.

On the day the blockade went into operation, it was known that twenty-five Russian ships were approaching Cuba, fourteen of which were thought to be carrying rockets. By that night Kennedy was able to tell the Prime Minister that some of these ships, probably those bringing military equipment, had turned back, but the others were still proceeding. The Americans had stopped one, but had let it go through because it was only a tanker carrying oil from the Black Sea. U Thant, the Secretary-General of the United Nations, now proposed a two-week pause for talks, during which no arms would be shipped into Cuba and the quarantine would be suspended. He wrote to the President asking him to avoid direct confrontation, to which

Kennedy replied that if the Russian ships kept out of the area, there would be no confrontation.

There remained the matter of the missiles already in Cuba, work on which was still continuing. Aerial reconnaissance revealed that the emplacements were being completed and the missiles put in position at great speed. Macmillan asked Kennedy whether it would be helpful if Britain offered to immobilize the missiles in the United Kingdom while talks took place and the President said he would invite the State Department to look at this suggestion. Soon afterwards a plausible proposal was received from the Russians to bargain, on a permanent basis, the dismantling of the missiles in Cuba for the removal of the American rockets in Turkey. This was preferable to a deal over Berlin but, had it been accepted, America's allies would have been justified in thinking that, to avoid the Cuban threat, the United States Government had bargained away their protection and Kennedy therefore rejected the suggestion,without, however, replying to it directly.

The letter proposing the Cuban–Turkish missile exchange was preceded the evening before by a diffuse and emotional appeal from Khrushchev, asking Kennedy to save the world from nuclear disaster and declaring that the ships at sea carried no missiles since these had already been delivered to Cuba. This was the first admission by the Russians that the weapons had in fact been installed on the island. The letter went on to say that if the President would give assurances that the United States would 'not participate in an attack on Cuba and that the blockade would be lifted', Khrushchev would agree not to send in any more weapons and would withdraw or destroy those already there.[8] This met Kennedy's demands in full and seemed to amount to complete capitulation by the Soviet leader. But alarming news followed next day. An American pilot was deliberately shot down over Cuba by a ground-to-air missile, which put at risk the whole reconnaissance system so essential to the United States.

Despite this, there were some signs that the Russian resolve was weakening. Approaches were being made to the British Government through minor officials of the Soviet Embassy in London, suggesting that Macmillan should mediate between the Russians and Americans. One of these emanated from the Soviet military attaché, Captain Ivanov, who persuaded a friend of his, Dr Stephen Ward, that 'Britain should prove she was no American pawn by immediately inviting Kennedy and Khrushchev to a summit in London to resolve the Cuban conflict.'[9] This seems to have been a rather amateurish attempt to drive a wedge between Britain and the United States. The Prime Minister had no intention of mediating and is reported to have said: 'When you begin to weaken, your first step is to send along your footman.'[10]

Late on Saturday, 27 October, Kennedy made an adroit move at the suggestion of his brother, Robert. Macmillan recounts how the President 'ingeniously ignoring Khrushchev's second letter, sent a message welcoming and accepting the suggestion made in the first'.[11] The Russian reply next day agreed to dismantle and withdraw the missles. This was surrender. By 12 November, forty-two missiles had been removed under inspection and the blockade was finally lifted on 20 November.

Macmillan paid a justified tribute to the President's skill, resourcefulness and courage in his conduct of the Cuban crisis.[12] If no other solution had been found, Kennedy was prepared to invade Cuba on 29 October, as soon as his forces were mobilized, but in the meantime he had played his diplomatic cards well and had emerged with credit and added prestige from the ordeal.

It is difficult to assess the importance of Macmillan's part in the story. 'It is not true', he told the House of Commons on 30 October, 'that we in this country played an inactive role in this great trial of strength'; but it was for the wider issues of general foreign policy and the repercussions in Europe, especially over Berlin, rather than for the actual decisions about Cuba, that Kennedy relied on Macmillan's greater knowledge and experience. He valued the Prime Minister's support and encouragement and was glad to be able to test his thoughts on someone of this stature, who was also outside his own immediate circle of sometimes conflicting counsellors. Kennedy put a high premium on Macmillan's advice. Indeed, had he not, the daily telephone conversations would not have been worth the time and trouble, since they went far beyond the requirements of co-operation between allies and were not in fact shared with other Western leaders.

Whatever the extent of his involvement, Macmillan certainly felt the weight of his responsibility as America's foremost friend. Speaking in the House of Commons many months later, he referred to it in these words:

... the week of the Cuban crisis – and I have been through some in peace and war – was the week of most strain I can ever remember in my life. It then seemed to many of us ... that in the struggle of wills between the Soviet Union and the Western powers, primarily the United States, the world might be coming to the brink of war.[13]

It could fairly be claimed that the outcome on this occasion was genuinely 'peace with honour'.

36
SKYBOLT AND POLARIS

Within two months of the safe conclusion of the Cuban crisis, Britain and the United States were involved in another nuclear issue which, though successfully resolved, might have had a serious effect on Anglo-American relations. It concerned Skybolt, a rocket fired from the air, which was being developed by the Americans and which President Eisenhower had agreed to supply to Britain in place of the fixed-site rocket, Blue Streak.

The arrangement with the former President was not merely a verbal understanding; it was a formal and binding agreement. If for any reason Skybolt proved unsatisfactory, Macmillan had been assured that, as an alternative, Polaris would be made available to be fitted to British-built submarines. Although there had been rumours of technical problems in the development of Skybolt, both President Eisenhower and later President Kennedy had informed the Prime Minister that they would be overcome, and in July 1962 an order for these rockets was placed by Britain and accepted in Washington; but by September the prospects for the survival of the weapon were poor.

In October, the Pentagon was so preoccupied with Cuba that little thought was given to the repercussions in Britain of discarding Skybolt. Sorensen thought that the President regarded the problem as technical rather than political and in any case, after Cuba, it seemed unimportant; all problems did. This evidence conflicts, however, with that of Schlesinger, who described Kennedy's reaction to McNamara's recommendation on 7 November that Skybolt should be cancelled. He reported that the President, realizing that this would be a severe blow to Macmillan, gave instructions that 'the British should be informed in ample time for them to prepare the ground before the decision was publicly announced'.[1] Next day McNamara told Ormsby-Gore, who, 'startled and appalled', said the news would be political dynamite in London. He must at once have reported the matter to the Foreign Office, yet in his own Memoirs the Prime Minister gave no indication of any foreknowledge of the cancellation until 'on 12 December Thorneycroft came to report his talks with McNamara in Paris. They had been wholly unsatisfactory; and the Minister of Defence had little doubt that the Americans meant to stop Skybolt altogether.'[2] Macmillan added the comment in his diary that 'there will be a great row in both countries'.[3]

It is extraordinary that the communication between President and Prime Minister, so close over Cuba only a short time before, should have been totally absent over Skybolt. In the weeks between 8 November and 12 December, neither Government made any approach to the other. David Bruce had been informed of the decision by McNamara, but had heard nothing from the State Department and, when he sent warnings, he received no instructions. Macmillan, McNamara and Rusk were all silent and no one except David Ormsby-Gore gave the President any warning of the British reaction. Indeed, Schlesinger reported Kennedy as complaining later that the Prime Minister 'should have warned me of the dangers ... we would have come up with a solution before publicity'.[4] Ironically, while Washington waited to hear from London, Macmillan was expecting an approach from the White House, so no one did anything.

On 13 December, a public announcement was made in Washington that Skybolt's future was uncertain owing to 'unforseen technical difficulties and rising costs'. The expected row promptly erupted in the British press and, when Thorneycroft made a statement in the House of Commons, even so moderate a Labour spokesman as George Brown suggested that it was time Britain gave up the attempt to have an independent nuclear deterrent.

Macmillan had already arranged to go to France in December for talks with de Gaulle and to Nassau immediately afterwards for a meeting with Kennedy. Accompanied by Lady Dorothy and Philip de Zulueta, he left for Paris on 13 December. During the course of his conversations with the French President, which were mainly concerned with the Common Market negotiations, he took the opportunity to inform de Gaulle that if Skybolt was cancelled he would press Kennedy to provide Britain with an adequate replacement, probably Polaris. It was afterwards suggested that the Prime Minister had deceived de Gaulle by concealing this intention and that the subsequent French veto of Britain's application to join the European Economic Community was due to the Nassau negotiations and Britain's purchase of Polaris as a result of them. This was not the reason and was never suggested by de Gaulle, but he allowed it to be said by others, although he was well aware of Macmillan's intentions.

When the Nassau meeting was arranged at the end of November, it had been intended to cover other, wider matters and Skybolt had not even been mentioned as a subject for discussion, but by 16 December, when Macmillan was due to leave for the Bahamas, it had become the first item on the agenda.

Even so, the failure of communication continued. When Kennedy declared publicly that Skybolt was not cost-effective, the decision was made in London to press instead for Polaris, but the Americans were not informed of this and nor was the British Ambassador:

On the 'plane to Nassau Ormsby-Gore warned Kennedy about the storm ... if the British believed the Americans were letting them down.... Within half an hour he and Ormsby-Gore worked out a proposal based on the assumption, created by the Thorneycroft–McNamara meeting and evidently not dispelled by London's instructions to its Ambassador, that Britain still wanted Skybolt.[5]

Schlesinger went on to record that it was only that evening that Macmillan told the President that he wanted Polaris and under conditions which would preserve the British claim to a national deterrent.

The Prime Minister was joined for the conference by Alec Home, Peter Thorneycroft and Duncan Sandys, with David Ormsby-Gore, Tim Bligh and Philip de Zulueta to help them. The American team consisted of McNamara, George Ball, McGeorge Bundy, David Bruce and Llewellyn Thompson, the American Ambassador to Moscow. Henry Brandon, the experienced United States correspondent for the *Sunday Times*, reported the strength of feeling in the British delegation, which he described as a '... resentment and suspicion of American intentions such as I have never experienced in all the Anglo-American conferences I have covered over the past twenty years.'

Macmillan opened the discussions on the morning of 19 December. After reviewing the history of Anglo-American nuclear co-operation and reminding Kennedy of Eisenhower's assurance that, if Skybolt failed, Britain could rely on obtaining Polaris, the Prime Minister dismissed the argument that this might upset the French by pointing out that a change from a missile fired from a bomber to one fired from a submarine was one of technique, not of principle. The President then suggested that the United States Government should pay half of any further development cost of Skybolt, estimated at two hundred million dollars, and the British the other half. Britain would have the right to buy the missiles, though America could not undertake to do so. Schlesinger considered this a wise and generous offer and in a sense this was true because the compromise would cost the United States one hundred million dollars for something they did not want; but it seemed a strange suggestion – Britain was being invited to spend the same sum on a weapon the Americans thought of doubtful viability. On the one hand, they were arguing that Skybolt would fail and must be abandoned; on the other, that it could be made to work, but they did not need it, because of Polaris, and would be ready to sell it to Britain.

Macmillan acknowledged that the United States were prepared to defend

Europe and had the means to do so, but would they always have the will? Britain, with her world-wide commitments, must continue to have an independent nuclear force; and he pressed hard for Polaris as the substitute for Skybolt. The arguments were intense, prolonged and sometimes painful and Macmillan described the three-day negotiation, fiercer than any previous one, as an exhausting experience. By the end of the first day, Kennedy realized that only Polaris would satisfy the British Government and thereafter he steered his delegation to find a formula to fit this requirement. As he said later to Sorensen: 'Looking at it from their point of view ... it might well be concluded that ... we had an obligation to provide an alternative.'[6] He felt unable to send the Prime Minister away without some substitute for the missiles Eisenhower had promised.

Macmillan wrote in his diary that the discussions turned largely on 'independence in national need' or an irrevocable commitment of the British force to NATO: 'I had to pull out all the stops – adjourn, reconsider, refuse one draft and demand another, etc. ...'[7] He was playing for high stakes. In the end Kennedy yielded on the major issue of Polaris; he was not prepared to face a break with the British, whose friendship he valued highly and with whom he had a far closer relationship than with any other ally. As Dean Rusk remarked later: 'We can't break with Britain. We have to be able to discuss world problems with someone.... We and the British don't always agree. But we discuss.'[8]

Eventually an arrangement was reached that Britain would be supplied with Polaris, for which she would make her own warheads. In return, the nuclear submarines would be assigned to NATO, except 'where Her Majesty's Government may decide that supreme national interests are at stake', in which event Britain reserved the right to use the deterrent independently.

This may have sounded like a concession by Britain. In fact, it was not, because of course the nuclear bomb would never be used except in a grave emergency where supreme national interests were at stake. There is no doubt that the outcome of this negotiation can be considered a victory for Macmillan.

The reaction of the British press was, as usual, conflicting. Some papers criticized the Government for clinging obstinately to a nuclear force, others attacked the agreement as a 'sell-out' to the United States. A *Times* commentator wrote that, 'apart from increased costs, Britain will not have a credible nuclear deterrent for some years'[9] and another article considered that '... President Kennedy can congratulate himself on establishing indivisible control of American and British nuclear forces, a bonus he obviously did not expect when he went to the Bahamas.'[10]

One Conservative Member of Parliament wrote that 'The Nassau arrangements ... present a culminating humiliation for the British people,' while most Labour Members took the view that Britain should not be in the nuclear business at all. Schlesinger had no doubt as to who had come off best: 'For Macmillan it was a great victory, marred only by the extent to which the Conservative Party and the London press had identified the British deterrent with Skybolt.'[11]

There were two postscripts to the Conference. Ironically, the day after it ended, a successful test of Skybolt was carried out, but this did not affect the United States' decision to concentrate on Polaris. The other addendum was an unexpected demand by the Americans, never mentioned at Nassau, that Britain should contribute to the future research and development costs of their new deterrent. Macmillan declined to carry this open-ended commitment and appealed personally to the President to overrule McNamara's request. The Prime Minister offered, instead, to add 5% to the retail cost, which was accepted. However hard the bargaining had been at the Conference, he was glad to feel, at the end of it, that no harm had been done to his own relations with Kennedy.

37

MACMILLAN AND EUROPE

Harold Macmillan's enthusiasm for a united Europe was a theme in his political thinking from the outbreak of the Second World War until his own retirement from public life twenty-five years later. In the third volume of his memoirs he reminded his readers that as long ago as 1897, in the year of the Diamond Jubilee, the then Prime Minister, Lord Salisbury, was looking ahead to a federal Europe as 'our sole hope of escaping from the constant terror and calamity of war. ... The Federation of Europe is the only hope we have.'[1] If Salisbury's statesmanship could have achieved it then, the tragedy of the two World Wars would have been avoided. In 1939, Harold Macmillan expressed the same view: 'If western civilization is to survive, we must look foreward to an organization, economic, cultural and perhaps even political, comprising all the countries of Western Europe.'[2]

In March 1943, Churchill broadcast a plan for the re-organization of Europe, with the creation of a Council of Europe as the first practical task. Three years later he delivered the famous Zurich speech, appealing for European unity: 'My counsel to Europe can be given in a single word: Unite.'[3] In 1947, he launched the United Europe Movement in a great meeting at the Albert Hall and formed a 'non-Party' managing committee which included Harold Macmillan. Its success was due mainly to the tenacity and perseverance of Duncan Sandys.

Unfortunately Eden stood aloof from these developments. At best, his attitude was one of neutrality. The Foreign Secretary, Ernest Bevin, was unhelpful and the Labour Government positively hostile. Ministers seemed to deprecate any Union which was not based on Socialism. Harold Macmillan was quick to see that Conservative fears and Socialist suspicions would prevent Britain playing her full part. 'No illusion is more dangerous', he pointed out, 'than that of a Socialist united front to resist Communism. It must be a democratic united front of all Parties and personalities who believe in freedom and democracy. We shall never unite Europe by dividing ourselves.'[4]

A successful international congress, held at The Hague in May 1948, resulted in the creation of the Council of Europe, comprising twelve member countries. The British Conservative delegation was led by Churchill and included Harold Macmillan. Spaak became President of the Assembly, which met at Strasbourg. It was consultative, with no powers of its own, but Churchill used it as a platform for his ideas, including a demand for the inclusion of a German delegation. Macmillan worked hard and successfully to implement this and regarded it as 'a decisive step . . . towards reconciliation and unity'.[5]

Two years later Robert Schuman, the French Foreign Minister, announced an imaginative and far-reaching plan for the co-operation of the iron, coal and steel industries of Western Europe. This was justified on economic grounds, but its real importance was political, because it linked France and Germany in an association of their heavy industries, which would make another war between them virtually impossible. Military power depends upon steel and the Schuman proposal had the double advantage of accepting Germany as an equal partner while at the same time giving the rest of Europe security against the possibility of future German aggression. Unfortunately, Bevin was unsympathetic and the British Government's reaction to the plan was therefore tepid. Macmillan was appalled by this lack of enthusiasm for an act of statesmanship which he saw as a turning point in Franco-German relations: 'If the plan is pursued,' he said, 'it will be a wonderful step forward. If it fails, it . . . will be more than a set-back. It will be a disaster.'[6]

The British Labour Government declined even to attend an international conference to discuss the Schuman proposals. This negative attitude was condemned by Macmillan, who declared that 'we may have to pay a terrible price for the isolationist policy which British Socialism has long practised and now openly dares to preach'.[7] He followed this speech with a strong minute to Churchill setting out the advantages of the plan and urging his leader to give it full support.

The issue was debated by the House of Commons in June 1950. During the course of it, a newly-elected Member spoke strongly in his maiden speech for co-operation with Europe. His name was Edward Heath. Churchill himself was scornful of the Socialist insularity and was prepared to accept some loss of national sovereignty in the cause of European unity; but in the division the Government view prevailed by a majority of 13 votes. Macmillan was unhappy at this outcome of what he described as 'the most important event in the post-war history of Europe'.[8] He and David Eccles worked hard to produce a compromise plan designed to make the Schuman proposals more democratic. This was received with sympathy and understanding by his European colleagues when the matter was debated in the Council of Europe.

'After what Churchill has done for you all,' he said, 'I have a right to ask it,' to which Maurice Schuman replied graciously with a reference to Macmillan's wartime work in North Africa: 'Yes, and Macmillan has a right to ask it in his own name. He has done more for France than any man, including Churchill.'

In April 1951, six countries signed the treaty establishing the Coal and Steel Community. It was sad that the greatest steel-making country in Europe, which also produced more coal than all the others combined, should have excluded herself from this brave new effort for European co-operation.

The next subject for debate was defence and the proposal to create a European Army, to which Germany would contribute. Of even greater significance was the decision of the American and Canadian Governments to send troops to Europe to help maintain the peace. Macmillan welcomed this warmly in a speech at Strasbourg in November 1950: 'The New World is to be called in to redress the balance of the Old, not after the catastrophy but before. It promises not liberation but security.'[9] The arrangements were confirmed by NATO the following month when Eisenhower was appointed as Supreme Commander with his Headquarters in Paris.

When the Conservative Government was elected in October 1951, there was naturally renewed hope and expectation in Europe that with Churchill again in charge, Britain would join both the Schuman coal and steel organization and the European Defence Community. Unfortunately the Cabinet was divided. Macmillan, Maxwell Fyfe, Eccles, Thorneycroft and Sandys were enthusiastic, but in November Eden declined to join the EDC and the other Ministers were at best ambivalent. Disappointingly, Churchill gave no positive lead. Macmillan wrote to him in protest and was disillusioned to the point of considering resignation from the Government. Only his ambition and his deep affection for and loyalty to Churchill influenced him to accept the negative position the majority of his colleagues had adopted.

Eden's attitude was the main barrier to progress and Macmillan made several appeals to him, both written and oral, 'but the Foreign Secretary was often abroad and even in discussion he was so well-informed and convincing upon any particular point that it was difficult to raise and defend more general concepts ... I felt that I could not make him understand the depth and scope of my anxieties. He was always looking for a solution of the short-term problem.'[10]

Eden's whole life had been devoted to foreign affairs. His knowledge of this area of politics was pre-eminent and his diplomatic skill unquestioned. Even Churchill was reluctant to oppose his judgement. Yet it was in foreign policy that he made his two greatest mistakes: Suez was the issue on which his career foundered, but in retrospect this was relatively unimportant compared with his consistent opposition to the Common Market and the whole concept of a united Europe. He underestimated from the outset the political will of the Six and for a quarter of a century Britain has paid and is still paying for his refusal to join the negotiations which led to the Treaty of Rome. At that time, first as Foreign Secretary and then as Prime Minister, he could have led Europe had he so wished and his grievous mistake in remaining aloof and declining to do so has cost his country dear.

Macmillan's own responsibility for the missed opportunity was less reprehensible. As Foreign Secretary he was inhibited and virtually impotent in the face of Eden's opposition and as Prime Minister, albeit tardily, he did his best to make amends for the wasted years. Nevertheless, when he became Foreign Secretary in 1955, it might have been expected that British policy towards Europe would change, particularly as this coincided in time with the momentous Messina Conference of the six member countries of the Coal and Steel Community. Indeed, as soon as he arrived in the Foreign Office, Macmillan made it known there that his purpose was the unity of Europe on a confederal basis and in his first speech in the House of Commons as Foreign Secretary he referred to the importance of 'the European idea'. But thereafter he did nothing to further it. The six Messina nations agreed in principle upon the creation of a common market and for a moment it appeared that British policy might become more positive.

When he addressed the Council of Europe in July 1955, Macmillan said they might have been 'making Europe without knowing it' and a *Sunday Times* editorial suggested that 'Mr Macmillan's optimism, even enthusiasm ... will have been taken by many as heralding a more forthcoming policy. ...'[11] In fact, the Six *were* making Europe, but without the support and co-operation of Britain. Their Foreign Ministers were all present at Messina and Macmillan was invited to attend, but did not do so. Instead, he sent a senior civil servant at the Board of Trade to represent the British Government. A committee was established to study the problems in implementing the Common Market and Britain was again invited, but again only sent the same official, and as a representative, not a delegate. In a cold Foreign Office reply Macmillan pointed out 'the special difficulties for this country' and only agreed to take part in this preparatory work 'without prior commitment'.[12]

The difficulties to which he referred were Britain's position in the sterling area and the Commonwealth, and her close ties with the United States, which in the opinion of the majority of the Cabinet, including the Prime Minister, precluded Britain from joining the EEC as a full member. The Foreign Office took the mistaken view that the problems were in any case too great and that the negotiations between the Six would prove abortive. Even Macmillan made it plain in a speech a year later that, in a choice between imperial preference and a European customs union, 'we could not hesitate. We must choose the Commonwealth.'[13]

The real purpose of the Common Market was political rather than economic. Its two most powerful members, France and Germany, saw it as the only certain insurance against another European war and as the best way of maintaining a lasting Franco-German alliance. When, as Prime Minister, Macmillan at last applied to join the Community in 1961, it was the political advantages which were also uppermost in his own mind. Until then, he had been more concerned with the creation of a system of European free trade, which would, he hoped, provide a degree of unity without political unification. He worked hard with Peter Thorneycroft, then President of the Board of Trade, and a team of officials to produce new proposals, known as 'Plan G', devised by Thorneycroft to cover all commodities except food. In order to safeguard Commonwealth trade, Macmillan proposed confining the free trade area to industrial goods; but not unnaturally France, as an agricultural exporter, thought this unfair and far too favourable to the United Kingdom and the Commonwealth. De Gaulle also feared that Britain would either become the Trojan horse for American interests or would take over the political leadership of Europe from France. Erhardt of Germany supported the British proposals, but was overruled by Chancellor Adenauer, who sided with de Gaulle. Those who, unlike de Gaulle, were federalists and supporters of a United States of Europe believed that this prospect would be prejudiced by the wider and looser association envisaged by Macmillan.

The Prime Minister was disingenuous in making it appear as though the aims of 'Plan G' were the same as those of the Six[14], which they were not. In so far as there was a European policy at all in the early years of his Administration, its objective was not, as he implied, to reach the same goal as the Messina Powers, although by a different route; it was, rather, to counter their proposals by the concept of a much looser economic umbrella to cover a much wider membership.

The Treaty of Rome was signed on 25 March 1957 and was to come into force on 1 January 1958. In June 1957 Macmillan minuted the Foreign Secretary: 'The present line is to let everything go along without effort until after ratification.' He realized the danger that '... when the Six have ratified, they may snap their fingers at the Free Trade Area and leave us in the lurch.'[15] In an interesting memorandum to Thorneycroft in July, he wrote:

We must not be bullied by the activities of the Six. We could ... fight their movement if it were to take the form of anything that was prejudicial to our interests. Economically, with the Commonwealth and other friends, including the Scandinavians, we could stand aside ... we must take positive action to ensure that the wider Free Trade

Area is more attractive than the narrower Common Market of the Six. We must take the lead either in widening their project or ... in opposing it.

Nevertheless, in the same memorandum, he expressed the view that:

... the pressure for European integration ... really derives from the strong desire of many European countries for some form of closer political association. We should take advantage of this, since ... we may well be able to show Europe that we are prepared for a closer political association.[16]

In August 1957, the Prime Minister appointed Reggie Maudling, who was not a dedicated European, as Minister responsible for British interests in Europe. As the year wore on, Macmillan became convinced that the British attempt to organize a wide Free Trade Area was being frustrated by France and in June 1958 he travelled to Paris to see de Gaulle. It was their first meeting since the wartime days in Algiers and he gave this impression of the General:

He has of course aged a lot. He has grown rather fat; his eyes are bad and he wears thick spectacles; he no longer smokes chains of cigarettes. His manner is calm, affable and rather paternal. But underneath this new exterior, I should judge that he is just as obstinate as ever. I spoke very strongly to him about the Free Trade Area, and the fatal political results which would follow the present French attitude. But he clearly was neither interested nor impressed.[17]

General de Gaulle expressed the opinion that Britain's history and geography made her a natural opponent of Continental unity and he thought her free trade tradition was inimical to the Common Market concept of a common external tariff and suitable arrangements for French agriculture. He quoted Macmillan as having declared at their meeting: 'The Common Market is the Continental system all over again. Britain cannot accept it. I beg you to give it up. Otherwise we shall be embarking on a war which will doubtless be economic at first, but which runs the risk of gradually spreading into other fields.'[18] It was not an argument which was likely to appeal to de Gaulle and he was no doubt sincere in believing that the British were not good Europeans. Moreover, he had a long memory and it was this sort of reaction to the Common Market which influenced him in vetoing Britain's application to join it four years later. He saw Macmillan's policies as 'keeping the Six in suspense and delaying the launching of the Community by proposing that the latter should be absorbed, and consequently dissolved, in a free trade area'.[19] He suspected the British of duplicity, while Macmillan saw the French as obstinate and obstructive.

France's position in 1958 was far weaker than it was to be in 1963, but no doubt Macmillan over-estimated both his own bargaining power and the influence of Germany in moderating French opposition to British policy. As Foreign Secretary, his ill-advised coolness towards the Common Market had contributed to European suspicions of his motives and Maudling's evident lack of sympathy with EEC aspirations cannot have been helpful. Britain had hovered on the side-lines at a crucial time and was later to pay the price for her hesitation. Her first attempt to join Europe was therefore flawed and half-hearted and led only to the short-lived European Free Trade Area of the 'Seven', a rival combination of non-EEC countries.

The EFTA Agreement was signed in Stockholm in November 1959 by Britain, Sweden, Norway, Denmark, Austria, Switzerland and Portugal. The negotiations which culminated in this compromise had been skilfully and patiently handled by Reggie Maudling, to whose 'equable temper and brilliant and fertile brain' Macmillan paid a well-deserved tribute;[20] but the opportunity to become a founder member of the EEC had been lost and EFTA was a second-best which could not long survive. At least part of the blame for Britain's unimaginative response to the Community initiative must rest with Macmillan, who, as Foreign Secretary and later Prime Minister, failed to maintain his own earlier enthusiasm for the unity of Europe.

During 1959, the formation of EFTA and the EEC's preoccupation with implementing the provisions of the Treaty of Rome precluded effective contact between Britain and the Six, but the Government's attitude was gradually becoming more flexible and, in January 1960, Selwyn Lloyd spoke to the Council of Europe:

I want to put to you as simply but as definitely as I can the British position. We regard ourselves as part of Europe ... The fact that the Alps and the Pyrenees have been more easily crossed in war then the Channel does not disqualify the United Kingdom from European status.[21]

Britain's mistake in not joining the Coal and Steel Community was frankly acknowledged.

There was a Foreign Office re-examination of policy during the year, in the course of which Churchill's 'three circles' concept was looked at again. This had presupposed a unique role for Britain as the common factor in the European, Commonwealth and American relationships; but even if this was still valid, the assumption that too close an association with Europe would necessarily weaken Britain's ties with the other two was regarded as questionable and at least subject to further investigation.

In the spring of 1960, Macmillan was in the United States, partly to encourage greater American interest in EFTA, and during this visit an unfortunate story appeared in the *Washington Post*, which reported that the Prime Minister had talked of Britain's historic role to crush Napoleonic ambitions for the integration of Europe. He was alleged to have added that if France and Germany continued along this road, Britain would have no alternative but to lead another alliance against them. Macmillan does not mention this in his memoirs, but the story, though denied by the Foreign Office, was widely publicized in Europe, where it served to strengthen suspicion of British policies.

During the spring and early summer, speculation mounted about Britain's relations with the EEC. The Beaverbrook press was, predictably, against any involvement and the *Daily Worker* took the same line though for different reasons; but most papers were in favour of closer collaboration with the Common Market and some already advocated joining it. Macmillan's mind was moving along the same lines. He was beginning to realize the dangers of remaining outside the EEC and to weigh these against the claims of EFTA, the Commonwealth and British agriculture. He instructed Duncan Sandys, the Commonwealth Secretary, to reconcile the European concept with Britain's Commonwealth ties and obligations and described this as 'perhaps the most urgent problem in the Free World to-day'. He could not have entrusted the task to anyone better qualified, for Sandys had been one of the founders of the European movement and its most ardent and consistent advocate. At the same time, Christopher Soames, another convinced European, became Minister of Agriculture; so the two key departments in the context of any Common Market negotiations which might eventuate were in the hands of Ministers who believed in the unity of Europe and were anxious to promote it. Edward Heath, another pro-Market man, was made Lord Privy Seal with special responsibility for European affairs.

These Government changes heralded a new emphasis on Europe and strengthened support in the Cabinet for those who believed Britain should make an approach to the Common Market countries with a view to negotiating entry into the Community; but this was not yet settled Government policy. There were still some sceptics in the Cabinet, notably Hailsham, Maudling and (because of his fears for British agriculture) Rab Butler, and a Right-wing group in the Conservative Party was strongly opposed to it.

There had been no mention of the Common Market in the 1959 Election Manifesto, so the decision, when it came, was breaking new ground, for which the Government had no mandate and Macmillan approached it with caution. Once his own mind was made up, he gradually edged first the Cabinet and then the Parliamentary Party into acquiescence. It was the biggest decision of his whole Premiership and he was careful to take it slowly and to run no risk of a serious split in the Conservative Party. This was wise because, as he himself put it: 'For the Conservative Party, so long and intimately linked with the ideal of Empire', it was a major change of direction, which would inevitably involve long, yet confidential discussion with the Governments of the Commonwealth.

Following a preliminary talk with President Kennedy in April 1961, Macmillan was able to inform Prime Ministers Diefenbaker, Menzies and Holyoake that the American Administration considered that the interests of the Western world would best be served by Britain's participation in the political as well as the economic arrangements of the Six. The problems for Commonwealth trade and British agriculture were formidable and it was questionable whether the Commonwealth could stand the strain of such a radical change of policy. It was fortunate that the office of Commonwealth Secretary should be occupied at this time by Duncan Sandys, always the keenest European in the Cabinet, who was in a good position to understand Commonwealth anxieties and interests and to satisfy them in the difficult negotiations which would soon be necessary. It was decided that he should personally visit Australia, New Zealand and Canada and that other Ministers would go to India, Pakistan, West Africa and the Caribbean.

It seemed right to consult Commonwealth Governments before rather than after a final Cabinet decision was taken and before detailed discussions opened between Britain and the Six. It was not simply a question of signing or not signing the Treaty of Rome. It had first to be decided, after genuine consultation with the Commonwealth, whether to enter into a negotiation at all. Thereafter, Britain could only join the EEC subject to satisfactory safeguards for her own agriculture and for the essential interests of her EFTA and Commonwealth partners. It would be necessary to hold a full Commonwealth Conference before a final decision could be taken, but this would only be of value when there were concrete propositions to discuss as a result of formal negotiations with the Community.

After the travelling Ministers had returned and made their reports to the Cabinet, it was unanimously agreed that the Government should apply to enter the Common Market. Accordingly, on the last day of July 1961, the Prime Minister announced to the House of Commons the Government's decision to apply formally to join the EEC. The detailed negotiations were entrusted to Edward Heath. Macmillan had sent advance copies of his statement to the Commonwealth Prime Ministers and to the President of the United States. Kennedy sent a generous reply expressing his goodwill and firm support and adding that, if there was any way in which America could be useful, 'you can count on us absolutely'. The Beaverbrook press was bitterly opposed to the application, but the other newspapers were sympathetic and in some cases enthusiastic.

The Common Market was debated on 2 and 3 August, on a Government motion inviting the House to support the Cabinet's decision to initiate negotiations, subject to suitable safeguards for British, Commonwealth and EFTA interests and subject ultimately to the approval of Parliament. The debate was opened by the Prime Minister, who dealt convincingly with the diversity of arguments against Britain's entry. There was only one perhaps inevitable illogicality when he referred to the division of Europe which, although 'of a commercial character, undoubtedly detracts from the political strength and unity'; yet he was the creator of EFTA, which had increased and formalized this division. He acknowledged Britain's tradition of isolationism, but drew attention to her abandonment of this attitude whenever Europe was in danger, as she now was once again due to Communist expansion. He argued for an outward-looking Europe, ready to help the underdeveloped countries, to which Britain with its worldwide ties could make a valuable contribution: 'I believe that our right place is in the vanguard of the movement towards the greater unity of the free world and that we can lead better from within than outside.'

He went on to claim that membership of the Community would strengthen Britain's economy and so enable her to help the Commonwealth more effectively. It would be a mistake, he thought, to regard her European and Commonwealth interests as conflicting – basically they were complementary. He believed the weight of opinion in British industry was in favour of joining the EEC, since it would provide a market comparable in size – after Britain's accession – to Russia or the United States. He demolished the argument of diminished national sovereignty by pointing out that every treaty was a limitation on a nation's freedom of action, but in this case he had noticed no loss of French or German national identity through the delegation of sovereignty which had been necessary; in practice it was a matter of degree, not of principle. Finally, he came down firmly against federalism, which was not envisaged in the Treaty of Rome and was not the policy of any of the leading European Governments, certainly not of France. A form of confederation was more attractive and with that Britain could willingly be associated.[22]

The speech was a great success and was acclaimed as such by the newspapers. Even Beaverbrook's *Evening Standard* described Macmillan as being 'back on top form'. The official Labour position was to sit firmly on the fence, although Michael Foot was violently opposed and Roy Jenkins was as strongly in support of the Government's policy. Jenkins maintained:

There is a real danger that we shall go into a kind of drab decline, rather detached from the main currents of life in the world, blaming other countries for our misfortunes and deluding ourselves, but no one else, with illusions of grandeur. I believe that the best prophylactic against that rather dismal happening is that we should go into Europe.[23]

Macmillan believed it too and for the last two years of his Premiership it was the centrepiece of Government policy, on the success of which he relied to revive the electoral fortunes of his Party and the economic performance of Britain.

The Prime Minister was gratified that his son, Maurice, made an effecitive speech which enhanced his reputation, but he reserved his highest praise for Harold Wilson's contribution which, though an attack on the Government, he considered 'the most brilliant speech of the debate'. He thought the House of Commons was at its best and that an exceptionally high standard of speaking was maintained throughout the whole two days. Those against the motion were drawn from the extreme left of the Labour Party, in paradoxical alliance with a few on the right of the Conservative Party. The official Opposition and about twenty Tories abstained on the substantive motion.

A strong team of able officials under Sir Pierson Dixon, the British Ambassador in Paris, was quickly recruited from appropriate Government departments to assist Heath in presenting the British case, which he set out in an impressive paper to the EEC meeting in Paris on 10 October. Butler took charge of a Ministerial committee to oversee the negotiations.

The next hurdle was the annual Party Conference at Brighton. This proved much easier to surmount than had been expected and when the vote was taken only about forty delegates out of four thousand opposed the Government's policy. The stage was now set for the European negotiations.

Britain's role of broker between the super powers was no longer an effective one and Macmillan sensed the need to look forward to new areas of political and economic vitality; to a wider sweep of ideas and events; and to the exciting prospects now opening in Europe. Britain's entry was to be the psychological fillip the people needed and he believed that membership would have a dynamic effect on her sagging economic performance. It would not be an easy road to prosperity, but it would be rewarding. British agriculture was efficient and industry would surely respond to the challenge of competition and the high rewards for success. Macmillan's own interest was mainly in the more influential political role which admission to and hopefully leadership of the EEC would enable Britain to play in the world. He regarded accession to the Community as his last major contribution in public life, which was to ensure his place in history as one of the nation's great peacetime Prime Ministers.

38

THE FRENCH VETO

It was not until January 1962 that, after weeks of continuous discussion, the Six succeeded in agreeing the next stage of their own agricultural policy, and it was only then that the British negotiations on temperate-zone foodstuffs could begin. Nevertheless, Ted Heath was hopeful that the arrangements for Britain's entry into the Common Market could be concluded by the end of July. Macmillan was less optimistic about the timing and thought the autumn a more realistic prospect. In April, a referendum in France resulted in an overwhelming victory for de Gaulle, with 90% of the electorate voting in his favour. Macmillan wrote him a warm letter of congratulation, expressing the hope that he could now turn his mind to the European problem and suggesting another personal meeting early in June.

Meanwhile, although discussions with the Commonwealth were proceeding satisfactorily on a bilateral basis, it was becoming necessary to plan a Prime Ministers' Conference and this was arranged for 10 September. In April, John McEwen, Deputy Prime Minister of Australia, visited England and Western Europe, where he was sympathetically received by the leading personalities, including de Gaulle; and Holyoake agreed to send one of his Ministers, Jack Marshall, to London for detailed talks about New Zealand's special trading position with Britain, which was so vital to her whole economy.

At the end of the month, Macmillan spent a few days in Canada, where he was given the Freedom of Toronto and warmly welcomed by a large crowd, as well as by the bankers and business men whom he met there. Only Diefenbaker made no attempt to disguise his hostility towards the European project. Bob Menzies was in London for a few days at the end of May and, although less obdurate than Diefenbaker, he was certainly not enthusiastic and issued an unhelpful statement which made headlines in the newspapers.

The next step was the meeting with de Gaulle, and Macmillan, accompanied by Lady Dorothy and Philip de Zulueta, arrived in Paris on 2 June. They stayed with the General at a lovely eighteenth-century house called the Château de Champs, which had once belonged to Madame de Pompadour. Macmillan summarized de Gaulle's attitude in a diary entry for 3 June: he did not want Britain in Europe for two main reasons:

1 It will alter the character of the Community. . . . Now it is a nice little club . . . under French hegemony.
2 Apart from our loyalty to the Commonwealth, we shall always be too intimately tied up with the Americans . . .[1]

By this time Macmillan had formed the impression that de Gaulle would not openly oppose the British application, but would instruct his negotiators to obstruct and delay or insist on terms so harsh to British agriculture or to the Commonwealth that they would be unacceptable.

Sir Pierson Dixon, who in the Prime Minister's judgement 'has the most subtle mind in Whitehall', had reported his view that 'de Gaulle has now definitely decided to exclude us', but that Britain might outwit him. Macmillan was not so sure that de Gaulle had finally made up his mind; it was always difficult to assess the thoughts and emotions of this enigmatic man.

Back in England, the Conservative opposition to the Common Market was organizing, led by Sir Derek Walker-Smith, Sir Robin Turton, both ex-Ministers, and Lord Hinchingbrooke (now Victor Montagu). Beaverbrook had also recruited Lord Montgomery to the anti-Market cause. A debate was arranged in the House of Commons, in which Heath, who opened for the Government, gave a most lucid exposition and showed a remarkable grasp of the complicated details of the negotiations. Unfortunately, a speech by McNamara in Michigan condemning all national nuclear forces (except, of course, that of the United States) enraged the French. As Macmillan shrewdly observed: 'The trouble with American Cabinet Ministers is that they are generally drawn either from the Board Room or the Common Room. But neither tycoons nor academics are very skilful or sensitive in politics, especially the politics of other countries.'[2]

At the beginning of August, the Brussels negotiations were adjourned for the holidays, having failed to reach agreement about temperate-zone food-stuffs. The principles were settled, but many loose ends were left untied. Good progress had, however, been made over manufactured goods from the older Commonwealth countries, imports from India, Pakistan and Ceylon, and associate status for the less-developed former colonial territories; so most aspects affecting the Commonwealth had been settled, or nearly settled, and although Heath's objective of an 'outline' agreement had not been reached, there was plenty for the Commonwealth Prime Ministers to discuss. Macmillan sent an account to them all of the position which had been reached in Brussels up to the time of the adjournment.

Before they began to assemble for the Conference, there was a curious conversation with Rab Butler, who had formally invited Macmillan to meet him for a meal at Bucks Club. It turned out to be a welcome if somewhat belated declaration of faith in the Common Market application. He said that, despite the objections of the farmers and the Commonwealth and the possible break-up of the Conservative Party, he had decided to support the policy. He repeated his conversion statement when the Cabinet met next day.

In the few days between the arrival of the Prime Ministers in London and the opening of the Conference at Marlborough House, which the Queen had presented to the Government as a centre for Commonwealth meetings, Macmillan prepared the ground by seeing most of his visitors for individual talks. These included Menzies, Holt and McEwen from Australia; Holyoake and Marshall from New Zealand, as well as Nash, the leader of the Opposition; Sir Alexander Bustamante, the Prime Minister of Jamaica; Dr Eric Williams of Trinidad; and President Ayub Khan of Pakistan, whom Macmillan described as 'a stage product of Sandhurst and the Indian cavalry, with all the language and phrases of the cavalry officers' mess'.[3] Diefenbaker lunched with him alone on 9 September, and Nehru, 'who looked old and tired', on the 10th, which was the first day of the Conference.

Macmillan opened the discussions with a speech of over an hour, followed by an hour and a half from Heath, whose grasp of the complicated issues affecting twenty countries and many commodities was remarkable. The reaction of the Prime Ministers, who occupied the next two days with their Second Reading speeches, is best described by Macmillan:

> It has been a broadside attack upon us, led by Diefenbaker. . . . Menzies wound up the first day with a very able and very damaging speech. Holyoake said New Zealand would be ruined. Nehru . . . was peevish. The Africans, who get everything they could want by 'association', are too proud . . . even to ask for it . . . the second day was better . . . able Dr Eric Williams talked good sense at great length, and Malaya was friendly.[4]

The inevitable leaks from this nominally private discussion and numerous press interviews with delegates ensured wide and unfavourable publicity in the newspapers, with the prevailing view that the Government must bow to the Commonwealth and abandon the project.

At the suggestion of Sir Norman Brook, however, Macmillan proposed setting up separate study groups, each under the chairmanship of the appropriate United Kingdom Minister, to deal with the special problems of Asia, Africa, the West Indies and the older Commonwealth countries. This committee stage, which continued for three days, lowered the temperature and compelled the Conference to face realities; but some of the Prime Ministers wished to speak again and Macmillan's characteristic diary entry read: 'it may be best to let them do so on Monday morning. Read *Kenilworth* – a splendid story.'[5] He and Philip de Zulueta worked all the evening on his own final speech, but for once there was trouble in the Garden Room: 'I dictated a long and splendid passage to one girl who seemed to take it down alright', but then could not decipher her own shorthand, 'had a nervous *crise* and burst into tears. However, we finished before midnight.'

The speech went well and after further contributions and a debate on world affairs in which all the Prime Ministers took part, the Conference turned to the preparation of a draft communiqué. This proved difficult because everyone wanted his own reservations inserted in it. The Conference was then adjourned for officials to work on a long and a short draft. Next day, the long draft, including all the reservations, looked absurd and was at once rejected. By lunchtime the short draft had been accepted and the Conference ended in an acquiescent, indeed friendly atmosphere. There was no question of the break-up of the Commonwealth and the most formidable problem in the Common Market negotiations had been overcome.

Next day the *Daily Express* was violently hostile and the *Manchester Guardian* priggish, but the other newspapers were favourable. Gaitskell compromised by seeming to accept the European idea in principle, while at the same time demanding such stringent conditions that any arrangement would have been impossible in practice.

The next task was to carry the Conservative Conference, and Ministers were asked to make pro-Market speeches throughout the autumn. In a letter to the Chairman of the Party, Freddie Erroll, the President of the Board of Trade, set out the economic arguments for joining and the difficulties British industry would face if we stayed out. He accompanied this by supporting Board of Trade papers, which were virtually, and most helpfully, speaker's notes for Ministers. Meanwhile, the Prime Minister himself issued an important pamphlet entitled 'Britain, the Commonwealth and Europe', which ranked with the 'wind of change' as a major policy pronouncement. It was based on his speeches to the Commonwealth Prime Ministers, with special emphasis on the political arguments for joining the EEC. The Common Market was at last being put forward by Ministers as a positive policy of overriding importance.

In his speech to the Party Conference at Llandudno, Macmillan made the European issue his main theme. At the Labour Conference the week before, Gaitskell had helped the collective Tory mind to focus and, by coming out against joining, had virtually ensured a massive Conservative vote in favour of doing so. Butler replied to Gaitskell's reference to a thousand years of history: 'For them, a thousand years of history books. For us, the future.' But Macmillan's speech was the outstanding performance. He made those who opposed the Market sound atavistic and out of tune with the times. 'Now is the opportunity and we must seize it,' he declared. It was his last great conference triumph and *The Times* commented the next day: 'In Cabinet, in the Parliamentary Party and in Conference, Mr Macmillan's victory, for the time being, has been complete.'[6]

After Llandudno, the Party's prospects looked better than for some time past. Macmillan had achieved his objectives of pacifying the Commonwealth and securing support for the European policy at constituency level. Although there might still be some trouble with the Party in the House of Commons, it would not be on such a scale as to threaten the future of the Government. The Prime Minister was poised to lead Britain into Europe and he hoped that this great enterprise would arouse enthusiasm national and crown his career. President de Gaulle's personal opposition was and remained the real obstacle.

As late as 6 January 1963, Heath told Macmillan that he was 'still hopeful of a successful outcome to the negotiations', but Sir Pierson Dixon reported from Paris that this would depend upon how far de Gaulle felt able to challenge the other members of the EEC, who all wished Britain to join the Community. Christopher Soames had probably discovered the real reason for de Gaulle's objection when he recounted to the Prime Minister a conversation with the French Minister of Agriculture, who had said:

Mon cher. C'est très simple. Maintenant, avec les six, il y a cinq poules et un coq. Si vous joignez (avec des autres pays) il y aura peut-être sept ou huit poules. Mais il y aura deux coqs. Alors – ce n'est pas aussi agréable.[7]

The General, with his proud and passionate patriotism for France, did not want any potential rival for the leadership of Europe.

On 14 January the blow fell. De Gaulle held a large press conference and announced majestically that the British application was not acceptable. Even Couve de Murville had not been informed of this sudden decision, but he was at once despatched to Brussels to bring the negotiations to an end. The General demanded that the Conference be adjourned *sine die* and, although attempts were made by the other Governments to resume the discussions, they were vetoed by the French and were formally abandoned on 29 January.

In a speech at Liverpool on 22 January, Macmillan declared with justifiable bitterness: 'Recrimination is useless, but the truth should be known. If there was any objection in principle to Britain's entry, we should, surely, have been told so from the start.'[8] Despairingly, he wrote in his diary:

All our policies at home and abroad are in ruins. ... European unity is no more; French domination of Europe is the new and alarming feature; our popularity as a Government is rapidly declining. We have lost everything except our courage and determination.[9]

The Prime Minister was especially sorry for Edward Heath: 'No one could have been a better negotiator and ambassador – but French duplicity has defeated us all.'[10] On 30 January Macmillan broadcast to the nation, with a brief historical survey of European division and conflict, the attempt to unite and the story of the French veto. He acknowledged that there was no ready-made alternative policy for Britain to pursue.

By ill chance, Princess Margaret had a long-standing engagement to visit Paris at this time, and was to have lunched privately with President de Gaulle while she was there. Lest this be interpreted as 'Britain coming to heel', Macmillan agreed to cancel the whole commitment. This led to some controversy in the press and, in retrospect, the Prime Minister felt his decision had been mistaken and that it would have been more dignified to allow the visit to take place.

After successful opening and winding-up speeches in an important House of Commons debate on the Nassau agreement, Macmillan himself paid a visit to Rome, which included an audience and an animated conversation with Pope John. On his return to London, he had to face another major debate on the failure of the Brussels negotiations. He explained why it was impossible to create a Commonwealth Common Market; but with a view to an increase in Commonwealth trade, he announced a meeting of its trade Ministers, to include close co-operation over the so-called 'Kennedy Round' of tariff cuts. He did not attempt to disguise his deep disappointment over the Brussels failure; but, while acknowledging 'with our heads that Britain's entry is not now capable of early realization, we should surely strive to keep the vision in our hearts'.[11]

It was a moving occasion for Harold Macmillan when, ten years later, he was invited to Brussels for the signing of the Treaty admitting Britain and three other countries to membership of the Community, this time with the full approval of Georges Pompidou's French Government. The wheel, as he said, had come full circle.

39

SECURITY

The Security Services in Britain are ultimately responsible to the Prime Minister. No system can ever be proof against every form of espionage and must always be balanced against infringements of individual liberty. As Harold Macmillan has himself written: 'It would indeed be a tragedy if we destroyed our freedom in the effort to preserve it. This is and must always be a dilemma facing the governments of free nations.'[1]

Apart from the defections of Burgess and Maclean, which occurred under the previous Labour Government but were revealed when Macmillan was Foreign Secretary, he had to deal with a number of security cases during his Premiership. The first was a conspiracy to obtain secret submarine information. It involved a Russian, two Poles and two Englishmen employed in the Underwater Weapons Establishment at Portland Bill, who were all arrested, charged and convicted in 1961. This was known as the Portland case and was followed by a committee of enquiry, presided over by Sir Charles Romer, which was appointed to investigate any weakness in security procedures.

Within a month of the Portland trial, George Blake, an employee in the Security Service although a convinced Communist, was found guilty of treachery and sentenced to forty-two years in prison, from which he subsequently escaped to re-emerge later in Russia. A fuller review was then undertaken by a committee under Lord Radcliffe's chairmanship, which published its report in April 1962. This revealed no major defects in the system, but found that a number of Civil Service staff associations and trade unions had been infiltrated by Communists and drew attention to the need to guard against people who were open to blackmail or intimidation by the Soviet authorities. The report recommended careful selection and periodic vetting of those in sensitive posts, and better security for secret documents. But much of the damage had already been done.

It will be remembered that when Marcus Lipton named Philby as 'the third man' in the Burgess and Maclean escape, no evidence could be found against him and Harold Macmillan was therefore obliged to exonerate him in the House of Commons. This had the effect of clearing him officially and enabled him to shelter behind the law of libel. He retired from the Foreign Service and went to live in Beirut, where he acted as correspondent for the *Observer*. In January 1963 he admitted that he was in fact the third man who had warned Burgess and Maclean; following this confession he left the Lebanon and reappeared later in Russia.

In the face of a barrage of Parliamentary questions, the Prime Minister saw the Leader of the Opposition and George Brown, and explained the difficulty of giving satisfactory answers in the House without prejudicing the work of the Secret Service. Harold Wilson supported Macmillan's request that the matter should be dealt with privately rather than in public and the Prime Minister was grateful for this courtesy and for Wilson's sense of responsibility.

Sixteen years later, interest in the case was revived by the revelation that Professor Blunt, Mr John Cairncross and others had also been involved. This côterie of Communists was recruited at Cambridge in the 1930s and over the subsequent twenty years many had attained positions of some significance in the Foreign and Secret Services. With hindsight, the Security Service should no doubt have noticed the growth of this outlook among young Cambridge intellectuals at that period and should have prevented their recruitment to the Government service; but such surveillance of an educational establishment would have been unusual and much resented and it would have been almost impossible to differentiate between ephemeral sympathizers and converts to Communism of a more serious kind.

In September 1962 another case of espionage was discovered in the Admiralty, where a civil servant called Vassall had been giving information to the Russians for some years. In this instance the motivation for treachery was fear rather than ideological commitment. In 1954, Vassall had been on the staff of the British Embassy in Moscow, where his homosexual tendencies were reported to KGB officers, who exploited this weakness by taking incriminating photographs of him and then blackmailing him into becoming a Soviet agent. By 1956 he was attached to Naval Intelligence in London, where positive vetting failed to reveal that he was a homosexual. He was able to abstract some secret documents and to photograph others until he was arrested and sentenced to eighteen years' imprisonment. His social contacts with individual Russians had been known at the British Embassy in Moscow and his homosexuality suspected, yet if these facts were reported to London they were ignored both by the Foreign Office and by the Admiralty for seven years.

The Prime Minister was always anxious about the effect on Anglo-American relations of any British spy caught working for the Russians and

Macmillan's reaction when Thorneycroft and Carrington reported the matter to him was: 'Oh, that's bad news. . . . You should never catch a spy. Discover him and then control him, but never catch him. A spy causes far more trouble once he's caught.'[2] And so it proved.

The case had serious repercussions for the Government because Vassall had been employed for a time as Private Secretary to Tam Galbraith, then Civil Lord of the Admiralty, who had since become an Under-Secretary of State in the Scottish Office. Rumours circulated that there had been a homosexual relationship between the two men. There was no evidence of this and no truth in it and after letters that had passed between them were published as a White Paper, the Annual Register commented that 'the most that could be said against Mr Galbraith was that he had suffered a socially pressing and plausible junior colleague a trifle too gladly'.

The Minister of Defence, Peter Thorneycroft, perhaps treated the matter a little too flippantly when it was debated in the House of Commons. It had been said that Vassall was living above his income in Dolphin Square, and Thorneycroft observed: 'We are all living above our incomes in all the London squares.'

The press accused Galbraith and Peter Carrington, the First Lord of the Admiralty, of negligence or worse, and the Prime Minister decided to appoint a tribunal, again under the chairmanship of Lord Radcliffe, which examined over 250 newspaper reports and reached the conclusion that not one of them could be justified. James Margach, who was himself a political correspondent of integrity, recalled that the editors and journalists concerned 'had been given every opportunity and offered the protection of privilege to justify their allegations'.[3] They failed to do so and in due course the tribunal completely vindicated both Ministers.

Macmillan had given Carrington his total support throughout the controversy, but in retrospect he felt he had acted a little unfairly in agreeing to accept Galbraith's resignation and, as soon as he was exonerated by the tribunal, the Prime Minister was glad to re-appoint him to the Government as Parliamentary Secretary to the Ministry of Transport.

During the hearing, two journalists had refused to disclose to the judges the sources of information on which they had based their reports. In fact, they could not do so because they had no sources – the stories were pure fiction. In Margach's words, 'the press had plumbed disgraceful depths of irresponsible character assassination . . .'[4] In March 1963, the two journalists were each sentenced to six months' imprisonment for contempt of court; but this made them martyrs in the eyes of many of their colleagues and Iain Macleod was right when he remarked that the press would not forgive or forget the incident for months to come. Relations between Whitehall and

Fleet Street were therefore already at a low ebb when the Vassall episode was speedily eclipsed by the Profumo scandal.

Rumours of the involvement of John Profumo, the Secretary of State for War, with a young woman called Christine Keeler began to circulate in early February and, by March 1963, were the subject of cocktail-party gossip in London. Profumo had met Miss Keeler in 1961 at a party at Cliveden to which she had been brought by Dr Stephen Ward, a friend of Lord Astor.

Following a court case in which she was concerned, the story was given a security connotation because Miss Keeler was said to have had a similar association at the same period with Captain Ivanov, the Naval Attaché at the Soviet Embassy. For this reason the Prime Minister's Principal Private Secretary, Tim Bligh, and Martin Redmayne, the Government Chief Whip, saw Profumo, who denied any impropriety. They accepted his explanation and reported the gist of the interview to the Prime Minister. At the same time, the Attorney-General, Sir John Hobson, had two personal talks with John Profumo, at the second of which Sir Peter (now Lord) Rawlinson, the Solicitor-General, was also present. Rawlinson suspected that Profumo was not telling the truth, but he could not be certain and there was no evidence to support the rumours, which might well have been as groundless as those which had prejudiced the reputation of Tam Galbraith.

The issue came to a head on the night of 21 March, when George (later Lord) Wigg, supported by Richard Crossman and Barbara Castle, raised it in the House of Commons, ostensibly as a matter of security, which it was not; in fact in order to embarrass the Government, which it did. There was never any doubt of Profumo's total loyalty, but Miss Keeler's name had been publicly coupled with 'a member of the Government' and in view of this it was decided that he must again be questioned. He had taken a strong sleeping-pill at midnight and, when awoken two hours later, was still in a state of sedation. When he arrived at the House of Commons at 2.45 a.m. he was interviewed by Iain Macleod, the Leader of the House, William Deedes, the Minister without Portfolio, the Chief Whip and the Law Officers of the Crown. It was his last chance to tell the truth. He either had to confess to an affair with Miss Keeler and resign from the Government or make a statement in the House refuting the charge. He again denied the allegations and the other Ministers accepted the word of a friend and colleague. They then helped him to prepare the personal statement he would have to make a few hours later from the Despatch Box. This was shown to the Prime Minister, who thought it clear and convincing, and approved it. Harold Macmillan is such an honourable man himself that he could not believe Profumo was not telling the truth. He went to the House the next morning to give the Secretary of State his support.

It has been argued by at least one member of the Cabinet that if the statement was a purely personal one, the other Ministers ought not to have assisted in its preparation. If, on the other hand, it was a Government statement, it should have been discussed in the Cabinet before being made. In practice it would have been difficult to call a Cabinet either late that night or early the following morning to allow adequate discussion before the House met at 11 a.m., when the statement, which had now become urgent, was due to be delivered. In any event, whatever their previous reservations, none of his colleagues doubted John Profumo's word once it became clear that he was ready to assert his innocence in the House of Commons and there is no reason to suppose that a meeting of the full Cabinet would have taken a different view.

The Prime Minister's confidence in Profumo was further strengthened by two successful libel actions which he immediately brought against a French and an Italian newspaper and their distributors in London. It did not seem credible that a responsible Minister could deliberately both mislead the House of Commons and commit perjury in a court of law. But everyone was mistaken; on 4 June, Profumo confessed to Tim Bligh and the Chief Whip that Miss Keeler had been his mistress and that this part of his statement in Parliament had therefore been untrue. But for this inexcusable action in lying to the House of Commons, the whole episode would have been of minor importance. Captain Ivanov's association with Miss Keeler was coincidental and no security risk was involved. It may be that John Profumo had not told his wife about his relationship with the girl and could not bear that she should hear it through a public statement in the House. Whatever the reason, it was a grievous mistake. If, at an earlier stage, he had quietly resigned as Secretary of State on grounds of health, he could probably have continued in public life, perhaps even returning to ministerial office after a suitable interval. This indeed was the advice which John Hobson had given him when trying to probe the truth of the matter before the statement was made. After his admission, however, Profumo had no alternative but to resign his appointment, his Privy Councillorship and his seat in Parliament. It was a heavy price to pay and a personal tragedy for John Profumo, who is an able man and had been a good Minister. He has never attempted to justify his conduct or to excuse his grave error of judgement in lying to the House. Instead, he has worked selflessly ever since for the unfortunate in the East End of London, work which has rightly been recognized by the conferment of a CBE.

Macmillan has been criticized for his handling of both the Vassall and Profumo affairs and in this respect they were not unconnected, because it may well have been the feeling that Galbraith had been unjustly accused in the first case that influenced the Prime Minister to give his Minister the benefit of the doubt in the second. In my view he was blamed unfairly, especially in the latter case. He either had to believe Profumo and accept his word of honour as a gentleman, given both privately and publicly in Parliament, or force him to resign despite his constant assertions of innocence.

It has been suggested that Macmillan should have seen Profumo personally in an attempt to elicit the truth, but it is doubtful that it would have made any difference had he done so. If Profumo could not bring himself to admit the facts to John Hobson, a friend and contemporary at Harrow, he was unlikely to be more forthcoming to someone of an older generation whom he did not know nearly as well and who was, moreover, the Prime Minister of Britain.

There may have been a further reason for Macmillan's reluctance to become personally involved. He was in some ways curiously unworldly and there was a puritanical strain in his character which gave rise to an inherent distaste for discussing sexual deviations. Such subjects embarrassed him and his instinct was to relegate them to the recesses of his mind, and certainly not to talk of them openly with a junior colleague.

The Profumo scandal was a gift to the press, which could now retaliate, and did, for the Vassall reverse. The vitriolic, often venomous newspaper attacks were directed mainly against the Prime Minister, who was said to be old, out-of-touch and incompetent. When Parliament re-assembled after the short Whitsun recess, he had to open the inevitable debate with a defence of himself and his Government in an atmosphere which seemed almost to threaten its continued existence. The case against him was put tersely by Jo Grimond, the leader of the Liberal Party: 'Either he knew the dangers of the company which his Secretary of State was keeping and did nothing about it, or he did not know and should have made effective inquiries. . . .'[5] More hurtful was the bitter personal attack made by Nigel Birch, who quoted from Browning's poem, *The Lost Leader*:

> Life's night begins: let him never come back to us!
> There would be doubt, hesitation and pain,
> Forced praise on our part – the glimmer of twilight,
> Never glad, confident morning again.

Twenty-seven Conservatives abstained when the division was called and at least two others were only persuaded by the Whips to vote for the Government on the assurance that Macmillan would retire as Prime Minister by the autumn. It was the most serious defection in the Parliamentary Party during the whole of Macmillan's premiership and, in his own words, 'the Government was generally believed to be tottering'.[6]

Even after the debate, the attacks and accusations continued. Rumours were rife in London, smearing other Ministers, some of them by name, with charges or innuendos of sexual promiscuity or perversion. As Macmillan recorded in his diary, 'a kind of Titus Oates atmosphere prevailed'.[7]

On 21 June, the Prime Minister announced that a Judicial Enquiry under Lord Denning would investigate every aspect of the Profumo affair and any other circumstances or information which might endanger national security. In August Macmillan himself gave evidence before the Enquiry and by the middle of September Lord Denning was able to complete his Report. All the slanderous rumours against Ministers were dismissed and the only criticism was contained in one paragraph which suggested that some blame could be attached to Profumo's colleagues for having been deceived by his denials. Even this should be set against Peter Rawlinson's subsequent comment that John Profumo was the most convincing liar he had ever encountered in his whole professional experience. The Prime Minister gave instructions for the Report to be published in full as soon as it could be printed.

The Keeler case, unimportant in itself, had been built up by the press into a *cause célèbre*; but the risk Macmillan took in placing the careers of his colleagues in the hands of Lord Denning had shown a confidence in their integrity which the outcome of the Enquiry fully justified. Nevertheless, the earlier series of security trials had alarmed the public and the discovery of spies and traitors was regarded as evidence of weakness in the system and was used to discredit the Prime Minister. This was unfair. The few failures of the Security Services are blazoned all over the world. Their many successes are perforce shrouded in silence.

In contrast to the first half of Macmillan's premiership, the last year of it was a period of almost unrelieved misfortune and even Rab Butler's remarkable diplomatic achievement at the Victoria Falls Conference was overshadowed by the Profumo scandal. Only the Test Ban Treaty, signed in Moscow on 5 August, recalled the heyday of Macmillan's many successes during his time as Prime Minister.

40

THE TEST BAN TREATY

On 27 November 1962, the Russian Ambassador in London delivered a long letter from Khrushchev on the subject of banning all nuclear tests and this was followed a month later by a letter to President Kennedy on the same lines, adding the offer of three on-site verification inspections each year. Although the President did not consider this an adequate number, he agreed that any offer of inspection marked a substantial advance.

In March 1963, the seventeen-nation Disarmament Committee reached deadlock in Geneva and Macmillan thought the time had come for a new Allied initiative; but before deciding on what form this should take, he sought the advice of David Ormsby-Gore in order to ascertain what line might be most acceptable to the Americans. The Ambassador did not think Kennedy would look with any favour on a proposal for another Summit meeting unless a constructive outcome was virtually assured; on the other hand an approach to the Soviet Government through normal diplomatic channels would not be productive. He thought Khrushchev assessed even Rusk's importance in the light of his own estimation of Gromyko's: 'That is to say, as someone who is a competent post-boy.' Ormsby-Gore therefore suggested sending two special emissaries to Moscow, one from Washington and one from London. On 16 March Macmillan wrote Kennedy a long letter, which, he claimed, was the basis on which the Test Ban Treaty was founded.

Both Schlesinger and Sorensen were inclined to question the extent of the Prime Minister's responsibility for the approach to Khrushchev and to give at least equal credit for this to Kennedy; but Longford and Nunnerley agreed that the initiative originated in London and that the President, overruling the doubts of his own advisers, then concurred with Macmillan's proposal.

In his letter to Kennedy, the Prime Minister suggested various ways in which progress might be made, including Ormsby-Gore's idea of special emissaries who, on the American side, might be Averell Harriman 'or even your brother, Bobby'.[1] The President rejected a Summit meeting, but sent

Macmillan the draft of a letter they might jointly send to Khrushchev, the text of which was agreed, not without difficulty, and despatched to Moscow on 15 April. It included the suggestion that 'President Kennedy and I would be ready to send in due course very senior representatives who would be empowered to speak for us and talk in Moscow directly with you', to be followed, if necessary, by 'a meeting of the three of us at which a definite agreement on a test ban could be made final'.[2]

Khrushchev replied on 8 May, agreeing 'to receive your highly-placed representatives' and, in a later letter, to open the negotiations.[3] The President welcomed this response in a public speech in Washington, announcing that high-level discussions would soon begin in Moscow and adding that the United States would carry out no further atmospheric tests as long as other nations refrained from doing so. In his diary Macmillan recorded his appreciation of David Ormsby-Gore's help, which had been

... quite invaluable. He has established a remarkable position with Kennedy, an intimate and trusted friend. It is most fortunate – and almost unprecedented – for a British ambassador to have this position....[4]

The Americans were always suspicious that Macmillan was prepared to concede more than was wise and Schlesinger wrote that before the meeting in Moscow:

The question whether we should try for a comprehensive or limited ban was still unresolved. The British were in favour of reducing the inspection quota still further, arguing that, even on the unlikely chance that the Russians were disposed to try a few clandestine tests underground, these tests could not possibly affect the balance of military power....[5]

Macmillan felt strongly that if agreement could be reached to ban tests in the atmosphere, in outer space and underwater, the omission of underground tests could be accepted, since they would probably be small and would not involve the pollution that had been such a source of public anxiety. An opportunity to discuss these and other points of difficulty arose when the President paid a short visit to Birch Grove House on 29 June, after a sentimental journey to the south of Ireland, from which his family had originally emigrated.

Kennedy flew in by helicopter, amid intense local excitement. Crowds had collected from far and wide, and the roads round Birch Grove and Chelwood Gate were packed with well-wishers to greet this gallant young figure, who seemed to exemplify all their hopes and idealism. To these were added, incongruously, a hundred CND marchers with banners demanding the abolition of nuclear tests. As this was the whole purpose of the President's visit, the demonstration seemed somewhat redundant.

Even with an overflow into Maurice Macmillan's house nearby, Kennedy's entourage and the Ministers and Foreign Office staff, including ambassadors, secretaries and typists, could not be adequately accommodated. Hotels and inns had to be commandeered and a communications centre established in Brighton. Throughout the twenty-four hours of the visit, helicopters were constantly in transit between London, Brighton and the Birch Grove landing-ground. Indoors the atmosphere was gay and informal. Despite the pain Kennedy suffered from his back (a special bed and rocking-chair were imported to ease it), his good humour and high spirits were infectious and the whole visit took on the character of a country-house party.

The talks were conducted personally between the two leaders, with no advisers present, and there was only one general session at the end of the day to which the large party of professionals was invited. Macmillan and Kennedy planned another meeting before Christmas and then 'hatless, with his brisk step, and combining that indescribable look of a boy on a holiday with the dignity of a President and Commander-in-Chief',[6] Kennedy walked to the waiting helicopter and was gone. Macmillan was never to see him again. Before the green summer leaves had turned to gold, he had fallen to an assassin's bullet in Dallas.

The two special representatives chosen for the Moscow negotiations were Averell Harriman for the United States and Lord Hailsham for Britain. Macmillan approved the choice of Harriman, whom he regarded as 'one of the ablest Americans with whom I have had to deal' and who possessed the qualities of 'patience, tact, courage and complete independence'[7] which were required for a mission of this kind. He was a shrewd negotiator, a former Ambassador to Moscow and a man of such stature and authority in the United States that in any crisis he could act on his own initiative.

The Americans were less enthusiastic about Quintin Hailsham. In a talk with him at Birch Grove, Kennedy had formed the impression that he wanted to play the role of mediator between the Russians and the Americans; and despite his distinguished legal background, Schlesinger thought that he was 'ill-prepared on the technicalities of the problem and was consumed by a desire to get a treaty at almost any cost'.[8] Macmillan's first thought for the assignment had been David Ormsby-Gore, but the Ambassador himself felt it would be better to send a Minister of Cabinet rank and someone not too closely associated with the American Administration. The Prime Minister thought Hailsham's energy and imagination would appeal to Khrushchev[9] and he is said to have told a journalist that Hailsham 'might amuse' the Soviet leader. Kennedy's apprehensions were met by arranging, 'with Macmillan's loyal help', that Harriman should lead for the West in the negotiations.[10] He lunched with the Prime Minister on his way to Moscow and the discussions began there on 15 July. They started badly with Khrushchev withdrawing his earlier offer of two or three on-site inspections a year.

The next development came from the United States. Kennedy was becoming concerned about de Gaulle's attitude to a test ban and, in order to pacify him and induce him to sign any treaty which might be negotiated, was now prepared to offer France important nuclear information, hitherto withheld. Macmillan reflected ruefully that such a suggestion made six months before might have averted de Gaulle's veto of the British Common Market application. He wrote to the President welcoming the principle and 'the bold sweep' of his proposal, which would, hopefully, have the effect of 'bringing France back into partnership', but counselling a more cautious form of words and a less definite offer in case de Gaulle accepted it without giving anything in return.[11] Kennedy agreed, and messages on the lines proposed by Macmillan were duly delivered in Paris by the British and American Ambassadors.

News now came from Moscow that the Russians wanted a non-aggression pact to be signed at the same time as a test ban treaty. Macmillan could see no objection to this, but Kennedy feared that France and Germany would distrust any expansion of the talks into wider issues. He was also against a non-dissemination pact, which the Prime Minister would have liked to include. Hailsham reported his opinion that the Soviet Government would not insist on linking a non-aggression pact with the test ban treaty and suggested, as a compromise, a reference to such a pact in the final communiqué, which he thought might satisfy the Russians. David Ormsby-Gore warned Macmillan that Congress was concerned lest proposals objectionable to the other Allies were included in the treaty, but on 25 July he reported to Alec Home that the President had agreed to Hailsham's suggestion for dealing with the non-aggression issue.

At the last minute there were technical arguments on peripheral matters of no real significance and Schlesinger wrote later that 'Harriman would not give ground; and as the negotiations dragged on, Hailsham became increasingly restive and unhappy.'[12] He complained to London that American rigidity might lose the whole treaty and this so alarmed Macmillan that he instructed David Ormsby-Gore to call on the President and express his anxiety and concern. At 5.30 p.m. on 25 July he telephoned Kennedy himself to explain why he had sent Ormsby-Gore to the White House; but in fact the President had just conceded the remaining point of difficulty and had instructed Harriman not to persist. 'With a broad smile on his face', he interrupted the Prime Minister to say: 'Don't worry. I've got David sitting right here beside me. We've just been on to Moscow. We've initialled the Treaty.'[13] Macmillan observed rather petulantly in his diary: 'He might have told us before and saved us a lot of anxiety.'[14] In fact, he had been informed the moment the President knew himself.

Later that night Macmillan made a short statement in Parliament, which was warmly received by the whole House, and the Conservative benches rose, waving their order papers, to cheer him as he left the Chamber. Next day, 26 July, the newspapers were virtually unanimous in their praise. The *Daily Mail* described the occasion as 'Mac's hour of triumph'; the *Daily Telegraph* thought the Treaty 'a considerable triumph for the world's leading statesmen, not least for the British Prime Minister, who has worked long and hard for this moment'; and the *Daily Express* was even more eulogistic: 'Mr Harold Macmillan has prepared for it by tireless diplomacy. He would never be discouraged. Not all the rebuffs and all the set-backs made him falter on the way. His pertinacity is rewarded.'

Writing recently, Harold Evans described the Test Ban Treaty as 'an event which will surely merit a place in the history books – and rank as a true Macmillan achievement. It was he – with his sense of history – who read the signs aright in Russia and saw the opportunities; who coaxed and prodded the Americans; who argued the case with Kruschev.'[15]

The Treaty was signed in Moscow on 5 August by the three Foreign Ministers and ratified on 8 October, which ironically was the same day on which Macmillan's illness forced him to retire from Office.

Perhaps the tribute he valued most was the letter of congratulation he received from President Kennedy:

Dear Friend,

This morning, as I signed the instrument of ratification of the Nuclear Test Ban Treaty, I could not but reflect on the extent to which your steadfastness of commitment and determined perseverance made this treaty possible.... History will eventually record your indispensable role in bringing about the limitation of nuclear testing; but I cannot let this moment pass without expressing to you my own keen appreciation of your signal contribution to world peace....[16]

It was the last great success of Macmillan's Premiership and not the least important.

41

RESIGNATION

As the session drew to an end, the Prime Minister addressed first the junior Ministers, then the 1922 Committee. Both speeches were successful and their enthusiastic reception was a heartening end to a distressing period in Parliament. Even the public opinion polls showed a gradual improvement, with Labour only 6% ahead as compared with 18% not long before, and Macmillan's own popularity-rating correspondingly higher than for many months.

At the beginning of August 1963 he and Lady Dorothy set out for Finland, which he had not visited since the Winter War twenty-three years earlier. The successful conclusion of the Test Ban Treaty, combined with helpful local press publicity about Macmillan's efforts to aid the Finns in 1940, ensured a warm welcome wherever they went and he was able to have useful, if somewhat tentative, talks with the President and the Prime Minister. Finland's relationship with Russia and the West has always been a delicate one and can only be maintained by flexible and skilful diplomacy.

On 9 August the Macmillans left for Stockholm, where they were joined by the Foreign Secretary, who conducted most of the inter-Governmental business so that, apart from informal talks with some of the Ministers and a visit to the King, the stay in Sweden was a short but agreeable holiday for Harold Macmillan and was followed, on his return to England, by ten days' grouse-shooting at Bolton Abbey and Swinton in Yorkshire.

It had by this time become necessary for the Prime Minister to consider his own future. He could resign just before the re-assembly of Parliament in October or continue in office up to and including the General Election which was due to be held not later than the autumn of 1964:

I was determined not to take any step which would bring my long premiership to an ignoble end or look as if I was afraid of facing any difficulties which might still confront us. I did not wish to go down to history as a Prime Minister who had been drowned by the flood of filth which had seeped up from the sewers of London.[1]

These words, written ten years later, show how deeply affected Macmillan was by the Profumo scandal, so alien to his own character and upbringing. Against his reluctance to resign at a low ebb in his career were the facts that he was very tired, with all the symptoms of failing health, that he was almost seventy years of age and that he did not feel strong enough to lead his Party in a hard-fought General Election. But there was also the important consideration that the succession to the Premiership was by no means settled or certain.

On 11 September Macmillan discussed the position with Rab Butler for four hours at Chequers without reaching any conclusion. He recorded in his diary:

I was careful not to give him any idea about which of several alternatives I would choose. . . . But I got a good idea of his own position. He would naturally (if I resign) accept the premiership if there was a general consensus of opinion for him. But he doesn't want another unsuccessful bid.[2]

Butler recalls that Macmillan had suggested that 'since my own prospects were uncertain in regard to the leadership I should do well as a king-maker. But my private diagnosis was that at this point he hoped and intended to remain as leader.'[3] Butler was correct in this assessment, but he wrote to Alec Home expressing the view that the Prime Minister had 'by no means made up his mind', partly because the succession was still in doubt.

A week later, Home was himself a guest at Chequers and advised Macmillan that, although there was no plot or pressure to oust him, he had – in the opinion of Home and other colleagues – 'lost too much ground to recover his winning form'. This view, expressed by a senior Minister who at that time clearly had no thought of becoming a candidate himself, was important, but Macmillan brushed it aside and talked of his determination to stay. After the evening at Chequers, Home said that he had no doubt that the Prime Minister had decided to go on, providing his health allowed him to.[4]

On 20 September Macmillan had an audience with the Queen and informed her that at the Party Conference three weeks later he would announce that there would be no General Election in 1963, but that he would not lead the Party in an election in 1964. This compromise solution would have involved a change of Prime Minister in the early months of that year. He recorded in his diary that the Queen felt the great importance of maintaining the royal prerogative and that he was 'determined at all costs to preserve the prerogative, which had been so useful in the past and which might be so valuable in the future'.[5] In Rab Butler's words, Macmillan did not want 'a diktat' from the 1922 Committee.

In fact, the prerogative will not be exercised again, because it could only be preserved, even theoretically, as long as the consultative procedure for choosing a new leader still prevailed. The Parliamentary Labour Party had long since elected its own leader by secret ballot and, once Alec Home introduced the same method for the Conservative Party, the Queen was obliged to accept as Prime Minister whoever had been chosen by the majority Party as its leader.

The last remaining prerogative of the Crown is the granting or withholding of a dissolution of the Parliament. In 1959 Harold Macmillan had drawn the Queen's attention to the difference between advising an election and asking for one. 'Advice', he said, 'the Crown must accept, but if the Prime Minister "asks" for a dissolution, the sovereign can agree to this or not, as seems best in the national interest.'

By the weekend of 5 October, Macmillan was again beginning to have doubts about his leadership decision. He had slept badly the previous night and sent a message to his son-in-law, Julian Amery, inviting him to Chequers. Philip de Zulueta was the only other guest and they talked in the Long Gallery till two a.m. on many subjects unconnected with Macmillan's personal problem, but the following morning the Prime Minister told Amery he was going to resign. When asked whom he would prefer as his successor, he replied, 'Quintin'.

'Do you think he would make a good Prime Minister?' Julian enquired.

'Possibly not, but he could win us the election.'

'What about Alec?' suggested Julian, but the idea was not pursued.[6] Soon afterwards Maurice Macmillan arrived at Chequers and they both urged the Prime Minister to stay on. After lunch on Sunday he agreed to do so. That evening he dined alone with Alec Home, who remained in favour of his earlier plan to retire in 1964.

On Monday morning, 7 October, Macmillan drove to London. By this time the Downing Street renovations had been completed and Lady Dorothy and the Prime Minister had returned there from Admiralty House. He first saw Tim Bligh, who reported that a large majority of the Cabinet wanted him to stay on and lead the Party at the election, and then Rab Butler, 'who would clearly prefer me to go on, for – in his heart – he does not expect the succession and fears it'.[7] Next, Macmillan saw the Lord Chancellor, the Chief Whip and Duncan Sandys, who all urged him to stay, and then Oliver Poole, the joint Chairman of the Party, who took the opposite view. Later in the evening they were joined by Dilhorne, Butler, Home and Sandys, who was 'very strong for me going on. Alec Home was balanced.'[8] Duncan Sandys stayed to dinner and the Chief Whip called again afterwards. By this time it was clear that the whole Cabinet would accept whatever course the Prime Minister proposed and on the night of 7 October he reached a firm decision to continue in office and fight the General Election. He was to inform his colleagues of this at a routine meeting of the Cabinet next morning.

Harold Macmillan had been unusually indecisive for several weeks and in retrospect he attributed this to the onset of the severe illness which, ironically, was to strike him that very night: 'I found it impossible to pass water and an excruciating pain when I attempted to do so. I was seized by terrible spasms.'[9] He was able to attend the Cabinet at ten o'clock next morning, but looked and felt so ill that he was obliged to leave the room before the business was completed. No one realized that the cause of the illness was a serious inflammation of the prostate gland and that an operation would be necessary, but his appearance alarmed his colleagues and after his departure they discussed the possibility of his resignation. Butler, supported by Alec Home and Reggie Maudling, advocated a temporizing speech by the Prime Minister to the Party Conference on the Saturday, but Iain Macleod led the majority of Ministers in preferring a clear-cut decision that Macmillan would stay on as their leader.

Nevertheless, contingency plans had to be considered, and the Lord Chancellor, Lord Dilhorne, told his colleagues about the arrangements Macmillan had already made for choosing a successor, and said that, as he was not a candidate, he would be available to take the views of members of the Cabinet if this became necessary. Lord Home broke in to say that he was in the same position as Dilhorne and would be ready to help in any way he could. He made this remark quite casually and was afterwards to regret having done so. 'If Macmillan did have to resign,' he recalled some years later, 'I had no more idea of competing than Reggie Dilhorne,'[10] and this was certainly true at the time. His observation was in fact lost in the general conversation round the Cabinet table and most of those present did not remember him making it; but Iain Macleod and Enoch Powell both heard and remembered it, and took it to be not a casual comment but a commitment. The consequences were to be unhelpful as the succession drama developed, and were to complicate the difficult situation which soon arose. The meeting broke up before lunch and some Ministers took the train to Blackpool, where the Party Conference was already assembling. Butler, Dilhorne and Home remained in London until the following day.

In the meantime, despite the pain he was enduring, Macmillan managed to appear at a party for his Downing Street staff which was being held to celebrate the return to No. 10. His doctors and Alec Badenoch, the leading surgeon in this field, had already decided that he must undergo an operation and, at nine o'clock that evening, he was admitted to King Edward VII Hospital, where a catheter was inserted to drain the bladder.

An announcement was made to the press that the Prime Minister was to have an operation for the removal of a prostatic obstruction and would be unable to go to Blackpool. The communiqué added that the Deputy Prime Minister, R.A. Butler, would be in charge of the Government during his absence from duty. It was the third occasion on which Butler had been invited to act during an incapacitating illness of a Prime Minister – for Churchill in 1953, Eden in 1956 and now Macmillan in 1963. Winston Churchill's serious stroke in 1953 had made it impossible for him to discharge his duties as Prime Minister for a period of two months, during which Butler had assumed the temporary responsibility, and it would have been better to have followed the same course ten years later.

Instead of resigning in the very week of the annual Party Conference, which inevitably distorted and over-publicized the normally private procedures for electing a new leader, Macmillan would have been wiser to delay his resignation at least until the Conference was over. His illness could not have come at a worse time:

Had it been a month earlier, the whole succession might have been settled quietly in accordance with past precedents, without any reference to the Party Conference and all the excitement that was caused at Blackpool. Had it been a month later, the Party Conference would have been satisfactorily past.[11]

The Prime Minister could easily have delayed the announcement of his resignation and much unfavourable publicity for the Party could have been avoided. There was no need to precipitate the leadership crisis which now ensued and it was a major error of political judgement to have done so. With quite unnecessary haste, however, the customary processes of consultation were put in hand as soon as the possible contenders for the leadership of the Party had declared themselves. These processes had lately been extended as a result of the Prime Minister's wish to increase the area of consultation. After Eden's resignation, Macmillan had himself been chosen by the Cabinet and although Members of Parliament were free to write to the then Chief Whip submitting their views on the succession, there was no formal consultation with the Parliamentary Party. There was much to be said for this method. Those who worked together closely in Cabinet had the best opportunity of assessing which of them would be most acceptable to his colleagues and would make the best leader of the Party and the best Prime Minister of the country.

Under the new arrangements, it had been decided that the Lord Chancellor should sound out the Cabinet; that the Chief Whip should invite the views of the junior Ministers and of some senior Conservative Members of the House of Commons; and that the other whips should ascertain the opinions of the MPs for whom they were responsible. The Chief Whip in the House of Lords would consult the Unionist peers; and the constituency chairmen, agents, candidates and leaders of the Young Conservatives would be given an opportunity of expressing their views through the Conservative Central Office. In the event, so far as the last category was concerned, where soundings were taken at all they were indecisive and played no part in the final decision.

Macmillan's operation was not performed until 15 October, and during the course of the previous day, the Prime Minister was able to see both the Lord Chancellor and the Foreign Secretary to inform them of his intention to resign. In his talk with the latter Macmillan indicated for the first time that he regarded Home as a possible successor. This astonished Alec Home, who pointed out that he was a peer, so the suggestion did not arise; in his own mind it was out of the question, but in fact, following the passage of the Peerage Act that summer, hereditary peers were allowed to renounce their titles and, if they wished, stand for election to the House of Commons. Acceptance of an amendment in the House of Lords that the Act was to come into operation not, as originally intended, after the next election but as soon as the Royal Assent was given on 31 July 1963, was to have a profound effect upon the leadership of the Conservative Party, since it permitted the candidatures of both Lord Hailsham and Lord Home. Without it, Butler would have been the almost automatic successor as Prime Minister.

Macmillan recorded:

I personally favoured either Hailsham or Macleod, preferably the former, for I felt that these two were the men of real genius in the Party who were the true inheritors of the Disraeli tradition of Tory radicalism which I had preached all my life. I regretfully had to admit that I did not feel that Butler could win an election or could receive the loyal support of the Party as a whole. I told Hailsham of my own views and hoped he would become a candidate.[12]

In this significant comment Macmillan publicly acknowledged his opposition to Butler, although he certainly understated it. It was appropriate that the Prime Minister's postal address at Chequers was Butler's Cross.[13]

During the last two years of his Premiership, Macmillan had brought forward three of the younger Ministers in the House of Commons, who were of sufficient experience and seniority to be considered for the leadership. Iain Macleod was Leader of the House of Commons and Chairman of the Party Organization; Reggie Maudling had been Chancellor of the Exchequer since Selwyn Lloyd's dismissal; and Edward Heath had been made responsible for the Common Market negotiations. Each had been given the opportunity, but none of them had emerged decisively as generally acceptable to the Party. Macmillan did not consider that any of the other members of his Cabinet in the House of Commons was even a possibility.

Heath had been a successful Chief Whip, but his departmental experience was limited and he was not yet a serious contender. Maudling's stock in the Parliamentary Party had been high when the House rose in July, but had waned in the intervening months and Macmillan did not consider he was ready for the Premiership because of his lack of experience in foreign affairs. Macleod was a controversial figure. He was, in Macmillan's words, 'the last of the orators in the Tory Party'.[14] His Colonial Secretaryship had evoked the enthusiasm and idealism of the Left wing in the Party and of the Young Conservatives, but it had antagonized the white settlers in Kenya and Rhòdesia and therefore the Right wing of the Party in Parliament. To lead a great political party, a candidate must be acceptable to all sections of it; Iain Macleod was not. Indeed, during and after the Colonial Secretaryship his name was anathema to many of his Parliamentary colleagues.

The obvious choice for the leadership in seniority and experience was Rab Butler and although he, too, had his critics, the course of events in the eight days between the announcement of Harold Macmillan's resignation and the Queen's invitation to Alec Home to form a Government can only be explained if it is accepted that Macmillan had long since resolved that Butler should not succeed him as Prime Minister.

Randolph Churchill wrote later: 'It can be argued that Macmillan did all he could during his seven years as Prime Minister to advance the fortunes of Butler.'[15] In a brilliantly caustic article in the *Spectator* in January 1964, Iain Macleod commented coldly:

Almost anything can no doubt be argued, but no one close to politics or to Harold Macmillan could seriously support this suggestion for a moment. Although incomparably the best qualified of the contenders, the truth is that at all times, from the first day of his premiership to the last, Macmillan was determined that Butler should not succeed him.

Macleod was right. It was well known in the House of Commons that Macmillan was implacably opposed to Butler as the future leader of the Party. There was nothing mean or ignoble in this attitude. Macmillan genuinely and no doubt correctly believed that, in Macleod's words, 'Butler had not in him the steel that makes a Prime Minister, nor the inspiration that a leader needs to pull his Party through a fierce general election.'[16] Many Conservative Members of Parliament shared this view. Others believed, like Macleod, that Butler had one important asset – he could attract 'wide understanding support from many people outside the Tory Party. And without such an appeal no general election can be won.'[18] It was this need to capture the centre, uncommitted ground in politics which influenced those who considered Butler the best candidate. Macmillan's appreciation was, however, accepted by others who mattered more – 'the magic circle'. This phrase, at once to become part of the political vocabulary, was used in the *Spectator* article to label the few men close to the Prime Minister who, in Macleod's opinion, engineered the outcome of the leadership crisis.

While there can be little doubt about Macmillan's determination that Butler should not succeed him, it is hard to believe in the existence of a magic circle as such, still less that it was created by the Prime Minister to secure his objective. The phrase was good, pungent journalism rather than a considered Macleod judgement. Certainly Macmillan's first choice as his successor, Lord Hailsham, was a personal and mistaken one, unsupported by any magic circle of influential colleagues.

Quintin Hailsham had been a splendid Chairman of the Party. He was uniquely capable of rousing the enthusiasm of the constituency workers and had made a significant contribution to the Conservative victory in 1959. He has a brilliant mind and, at his best, his speeches can be moving and most eloquent. But his advice is erratic and many of his Cabinet colleagues would have been reluctant to serve under him. They acknowledged that he would make an inspiring leader of the Party at an election. Their fear was that, if he won it, his judgement as the leader of the nation would be suspect. Nevertheless, the Hailsham bandwagon was set in motion.

Maurice Macmillan and Julian Amery departed for Blackpool to canvass support for the Prime Minister's candidate in the presidential type of campaign which Macmillan's resignation had now made inevitable. Their efforts were assisted (or prejudiced) by the extraordinary performance of Randolph Churchill, recently returned from the United States, who did little to improve Hailsham's prospects by peddling 'Q' lapel badges round Blackpool, some of which he even presented to Butler, who quickly consigned them to the wastepaper basket.

On Thursday evening, 10 October, Hailsham was to address a large meeting organized by the Conservative Political Centre. It seemed the obvious opportunity to declare his candidature. He had already issued his speech to the press, and so was obliged to adhere to the text of it. It was rather dull; but in response to the somewhat perfunctory applause, he added an emotional postscript announcing his decision to give up his peerage and to stand for election to the House of Commons. He left the hall to a great burst of cheering from his excited supporters and hurried to a Young Conservative dance. The demonstration which greeted him there was described to Rab Butler as being 'reminiscent of a Nuremberg rally'[18] and as one 'more often accorded by teenage girls to pop singers than to potential Prime Ministers'.[19]

Hailsham's undignified exuberance and Randolph Churchill's crude canvassing on his behalf combined to create a reaction against him and alienated more support than it attracted. His lack of judgement seemed confirmed and his too-evident eagerness for the premiership ensured that he would never achieve it. His bandwaggon came to a halt almost as soon as it had started to roll. The Prime Minister was too skilled a tactician to run two candidates at the same time, but when his horse fell at the first fence his bet was switched to another from the same stable. His second choice was the Earl of Home.

That Thursday afternoon, as President of the National Union, Alec Home had been entrusted by Macmillan with the task of announcing to the Conference the news of the Prime Minister's resignation; and on the Friday morning he began a good speech on foreign affairs by saying: 'I am offering a prize to any newspaper man who can find a clue in my speech that this is Lord Home's bid for the leadership.' This disarming remark delighted the delegates. He has always been immensely popular with the constituency associations and, when he sat down, the prolonged applause was as much for the man as for the performance.

Even before this, rumours were circulating in the Imperial Hotel that Home might be drafted as the compromise candidate to break the deadlock between Butler and Hailsham. Sir Reginald Bennett, then MP for Gosport and Fareham, reported this to Macleod. 'Don't be so bloody ridiculous,' Iain replied. 'Alec told us in Cabinet that he wasn't a runner.' When Bennett pointed out that, while Home no doubt meant this at the time, he might have come under considerable pressure since then to allow his name to go forward, Macleod still rejected the idea out of hand. In fact, Reggie Bennett was right.

Although Alec Home told Butler on more than one occasion that he could not contemplate leaving the House of Lords, he was already being pressed privately to accept nomination. A stream of visitors to his hotel bedroom included three Cabinet colleagues – Lord Dilhorne, Duncan Sandys and John Hare – and several senior Back Benchers, among them Selwyn Lloyd (on three occasions), Sir William Anstruther-Gray (later Lord Kilmany), Sir Charles Mott-Radclyffe and Colonel 'Juby' Lancaster. None of these felt able to support either Butler or Hailsham and they begged Home to enter the contest. He gave no commitment to do so, but agreed to consult his doctor as to whether he would be fit enough to assume the Premiership. This indicated a considerable change of attitude but, as late as Saturday, 12 October, he remarked to Hailsham, 'I think you've got a pretty good chance.'[20]

By this time a groundswell was gradually developing in Home's favour. With a third of the Members of Parliament against Butler and more than a third against Hailsham, Home was being cast in the role of Bonar Law fifty years earlier as the Party unifier against whom there were the fewest objectors. But when this was suggested to Iain Macleod he still refused to take it seriously. He did not know that John Morrison, the Chairman of the 1922

Committee, was taking soundings among colleagues in the Parliamentary Party and that these revealed considerable opposition to Rab Butler's candidature. Morrison saw Butler and gave him this information; he also convened a special meeting of the Executive of the 1922 Committee to discuss the situation. The Executive consists of the Chairman and officers of the main Committee and a dozen senior Members elected by the whole Parliamentary Party to represent its views. It is the most powerful and influential Conservative group outside the Cabinet and even Macleod would have realized the growing extent of support for the Foriegn Secretary had he known that the majority of its members shared Morrison's own preference for Alec Home.

By now the Imperial Hotel was a hot-house of gossip and intrigue. Small groups gathered in corners or in hotel bedrooms, discussing the prospects of their respective nominees and criticizing the other contenders. Apart from Rab Butler, the only other House of Commons candidate with any chance of gaining the prize was Reggie Maudling; indeed, in different circumstances he would have commanded support as the most likely contender from the younger political generation. But, on this occasion, the Conference had an unusual influence upon Members of Parliament and Maudling was not the sort of speaker to arouse the enthusiasm of a large audience. He and Macleod had a private pact that they would not oppose each other. Knowing that Maudling's chances were better than his own, Iain tried with selfless generosity to help Reggie with his Conference speech. He coached him tactfully with the timing, the pauses, the turn of phrase and the peroration, but to no avail. Maudling's performance was pedestrian and his hopes slipped away as the speech sagged heavily to its conclusion. No one felt that he could convert the uncommitted or inspire the faithful. A better candidate must be found and, to the uninformed, Butler still looked the obvious choice.

Just before the last Conference session on Saturday, Alec Home went to see Rab Butler to inform him that he intended to consult his doctor the following week. It was a polite way of saying that he was now a rival candidate. That afternoon Butler made the Leader's speech at the mass meeting which concluded the Conference. It was a competent, though not particularly impressive performance and did not enhance his claims. In the course of a short speech introducing Butler, Home made a curious observation: 'We choose our leader,' he said, 'not for what he does or does not do at the Party Conference, but because the leader we choose is in every respect a whole man who in all circumstances is fit to lead the nation.'[21] This was in no way derogatory to Butler, but it was an unlikely remark if, at that moment, Home regarded himself as a candidate.

On Monday, 14 October, Home's doctor declared him fit to undertake the leadership and he reported this to the Prime Minister, who had in the meantime been informed from the Palace that the Queen would ask for his advice as to the succession. The new processes of consultation were therefore put in hand and a minute to this effect was sent by Macmillan to Butler with copies to the Queen, the Lord Chancellor, the Chief Whip, Iain Macleod, Lord St Aldwyn and Lord Poole. Butler read the minute to the Cabinet the following morning and the procedure it outlined was approved.

The Prime Minister had already seen Rab Butler on Monday. On Tuesday, 15 October, he saw Home, Macleod, Hailsham, Maudling and Heath, and on Wednesday the 16th, Thorneycroft, Boyle, Soames, Hare, Brooke, Joseph and Sandys. He recorded in his diary: 'Practically all these Ministers, whether Hoggites or Butlerites or Maudlingites, agreed that if Lord Home would undertake the task of Prime Minister the whole Cabinet and the whole Party would cheerfully unite under him.'[22] He also saw Selwyn Lloyd, who was not at that time a member of the Cabinet.

A *Daily Express* poll on 16 October showed Butler in the lead with $39\frac{1}{2}$ points to $21\frac{1}{2}$ for Hailsham, 11 for Maudling and $9\frac{1}{2}$ for Home. In an effort to keep the door open, Butler pointed out to the Prime Minister the difficulty of bringing in a peer, not only because of the delay this would involve, but also because of the psychological impact such a step would be likely to have in the country. It did indeed seem strange that, after twelve years in power, the Conservative Party was admitting that, out of a Parliamentary membership of 363, no one could be found in the House of Commons who would be acceptable as Prime Minister.

While Macmillan was seeing the Cabinet, the whips had been taking their soundings among the junior Ministers and Back-Bench Members of the Parliamentary Party. At first Redmayne had not underlined the fact that Alec Home was now a certain runner and St Aldwyn suggested that his name should be mentioned to MPs as the candidate most likely to unite the Party. The Chief Whip adopted this proposal on his own responsibility without any prompting from the Prime Minister. Indeed, Macmillan did little to influence the selection at this stage except in his talks with members of the Cabinet, to many of whom he implied (when he did not actually state) that Home was his own choice.

Following Michael St Aldwyn's suggestion, most Members were again approached and asked if their order of preference would be different if they knew for certain – as they were now informed – that Home would renounce his peerage and was a firm candidate who alone could unite the Party. Home knew nothing of this second round but, as a result of it, several Members revised their lists, raising his name from third to second or second to first as the case might be. Iain Macleod was right when he wrote in the *Spectator* article that the Whips were working quietly but effectively to influence the votes in favour of Home. Many senior Back-Benchers were doing the same. This is not a criticism; they were perfectly entitled to ensure, if they could, the election of the man whom they thought best able to unite the Party and best fitted to lead the country.

In making his report to the Prime Minister, the Chief Whip acknowledged in an interview in the *Listener*, on 19 December 1963, that he gave weight 'to people on whose opinion one would more strongly rely than on others'. It is at least questionable whether he should have made so personal a judgement about his colleagues in the Party, but on that basis he was able to report that in first choices Home was 'marginally' ahead and became 'outstandingly so as you took it further through the field'. Michael St Aldwyn, the Chief Whip in the House of Lords, was on stronger ground when he said that the peers were 'overwhelmingly for Home'. It would have been surprising if they were not.

The Cabinet soundings were far the most important. No one who was unacceptable to his colleagues could have become their leader, and when Dilhorne reported an overwhelming Cabinet consensus for Home, it was decisive. But it is not easy to understand who comprised this large majority; apart from Macmillan, the Cabinet consisted of twenty members. Macleod wrote in the *Spectator*: 'From my personal knowledge, eleven were for candidates other than Lord Home.' As the position crystallized between Butler and Home, with the other two candidates in effect withdrawing from the contest, at least nine members of the Cabinet (Boyd-Carpenter, Boyle, Brooke, Butler, Erroll, Hailsham, Macleod, Maudling and Powell) were for Butler. At least four (Dilhorne, Hare, Home and Sandys) were for Home and it is almost certain that Heath and Soames were also Home supporters. The views of the remaining five were not know, but even if all were for Home it is impossible to reconcile the figures with 'an overwhelming consensus'.

On the morning of 17 October, the Prime Minister saw, separately, the Lord Chancellor, the Chief Whip, John Morrison, the Chairman of the 1922 Committee (now Lord Margadale), Lord St Aldwyn and (together) Lord Poole, Mrs Peggy Shepherd, the Chairman of the National Union, and Lord Chelmer, to receive the reports of the various soundings. After lunch he again saw Dilhorne, Redmayne, St Aldwyn and Poole, this time together, to co-ordinate the reports. He then dictated a memorandum for the Queen on the outcome and also signed his formal letter of resignation. To help the patient accomplish so much in these three tiring days, Tim Bligh had set up an office in the hospital, and on 17 October this was manned all day by two Downing Street typists.

During the day it became known through personal contacts and reliable press sources that the decision was for Home. When this was confirmed, Maudling and Powell met at Macleod's flat, where they were joined by Toby

Aldington. Later that evening Macleod and Powell both spoke to Alec Home on the telephone and told him they could not serve under him. They had at last realized that Home was not only a certain runner but the probable winner in the leadership stakes and they were determined to prevent this.

Macleod, Maudling, Erroll and Aldington gathered at Powell's house in South Eaton Place after their dinner engagements for what became known as 'the midnight meeting'. Hailsham kept in touch with them by telephone and was by this time in agreement with the others that Butler would be preferable to Home as Prime Minister. Rab was informed of this development and those at the meeting assured him of their support. The understanding between Butler, Hailsham and Maudling, three of the four principal candidates, seemed of importance, and the Chief Whip was invited to call at Powell's house to discuss the matter. He undertook to inform Macmillan of their views. Butler wrote later:

One presumes and hopes that the Chief Whip informed the Prime Minister, as he was requested to do, that seven or eight members of the Cabinet were opposed to the choice of Home. What is certain is that Macmillan decided to ignore this powerful objection and acted ... with utter determination and dispatch, making a definite recommendation of Home.[23]

Redmayne, Dilhorne and Selwyn Lloyd had spent the earlier part of the evening at the Foreign Secretary's house in Carlton Gardens. The opposing camps were aligning their forces for the final decision, but although the Butler faction seemed formidable, Home's supporters had the Prime Minister's ear. When Hailsham telephoned to say he would not serve under Home, Selwyn Lloyd, who answered the telephone, warned him that this would look like sour grapes. At the same time he advised Alec not to lose his nerve. Home was not unnaturally aggrieved by the turn events were taking and reminded the Prime Minister on the telephone that he had been asked to come forward in the interests of Party unity and that he now felt like withdrawing from the contest. Macmillan urged him not to do so and added 'If we give in to this intrigue, there will be chaos ... go ahead and get on with it.' From his hospital bed, ill as he was, the Prime Minister was still in control of the situation.

Next day, Edward Boyle told Macleod and Powell that he too would decline to join a Home administration, but by Saturday he had changed his mind, partly as the result of a talk with Butler, partly because there were important decisions pending at the Ministry of Education which he was anxious to take.

On the morning of Friday, 18 October, Butler telephoned the Lord Chancellor to invite him to convene a meeting of the rival candidates to sort out the situation. Dilhorne tried both the hospital and 10 Downing Street to obtain Macmillan's approval for taking the chair at this meeting, but received no reply. In the meantime, and on his own initiative, Macleod had arranged to bring Hailsham and Maudling to Butler's office, where they pledged their support for him. But, forewarned by Redmayne, the Prime Minister was too quick for them. He sent his letter of resignation by hand to the Palace at 9.30 a.m. and the Queen visited him in the hospital at 11 a.m.

Harold Macmillan received his sovereign in bed in the board room. As he was still too ill to carry on a conversation of any length, he read her the memorandum he had already dictated which incorparated the reports submitted to him by Dilhorne, Redmayne and St Aldwyn. Since these recommended Home, not merely as the Prime Minister's personal preference but as the collective choice of the Cabinet and the Conservative Party in both Houses, there could be no question of seeking further advice and the Queen had no option but to send for Lord Home. Macmillan had warned her of the move in favour of Rab Butler and suggested that speed was important and that she should therefore see Home as soon as possible. She agreed to do so and at 12.15 the Foreign Secretary was summoned to the Palace and invited to form a Government. Acting on Macmillan's advice she did not appoint Home as Prime Minister until he had had an opportunity to see his principal colleagues and ascertain whether they would be willing to serve under him.

As soon as the Queen left the hospital, the 'scrambler' was removed from Macmillan's bedside telephone. He commented ruefully to John Wyndham: 'Nothing rolls up as quickly as the red carpet.'[24]

Alec Home began his interviews after lunch. At first Butler, Hailsham, Macleod, Maudling and Powell all declined to join a Government. In the face of a defection of senior Ministers on this scale, Home would have had to abandon the attempt. Butler was the key; he had only to persist in his refusal to make the position impossible. Home told him frankly that the outcome depended on the decision he and Maudling had to make; he offered the Foreign Office to Butler, who undertook to consider this proposal. At a meeting that evening between Home, Hailsham, Butler and Maudling, Hailsham said that, although he would prefer Butler, he would be willing to serve under Home. He felt that, as a candidate himself, he would be criticized for not doing so on grounds of personal pique.

Everything still depended on Rab's decision. Mollie Butler, who is devoted to her husband and was more ambitious for him than he was for himself, urged him to stand firm. 'But the knives are very sharp at the top,' she commented.[25] William Rees-Mogg, later editor of *The Times*, was also a supporter of Butler. But Rab considered that Quintin Hailsham's defection amounted to an erosion of support and next morning he agreed to come in.

He was genuinely concerned not to split the Party and this was no doubt his main motivation, but there was another reason for his capitulation. In the final analysis he lacked the personal ambition and the ruthlessness to fight his own corner. This is an endearing characteristic in the man; it was a fatal flaw in the politician. Macmillan sensed this, and this may explain his determination that Butler should not succed him.

When Maudling heard that Butler had agreed to join the new Government, he himself followed on the not unreasonable grounds that it was pointless to be more royal than the king. Only Macleod and Powell remained adamant. Alec Home saw each of them again in an attempt to persuade them to change their minds, but they felt unable to do so. Macmillan 'was sad that Macleod, for whom I had the highest regard, did not feel able to join.'[26] He did not mention Enoch Powell.

Five resignations, and especially Butler's, would have made it impossible for Home to form an administration. Two were a pity but could be accepted. By lunchtime on Saturday, 19 October, Home was able to drive to the Palace and accept his appointment as First Lord of the Treasury. The leadership crisis was over.

Thus ended Harold Macmillan's Premiership of six years and nine months. He received a generous and most gracious letter of appreciation for his services from the Queen and countless other messages of affection and good wishes, among which he prized especially a telegram from Churchill and a warm letter from Lord Beaverbrook. Perhaps the most touching was one on their private wire from John Kennedy, the last he was to receive from the President only a few weeks before his assassination at Dallas.

Macmillan's own future still had to be settled. The Queen offered him an earldom, 'on her authority (that is not on "advice") if I ever wanted it'. Many of his admirers have urged him to take this honour, which would have preserved the hereditary concept by the creation of perhaps the only new peerage of this kind that would be generally acceptable in this egalitarian age. But he did not wish to go to the House of Lords. He had been a Member of the House of Commons for forty years, seventeen of them in Office, and he preferred to end his political life where it had begun and take no further part in public affairs. As he wrote:

It has always seemed to me more artistic, when the curtain falls on the last performance, to accept the inevitable 'E finita la commedia'. It is tempting, perhaps, but unrewarding to hang about the green room after the final retirement from the stage.[27]

He did not leave the House of Commons until the end of the Parliament, because it seemed unnecessary to inflict a by-election on his constituents when a General Election was certain to be held within a year; but he only made three short speeches there after leaving Downing Street – the first in November 1963 after the murder of President Kennedy, the second after the publication of the Denning Report and the last in July 1964 to pay tribute to Winston Churchill.

42
RETIREMENT

When Harold Macmillan was well enough to leave the King Edward VII Hospital, he had nowhere to stay in London and Sir Hugh Wontner, a former Lord Mayor, who was chairman of the Savoy group of hotels, kindly lent the Macmillans his own suite of rooms at Claridges. By coincidence, Winston Churchill had also stayed at Wontner's Claridges penthouse after his election defeat in 1945. As soon as he entered the sitting-room, Macmillan went straight to the book-case. When Alec Home visited the same room on a later occasion, his first instinct was to look at two pictures of birds on one of the walls. It was indicative of the personal interests of the two men.

Within a few years of his retirement, in 1966, Harold Macmillan was stricken with grief by the sudden death of Lady Dorothy. This unhappy family event left him bereft and lonely. She had been a wonderful support to him throughout his career, especially in the early days at Stockton and later when he became Prime Minister.

Macmillan's attitude to other women has always been detached. He does not really like them or feel at ease in their company, although this has become less pronounced in recent years. There have been some exceptions: he was devoted to Lady Londonderry, who was kind, helpful and always loyal – she was not, like some other great hostesses, merely a barometer of a young man's success or popularity. In later years, Ava, Lady Waverley, was a close friend who flattered him and played a part in his life. He admired and respected Lady Rhys-Williams' mind, and welcomed her advice on economic policy, though he did not always agree with or take it. And, although she was of a younger generation, he became fond of John Wyndham's wife, Pamela Egremont. But these friendships were peripheral and he never became romantically attached to anyone except Dorothy. He loved her always and was deeply unhappy when she died.

Since then he has handed over Birch Grove House to his son, Maurice, and now lives in what used to be the butler's quarters. This flat can only be reached through the kitchens and by a steep stairway with a rope hand-rail. It consists of three small rooms and a bathroom. He also has the use, when he has guests, of his old study on the ground floor.

Much of Macmillan's time between 1964 and 1974 was occupied in writing his memoirs. He dictated them at Birch Grove, then revised the drafts with meticulous care. It is always a joy and an intellectual treat to listen to him talking, but the written words fall far below the spoken. They lack the style, the light and shade, much of the humour and, inevitably, the pauses and the perfect timing which made him such a brilliant conversationalist and such a fascinating performer on the television.

The books are a disappointment because they reveal so little of the man. He is a very private person (as was his brother Daniel), unwilling to disclose his thoughts, doubts, fears and feelings. Nor is he very candid in his assessment of his own leading contemporaries in public life, so the autobiography loses much of its potential value. It is a very long (six volumes of about 700 pages each) and not always very readable catalogue of events and his part in them. There are nuggets of gold, but one must wade through over two million words to find them.

Very different, and much better written, are his short book, *The Past Masters*, about some of his predecessors in public life, and a delightful essay entitled *Oxford Remembered*, published in *The Times* in October 1975, which provided a nostalgic picture of the University during his time as an undergraduate at Balliol.

It is not without interest that the political memoirs of some other former Prime Ministers have been even less rewarding, notably those of Anthony Eden and Harold Wilson, though their later books, such as Eden's *Another World* and Wilson's *A Prime Minister on Prime Ministers*, have been, like *The Past Masters*, far more readable in their different ways. The exception was Winston Churchill, whose magnificent prose and superb command of the English language ensured success in whatever subject or period he chose to write about. But Churchill, in this as in so many spheres, was *sui generis* and incomparable.

Macmillan's other principal preoccupation during the decade after his retirement from public life was the publishing house. His brother Daniel was dead and by 1963 the firm, which had depended largely on Daniel's personal control and administration, was at a low ebb in its fortunes. The business was declining and was reliant mainly upon its backlist. At this critical juncture, Macmillan's retirement enabled him to take over the chairmanship as soon as he was well enough to do so.

The choice lay between continuing as a relatively small family concern with diminishing prospects or taking 'a great leap forward'. Harold Macmillan has always been ready to gamble, so the decision was not a difficult one. He negotiated a large loan from the bank and embarked on a major programme of investment. The old premises in St Martin Street were sold and new offices were purchased in Little Essex Street. At the same time an operational centre, with warehousing and more offices, was built at Basingstoke. The older members of the staff were retired with good pensions and new staff were recruited for the expansion programme. It was said at the time that 'if Macmillan's gamble pays off it will be the greatest high-wire act since Blondin crossed the Niagara Falls'.[1] In the end, both turn-over and profits increased dramatically and the group structure has been reorganized with a holding company (Macmillan Limited), a sub-holding company (Macmillan Publishers) and operating companies in the United Kingdom, which include Macmillan, London; Macmillan Press; Macmillan Educational and Macmillan Journals. Overseas companies are doing good business in Australia, India, Nigeria and Hong Kong, and there is a company in the United States called St Martin's Press. In all, there are now thirty-four subsidiaries.

From 1964 until 1967, Harold Macmillan was an active chairman of the group. For the next three years, until 1970, he concentrated on his memoirs, and his son Maurice ran the business; but with the return of a Conservative Government in the 1970 election, Maurice became a Minister and Harold again took charge of the company. He was joined by his grandson, Alexander, and they worked closely together until 1974. During that period he went to the office at least twice, often three times a week from Birch Grove. Although a generous man, he is mean to himself in small ways and used to take a bus or the underground from Victoria to Little Essex Street, rather than hire a taxi, until this became known and the managing director insisted on sending a car to meet him at the station.

When Heath's Government fell in March 1974, Maurice returned to the firm as chairman with Alexander as deputy chairman. Macmillan became president and has held that position ever since. In the last few years his visits to the office have become less frequent and he usually only goes there when other interests have taken him to London. He is entitled to attend board meetings, but although he seldom does so (and pretends he is not allowed to), he usually goes to the luncheons of the holding company which are held after the board meetings and on these occasions senior executives are invited to meet him on a rotational basis.

As president, Macmillan is still consulted on major matters of policy and no large investment is made before seeking his advice. Any documents of importance are sent to him to read and he takes a keen interest in and comments on the shape of the list. He sees the essence of a problem very quickly and is always ready to give an opinion or make a decision when asked to do so. One of his remaining responsibilities is to visit the bank on the firm's behalf whenever this is necessary and his grandson maintains that no bank manager has ever been known to refuse him. He retains a small office at Little Essex Street, which provides a base for his secretary, Miss Aimetti, and a place for him to dictate and keep his files.

Macmillan finds it difficult to adjust to modern commercialism in publishing and to the use by many authors of an agent to negotiate their contracts, as compared with the older and more agreeable concept that the publisher should be the author's friend and should establish a personal relationship with him. Nor has he appreciated that television can be a useful medium for popularizing an author or a book. He did not understand, for instance, why the autobiography of a television newscaster should be an instant success. He was even more surprised when Alexander informed him that their staid and respectable firm had published two books about sex; but, although startled, he was somewhat mollified when told they were both selling well and making useful profits.

Macmillan's long publishing memory can be helpful, as when the firm was having trouble with an authoress and feared that it might lose her because of the disagreement. He recalled that much the same situation had arisen with H.G. Wells and was able to direct research to the old file where a copy of a propitiatory letter to Wells, which had induced him to remain with Macmillan's, was duly discovered. A letter was sent to the authoress in the same vein and with the same result.

Harold Macmillan's academic contacts are unrivalled and are sometimes useful in attracting new authors to the list. As Chancellor of Oxford University, he is also the titular head of a competitor, the Oxford University Press, whose quint-centenary celebrations at All Souls he presided over, but this is a sinecure post, so no conflict of interest arises. Apart from his autobiography and the publishing business, Oxford has been Harold Macmillan's main and continuing interest in his retirement. Although the role of Chancellor can be considered formal and ornamental, he should be available to give advice when this is sought and to that extent is rather more than a figure-head.

By common consent, Macmillan has been a consummate constitutional monarch. He likes to be informed about University news and views and sometimes sits late into the night in long discussions with the Vice-Chancellor, Sir Rex Richards; but his interest, though keen, is unobtrusive and he never interferes. When he receives university correspondence it is sent on to Richards to deal with, though it is often accompanied by a diffident and always courteous comment.

The Chancellor is expected to be present on a number of regular as well as special occasions and Macmillan never refuses an invitation. He visits Oxford about three times a term and is always delighted to be asked, but does not go unless invited to do so. He presents the honorary degrees and invariably attends encaenia, the annual commemoration of founders and benefactors, which is held in June and conducted in Latin. Harold Macmillan's pronunciation of Latin is considered idiosyncratic to the point of eccentricity.

The Chancellor is invited to open new buildings, to receive foreign Heads of State and Prime Ministers when they visit Oxford and to make appropriate speeches on formal occasions. Macmillan's are always excellent, carefully prepared and perfectly delivered. During one dinner at which he was to speak, he fell fast asleep. Sir Rex Richards instructed the waiters to ignore this and to go on serving the meal, replacing each uneaten course by the next; but when the time came for the speech Macmillan awoke unperturbed and delivered a brilliant oration. By contrast, Oxford colleagues usually find it difficult to persuade him to go to bed before one or two o'clock in the morning. He loves conversation and Lord Goodman has remarked on his didactic political comments, often accompanied by deliberately outrageous observations but always expressed without a shred of malice or arrogance.

Sir Max Beloff considers him the most assiduous Chancellor in living memory and a great asset to the University. Most of those who were critical of the election to the Chancellorship of a Prime Minister have since changed their minds and are now full of praise for the felicitous way in which he has discharged his duties. Harold Macmillan has become an Oxford legend in his own lifetime and is especially popular with the undergraduates, who stop and clap him in the streets. On a visit one August he asked where all the students were and on being reminded that it was the long vacation, he jokingly observed, 'Ah, yes, I suppose they have all gone north for the grouse shooting.' His mind often reverts to the memories of his youth and in a letter to Hermione Lyttelton he wrote nostalgically: 'Even at the end of a life ... it is to those glorious Oxford days that I look back.'

In view of his long tenure of the Chancellorship and of the affection and respect in which he is held, it was decided to have his portrait painted. A well-known artist was approached who said he would be honoured to do it without payment, but when Macmillan was told of the proposal he expressed a strong preference for Graham Sutherland as the painter. This put Sir Rex Richards in a difficult position because only a year earlier he had asked Sutherland to paint a portrait for the Royal Society for a nominal fee and he felt he could not repeat the request. Sutherland's usual charge was about £30,000, which the University could not afford. Surprisingly, in view of the Churchill family's reaction to Sir Winston's portrait by the same artist, Macmillan was adamant, so Lord Goodman telephoned Sutherland, then in the South of France, who agreed to do the painting for whatever the

University could afford to pay. When told of this in January 1980, Macmillan was delighted and described it as 'the best news of the New Year'. He was correspondingly distressed when Graham Sutherland died soon afterwards. Bryan Organ was then invited to paint the portrait, which has now been completed and is a brilliant composition.

Macmillan's efforts to raise money for the Oxford Union are typical of the personal trouble he is prepared to take in any cause connected with the University. The Society's nineteenth-century building is unsaleable and cannot be demolished because it houses some Rosetti murals and is subject to a preservation order; but the high cost of maintaining it has become a heavy burden on the Union's depleted finances. In view of this Macmillan launched an appeal, which has raised £100,000. Half of it accrued in one evening as the result of a fund-raising dinner in the United States in 1977. Accompanied by Lord Goodman and Lord Barnetson, Macmillan flew to Washington, made a successful speech, persuading his audience that the future of the Western world depended on the undergraduates of Oxford University, and flew back to England the same night. It was a remarkable endeavour for someone of his age.

In October 1979, he undertook an even more arduous journey to China in his dual capacity as president of the publishing house and Chancellor of Oxford University. It was primarily a business visit designed to explore the development of a Chinese market. The firm was wise to entrust this task to its most famous partner, whose international prestige ensured his reception at the highest level. He flew out via Hong Kong and arrived in Peking on 21 October with the managers of the company's academic division and of its Hong Kong subsidiary. A banquet was given in his honour that evening and during the following week he saw the Great Wall and met the Chancellor of Peking University and other leading academics. Chairman Hua was away on a tour of Europe, but Macmillan had talks with the senior Vice-Premier, Teng Hsiaoping, and with Vice-Premier Fang Yi, the president of the Chinese Academy of Sciences. He thought Teng had beautiful manners and was 'rather jolly' as well as being extremely well informed, even on detailed matters. He visited Shanghai, then left for Japan, where he spent four days before flying back to London.

After a few hours' sleep at Little Essex Street, he was ready to receive Chairman Hua at Oxford. The Chinese leader had expressed a wish both to meet Macmillan and to see the University, so it was decided to combine the two; but on the day of his own departure for China, Macmillan had heard for the first time that the lunch in Hua's honour was to take place at the Randolph Hotel. This Victorian building is not renowned for its architectural beauty and he was amused and amazed that it should have been chosen: 'You mean to say', he protested, 'that Hua is coming 25,000 miles from China to the great historic city of Oxford to be given lunch at the Randolph!'[2] However, Trust House Forte, which owns the hotel, sent down chefs and waiters from London, and the occasion was a great success.

The visit to China was not Macmillan's only tour of this kind. He is often accompanied by his grandson, Alexander, and on his extensive travels, which have included Australia, he is recognized wherever he goes. In the United States, porters and taxi drivers greet him by name, and in French provincial towns, a short walk through the streets becomes almost a royal progress. On a visit to the Far East, partly to promote the first volume of his memoirs, Macmillan was interviewed by journalists who wanted him to answer questions about the Vietnam war, whereas he was only anxious to talk about his book. 'Don't you realize, Mr Macmillan, that U Thant is coming here tomorrow to try and settle the war?' asked one reporter. 'Have you no comment to make on this important event?' Macmillan's typical throw-away reply was 'Oh, how good of him.'

Harold Macmillan has always enjoyed club life, because he likes the company and conversation of men of the same social and intellectual background. He has been a member of many London clubs, including the Carlton, the Beefsteak, Bucks, Pratts and the Turf. He likes lunching at Bucks and dining at Pratts, but it is with the Carlton that his name is usually associated. He became its chairman in April 1977 and carried through the merger with the Junior Carlton, followed by a systematic regeneration of the combined club, including the enhancement of its political activities and the recruitment of new and younger members. It was decided that, to achieve these changes, a unifying figure of great prestige was required and Alexander Macmillan suggested his grandfather, who was accordingly approached by Lord Ashdown, Lord Chelmer and Sir Desmond Plummer on behalf of the Committee. He accepted on the understanding that the work would devolve mainly on the Vice-Chairman, but Lord Ashdown, who filled that position, died shortly afterwards and Macmillan assumed the full responsibilities of the chairmanship.

Some members disapproved of the merger with the Junior Carlton, which might not have gone through without Macmillan's calm influence and leadership. He justified the amalgamation on the grounds that it is better to be a member of one large, solvent club than of two smaller ones which are both becoming bankrupt. Kenneth Lewis, MP for Rutland and a member of the Committee, has stated that the closure of the Junior Carlton and the sale of its premises produced a net figure of £700,000, so the financial problem has been resolved. Another member of the Committee, Raymond Grumbar, has paid tribute to Macmillan's chairmanship of it: 'He presides over the monthly meetings, listens carefully to the contributions and sums up the consensus with skill and good judgement. He is always alert and full of ideas.'[3]

During his chairmanship of the club, Macmillan spent at least one night a week there, always using the same room. Next morning he was usually unapproachable behind *The Times* newspaper, but he made a point of going to the bar at lunchtime to talk to other members. He enjoys teasing those who take themselves too seriously and care is taken to ensure that he is not monopolized. When he was unveiling a bust of Margaret Thatcher, he glanced round the room at the portraits of former Party leaders staring sternly from the walls and observed that 'some of them would have been glad, some would have been sorry – but not Disraeli, who preferred the ladies – all would have been surprised'.[4]

Macmillan was indefatigable in performing his duties as chairman and when the club held a party to celebrate the Queen's Jubilee, he stood from 9.00 till 10.15 p.m. personally receiving (with his habitually limp handshake) at least 400 guests. At 1.45 a.m. he was still in animated conversation, but at this point a note was handed to someone who was about to approach him. It read: 'Please do not talk to the chairman. It is past his bed-time.'

Macmillan resigned as chairman at the end of December 1979, and was succeeded by Lord Boyd-Carpenter. The club paid him the unique compliment of holding an extraordinary general meeting in order to change the rules, so that he could be elected president for life; and on 10 March 1980 he was the guest of honour at a dinner to thank him for his services as chairman and to celebrate his appointment as the club's first president.

Other honours have come his way since his retirement from public life. In March 1968 he was given the Freedom of Stockton-on-Tees in recognition of his services as Member of Parliament for the Borough and later as Prime Minister; and in 1976 he was awarded the Order of Merit. He had always declined any title, but was glad to accept membership of this distinguished Order, which was instituted in 1902 and is the personal gift of the sovereign. It is limited to a maximum of twenty-four members.

Later he was paid a compliment by British Railways which invited him to christen a new locomotive named after himself. He had served on the board of the Great Western Railway from 1929 to 1940 and again from 1945 till its nationalization in 1947. The then chairman, Lord Portal, declined compensation for his fellow directors but asked instead that they should be allowed to retain gold passes which permitted them to travel free on any train in Britain. Macmillan still uses his pass to this day.

At a centenary dinner to commemorate Walter Bagehot, Macmillan made one of his now rare speeches, in the course of which he indulged in a flight of fantasy arising from a report of his own death which had appeared in a national newspaper. 'When I died last summer,' he told his audience,

I was tempted to bring it all to an end. I thought I'd go to Coutts bank, draw out my money and disappear. I'd live in Provence. After lunch I could play a game of boule or dominoes and read the *Echo de Lyons*. I would not exist. But it all went wrong when people started ringing up. One man said, 'The *Daily Telegraph*, which is a very respectable paper, says you are dead, so you must be.' I replied, 'Like Mark Twain, the reports of my death have been greatly exaggerated,' at which the young man asked, 'Who is Mark Twain?' I think that would have amused Bagehot.

After he retired from politics, Macmillan made a strict rule, which he kept for nearly twelve years, not to appear again on a political platform. He broke it for the first and almost the only time when he gave the fifth Iain Macleod Memorial lecture to a Young Conservative Conference at Hastings in 1975, and then only 'because of my deep respect and affection for Iain ... the last of the great orators ... a great Secretary of State'. After appealing for the unity of ownership, management and men in British industry, which he said had not been achieved in the nationalized public sector, he turned to his main theme of a united Europe. He deplored the haggling over relatively minor economic matters and reminded his audience that Europeans, the creators of modern civilization, had torn their continent apart in two world wars. His vision was of a Europe with common defence and foreign policies, allied to the United States, but strong in its own right through its unity. He spoke again on the same lines in the European referendum that summer and made his last major speech at Bradford in June 1979 during the European election campaign.

These public appearances have been the exception, but he has given several successful television interviews since his resignation, which have been consistently brilliant in his own inimitable style. His performances when in office were not often outstanding, but once he had learned the techniques of television, he became an acknowledged master of this form of communication. This has enabled huge audiences to enjoy his conversation in almost as intimate a way as we used to, years ago, in the Smoking Room of the House of Commons. Despite his own prowess as a performer, he never watches television and does not even possess a set.

Macmillan's first mentor was Norman Collins at the time of the 1959 General Election. Just before his broadcast Macmillan asked how many people would be watching it and someone said seven million. Collins quickly corrected this. There would be only two people, he explained – a girl who would be half-way out of the door on her way to a dance and her mother who would be about to go into the kitchen to cook supper. This was the audience whose attention and interest the Prime Minister had to hold.

Since those days Macmillan has learned how best to produce his own broadcasts. In order to establish direct communication with the viewer, he sits three-quarters to camera, with one quarter to his partly concealed interrogator. He prefers to be interviewed at home, and if possible the same film crew is used on each occasion. A list of their names is sent in advance to enable him to greet them individually and thus create a relaxed atmosphere. His grandson, Alexander, is usually present and sits next to the director to ensure that there are no shots from a low angle. When making an important point Macmillan tends to talk quietly, so that the listener has almost to strain to hear him and, when he uses a gesture for emphasis, it is a vigorous one. His most effective attribute as a speaker, whether on a public platform, on television or in private conversation, is his skilful use of the pause. Alexander timed the one which followed the words 'and ere the leaves had turned' in the tribute to President Kennedy. It lasted for thirteen seconds. Eric Morcombe and Ernie Wise were in the studio for their own broadcast which was to follow Macmillan's and Alexander saw tears in their eyes. They said there was not an entertainer in the world who would have dared hold a pause for that length of time.

In October 1976, Macmillan broke his self-imposed silence on contemporary politics by giving Robin Day an important BBC television interview entitled 'Britain in Crisis'. After referring to the growing military strength of the Soviet Union, the low morale of the United States following Vietnam and Watergate, and the reduced power of the President in relation to Congress, he dealt in detail with the decline in the British economy and the reasons for it. In 1960, 40% of the national income had been spent by central and local government on the public services. Sixteen years later this had risen to 60%, leaving only 40% for the production of wealth, upon which everything else depended. He pointed out that of the three-fifths of the population who are of working age, only half are producers, the rest distributors. He agreed that public spending had to be cut, but with the objective of releasing more resources for higher production. Interest rates were too high and profits too low to allow adequate investment in industry.

The second half of the broadcast consisted of a call for 'a Government of National Unity', by which Macmillan meant a government of the centre, drawn from all parties, to cope with the crisis in the nation's affairs. He warned that unpopular measures would be necessary, that there would be higher unemployment for a time and that economic recovery would take three years. He was recommending, in 1976, most of the policies now being implemented by Margaret Thatcher. He differed from her only in the belief that no Party government could command the national support needed to carry them through.

When Robin Day asked him who could lead a National Government and suggested that he might himself still do so, he replied: 'You're tempting me.... Mr Gladstone formed his last Government when he was eighty-three. I'm only eighty-two. You mustn't put temptation in my way.' It was said in jest, but he was talking privately and half-seriously at that time of standing for the House of Commons as a national candidate in order to play a part in forming an all-Party Government; and when I met him one summer evening at the Churchill centenary exhibition at Somerset House, he asked me whether I thought such a step would appear ridiculous to my political generation. He added that he would first consult Anthony Eden, both to seek his advice and in order not to pre-empt any ideas on the same lines which Eden might himself have been considering. Shortly after this conversation, Clarissa Avon has said that he did in fact make the journey to Wiltshire to discuss the project; but the IMF loan saved the country from collapse and gave the Labour Government a further lease of life.

For progressive Conservatives before the war and since, the middle ground was one thing, but Socialist policies were quite another. Macmillan's views on economic issues in the 1930s were far to the Left of those held by almost all his Conservative colleagues in Parliament. So much so, indeed, that the late James Margach, a most experienced and level-headed *Times* lobby correspondent, believed Macmillan might have 'crossed the floor' at that time and joined the Labour Party. Margach quotes a conversation said to have taken place between Clement Attlee and Sir David Llewellyn, then a Conservative MP, on a train journey from Cardiff to Paddington. On that occasion, according to Margach, Attlee described Macmillan as

... by far the most radical man I've known in politics. If it hadn't been for the war, he'd have joined the Labour Party.... If that had happened ... Macmillan would have been Labour's Prime Minister and not me.... He was a real left-wing radical in his social, human and economic thinking.... His experiences of the depression, the hunger, the poverty, fathers on the dole, kids not getting food, changed Macmillan completely.[5]

Harold Macmillan has never categorically confirmed or denied this story. When questioned about it, he has acknowledged that it might have had some basis of truth 'in the slump, but not later'. It is difficult to believe that he would in fact have ever taken this step. He may well have been drawn to Labour's policies in the conditions of the 1930s, but his consistent and lasting inclination has been towards progressive Conservatism in times of tranquillity and to the concept of coalition government in times of national crisis in war or peace.

Macmillan gave another television interview, this time with Robert

McKenzie, on the eve of his eighty-fifth birthday in February 1979. Naturally on such an occasion it was partly reminiscent of his youth, his war service and his career in politics, but he soon returned to his dream of a united Europe, comparing its component countries with the city states of ancient Greece, which fought each other and fell victim first to Alexander the Great and later to the Romans. He stressed that a Europe with a single foreign policy, a single defence policy and a single economic policy could be the equal of the two great super powers. He expressed concern about the SALT negotiations, which he considered endangered Europe, and about the reduced power of the United States, the abandonment of Aden and the Russian invasion of Afghanistan. He believed that the West must keep up its guard and make no further concessions.

On home policy he again emphasized the need for a consensus, without which a modern democratic society cannot work well. He did not care for wage control or money control, which could only have a depressing effect on enterprise and production. He was optimistic about the future and about the character of the British people, who needed only leadership to restore by their own endeavour the prestige and prosperity of the nation.

Mentally, Macmillan is at least twenty years younger than his age. Physically, he is photogenic and there is hardly a bad photograph of him in existence; but he makes a show of being feeble and decrepit. He has been described as a poseur, and his 'old man' act is an affectation, but it is a harmless one which suits his style better now than when he was younger. Humphry Berkeley recalled meeting him for the first time in 1948 at Cambridge, where he was addressing a University audience; he was then only fifty-four. Berkeley saw him off at the station after the meeting. He was wearing a cap and an old coat and was almost tottering towards the ticket barrier when he suddenly realized that the train was on the point of leaving. 'With the agility of Christopher Chataway', Berkeley wrote, 'he at once leapt towards the train and caught it as it was moving out of the station.'[6]

I had much the same experience myself many years later when visiting him at Birch Grove House. Indoors, he had been leaning on a stick, which he forgot to take with him when we were walking round the garden after luncheon. 'I am glad to see you walking so well,' I remarked innocently, whereupon he resumed his shuffling gait and asked me to return to the house for the stick, which he said he could scarcely manage without. An hour later he had again forgotten it and led the way upstairs at a brisk pace to show me the portrait his Parliamentary colleagues had given him when he retired from the House of Commons. When I complimented him for the second time, he looked a little embarrassed and said, 'Well, they are very shallow stairs.' In fact he is not at all lame, but his eyesight is bad and it is this which causes the difficulty.

On another occasion he had been giving the Address at a memorial service and shuffled (rather than walked) down the aisle of St Margaret's, Westminster, just behind the family, while the rest of the congregation waited to leave. He was leaning on his stick with one hand and on the arm of a grandson with the other, when Rab Butler was heard to exclaim in his well-known and penetrating stage whisper, audible to half the church: 'It's all put on, you know.'

Macmillan's sense of humour is always a joy. After the Guildhall luncheon which followed the St Paul's service for the Queen's Jubilee, he remarked to a courtier: 'I hope you'll give us all a medal. Dickie [Mountbatten] will be so disappointed if you don't.' When a Jubilee medal duly arrived later, Macmillan observed, 'I'm afraid the fellow must have taken me seriously.'

In his retirement Harold Macmillan has retained a keen interest in politics and in the leaders of his own Party who have succeeded him. He has a real affection for Alec Home, whom he respects and whom he thinks of as representing the best aspects of the old aristocratic tradition in public life. He considered Edward Heath a brilliant staff officer and an able Minister and was much impressed by Heath's patience, skill and mastery of detail in his conduct of the Common Market negotiations.

Although Margaret Thatcher had served efficiently as a junior Minister in his Government, Macmillan scarcely knew her at that time. After her election as leader of the Party in 1975, he heard she was working too hard and said he hoped she would take a holiday during the summer recess. When told that she had a long list of speaking engagements and was also planning visits to various European countries, he commented drily: 'She would do much better to stay at home in her garden – has she got a garden? – and read Moneypenny and Buckle's life of Disraeli.' While the Party was in Opposition she found time to visit him at Birch Grove on several occasions, which he appreciated, and he grew to like and admire her. In a later conversation with the author after she became Prime Minister, he compared her with Heath: 'Ted was a very good No. 2 [pause]. Not a leader [pause]. Now, you have a *real* leader [long pause]. Whether she is leading you in the right direction ...'[7]

Macmillan's television broadcast in October 1980 was an impressive performance by any standard. For a man of eighty-seven, who has been living in retirement for seventeen years, it was remarkable. He expressed, for the first time publicly, his doubts and fears about the present Government's handling of the economy. His reflationary theme was in striking, if courteous, contrast to Margaret Thatcher's policy. At a time of world recession, the deepest since the 1930s, he felt strongly that the Government should not deliberately superimpose a self-inflicted domestic recession, the whole burden of which has fallen on wealth-creating private industry.

In the public sector the Government is the banker and must subsidize the railways and the steel industry or close them down, which it dare not do. Instead of keeping men and machines idle, Macmillan maintained that the taxpayer's money should be used to sustain these basic industries. He was advocating a return to the Keynesian economics in which he has always believed. No doubt this was right for the 1930s when prices were stable or falling. His interviewer, Robert McKenzie, did not put to him the problem of spending the nation out of a recession at a time of high inflation, which his policy could only increase. Although his instinctive attitude towards the management of the economy is the opposite of Margaret Thatcher's, he recognizes her qualities of courage, determination and leadership.

In his retirement, Harold Macmillan has shown dignity and style. He has always been constructive, good-humoured, good-mannered, and though no longer in the centre of the stage, he has continued to be an asset to the Party and the country he led with such distinction for nearly seven years.

43
THE STYLE AND THE
SUBSTANCE

In assessing Harold Macmillan as a man and a statesman it may be best to begin with the sort of pen picture that the Duc de la Rochefoucauld gave of himself and of Cardinal de Retz; and then try to determine whether this is the façade or the real man, the style or the substance.

In appearance, as a young man, Macmillan was elegant, neat and notably well dressed. Then and in middle life his suits were made by a good tailor and his soldierly bearing, a legacy of his service in the Grenadier Guards, was maintained into his seventies. In the House of Commons he almost invariably wore an Old Etonian or Brigade of Guards tie. (This set a trend which those of us in the Parliamentary Party who were entitled to do so soon followed. When Edward Heath became leader of the Party, the fashion quickly faded and has not since been revived.)

Later Macmillan became less careful of his appearance and even as Prime Minister his clothes, though always well cut, were usually old and often unkempt. He sometimes wore trousers and a coat from different suits, which might be accompanied, even in London, by an ancient and apparently egg-stained cardigan. His eyes are hooded and he has a habit of displaying discoloured teeth in a bared grimace, but nothing can change the impression he creates of casual, careless elegance, and whatever he wears or does he still looks the *grand seigneur*.

In character, Harold Macmillan is complex, almost chameleon. He is a shy, sensitive man, reserved and undemonstrative in his personal relationships, unwilling to discuss intimate matters and uneasy if obliged to do do. He is a good host, always courteous, agreeable and hospitable but he keeps his distance, does not court close friendships outside his immediate family and discourages any attempt to invade his innate privacy of mind. Yet he enjoys the company of intelligent men and is a brilliant raconteur and conversationalist, witty but also wise, with a sense of humour and a sense of fun. At the same time there is a strong strain of irony, partly attributable to his feeling that life is transitory and impermanent. He is a very honourable man of deep and sincere religious conviction and high moral standards, who admires and possesses the old virtues to the point of being strait-laced and almost puritanical in his reactions to modern morals and to the subject of sex, which he dislikes discussing. This was certainly one of the reasons for his reluctance to talk personally to John Profumo. Despite this, he can give the impression of worldly cynicism and his personality reflects the mixture of the romantic and the cynic in his nature. Not long ago he was reported as saying, 'Sometimes to do the right thing is the right thing to do.' He is perhaps more sentimental than compassionate, yet he has great generosity of spirit. He is loyal to his friends, to those who have worked for him and to his own convictions. He has always been prepared to seek the solution of a problem through subtle means and methods, but he would never compromise over a matter of principle. One of his most outstanding attributes is his courage. James Barrie once said: 'Courage is the thing – if that goes, all goes.' It is a quality Harold Macmillan has never lacked in peace or in war.

As is clear from *The Past Masters*, he has always been drawn to the background and life-style of the Whig grandees and he admires the best characteristics of the old aristocracy – the sense of service and of *noblesse oblige*. This influenced the high esteem in which he has always held Alec Home. But one of his former ministerial colleagues has suggested that there is also a commonplace side to his personality, due no doubt to the trichotomy, sometimes difficult to reconcile, between his peasant ancestry, his upper middle-class professional background and his aristocratic marriage.

The passage of the years has not dimmed the quality of Macmillan's mind, though his style of presentation has altered. In the two decades between the wars, he seemed an earnest, donnish intellectual. As a Minister, and especially as Prime Minister, he had become polished, witty, courtly and urbane. Throughout his life his perceptions have been quick and his brain, sharp as a razor, is based on a distinguished academic foundation. He had the administrative ability, the oratorical skill and the intellectual force, as well as the courage and strength of character, to ensure his success in public life. To these were added his capacity for hard work and his driving ambition, which took him to the pinnacle of power.

Harold Macmillan is an actor, as any successful speaker and politician must be to some extent, and especially during the period of his Premiership he has played many parts. One was the semblance of effortless government by a gifted amateur, whereas in reality he was always a dedicated, hard-working professional. Harold Wilson has suggested that in this respect Macmillan's role as a poseur was itself a pose. Another was the 'unflappable' Prime Minister, who read Trollope and Jane Austen (and, as Rab Butler has affirmed, Plutarch and even Livy) in times of crisis, both in order to relax his own apprehensions and to conceal from others the nervous strain he often felt before an important speech or a difficult interview. The 'old man' act in more recent years has served to disguise a mind as shrewd and alert as ever. He played any part equally well and, adapting to his audience, could pull out all the stops as the crofter, the business man, the intellectual or the aristocrat. His style of acting is not a modern one; it is almost ham, but so good that it is effective as well as amusing.

In matters which were important to him, however, he has never cloaked his concern or the sincerity of his feelings – for instance, his identification with the Brigade of Guards and the Grenadier Guards in particular, which derived from his experiences in the First World War; his horror of mass unemployment and its effects on the spirit and well-being of the people; his association with Churchill's warning of German aggression before the Second World War; his dedication in the search for *détente* with Russia, which reflected his anxiety to avoid a third world war; and the strength of his support for a united Western Europe, which was part of the same strand of policy. George Hutchinson rightly wrote that the memory of war inspired in Macmillan a commitment to the preservation of peace, just as the memory of Stockton influenced instinctively his handling of the economy.

As a speaker, Harold Macmillan is in the highest class. He is not a natural orator as were Lloyd George and Aneurin Bevan, but he has a gift for the use of words and a perfect sense of timing. He is a good communicator in any medium, though at his best in private conversation and latterly on the television. His philosophic mind, the epigrammatic, often ironic turn of phrase, the historical and literary analogies, all expressed with a languor of voice and manner, make his monologues a joy and an intellectual treat for any listener. He is an acknowledged master of the difficult art of after-dinner speaking, for which George Hutchinson described his technique as 'informal, yet mannered, stylized, a beguiling combination of the colloquial and the classic, often discursive, invariably apt'.[1] His speeches in Parliament or at large public meetings were elegant, well delivered and almost always of a high standard. He carried great authority in the House of Commons and at his best few cared to challenge him in debate. John Wyndham considered that some of his impromptu contributions were even better than those which had been carefully prepared.

Macmillan was an able administrator in any Department over which he presided and was full of ideas which were not always practicable (or even very seriously intended), but which made him a stimulating Minister to work for and advise. He understood how to delegate and he guided and controlled the Cabinet with great skill; but he did not care for the role of Opposition spokesman, although he was good at it. He was essentially a man of Government, interested in achieving results and in the exercise of power. If he could take the decisions, others could claim the credit.

Macmillan much enjoyed being Prime Minister in the lighter as well as in the more serious aspects of the Office. 'Interesting work,' he is reported to have remarked to James Callaghan. 'Fine town house. Nice place in the country. Servants. Plenty of foreign travel. I wouldn't give it up if I were you.' He also enjoyed presenting himself in the role of Prime Minister, just as in the years of retirement he enjoyed giving a good performance on the television. Yet he was quite without vanity and although he gave much time to reading the newspapers, Pamela Egremont confirms that he seldom read press comment about himself, even when it was favourable.

Lord Fraser of Kilmorack, who served five Conservative Prime Ministers, considered Macmillan 'the best "all-rounder". Not a genius like Churchill, but a supremely competent player. A real professional with all the strokes.' Charles Hill, a shrewd observer of the political scene, named the three Conservative statesmen who had made the greatest impression on him. They were Macmillan, Butler and Macleod.

As Prime Minister, Macmillan had a talent for pursuing progressive policies but presenting them tactfully in a Conservative tone of voice. This disarmed Right-wing criticism of his Left-wing actions, especially on colonial issues. Like Peel, Disraeli and Churchill in their different ways, he was a Tory radical, whose own inclinations blended with what he saw as the best political position for his Party. He wrote

A successful Party of the Right must continue to recruit from the Centre and even from the Left Centre. Once it begins to shrink into itself like a snail, it will be doomed.[2]

He believed that a Conservative Government is best managed from a position just to the left of centre and that any Party yields the middle ground in politics at its peril. This view (which applied, in reverse, in the Labour Party) prevailed for more than three decades after the Second World War. The fact that it has now become unfashionable has led to the present polarization of politics in Britain.

Macmillan sought consistently – as did Disraeli, whom he so much admired – to identify the Conservative Party with the manual workers and their families. He had no sympathy with *laissez-faire* Liberalism or Whig support for the powerful manufacturing interests in the last century. His purpose was to win working-class support for his Party and for the traditional social structure of Britain.

Although as a young man his main interest was economic planning, after he reached Downing Street he devoted three-quarters of his time and concern to foreign affairs. He liked thinking in a broad, historical context and his sense of history enabled him to assess Britain's place in a changing world and to give his country greater influence than her diminished economic and military resources really warranted. He used all his diplomatic skill to compensate for Britain's post-war lack of material power. When he became Prime Minister Macmillan had two immediate objectives. The first was to secure the survival of his Government by reviving the morale of the Conservative Party and of the nation in the aftermath of Suez. He soon succeeded in this task. It was equally essential to restore Anglo-American accord and in this – assisted by his personal friendship with President Eisenhower – he was also speedily successful.

At home, his longer-term preoccupation was to adapt Disraeli's philosophy of One Nation by expanding and stimulating the economy in order to bring greater well-being and happiness into the lives of the people, even if this involved some sacrifice of strict fiscal responsibility. In the Commonwealth, his purpose was to accelerate colonial advance to self-government, especially in Africa, and this was achieved with goodwill and without bloodshed. Internationally, he consistently sought a workable relationship with the Soviet Union, in which he was at least partially successful. His last major foreign policy initiative was the attempt to join the European Economic Community. The failure to do so at that time – due more to Eden's initial error and to the intransigence of General de Gaulle than to any fault of his own – was the most bitter disappointment of Macmillan's career. By clinging to Churchill's 'three circles' concept of co-ordinator between the United States, the Commonwealth and Europe, Britain failed to find an effective role. Instead, she became America's junior partner, the new Commonwealth lacked the cohesion of the old Empire and we were too late in joining Europe to lead it. Nevertheless, Macmillan's successes in influencing the outcome of international issues far outweighed his failures.

It is for his direction of the economy, in the light of the inflation which has since risen so steeply and which he did too little to discourage, that he may be criticized. It must be remembered, however, that the period of his Premiership was one of prosperity, during which inflation and unemployment were low and the standard of living high for the large majority of the British people. History will assess whether it was a time of real achievement or of missed opportunities, disguised by Macmillan's own inimitable style. The conclusion may be that it was a combination of the two; that genuine gains were made but that the chance to modernize the industrial structure of Britain was not fully taken.

Macmillan and Butler were the Conservative leaders of the post-war Keynesian consensus on social and economic problems, personified in the

Labour Party by Hugh Gaitskell. In those days policy was relatively bi-partisan. Planning and aid to industry, especially in its regional emphasis, were not politically controversial and Macmillan's thinking was never dog-matic. No one would suggest that this consensus still exists in the 1980s. The Labour Party has swung strongly to the Left and Margaret Thatcher's brand of Conservatism is very different from Macmillan's.

Influenced politically by the pre-war poverty and widespread unemploy-ment at Stockton-on-Tees and economically by the views of Maynard Keynes and Roy Harrod, Macmillan was always an expansionist. Margaret Thatcher, appalled by the growth of inflation and Government expenditure, believes that salvation can only come through retrenchment and that high unemploy-ment must be endured in the meantime. For her, a cure for inflation is the first priority; for Macmillan unemployment was to be avoided at almost any other cost.

The assessment by former colleagues and political journalists of Harold Macmillan's contribution to the Conservative Party and to the nation will depend to some extent on the success or failure which Margaret Thatcher's Government has in the meantime achieved in reversing the steady decline since his retirement. If her policies succeed in restoring Britain's prosperity at home and prestige abroad, his own management of the economy will be seen in an unfavourable light; if she has failed, critics may look back nostalgically to the different days and ways in which Macmillan conducted the country's affairs. The comparison will, however, be short-term, in a sense superficial, and therefore invalid in a broader perspective, because the prevailing circum-stances of the two periods were so unlike. Whatever the outcome and despite the differences in policy, both these Prime Ministers have the same qualities of courage and leadership which each admires in the other.

I have tried to outline Macmillan's achievements and his character and capacity which made them possible, but in spite of these more important attributes, it is his style and his presentation of himself which people enjoy and to which commentators constantly refer. It has a bygone, patrician distinction which he has cultivated and perfected because he saw how effective it was and how much it pleased and impressed the House of Commons, the electorate and even the world figures with whom he worked and negotiated. He became a 'character' and there are all too few in public life since he left it.

I think George Hutchinson was mistaken in describing Macmillan as 'the last Edwardian at No. 10'. In fact he was a very modern Prime Minister. It was only his style which was Edwardian, not the man himself, still less the statesman. Yet in any assessment of the part he played on the world stage, both the style and the substance must be accorded their place. I believe that the style, elaborately acted, was a cover for both the private man and the Prime Minister. It served to protect his privacy of mind as a person and to conceal his thoughts and intentions in his negotiations with other national leaders. It was useful and it was attractive. People liked it, and so long and successfully was it practised that eventually the style merged with the man and became part of his personality.

The direction and management of public affairs is dictated by events to which men must react, but the destinies of nations are also guided by the policies and influence of their leaders and in this Macmillan's style was an important asset. It worked greatly to his own and Britain's advantage, for example, in the impression it made on President Kennedy, who was delighted and intrigued by it.

Some contemporary critics who have not studied his career with any care have concluded that Macmillan was all style and no substance. This is a shallow view unsupported by the evidence. I set against it the opinion of another Prime Minister, Sir Harold Wilson, who wrote 'behind that public nonchalance was the real professional' and who added that 'few Prime Ministers have worked so hard.... Few have had so wide-ranging a grip on every aspect of Government or so clear ... a command over their colleagues....'[3] In fact no one can get to the top in British politics without ability, character, hard work and experience and even Macmillan's style would have been of little value without the substance which lay behind it.

Harold Macmillan is a very civilized man of generous sympathies and outstanding intellect. He combines the shrewdest political brain in Britain since Baldwin with a philosophical statesmanship of impressive range. But even these attributes would have been far less effective without his skilful presentation of his own personality – so style and substance have each played an essential part in the contribution Macmillan has made and for which I believe he will be remembered as one of the great peacetime Prime Ministers of his country.

SELECT BIBLIOGRAPHY

Books by Harold Macmillan; published by Macmillan:

Industry and the State, 1927
Reconstruction: A Plea for a National Policy, 1933
Planning for Employment and *The Next Five Years*, 1935
The Middle Way, 1938, re-issue 1966
Winds of Change 1914-1939, 1966
The Blast of War 1939-1945, 1967
Tides of Fortune 1945-1955, 1969
Riding the Storm 1956-1959, 1971
Pointing the Way 1959-1961, 1972
At the End of the Day 1961-1963, 1973
The Past Masters, 1975

Abel, Elie, *The Missiles of October*, MacGibbon & Kee, 1966
Barrow, Andrew, *Gossip 1920-1970*, Hamish Hamilton, 1978
Beer, S.H., *Modern British Politics*, Faber, 1965
Berkeley, Humphry, *The Powers of the Prime Minister*, Allen & Unwin, 1968
    Crossing the Floor, Allen & Unwin, 1972
Boothby, Lord, *My Yesterday, Your Tomorrow*, Hutchinson, 1962
Brittan, S., *Steering the Economy*, Secker & Warburg, 1969
Bryant, Arthur, *Triumph in the West 1943-1946*, based on the diaries and
    notes of Viscount Alanbrooke, Collins, 1959
Butler, Lord, *The Art of the Possible*, Hamish Hamilton, 1971
Colville, John, *Footprints in Time*, Collins, 1976
    The Churchillians, Weidenfeld, 1981
Cooper, Diana, *Trumpets from the Steep*, Michael Russell, 1960
Coote, C.R., *Editorial*, Eyre & Spottiswoode, 1965
Cosgrave, P. *Margaret Thatcher*, Hutchinson, 1978

de Gaulle, Charles, *Memoirs of Hope*, Weidenfeld, 1971

Eden, Anthony, *Full Circle*, Cassell, 1960

Egremont, Lord, *Wyndham and Children First*, Macmillan, 1968

Eisenhower, D.D., *Waging Peace 1956–1961*, Heinemann, 1966

Evans, Harold, *Downing Street Diary*, Hodder & Stoughton, 1981

Faulkner, Brian, *Memoirs of a Statesman*, Weidenfeld, 1978

Fisher, Nigel, *The Tory Leaders*, Weidenfeld, 1977
 Iain Macleod, Deutsch, 1975

Gamble, A., *The Conservative Nation*, Routledge & Kegan Paul, 1974

Gilbert, M., *Plough My Own Furrow*, Longmans, 1965

Gore-Allen, W., *The Reluctant Politician – Derick Heathcoat Amory*, Christopher Johnson, 1958

Grimond, Jo, *Memoirs*, Heinemann, 1979

Hailsham, Lord, *The Door Wherein I Went*, Collins, 1975

Hill, Lord, *Both Sides of the Hill*, Heinemann, 1964

Hollis, C., *The Oxford Union*, Evans, 1965

Home, Lord, *The Way the Wind Blows*, Collins, 1976

Hughes, Emrys, *Macmillan: Portrait of a Politician*, Allen & Unwin, 1962

Hutchinson, George, *The Last Edwardian at No. 10*, Quartet, 1980

James, R.R. (ed.), *Chips: The Diaries of Sir Henry Channon*, Weidenfeld, 1967

Jones, T., *A Diary with Letters 1931–1950*, Oxford, 1954

Kilmuir, Lord, *Political Adventure*, Weidenfeld, 1964

Knox, R., *A Spiritual Aeneid*, Burns & Oates, 1958

Laqueur, Walter (ed.), *A Dictionary of Politics*, Weidenfeld, 1973

Lloyd, Selwyn, *Suez, 1956*, Cape, 1976

Longford, Lord, *Kennedy*, Weidenfeld, 1976

Mallaby, G., *From My Level*, Hutchinson, 1965

Margach, James, *The Abuse of Power*, W.H. Allen, 1978

McKenzie, R.T., *British Political Parties*, Heinemann, 1964

Mosley, Oswald, *My Life*, Nelson, 1968

Murphy, Robert, *Diplomat Among the Warriors*, Collins, 1964

Nicolson, Harold, *Diaries and Letters 1930–1939*, 1966

Nixon, Richard, *The Memoirs of Richard Nixon*, Sidgwick & Jackson, 1978

North, Lord (ed.), *The Alexander Memoirs*, Cassell, 1962

Nunnerley, David, *President Kennedy and Britain*, Bodley Head, 1972

Proudfoot, M., *British Politics and Government 1951–1970*, Faber, 1974

Roth, A., *Heath and the Heathmen*, Routledge & Kegan Paul, 1972

Sampson, Anthony, *Macmillan: A Study in Ambiguity*, Allen Lane, 1967

Schlesinger, Arthur, M., Jr., *A Thousand Days*, Deutsch, 1965

Smith, Dudley, *Harold Wilson*, Hale, 1964

Sorenson, Theodore, C., *Kennedy*, Hodder & Stoughton, 1965
Swinton, Lord, *Sixty Years of Power*, Hutchinson, 1966
Usborne, R., *A Century of Summerfields*, Methuen, 1964
Waugh, Evelyn, *The Life of Ronald Knox*, Chapman & Hall, 1959
Wilson, Harold, *A Prime Minister on Prime Ministers*, Weidenfeld, 1977
Woodhouse, C.M., *Post-War Britain*, Bodley Head, 1966
Wright, Sir Michael, *Disarm and Verify*, Chatto, 1964
Young, Kenneth, *Sir Alec Douglas-Home*, Dent, 1970

Articles
Political Quarterly, Volume 32, 1961
    April 1961, S.H. Beer, 'Democratic One-Party Government for Britain'
    July 1961, Editorial, 'The Adaptable Party'
    July 1961, C. Hollis, 'The Conservative Party in History'
    July 1961, D. Hennessey, 'The Communication of Conservative Policy 1957-1959'

SOURCE NOTES

CHAPTER 1
1. Extract from a contribution by Sir Olaf Caroe in *A Century of Summerfields*.
2. Extract from a contribution by A.D. Finney in *A Century of Summerfields*, pp. 62-3.
3. Extract from a contribution by Lord Norrie in *A Century of Summerfields*.
4. *Winds of Change*, p. 41.
5. See *A Spiritual Aeneid* for an account of this.
6. *The Life of Ronald Knox*, Evelyn Waugh.
7. *Winds of Change*.
8. *The Past Masters*.
9. *Editorial*, C.R. Coote, 1965.

CHAPTER 2
1. *Editorial*.
2. The phrase 'two nations' refers to a quote from *Sybil* by Disraeli: 'I was told that the Privileged and the People formed Two Nations.'

CHAPTER 3
1. *Macmillan: A Study in Ambiguity*, Anthony Sampson.

CHAPTER 4
1. *The House of Macmillan*, 1943.
2. *The House of Macmillan*.
3. *The House of Macmillan*.
4. *Winds of Change*, p. 186.
5. *Winds of Change*, p. 483.

6. Lord Snow in conversation with the author.

CHAPTER 5
1. *Winds of Change*, p. 146.

CHAPTER 6
1. *On Pitt's Maiden Speech in the House of Commons*, 1781.
2. *Winds of Change*, p. 222.
3. *Industry and the State*.
4. *Winds of Change*, p. 224.
5. *Winds of Change*, p. 224.
6. *Winds of Change*, p. 224.
7. *Winds of Change*, p. 225.
8. Macmillan in the House of Commons. *Hansard*, 2 May 1927.
9. Neville Chamberlain's diary quoted in Sir Keith Feiling's biography *The Life of Neville Chamberlain*, 1947.
10. *One Hundred Commoners*, James Johnstone, 1931.
11. *Winds of Change*.
12. *Saturday Review*, November 1929.
13. *My Life*, Oswald Mosley.
14. Thomas Jones to a member of the Foreign Policy Association in Washington, 1931.

CHAPTER 7
1. *Winds of Change*, pp. 311, 312, 518.
2. *The Past Masters*, p. 122.
3. *The Past Masters*.
4. *Winds of Change*, p. 315.
5. *Winds of Change*, p. 285.
6. *Winds of Change*, p. 286.

7. Speech in the House of Lords,
   5 March 1881.
8. Macmillan in the House of
   Commons. *Hansard*, 22 November
   1934.
9. *Winds of Change*, p. 302.
10. Macmillan in the House of
    Commons. *Hansard*, 9 July 1935.
11. Letter from Keynes to Macmillan, 6
    June 1932. *Winds of Change*, p. 363.
12. Macmillan in the House of
    Commons. *Hansard*, 8 March 1933.
13. *A Diary with Letters 1931–1950*,
    T. Jones, 1956.
14. *Home and Abroad*, Lord Strang,
    p. 61.
15. *A Diary with Letters 1931–1950*.
16. *Winds of Change*, p. 354.
17. *Winds of Change*, pp. 426–31.
18. *Winds of Change*, p. 428.
19. *The Times*, 17 September 1935.
20. *Winds of Change*, p. 430.
21. *Winds of Change*, p. 431.
22. *Winds of Change*, p. 434.
23. *Winds of Change*, p. 437.
24. *Winds of Change*, p. 448.
25. *Winds of Change*, p. 454.
26. Article in the *Star*, 20 March 1936.
27. *Winds of Change*, p. 470.
28. For Macmillan's views on the
    Spanish Civil War, see *Winds of
    Change*, pp. 471–6.
29. For Macmillan's views on the
    abdication, see *Winds of Change*,
    pp. 477–8.

CHAPTER 8
1. From the introduction to reissue of
   The Middle Way.
2. *The Middle Way*.
3. *The Middle Way*.
4. *The Middle Way*.
5. *The Middle Way*.
6. Quoted in *Winds of Change*, p. 502.
7. *The Middle Way* (1966), pp. 23–4.
8. *The Middle Way* (1966), p. 20.

CHAPTER 9
1. *Winds of Change*, p. 527.
2. *Winds of Change*.
3. *Winds of Change*, p. 573.

4. *Winds of Change*, p. 584.
5. *The Times*, 21 March 1939.
6. *Diaries and Letters 1930–1939*,
   Harold Nicolson, 1966.
7. *Winds of Change*, p. 606.

CHAPTER 10
1. *The Tory Leaders*, Nigel Fisher.
2. *The Blast of War 1939–1945*.
3. Debate in the House of Commons.
   Hansard, 18 October 1939.
4. *The Tory Leaders*.
5. Speech in the House of Commons.
   Hansard, 17 January 1940.
6. Speech in the House of Commons.
   Hansard, 19 March 1940.
7. *The Tory Leaders*, Chamberlain's
   diary for 4 May 1940.
8. *The Tory Leaders*, Halifax, 6 May
   1940.
9. *The Blast of War*, p. 69.
10. Amery in the House of Commons.
    Hansard, 7 May 1940.
11. *The Gathering Storm*, Winston
    Churchill.
12. *My Political Life*, Leo Amery.
13. Neville Chamberlain in the House of
    Commons. *Hansard*, 8 May 1940.
14. *The Tory Leaders*, p. 43.
15. *The Blast of War*, p. 75.
16. *Halifax*, Lord Birkenhead.
17. *The Gathering Storm*.
18. *The Blast of War*, p. 78.

CHAPTER 11
1. *The Blast of War*, p. 78.
2. *The Blast of War*, p. 81.
3. *The Blast of War*, p. 93.
4. *Macmillan – A Study in Ambiguity*.
5. *The Blast of War*, p. 82.
6. *The Blast of War*, pp. 82–3.
7. *The Blast of War*, p. 82.
8. *The Blast of War*, p. 83.
9. *The Blast of War*, p. 85.
10. *The Blast of War*.
11. *The Blast of War*, pp. 159–60.

CHAPTER 12
1. *The Blast of War*, p. 161.
2. *The Blast of War*, p. 161.

3. Speech in the House of Commons. *Hansard*, 24 June 1942.
4. *Birmingham Post*, 25 June 1942.
5. *The Blast of War*, pp. 179–80.
6. *The Blast of War*, p. 165.
7. *The Blast of War*, p. 217.

CHAPTER 13
1. *Diplomat among Warriors*, Robert Murphy.
2. *The Blast of War*, p. 243.
3. Sir Pierson Dixon's private diaries.
4. *The Blast of War*, p. 249.
5. Sir Pierson Dixon's private diaries.
6. *Wyndham and Children First*, Lord Egremont.
7. *The Blast of War*, p. 271. Diary entry for 23 February 1943.
8. *The Blast of War*, p. 280.
9. *The Blast of War*, p. 293.
10. *The Blast of War*, p. 298.
11. *Diplomat Among Warriors*.
12. *The Blast of War*, p. 345.
13. *The Blast of War*, pp. 345–6. Diary entry for 14 June 1943.
14. *The Blast of War*, p. 346.
15. *History of the Second World War: Civil Affairs and Millitary Government*, F.S.V. Donnison, HMSO, 1966, p. 57.
16. *History of the Second World War: Civil Affairs and Military Government*, p. 59.
17. *The Blast of War*, p. 348.
18. *The Blast of War*, p. 351. Diary entry for 23 June 1943.
19. *Wyndham and Children First*.
20. *The Blast of War*, p. 441. Diary entry for 23 December 1943.
21. *The Blast of War*, p. 442. Diary entry for 23 December 1943.
22. *The Blast of War*, p. 445. Diary entry for 25 December 1943.
23. *The Blast of War*, p. 445.
24. *The Blast of War*, p. 449.
25. *The Blast of War*, pp. 449–50.
26. Lord Sherfield in conversation with the author.
27. *Trumpets from the Steep*, Diana Cooper, 1960.

28. 'Mr Macmillan and the Edwardian Style', an essay by L.A. Siedentrop.
29. *Sunday Telegraph*, 9 February 1964.
30. *Sunday Telegraph*, 9 February 1964.
31. *The Blast of War*, p. 386.
32. *Diplomat Among Warriors*.
33. *Triumph in the West 1943–1946*, Arthur Bryant. Alan Brooke's diary notes for 8 December 1943.

CHAPTER 14
1. *The Blast of War*, p. 376. Diary entry for 18 July 1943.
2. *Diplomat Among Warriors*, p. 243.
3. *Diplomat Among Warriors*, p. 247.
4. *The Blast of War*, p. 461.
5. *The Blast of War*, p. 468. Diary entry for 29 November 1943.
6. *The Blast of War*, pp. 472–3.
7. *The Blast of War*, p. 476.
8. *The Alexander Memoirs*, ed. Lord North.
9. *The Blast of War*, p. 499. Diary notes for 4 June 1944.
10. *The Blast of War*, p. 500.
11. *The Blast of War*, p. 511.
12. *The Blast of War*, p. 525. Diary entry for 1 August 1944.
13. *The Blast of War*, p. 547.
14. *The Blast of War*.
15. *The Blast of War*, p. 547. Diary entry for 22 August 1944.
16. *The Blast of War*, p. 547.
17. *The Blast of War*, p. 547.
18. *The Blast of War*, p. 553.
19. *The Blast of War*, p. 603. Diary notes for 8 December 1944.
20. Letter from Churchill to Macmillan, 8 December 1944. *The Blast of War*, p. 606.
21. *The Blast of War*, p. 611.
22. *When Greek Meets Greek*, Rex Leeper.
23. *The Blast of War*, p. 702. Diary notes for 23 April 1945.
24. *The Blast of War*.
25. *Tides of Fortune*, p. 17.
26. *Victims of Yalta*, Nicholai Tolstoy.
27. *Tides of Fortune*, p. 17.
28. Harold Macmillan in conversation with the author.

29. *My Yesterday, Your Tomorrow*, Lord Boothby.
30. *Wyndham and Children First*.

CHAPTER 15
1. *Tides of Fortune*, p. 28.
2. *Tides of Fortune*, p. 31.
3. *Triumph and Tragedy*, Winston Churchill, p. 583.
4. *Tides of Fortune*.
5. *Tides of Fortune*, pp. 53–67.
6. *Tides of Fortune*, p. 70.
7. *Sunday Telegraph*, 9 February 1964.
8. *Macmillan – Portrait of a Politician*.
9. *Tides of Fortune*, p. 48.
10. Speech by Macmillan, 1 September 1946.
11. Speech in the House of Commons. *Hansard*, 20 November 1946.
12. *Tides of Fortune*, p. 302.
13. *Tides of Fortune*, p. 307.
14. Speech by Macmillan at Church House, Westminster, 14 June 1947.
15. *Sunday Express*, 15 May 1947.
16. *Tides of Fortune*, p. 318. Diary entry for 5 October 1950.
17. *Tides of Fortune*, p. 318.
18. *Tides of Fortune*, p. 322. Diary entry for 16 July 1951.
19. Churchill in conversation with his guests (including the author), at a lunch party at his house in Hyde Park Gate.
20. *Tides of Fortune*, p. 358.
21. *Macmillan: Portrait of a Politician*, Emrys Hughes.
22. *Macmillan – A Study in Ambiguity*.
23. *High Tide and After*, Hugh Dalton, p. 327.
24. 'Mr Macmillan and the Edwardian Style', L.A. Siedentrop.

CHAPTER 16
1. *Tides of Fortune*, p. 364. Diary entry for 28 October 1951.
2. Macmillan in conversation with the author.
3. Macmillan in conversation with the author.
4. Macmillan in conversation with the author.

5. *Tides of Fortune*, p. 460.
6. *Tides of Fortune*, p. 399. Diary entry for 8 January 1952.
7. *Tides of Fortune*, p. 395.
8. *Tides of Fortune*, p. 397. Diary entries for 19–24 November 1951.
9. *Tides of Fortune*, p. 460.
10. *Tides of Fortune*, p. 400. Diary entry for 13–14 March 1952.
11. Macmillan in conversation with the author.
12. *Tides of Fortune*, p. 410. Diary entry for 29 March 1952.
13. Speech to the Party Conference at Scarborough, October 1952.
14. *Macmillan – Portrait of a Politician*.
15. *Full Circle*, Anthony Eden.
16. *The Economist*, 24 December 1955.
17. *The Churchillians*, Sir John Colville, p. 133.

CHAPTER 17
1. *Tides of Fortune*, p. 560. Diary entry for 29 October 1954.
2. *Full Circle*.
3. *Tides of Fortune*, p. 572. Diary entry for 30 November 1954.
4. Speech by Churchill in the House of Commons. *Hansard*, 1 March 1955.
5. *Tides of Fortune*, p. 579. Diary entry for 2 March 1955.
6. *Riding the Storm*, p. 11. Diary entry for 29 January 1956.
7. *Tides of Fortune*, p. 567. Diary entry for 25 November 1954.
8. *Tides of Fortune*, p. 541.
9. *Footprints in Time*, John Colville.
10. *Tides of Fortune*, p. 544. Diary entry for 1 October 1954.
11. *Tides of Fortune*, p. 552.
12. *Spectator*, 28 October 1955.
13. *New Statesman*, 5 November 1955.
14. *The Churchillians*, p. 188.
15. *The Economist*, 16 April 1955.

CHAPTER 18
1. *Full Circle*.
2. *Macmillan – Portrait of a Politician*.
3. *Spectator*, 15 April 1955.
4. *Tides of Fortune*, p. 603.

5. Speech in the House of Commons. *Hansard*, 27 July 1955.
6. *Tides of Fortune*, p. 669. Diary entry for 1 September 1955.
7. *Spectator*, 23 December 1955.
8. *Daily Telegraph*, 3 January 1956.
9. *Spectator*.
10. *Tides of Fortune*, p. 692. Letter to Eden, 24 October 1955.
11. *Tides of Fortune*, pp. 693-4.
12. *Political Adventure*, Lord Kilmuir.
13. *Tides of Fortune*, p. 696.
14. *Full Circle*.

CHAPTER 19
1. Sir Harold Wilson in conversation with the author.
2. *Steering the Economy*, S. Brittan.
3. *The Economist*, 24 December 1955.
4. *Spectator*, 30 December 1955.
5. *Financial Times*, 22 December 1955.
6. *Riding the Storm*, p. 19.
7. Letter from Macmillan to Eden, *Riding the Storm*.
8. *Riding the Storm*, p. 2.
9. *British Economic Policy Since the War*, Andrew Shonfield.
10. Budget speech in the House of Commons. *Hansard*, 17 April 1956.
11. *Riding the Storm*, p. 13. Diary entry for 14 February 1956.
12. *The Economist*, 25 February 1956.
13. *Spectator*, 24 February 1956.
14. *Riding the Storm*.

CHAPTER 20
1. Speech in the House of Commons. *Hansard*, 2 August 1956.
2. *Full Circle*.
3. Eden's message to Eisenhower. *Riding the Storm*, p. 103.
4. *Diplomat Among Warriors*, p. 462.
5. *Diplomat Among Warriors*.
6. *Suez 1956*, Selwyn Lloyd.
7. *Riding the Storm*, p. 105.
8. *Riding the Storm*.
9. Anthony Eden in the House of Commons. *Hansard*, 30 July 1956.
10. *Riding the Storm*, p. 106. Diary entry for 1 August 1956.

11. *Riding the Storm*, p. 108.
12. *Riding the Storm*, p. 109.
13. *Riding the Storm*, p. 117.
14. *Riding the Storm*, p. 136.
15. *No End of a Lesson*, Anthony Nutting, Constable, 1967.
16. *Story of My Life*, Moshe Dayan, Weidenfeld, 1976.
17. *With Great Truth and Respect*, Lord Gore-Booth.
18. *Riding the Storm*, p. 157.
19. *Riding the Storm*, p. 166.
20. *Suez, 1956*.
21. *Suez, 1956*.
22. *The Art of the Possible*, R.A. Butler.
23. *Riding the Storm*, p. 163.
24. Macmillan to Gwilym Lloyd George and the author.
25. *Full Circle*.
26. *Suez, 1956*.
27. Lord Duncan-Sandys in conversation with the author.

CHAPTER 21
1. *Political Adventure*.
2. *The Art of the Possible*.
3. *The Tory Leaders*, Nigel Fisher, p. 85.
4. *The Tory Leaders*, p. 85.
5. *The Art of the Possible*.
6. *Tides of Fortune*, p. 302.
7. Macmillan in conversation with the author.
8. Macmillan in conversation with the author.
9. *Wyndham and Children First*, p. 161.
10. *Riding the Storm*, p. 186.
11. *The Art of the Possible*.
12. *Riding the Storm*, p. 196.
13. Speech to the Party meeting on his election as leader. *Riding the Storm*, p. 203.
14. Lady de Zulueta in conversation with the author.
15. Particularly by Mary Proudfoot in *British Politics and Government 1951-1970*.
16. Lord Hill in conversation with the author.
17. Lord Hill in conversation with the author.

18. *Riding the Storm*, p. 228.
19. *Political Adventure*.
20. *Riding the Storm*, p. 235. Diary entry for 14 May 1957.
21. *Waging Peace, 1956–1961*, D.D. Eisenhower, p. 122.
22. *Riding the Storm*, pp. 251–4.
23. *Waging Peace*, p. 124–5.
24. *Riding the Storm*.
25. *Western Mail*, 5 April 1957.
26. *Riding the Storm*, p. 263.
27. *Riding the Storm*, p. 245.
28. Defence debate in the House of Commons. *Hansard*, 16–17 April 1957.
29. *Riding the Storm*, p. 238. Diary entry for 17 May 1957.
30. *Wyndham and Children First*.
31. *The Door Wherein I Went*, Lord Hailsham.
32. *Iain Macleod*, Nigel Fisher, 1973, p. 118.
33. *Riding the Storm*, p. 345.
34. *Five-up*, P.B. Lucas.
35. *Riding the Storm*, p. 354. Diary entry for 29 August 1957.
36. *The Door Wherein I Went*.
37. *Riding the Storm*, p. 416. Diary entry for 29 August 1957.
38. *Riding the Storm*, p. 285.
39. *Riding the Storm*, p. 319.
40. *Riding the Storm*, p. 354. Diary entry for 4 September 1957.
41. *Riding the Storm*, p. 356–7.
42. *Riding the Storm*, p. 363. Diary entry for 22 December 1957.
43. *Riding the Storm*, p. 365.
44. *Riding the Storm*, p. 367. Diary entry for 6 January 1958.
45. *Wyndham and Children First*.
46. Viscount Amory in conversation with the author.
47. *Riding the Storm*, p. 374.
48. Iain Macleod in conversation with the author. *Iain Macleod*, Nigel Fisher, p. 122.

CHAPTER 22
1. *The Times*, 6 July 1957.
2. *Riding the Storm*, p. 389. Diary entry for 19 January 1958.

3. *Macmillan – A Study in Ambiguity*, p. 137.
4. Malcolm Macdonald in conversation with the author.
5. *Riding the Storm*, p. 401.
6. Lord Carrington in conversation with the author.
7. *Riding the Storm*, pp. 412–13.
8. *Wyndham and Children First*.
9. *Macmillan – A Portrait of a Politician*.
10. *Riding the Storm*, pp. 410–14.

CHAPTER 23
1. *Riding the Storm*, p. 708. Diary entry for 27 February 1958.
2. *Riding the Storm*, p. 715.
3. Conversation in the House of Commons, 8 May 1958. *Iain Macleod*, p. 128.
4. *Riding the Storm*, p. 713. Diary entry for 8 May 1958.
5. *Riding the Storm*, p. 721. Diary entry for 23 August 1958.
6. *Riding the Storm*, pp. 729–30.
7. Budget speech 1959.
8. *Iain Macleod*, p. 136.

CHAPTER 24
1. *Riding the Storm*, p. 703.
2. *Riding the Storm*, p. 521. Diary entry for 17 July 1958.
3. *Riding the Storm*, p. 572.
4. *Waging Peace*.
5. *Riding the Storm*, p. 646.
6. *Riding the Storm*, p. 650.
7. Macmillan in the House of Commons. *Hansard*, 19 June 1958.

CHAPTER 25
1. Election speech by Macmillan, 1 October 1959.
2. Macmillan's theme in the 1959 Election.
3. *Wyndham and Children First*.
4. *Wyndham and Children First*.
5. *The Times*, 10 October 1959.
6. Butler and Rose comment on the election result.
7. *Pointing the Way*, p. 16. Diary entry for 11 October 1959.

CHAPTER 26
1. *Crossing the Floor*, Humphry Berkeley.
2. *Pointing the Way*, p. 19.
3. *Pointing the Way*, p. 30.
4. *Pointing the Way*, p. 33.
5. David Harlech in conversation with the author.
6. Julian Amery in conversation with the author.
7. *Pointing the Way*, p. 233.
8. Macmillan in conversation with the author.
9. *Pointing the Way*, p. 223. Diary entry for 11 March 1960.
10. *Sir Alec Douglas-Home*, Kenneth Young.
11. *Pointing the Way*, p. 230.
12. 'Mr Macmillan and the Edwardian Style', L.A. Siedentrop.

CHAPTER 27
1. *Spectator*, January 1964.
2. *Critical and Historical Essays*, Lord Macauley, London, 1851, p. 19.
3. *Pointing the Way*, p. 119.
4. *Crossing the Floor*, Humphry Berkeley.
5. *Pointing the Way*, p. 119.
6. Speech in Southern Rhodesia, 19 January 1960.
7. *Iain Macleod*, p. 160.
8. *Iain Macleod*, p. 158.
9. *Pointing the Way*, p. 150.
10. *Pointing the Way*, p. 152.
11. *Pointing the Way*, p. 154.
12. Speech to the South African Parliament, 3 February 1960.
13. *The Pendulum Years*, Bernard Levin, Cape, 1970.
14. *Pointing the Way*, p. 160.
15. Letter from Eisenhower to Macmillan, 15 February 1960. *Pointing the Way*, p. 164.

CHAPTER 28
1. *Pointing the Way*, p. 172. Diary entry for 4 May 1960.
2. *Pointing the Way*, p. 172. Diary entry for 5 May 1960.

3. Macmillan to the Queen, 3 April 1960. *Pointing the Way*, p. 169.
4. *Pointing the Way*, p. 293. Diary entry for 16 November 1960.
5. *Pointing the Way*, p. 165. Diary entry for 21 February 1960.
6. Iain Macleod in a television interview in February 1965.
7. Duncan Sandys in conversation with the author.
8. *At the End of the Day*, p. 298. Diary entry for 4 August 1960.
9. *At the End of the Day*, p. 314. Diary entry for 4 June 1961.
10. Macmillan in conversation with the author.
11. *At the End of the Day*, p. 318.
12. *At the End of the Day*, p. 323. Diary entry for 9 October 1962.
13. *At the End of the Day*, p. 324.
14. *At the End of the Day*, p. 324. Diary entry for 26 December 1962.

CHAPTER 29
1. *Pointing the Way*, p. 112. Diary entry for 22 December 1959.
2. *Pointing the Way*, p. 113.
3. *Pointing the Way*, p. 181. Diary entry for 13 March 1960.
4. *Political Adventure*, Lord Kilmuir.
5. *Pointing the Way*, p. 214.
6. *Pointing the Way*, pp. 215-16
7. Speech in the House of Commons. *Hansard*, 20 May 1960.
8. *Pointing the Way*, p. 250.
9. *Pointing the Way*, p. 253.

CHAPTER 30
1. Macmillan in conversation with the author.
2. *Pointing the Way*, p. 308. Diary entry for 28 November 1960.
3. *Kennedy*, Lord Longford.
4. *Pointing the Way*, p. 336.
5. *President Kennedy and Britain*, David Nunnerey.
6. *Pointing the Way*, p. 337. Diary entry for 26 March 1961.
7. *Pointing the Way*, p. 338. Diary entry for 26 March 1961.

8. *Pointing the Way*, p. 339. Diary entry for 26 March 1961.
9. *Pointing the Way*, p. 339.
10. *Pointing the Way*, p. 341.
11. *Pointing the Way*, p. 343. Diary entry for 30 March 1961.
12. *Pointing the Way*, p. 348.
13. *Pointing the Way*, p. 349. Diary entry for 5 April 1961.
14. *A Thousand Days*, Arthur Schlesinger.
15. *J.F.K.; the Man and the Myth*, Victor Lasky.
16. *J.F.K.; the Man and the Myth*.
17. *Pointing the Way*, p. 351. Diary entry for 5 April 1961.
18. *Pointing the Way*, pp. 352–3. Diary entry for 12 April 1961.
19. *Pointing the Way*, p. 353. Diary entry for 12 April 1961.
20. *Pointing the Way*, p. 353.
21. *President Kennedy and Britain*.
22. *Pointing the Way*, p. 358. Diary entry for 11 June 1961.
23. *A Thousand Days*.
24. *Pointing the Way*, p. 359. Diary entry for 11 June 1961.

CHAPTER 31
1. Macmillan in conversation with the author.
2. *Steering the Economy*.
3. *Political Adventure*.
4. *Political Adventure*.
5. *At the End of the Day*, p. 45.
6. *At the End of the Day*, p. 69.
7. *At the End of the Day*, p. 72. Diary entry for 17 June 1962.

CHAPTER 32
1. *The Art of the Possible*.
2. *The Art of the Possible*.
3. Letter to Macmillan from Iain Macleod, 11 July 1962. *Iain Macleod*, p. 220.
4. *At the End of the Day*, p. 92. Diary entry for 8 July 1962.
5. Selwyn Lloyd in conversation with the author.
6. Lord Amory in conversation with the author.

7. *The Art of the Possible*.
8. *At the End of the Day*, p. 96.
9. *At the End of the Day*, p. 92.
10. Article by Derek Marks, *Daily Express*, 20 July 1962.
11. *At the End of the Day*, p. 98.
12. *Political Adventure*.
13. *Daily Express*, 20 July 1962.
14. *Iain Macleod*, p. 221.
15. *At the End of the Day*, p. 97. Diary entry for 14 July 1962.
16. *At the End of the Day*, p. 101. Diary entry for 19 July 1962.
17. Speech in the House of Commons. *Hansard*, 26 July 1962.

CHAPTER 33
1. *Pointing the Way*, p. 418.
2. *Pointing the Way*, p. 411.
3. *Pointing the Way*, p. 426. Diary entry for 29 November 1961.
4. *Pointing the Way*, p. 428. Diary entry for 29 November 1961.
5. *At the End of the Day*, p. 34.

CHAPTER 34
1. *At the End of the Day*, p. 146. Diary entry for 23 November 1961.
2. *Kennedy*, Lord Longford.
3. *A Thousand Days*.
4. *At the End of the Day*, p. 148.
5. *Kennedy*, Theodore Sorenson.
6. *At the End of the Day*, p. 147.
7. *Kennedy*, Theodore Sorenson.
8. *A Thousand Days*.
9. *Kennedy*, Theodore Sorenson, p. 559.
10. *A Thousand Days*, pp. 433–4.
11. *A Thousand Days*.
12. *A Thousand Days*.
13. Macmillan in conversation with the author.
14. *A Thousand Days*.

CHAPTER 35
1. Iain Macleod in conversation with the author.
2. Duncan Sandys explained Macmillan's policy to the author, as the author was responsible to him for the colony at the time.

3. *President Kennedy and Britain.*
4. *At the End of the Day*, p. 182.
5. *A Thousand Days.*
6. *President Kennedy and Britain.*
7. *At the End of the Day*, p. 199.
8. *At the End of the Day*, p. 213.
9. *President Kennedy and Britain.*
10. *Kennedy*, Lord Longford.
11. *At the End of the Day*, p. 214.
12. *At the End of the Day*, p. 219.
13. *The Missiles of October*, Elie Abel, p. 136.

CHAPTER 36
1. *A Thousand Days.*
2. *At the End of the Day*, p. 343.
3. *At the End of the Day*, p. 343. Diary entry for 11 December 1962.
4. *A Thousand Days.*
5. *A Thousand Days.*
6. *Kennedy*, Theodore Sorenson.
7. *At the End of the Day*, p. 360. Diary entry for 23 December 1962.
8. *Kennedy*, Theodore Sorenson.
9. *The Times*, 27 December 1962.
10. *Kennedy*, Theodore Sorenson.
11. *A Thousand Days.*

CHAPTER 37
1. *Salisbury 1830-1903*, A.L. Kennedy, 1953, p. 273.
2. *Tides of Fortune*, p. 152.
3. *Tides of Fortune*, p. 154.
4. *Tides of Fortune*, p. 160.
5. *Tides of Fortune*, p. 184.
6. *Tides of Fortune*, p. 189.
7. *Tides of Fortune*, p. 192.
8. *Tides of Fortune*, p. 201.
9. *Tides of Fortune*, p. 222.
10. *Tides of Fortune*, p. 465.
11. *Sunday Times*, 10 July 1955.
12. Cmd 9525, London, HMSO, 1955.
13. Speech by Macmillan in London. *The Times*, 4 October 1956.
14. *Riding the Storm*, pp. 435-6.
15. *Riding the Storm*, pp. 435-6.
16. *Riding the Storm*, p. 436.
17. *Riding the Storm*, p. 448. Diary entry for 29-30 June 1958.
18. *Memoirs of Hope*, General de Gaulle.

19. *Memoirs of Hope.*
20. *Pointing the Way*, pp. 57-8.
21. *Pointing the Way.*
22. Speech in the House of Commons. *Hansard*, 2 August 1961.
23. *At the End of the Day*, p. 26. Diary entry for 5 August 1961.

CHAPTER 38
1. *At the End of the Day*, p. 120. Diary entry for 3 June 1962.
2. *At the End of the Day*, p. 123.
3. *At the End of the Day*, p. 130. Diary entry for 8 September 1962.
4. *At the End of the Day*, p. 131. Diary entry for 12 September 1962.
5. *At the End of the Day*, p. 134. Diary entry for 15 September 1962.
6. *The Times*, 13 October 1962.
7. *At the End of the Day*, p. 365. Diary entry for 12 January 1963.
8. *At the End of the Day*, p. 367.
9. *At the End of the Day*, p. 367. Diary entry for 28 January 1963.
10. *At the End of the Day*, p. 368. Diary entry for 4 February 1963.
11. Speech in the House of Commons. *Hansard*, 11 February 1963.

CHAPTER 39
1. *At the End of the Day*, p. 423.
2. *Inside Story*, Chapman Pincher.
3. *The Abuse of Power*, James Margach.
4. *The Abuse of Power.*
5. *Memoirs*, Jo Grimond.
6. *At the End of the Day*, p. 443. Diary entry for 7 July 1963.
7. *At the End of the Day*, p. 443. Diary entry for 7 July 1963.

CHAPTER 40
1. Macmillan's letter to President Kennedy, 16 March 1963. *At the End of the Day*, p. 463.
2. *At the End of the Day*, p. 468.
3. Letter from Khrushchev, 8 May 1963. *At the End of the Day*, p. 469.
4. *At the End of the Day*, p. 469. Diary entry for 20 May 1963.
5. *A Thousand Days.*

6. *At the End of the Day*, p. 475.
7. *At the End of the Day*, p. 470.
8. *A Thousand Days.*
9. *At the End of the Day*, p. 470.
10. *Kennedy,* Theodore Sorenson.
11. *At the End of the Day*, p. 478.
12. *A Thousand Days.*
13. *President Kennedy and Britain,* David Nunnerley, p. 107.
14. *At the End of the Day*, p. 483. Diary entry for 25 July 1963.
15. *Downing Street Diary,* Harold Evans, p. 285.
16. A private letter from Kennedy to Macmillan, which was published when the President heard of Macmillan's illness.

CHAPTER 41
1. *At the End of the Day*, p. 491–2.
2. *At the End of the Day*, p. 494. Diary entry for 11 September 1963.
3. *The Art of the Possible.*
4. Home in *Sir Alec Douglas-Home.*
5. *At the End of the Day*, p. 495.
6. Julian Amery in conversation with the author.
7. *At the End of the Day*, p. 499. Diary entry for 7 October 1963.
8. *At the End of the Day*, p. 499. Diary entry for 7 October 1963.
9. *At the End of the Day*, p. 501. Diary entry for 8 October 1963.
10. *The Way the Wind Blows,* Lord Home.
11. *At the End of the Day*, p. 505.
12. *At the End of the Day*, p. 496.
13. *Sir Alec Douglas-Home.*

14. *Iain Macleod,* p. 25.
15. *The Fight for the Tory Leadership,* Randolph Churchill, 1964.
16. *Spectator,* 17 January 1964.
17. *Spectator,* 17 January 1964.
18. *The Art of the Possible.*
19. *Sir Alec Douglas-Home.*
20. *The Door Wherein I Went.*
21. Speech by Lord Home at the Blackpool Conservative Conference, 1963.
22. *At the End of the Day*, p. 513. Diary entry for 16 October 1963.
23. *The Art of the Possible.*
24. *Wyndham and Children First.*
25. In a letter to the author's wife.
26. *At the End of the Day*, p. 516.
27. *At the End of the Day*, p. 520.

CHAPTER 42
1. Malcolm Oran in an article in the *Bookseller.*
2. Sir Rex Richards in conversation with the author.
3. In conversation with the author.
4. Quoted by Norman St John Stevas in a speech at the Carlton Club.
5. *The Abuse of Power.*
6. *Crossing the Floor.*
7. Macmillan in conversation with the author.

CHAPTER 43
1. *The Last Edwardian at No. 10,* George Hutchinson.
2. *The Past Masters.*
3. *A Prime Minister on Prime Ministers,* Harold Wilson.

INDEX

Personal titles are given as in the text and as appropriate to the period covered.